A Book For All Readers: Designed As An Aid To The Collection, Use, And Preservation Of Books, And The Formation Of Public And Private Libraries

Ainsworth Rand Spofford

A Book for All Readers

DESIGNED AS AN AID TO THE

COLLECTION, USE, AND PRESERVATION
OF BOOKS

AND THE

FORMATION OF PUBLIC AND PRIVATE LIBRARIES

BY

AINSWORTH RAND SPOFFORD

G. P. PUTNAM'S SONS
NEW YORK & LONDON
1900

TABLE OF CONTENTS.

A BOOK FOR ALL READERS

CHAPTER 1.

THE CHOICE OF BOOKS.

When we survey the really illimitable field of human
knowledge, the vast accumulation of works already printed, and the ever-increasing flood of new books poured out
by the modern press, the first feeling which is apt to arise
in the mind is one of dismay, if not of despair. We ask—
who is sufficient for these things? What life is long
enough—what intellect strong enough, to master even a
tithe of the learning which all these books contain? But
the reflection comes to our aid that, after all, the really important books bear but a small proportion to the mass.
Most books are but repetitions, in a different form, of what
has already been many times written and printed. The
rarest of literary qualities is originality. Most writers are
mere echoes, and the greater part of literature is the pouring out of one bottle into another. If you can get hold of
the few really best books, you can well afford to be ignorant
of all the rest. The reader who has mastered Kames's
"Elements of Criticism," need not spend his time over the
multitudinous treatises upon rhetoric. He who has read
Plutarch's Lives thoroughly has before him a gallery of
heroes which will go farther to instruct him in the elements of character than a whole library of modern biographies. The student of the best plays of Shakespeare
may save his time by letting other and inferior dramatists
alone. He whose imagination has been fed upon Homer,
Dante, Milton, Burns, and Tennyson, with a few of the
world's master-pieces in single poems like Gray's Elegy,
may dispense with the whole race of poetasters. Until you

have read the best fictions of Scott, Thackeray, Dickens, Hawthorne, George Eliot, and Victor Hugo, you should not be hungry after the last new novel,—sure to be forgotten in a year, while the former are perennial. The taste which is once formed upon models such as have been named, will not be satisfied with the trashy book, or the spasmodic school of writing.

What kind of books should form the predominant part in the selection of our reading, is a question admitting of widely differing opinions. Rigid utilitarians may hold that only books of fact, of history and science, works crammed full of knowledge, should be encouraged. Others will plead in behalf of lighter reading, or for a universal range. It must be admitted that the most attractive reading to the mass of people is not scientific or philosophical. But there are many very attractive books outside the field of science, and outside the realm of fiction, books capable of yielding pleasure as well as instruction. There are few books that render a more substantial benefit to readers of any age than good biographies. In them we find those personal experiences and adventures, those traits of character, that environment of social and domestic life, which form the chief interest in works of fiction. In fact, the novel, in its best estate, is only biography amplified by imagination, and enlivened by dialogue. And the novel is successful only when it succeeds in depicting the most truly the scenes, circumstances, and characters of real life. A well written biography, like that of Dr. Johnson, by Boswell, Walter Scott, by Lockhart, or Charles Dickens, by Forster, gives the reader an insight into the history of the times they lived in, the social, political, and literary environment, and the impress of their famous writings upon their contemporaries. In the autobiography of Dr. Franklin, one of the most charming narratives ever written, we are taken into the writer's confidence, sympathize with his early struggles, mistakes, and successes, and learn how he made himself, from a poor boy selling ballads on Boston streets, into a leader among men, whom two worlds have delighted to honor. Another most interesting book of biography is that of the brothers William and Robert Chambers, the famous publishers of Edinburgh, who did more to diffuse useful knowledge, and to educate the people, by their manifold cheap issues of improving and entertaining literature, than was ever done by the British Useful Knowledge Society itself.

The French nation has, of all others, the greatest genius for personal memoirs, and the past two centuries are brought far more vividly before us in these free-spoken and often amusing chronicles, than in all the formal histories. Among the most readable of these (comparatively few having been translated into English) are the Memoirs of Marmontel, Rousseau, Madame Rémusat, Amiel, and Madame De Staël. The recently published memoirs by Imbert de St. Amand, of court life in France in the times of Marie Antoinette, Josephine, Marie Louise, and other periods, while hastily written and not always accurate, are lively and entertaining.

The English people fall far behind the French in biographic skill, and many of their memoirs are as heavy and dull as the persons whom they commemorate. But there are bright exceptions, in the lives of literary men and women, and in some of those of noted public men in church and state. Thus, there are few books more enjoyable than Sydney Smith's Memoirs and Letters, or Greville's Journals covering the period including George IV to Victoria, or the Life and Letters of Macaulay, or Mrs. Gaskell's Charlotte Brontë, or the memoirs of Harriet Martineau, or Boswell's Life of Dr. Johnson. Among the briefer biographies worthy of special mention are the series of English Men of Letters, edited by John Morley, and written by some of the best of contemporary British writers. They embrace memoirs of Chaucer, Spenser, Bacon, Sidney, Milton, De Foe, Swift, Sterne, Fielding, Locke, Dryden, Pope, Johnson, Gray, Addison, Goldsmith, Burke, Hume, Gibbon, Bunyan, Bentley, Sheridan, Burns, Cowper, Southey, Scott, Byron, Lamb, Coleridge, Keats, Shelley, Wordsworth, De Quincey, Macaulay, Landor, Dickens, Thackeray, Hawthorne, and Carlyle. These biographies, being quite compendious, and in the main very well written, afford to busy readers a short-hand method of acquainting themselves with most of the notable writers of Britain, their personal characteristics, their relation to their contemporaries, and the quality and influence of their works. Americans have not as yet illustrated the field of biographic literature by many notably skilful examples. We are especially deficient in good autobiographies, so that Dr. Franklin's stands almost alone in singular merit in that class. We have an abundance of lives of notable generals, professional men, and politicians, in which indiscriminate eulogy and partisanship too often usurp the place of actual facts, and the truth of history is distorted to glorify the merits of the subject of the biography. The great success of General Grant's own Memoirs, too, has led publishers to tempt many public men in military or civil life, into the field of personal memoirs, not as yet with distinguished success.

It were to be wished that more writers possessed of some literary skill, who have borne a part in the wonderful drama involving men and events enacted in this country during the century now drawing to a close, had given us their sincere personal impressions in autobiographic form. Such narratives, in proportion as they are truthful, are far more trustworthy than history written long after the event by authors who were neither observers nor participants in the scenes which they describe.

Among American biographies which will help the reader to gain a tolerably wide acquaintance with the men and affairs of the past century in this country, are the series of Lives of American Statesmen, of which thirty volumes have been published. These include Washington, the Adamses, Jefferson, Franklin, Hamilton, Jay, Madison, Marshall, Monroe, Henry, Gallatin, Morris, Randolph, Jackson, Van Buren, Webster, Clay, Calhoun, Cass, Benton, Seward, Lincoln, Chase, Stevens, and Sumner. While these Memoirs are of very unequal merit, they are sufficiently instructive to be valuable to all students of our national history.

Another very useful series is that of American Men of Letters, edited by Charles Dudley Warner, in fifteen volumes, which already includes Franklin, Bryant, Cooper, Irving, Noah Webster, Simms, Poe, Emerson, Ripley, Margaret Fuller, Willis, Thoreau, Taylor, and Curtis.

In the department of history, the best books for learners are not always the most famous. Any mere synopsis of universal history is necessarily dry reading, but for a constant help in reference, guiding one to the best original sources, under each country, and with very readable extracts from the best writers treating on each period, the late work of J. N. Larned, "History for Ready Reference," five volumes, will be found invaluable. Brewer's Historic Note Book, in a single volume, answers many historic queries in a single glance at the alphabet. For the History of the United States, either John Fiske's or Eggleston's is an excellent compend, while for the fullest treatment, Bancroft's covers the period from the discovery of America up to the adoption of the constitution in 1789, in a style at once full, classical, and picturesque. For continuations,

McMaster's History of the People of the United States covers the period from 1789 to 1824, and is being continued. James Schouler has written a History of the United States from 1789 to 1861, in five volumes, while J. F. Rhodes ably covers the years 1850 to the Civil War with a much more copious narrative.

For the annals of England, the Short History of England by J. R. Green is a most excellent compend. For more elaborate works, the histories of Hume and Macaulay bring the story of the British Empire down to about 1700. For the more modern period, Lecky's History of England in the 18th century is excellent, and for the present century, McCarthy's History of Our Own Time, and Miss Martineau's History of England, 1815-52, are well written works. French history is briefly treated in the Student's History of France, while Guizot's complete History, in eight volumes, gives a much fuller account, from the beginnings of France in the Roman period, to the year 1848. Carlyle's French Revolution is a splendid picture of that wonderful epoch, and Sloane's History of Napoleon gives very full details of the later period.

For the history of Germany, Austria, Russia, France, Spain, Italy, Holland, and other countries, the various works in the "Story of the Nations" series, are excellent brief histories.

Motley's Rise of the Dutch Republic and his United Netherlands are highly important and well written historical works.

The annals of the ancient world are elaborately and ably set forth in Grote's History of Greece, Merivale's Rome, and Gibbon's Decline and Fall of the Roman Empire.

Another class of books closely allied to biography and history, is the correspondence of public men, and men of letters, with friends and contemporaries. These familiar letters frequently give us views of social, public, and professional life which are of absorbing interest. Among the best letters of this class may be reckoned the correspondence of Horace Walpole, Madame de Sévigné, the poets Gray and Cowper, Lord Macaulay, Lord Byron, and Charles Dickens. Written for the most part with unstudied ease and unreserve, they entertain the reader with constant variety of incident and character, while at the same time they throw innumerable side-lights upon the society and the history of the time.

Next, we may come to the master-pieces of the essay-writers. You will often find that the best treatise on any subject is the briefest, because the writer is put upon condensation and pointed statement, by the very form and limitations of the essay, or the review or magazine article. Book-writers are apt to be diffuse and episodical, having so extensive a canvas to cover with their literary designs. Ambng the finest of the essayists are Montaigne, Lord Bacon, Addison, Goldsmith, Macaulay, Sir James Stephen, Cardinal Newman, De Quincey, Charles Lamb, Washington Irving, Emerson, Froude, Lowell, and Oliver Wendell Holmes. You may spend many a delightful hour in the perusal of any one of these authors.

We come now to poetry, which some people consider very unsubstantial pabulum, but which forms one of the most precious and inspiring portions of the literature of the world. In all ages, the true poet has exercised an influence upon men's minds that is unsurpassed by that of any other class of writers. And the reason is not far to seek. Poetry deals with the highest thoughts, in the most expressive language. It gives utterance to all the sentiments and passions of humanity in rhythmic and harmonious verse. The poet's lines are remembered long after the finest compositions of the writers of prose are forgotten.

They fasten themselves in the memory by the very flow and cadence of the verse, and they minister to that sense of melody that dwells in every human brain. What the world owes to its great poets can never be fully measured. But some faint idea of it may be gained from the wondrous stimulus given through them to the imaginative power, and from the fact that those sentiments of human sympathy, justice, virtue, and freedom, which inspire the best poetry of all nations, become sooner or later incarnated in their institutions. This is the real significance of the oft-quoted saying of Andrew Fletcher, that stout Scotch republican of two centuries ago, that if one were permitted to make all the ballads of a nation, he need not care who should make the laws.

In the best poetry, the felicity of its expressions of thought, joined with their rhythmical form, makes it easy for the reader to lay up almost unconsciously a store in the memory of the noblest poetic sentiments, to comfort or to divert him in many a weary or troubled hour. Hence time is well spent in reading over and over again the great poems of the world. Far better and wiser is this, than to waste it upon the newest trash that captivates the popular fancy, for the last will only tickle the intellectual palate for an hour, or a day, and be then forgotten, while the former will make one better and wiser for all time.

Nor need one seek to read the works of very many writers in order to fill his mind with images of truth and beauty which will dwell with him forever. The really great poets in the English tongue may be counted upon the fingers. Shakespeare fitly heads the list—a world's classic, unsurpassed for reach of imagination, variety of scenes and characters, profound insight, ideal power, lofty eloquence, moral purpose, the most moving pathos, alternating with the finest humor, and diction unequalled for strength and beauty of expression. Milton, too, in his minor poems, has given us some of the noblest verse in the language. There is poetry enough in his L'Allegro and Il Penseroso to furnish forth a whole galaxy of poets.

Spenser and Pope, Gray and Campbell, Goldsmith and Burns, Wordsworth and the Brownings, Tennyson and Longfellow,—these are among the other foremost names in the catalogue of poets which none can afford to neglect. Add to these the best translations of Homer, Virgil, Horace, Dante, and Goethe, and one need not want for intellectual company and solace in youth or age.

Among the books which combine entertainment with information, the best narratives of travellers and voyagers hold an eminent place. In them the reader enlarges the bounds of his horizon, and travels in companionship with his author all over the globe. While many, if not the most, of the books of modern travellers are filled with petty incidents and personal observations of no importance, there are some wonderfully good books of this attractive class. Such are Kinglake's "Eothen, or traces of travel in the East," Helen Hunt Jackson's "Bits of Travel," a volume of keen and amusing sketches of German and French experiences, the books of De Amicus on Holland, Constantinople, and Paris, those on England by Emerson, Hawthorne, William Winter, and Richard Grant White, Curtis's Nile Notes, Howell's "Venetian Life," and Taine's "Italy, Rome and Naples."

The wide domain of science can be but cursorily touched upon. Many readers get so thorough a distaste for science in early life—mainly from the fearfully and wonderfully dry text-books in which our schools and colleges have abounded—that they never open a scientific book in later years. This is a profound mistake, since no one can afford to remain ignorant of the world in which we live, with its myriad wonders, its inexhaustible beauties, and its unsolved problems. And there are now works produced in every department of scientific research which give in a popular and often in a fascinating style, the revelations of nature which have come through the study and investigation of man. Such books are "The Stars and the Earth," Kingsley's "Glaucus, or Wonders of the Shore," Clodd's "Story of Creation," (a clear account of the evolution theory) Figuier's "Vegetable World," and Professor Langley's "New Astronomy." There are wise specialists whose published labors have illuminated for the uninformed reader every nook and province of the mysteries of creation, from the wing of a beetle to the orbits of the planetary worlds. There are few pursuits more fascinating than those that bring us acquainted with the secrets of nature, whether dragged up from the depths of the sea, or demonstrated in the substance and garniture of the green earth, or wrung from the far-off worlds in the shining heavens.

A word only can be spared to the wide and attractive realm of fiction. In this field, those are the best books which have longest kept their hold upon the public mind. It is a wise plan to neglect the novels of the year, and to read (or to re-read in many cases) the master-pieces which have stood the test of time, and criticism, and changing fashions, by the sure verdict of a call for continually new editions. Ouida and Trilby may endure for a day, but Thackeray and Walter Scott are perennial. It is better to read a fine old book through three times, than to read three new books through once.

Of books more especially devoted to the history of literature, in times ancient and modern, and in various nations, the name is legion. I count up, of histories of English literature alone (leaving out the American) no less than one hundred and thirty authors on this great field or some por-

tion of it. To know what ones of these to study, and what
to leave alone, would require critical judgment and time
not at my command. I can only suggest a few known by
me to be good. For a succinct yet most skilfully written
summary of English writers, there is no book that can compare with Stopford A. Brooke's Primer of English Literature. For more full and detailed treatment, Taine's History of English Literature, or Chambers' Cyclopaedia of
English Literature, two volumes, with specimens of the
writers of every period, are the best. E. C. Stedman's Vic-
torian Poets is admirable, as is also his Poets of America.
For a bird's eye view of American authors and their works,
C. F. Richardson's Primer of American Literature can be
studied to advantage, while for more full reference to our
authors, with specimens of each, Stedman's Library of
American Literature in eleven volumes, should be consulted. M. C. Tyler's very interesting critical History of the
Early American Literature, so little known, comes down
in its fourth volume only to the close of the revolution in
1783.

For classical literature, the importance of a good gen-
eral knowledge of which can hardly be overrated, J. P. Ma-
haffy's History of Greek Literature, two volumes, and G.
A. Simcox's Latin Literature, two volumes, may be com-
mended. On the literature of modern languages, to refer
only to works written in English, Saintsbury's Primer of
French Literature is good, and R. Garnett's History of
Italian Literature is admirable (by the former Keeper of
Printed Books in the British Museum Library). Lublin's
Primer of German Literature is excellent for a condensed
survey of the writers of Germany, while W. Scherer's History of German Literature, two volumes, covers a far wider
field. For Spanish Literature in its full extent, there is
no work at all equal to George Ticknor's three volumes,

but for a briefer history, H. B. Clark's Hand-book of Spanish Literature, London, 1893, may be used.

I make no allusion here to the many works of reference in the form of catalogues and bibliographical works, which may be hereafter noted. My aim has been only to indicate the best and latest treatises covering the leading literatures of the world, having no space for the Scandinavian, Dutch, Portuguese, Russian, or any of the Slavonic or oriental tongues.

Those who find no time for studying the more extended works named, will find much profit in devoting their hours to the articles in the Encyclopaedia Britannica upon the literatures of the various countries. These are within reach of everyone.

The select list of books named in this chapter does not by any means aim to cover those which are well worth reading; but only to indicate a few, a very few, of the best. It is based on the supposition that intelligent readers will give far less time to fiction than to the more solid food of history, biography, essays, travels, literary history, and applied science. The select list of books in the fields already named is designed to include only the most improving and well-executed works. Many will not find their favorites in the list, which is purposely kept within narrow limits, as a suggestion only of a few of the best books for a home library or for general reading. You will find it wise to own, as early in life as possible, a few of the choicest productions of the great writers of the world. Those who can afford only a selection from a selection, can begin with never so few of the authors most desired, or which they have not already, putting in practice the advice of Shakespeare:

"In brief, sir, study what you most affect."

Says John Ruskin: "I would urge upon every young man

to obtain as soon as he can, by the severest economy, a restricted and steadily increasing series of books, for use through life; making his little library, of all his furniture, the most studied and decorative piece." And Henry Ward Beecher urged it as the most important early ambition for clerks, working men and women, and all who are struggling up in life, to form gradually a library of good books. "It is a man's duty," says he, "to have books. A library is not a luxury, but one of the necessaries of life."

And says Bishop Hurst, urging the vital importance of wise selection in choosing our reading: "If two-thirds of the shelves of the typical domestic library were emptied of their burden, and choice books put in their stead, there would be reformation in intelligence and thought throughout the civilized world."

SELECTION OF BOOKS FOR PUBLIC LIBRARIES.

Let us now consider the subject of books fitted for public libraries. At the outset, it is most important that each selection should be made on a well considered plan. No hap-hazard, or fitfully, or hastily made collection can answer the two ends constantly to be aimed at—namely, first, to select the best and most useful books, and, secondly, to economize the funds of the library. No money should be wasted upon whims and experiments, but every dollar should be devoted to the acquisition of improving books.

As to the principles that should govern and the limitations to be laid down, these will depend much upon the scope of the library, and the amount of its funds. No library of the limited and moderate class commonly found in our public town libraries can afford to aim at the universal range of a national library, nor even at the broad selections proper to a liberally endowed city library.

But its aims, while modest, should be comprehensive enough to provide a complete selection of what may be termed standard literature, for the reading public. If the funds are inadequate to do this in the beginning, it should be kept constantly in view, as the months and years go on. Every great and notable book should be in the library sooner or later, and if possible at its foundation. Thus will its utility and attractiveness both be well secured.

Taking first the case of a small public library about to be started, let us see in a few leading outlines what it will need.

1. A selection of the best works of reference should be the corner-stone of every library collection. In choosing these, regard must be had to secure the latest as well as the best. Never buy the first edition of Soule's Synonymes because it is cheap, but insist upon the revised and enlarged edition of 1892. Never acquire an antiquated Lempriere's or Anthon's Classical Dictionary, because some venerable library director, who used it in his boyhood, suggests it, when you can get Professor H. T. Peck's "Dictionary of Classical Antiquities," published in 1897. Never be tempted to buy an old edition of an encyclopaedia at half or quarter price, for it will be sure to lack the populations of the last census, besides being a quarter of a century or more in arrears in its other information. When consulting sale catalogues to select reference books, look closely at the dates of publication, and make sure by your American or English catalogues that no later edition has appeared. It goes without saying that you will have these essential bibliographies, as well as Lowndes' Manual of English Literature first of all, whether you are able to buy Watt and Brunet or not.

2. Without here stopping to treat of books of reference in detail, which will appear in another place, let me refer

to some other great classes of literature in which every library should be strong.   History stands fairly at the head, and while a newly established library cannot hope to possess at once all the noted writers, it should begin by securing a fine selection, embracing general history, ancient and modern, and the history of each country, at least of the important nations.   For compendious short histories, the "Story of the Nations" series, by various writers, should be secured, and the more extensive works of Gibbon, Grote, Mommsen, Duruy, Fyffe, Green, Macaulay, Froude, McCarthy, Carlyle, Thiers, Bancroft, Motley, Prescott, Fiske, Schouler, McMaster, Buckle, Guizot, etc., should be acquired.   The copious lists of historical works appended to Larned's "History for Ready Reference" will be useful here.

3. Biography stands close to history in interest and importance.   For general reference, or the biography of all nations, Lippincott's Universal Pronouncing Dictionary of Biography is essential, as well as Appleton's Cyclopaedia of American Biography, for our own country.   For Great Britain, the "Dictionary of National Biography" is a mine of information, and should be added if funds are sufficient. Certain sets of collective biographies which are important are American Statesmen, 26 vols., Englishmen of Letters, — vols., Autobiography, 33 vols., Famous Women series, 21 vols., Heroes of the Nation series, 24 vols., American Pioneers and Patriots, 12 vols., and Plutarch's Lives. Then of indispensable single biographies there are Boswell's Johnson, Lockhart's Scott, Froude's Carlyle, Trevelyan's Macaulay, Froude's Caesar, Lewes' Goethe, etc.

4. Of notable essays, a high class of literature in which there are many names, may be named Addison, Montaigne, Bacon, Goldsmith, Emerson, Lamb, De Quincey, Holmes, Lowell, etc.

5. Poetry stands at the head of all the literature of imagination. Some people of highly utilitarian views decry poetry, and desire to feed all readers upon facts. But that this is a great mistake will be apparent when we consider that the highest expressions of moral and intellectual truth and the most finely wrought examples of literature in every nation are in poetic form. Take out of the world's literature the works of its great poets, and you would leave it poor indeed. Poetry is the only great source for the nurture of imagination, and without imagination man is a poor creature. I read the other day a dictum of a certain writer, alleging that Dickens's Christmas Carol is far more effective as a piece of writing than Milton's noble ode "On the Morning of Christ's Nativity." Such comparisons are of small value. In point of fact, no library can spare either of them. I need not repeat the familiar names of the great poets; they are found in all styles of production, and some of the best are among the least expensive.

6. Travels and voyages form a very entertaining as well as highly instructive part of a library. A good selection of the more notable will prove a valuable resource to readers of nearly every age.

7. The wide field of science should be carefully gleaned for a good range of approved text-books in each department. So progressive is the modern world that the latest books are apt to be the best in each science, something which is by no means true in literature.

8. In law, medicine, theology, political science, sociology, economics, art, architecture, music, eloquence, and language, the library should be provided with the leading modern works.

9. We come now to fiction, which the experience of all libraries shows is the favorite pabulum of about three readers out of four. The great demand for this class of read-

ing renders it all the more important to make a wise and improving selection of that which forms the minds of multitudes, and especially of the young. This selection presents to every librarian and library director or trustee some perplexing problems. To buy indiscriminately the new novels of the day, good, bad, and indifferent (the last named greatly predominating) would be a very poor discharge of the duty devolving upon those who are the responsible choosers of the reading of any community. Conceding, as we must, the vast influence and untold value of fiction as a vehicle of entertainment and instruction, the question arises—where can the line be drawn between the good and improving novels, and novels which are neither good nor improving? This involves something more than the moral tone and influence of the fictions: it involves their merits and demerits as literature also. I hold it to be the bounden duty of those who select the reading of a community to maintain a standard of good taste, as well as of good morals. They have no business to fill the library with wretched models of writing, when there are thousand of good models ready, in numbers far greater than they have money to purchase. Weak and flabby and silly books tend to make weak and flabby and silly brains. Why should library guides put in circulation such stuff as the dime novels, or "Old Sleuth" stories, or the slip-slop novels of "The Duchess," when the great masters of romantic fiction have endowed us with so many books replete with intellectual and moral power? To furnish immature minds with the miserable trash which does not deserve the name of literature, is as blameworthy as to put before them books full of feverish excitement, or stories of successful crime.

We are told, indeed (and some librarians even have said it) that for unformed readers to read a bad book is better

than to read none at all. I do not believe it. You might
as well say that it is better for one to swallow poison than
not to swallow any thing at all. I hold that library pro-
viders are as much bound to furnish wholesome food for
the minds of the young who resort to them for guidance,
as their parents are to provide wholesome food for their
bodies.

But the question returns upon us—what is wholesome
food? In the first place, it is that great body of fiction
which has borne the test, both of critical judgment, and of
popularity with successive generations of readers. It is
the novels of Scott, Austen, Dickens, Thackeray, George
Eliot, Cooper, Hawthorne, Kingsley, Mulock-Craik, and
many more, such as no parents need blush to put into the
hands of their daughters. In the next place, it is such a
selection from the myriads of stories that have poured
from the press of this generation as have been approved by
the best readers, and the critical judgment of a responsible
press.

As to books of questionable morality, I am aware that
contrary opinions prevail on the question whether any
such books should be allowed in a public library, or not.
The question is a different one for the small town libraries
and for the great reference libraries of the world. The
former are really educational institutions, supported at the
people's expense, like the free schools, and should be held
to a responsibility from which the extensive reference libraries in the city are free. The latter may and ought to
preserve every form of literature, and, if national libraries,
they would be derelict in their duty to posterity if they did
not acquire and preserve the whole literature of the country, and hand it down complete to future generations.
The function of the public town library is different. It
must indispensably make a selection, since its means are

not adequate to buy one-tenth of the annual product of
the press, which amounts in only four nations (England,
France, Germany, and the United States) to more than
thirty-five thousand new volumes a year. Its selection,
mainly of American and English books, must be small, and
the smaller it is, the greater is the need of care in buying.
In fact, it is in most cases, compelled to be a selection from
a selection. Therefore, in the many cases of doubt arising
as to the fit character of a book, let the doubt be resolved
in favor of the fund, thus preserving the chance of getting
a better book for the money.

With this careful and limited selection of the best, out
of the multitude of novels that swarm from the press, the
reading public will have every reason to be satisfied. No
excuse can be alleged for filling up our libraries with poor
books, while there is no dearth whatever of good ones. It
is not the business of a public library to compete with the
news stands or the daily press in furnishing the latest short
stories for popular consumption; a class of literature whose
survival is likely to be quite as short as the stories themselves.

Take an object lesson as to the mischiefs of reading the
wretched stuff which some people pretend is "better than
no reading at all" from the boy Jesse Pomeroy, who perpetrated a murder of peculiar atrocity in Boston. "Pomeroy confessed that he had always been a great reader of
'blood and thunder' stories, having read probably sixty
dime novels, all treating of scalping and deeds of violence.
The boy said that he had no doubt that the reading of
those books had a great deal to do with his course, and he
would advise all boys to leave them alone."

In some libraries, where the pernicious effect of the
lower class of fiction has been observed, the directors have
withdrawn from circulation a large proportion of the

novels, which had been bought by reason of their popularity. In other newly started libraries only fiction of the highest grade has been placed in the library from the start, and this is by far the best course. If readers inquire for inferior or immoral books, and are told that the library does not have them, although they will express surprise and disappointment, they will take other and improving reading, thus fulfilling the true function of the library as an educator. Librarians and library boards cannot be too careful about what constitutes the collection which is to form the pabulum of so many of the rising generation.

This does not imply that they are to be censors, or prudes, but with the vast field of literature before them from which to choose, they are bound to choose the best.

The American Library Association has had this subject under discussion repeatedly, and while much difference of opinion has arisen from the difficulty of finding any absolute standard of excellence, nearly all have agreed that as to certain books, readers should look elsewhere than to the public free library for them. At one time a list of authors was made out, many of whose works were deemed objectionable, either from their highly sensational character, or their bad style, or their highly wrought and morbid pictures of human passions, or their immoral tendency. This list no doubt will surprise many, as including writers whose books everybody, almost, has read, or has been accustomed to think well of. It embraces the following popular authors, many of whose novels have had a wide circulation, and that principally through popular libraries.

Here follow the names:

Mary J. Holmes, Mrs. Henry Wood, C. L. Hentz, M. P. Finley, Mrs. A. S. Stephens, E. D. E. N. Southworth, Mrs. Forrester, Rhoda Broughton, Helen Mathers, Jessie Fothergill, M. E. Braddon, Florence Marryat, Ouida, Horatio

Alger, Mayne Reid, Oliver Optic, W. H. S. Kingston, E. Kellogg, G. W. M. Reynolds, C. Fosdick, Edmund Yates, G. A. Lawrence, Grenville Murray, W. H. Ainsworth, Wilkie Collins, E. L. Bulwer-Lytton, W. H. Thomes, and Augusta Evans Wilson.

Bear in mind, that only English and American novels are included, and those only of the present century: also, that as to many which are included, no imputation of immorality was made. Such a "black list" is obviously open to the charge of doing great injustice to the good repute of writers named, since only a part of the works written by some of them can properly be objected to, and these are not specially named. Bulwer-Lytton, for example, whose "Paul Clifford" is a very improper book to go into the hands of young people, has written at least a dozen other fictions of noble moral purpose, and high literary merit.

Out of seventy public libraries to which the list was sent, with inquiry whether the authors named were admitted as books of circulation, thirty libraries replied. All of them admitted Bulwer-Lytton and Wilkie Collins, all but two Oliver Optic's books, and all but six Augusta Evans Wilson's. Reynolds' novels were excluded by twenty libraries, Mrs. Southworth's by eleven, "Ouida's" by nine, and Mrs. Stephens's and Mrs. Henry Wood's by eight. Other details cannot find space for notice here.

This instance is one among many of endeavors constantly being made by associated librarians to stem the ever increasing flood of poor fiction which threatens to submerge the better class of books in our public libraries.

That no such wholesome attempt can be wholly successful is evident enough. The passion for reading fiction is both epidemic and chronic; and in saying this, do not infer that I reckon it as a disease. A librarian has no right to banish fiction because the appetite for it is abused. He is not to set up any ideal and impossible standard of selection. His most useful and beneficent function is to turn into better channels the universal hunger for reading which is entertaining. Do readers want an exciting novel? What can be more exciting than "Les Miserables" of Victor Hugo, a book of exceptional literary excellence and power? Literature is full of fascinating stories, admirably told, and there is no excuse for loading our libraries with trash, going into the slums for models, or feeding young minds upon the unclean brood of pessimistic novels. If it is said that people will have trash, let them buy it, and let the libraries wash their hands of it, and refuse to circulate the stuff which no boy nor girl can touch without being contaminated.

Those who claim that we might as well let the libraries down to the level of the poorest books, because unformed and ignorant minds are capable of nothing better, should be told that people are never raised by giving them nothing to look up to. To devour infinite trash is not the road to learn wisdom, or virtue, or even to attain genuine amusement. To those who are afraid that if the libraries are purified, the masses will get nothing that they can read, the answer is, have they not got the entire world of magazines, the weekly, daily, and Sunday newspapers, which supply a whole library of fiction almost daily? Add to these plenty of imaginative literature in fiction and in poetry, on every library's shelves, which all who can read can comprehend, and what excuse remains for buying what is neither decent nor improving?

Take an example of the boundless capacity for improvement that exists in the human mind and human taste, from the spread of the fine arts among the people. Thirty years ago, their houses, if having any decoration at all, exhibited those fearful and wonderful colored lithographs

and chromos in which bad drawing, bad portraiture, and
bad coloring vied with each other to produce pictures
which it would be a mild use of terms to call detestable.
Then came the two great international art expositions at
Philadelphia and Chicago, each greatly advancing by the
finest models, the standard of taste in art, and by new economies of reproduction placing the most beautiful statues
and pictures within the reach of the most moderate purse.
What has been the result? An incalculable improvement
in the public taste, educated by the diffusion of the best
models, until even the poor farmer of the backwoods will
no longer tolerate the cheap and nasty horrors that once
disfigured his walls.

The lesson in art is good in literature also. Give the
common people good models, and there is no danger but
they will appreciate and understand them. Never stoop
to pander to a depraved taste, no matter what specious
pleas you may hear for tolerating the low in order to lead
to the high, or for making your library contribute to the
survival of the unfittest.

Is it asked, how can the librarian find out, among the
world of novels from which he is to select, what is pure and
what is not, what is wholesome and what unhealthy, what
is improving and what is trash? The answer is—there are
some lists which will be most useful in this discrimination,
while there is no list which is infallible. Mr. F. Leypoldt's little catalogue of "Books for all Time" has nothing
that any library need do without. Another compendious
list is published by the American Library Association.
And the more extensive catalogue prepared for the World's
Fair in 1893, and embracing about 5,000 volumes, entitled
"Catalogue of A. L. A. Library: 5,000 vols. for a popular
library," while it has many mistakes and omissions, is a tolerably safe guide in making up a popular library. I may

note that the list of novels in this large catalogue put forth by the American Library Association has the names of five only out of the twenty-eight writers of fiction heretofore pronounced objectionable, and names a select few only of the books of these five.

As for the later issues of the press, and especially the new novels, let him skim them for himself, unless in cases where trustworthy critical judgments are found in journals. Running through a book to test its style and moral drift is no difficult task for the practiced eye.

Let us suppose that you are cursorily perusing a novel which has made a great sensation, and you come upon the following sentence: "Eighteen millions of years would level all in one huge, common, shapeless ruin. Perish the microcosm in the limitless macrocosm! and sink this feeble earthly segregate in the boundless rushing choral aggregation!" This is in Augusta J. Evans Wilson's story "Macaria", and many equally extraordinary examples of "prose run mad" are found in the novels of this once noted writer. What kind of a model is that to form the style of the youthful neophyte, to whom one book is as good as another, since it was found on the shelves of the public library?

I am not insisting that all books admitted should be models of style; even a purist must admit that one of the greatest charms of literature is its infinite variety. But when book after book is filled with such specimens of literary lunacy as this, one is tempted to believe that Homer and Shakespeare, to say nothing of Thackeray and Haw-thorne, have lived in vain.

Never fear criticism of those who find fault with the absence from your library of books that you know to be nearly worthless; their absence will be a silent but eloquent protest against them, sure to be vindicated by the utter oblivion into which they will fall. Many a flaming reputation has been extinguished after dazzling callow admirers for six months, or even less. Do not dread the empty sarcasm, that may grow out of the exclusion of freshly printed trash, that your library is a "back number." To some poor souls every thing that is great and good in the world's literature is a "back number"; and the Bible itself, with its immortal poetry and sublimity, is the oldest back number of all. It is no part of your business as a librarian to cater to the tastes of those who act as if the reading of endless novels of sensation were the chief end of man. As one fed on highly spiced viands and stimulating drinks surely loses the appetite for wholesome and nourishing food, so one who reads only exciting and highly wrought fictions loses the taste for the master-pieces of prose and poetry.

Let not the fear of making many mistakes be a bug-bear in your path. If you are told that your library is too exclusive, reply that it has not means enough to buy all the good books that are wanted, and cannot afford to spend money on bad or even on doubtful ones. If you have excluded any highly-sought-for book on insufficient evidence, never fail to revise the judgment. All that can be expected of any library is approximately just and wise selection, having regard to merit, interest, and moral tone, more than to novelty or popularity.

In the matter of choice, individual opinions are of small value. Never buy a book simply because some reader extols it as very fine, or "splendid," or "perfectly lovely." Such praises are commonly to be distrusted in direct proportion to their extravagance.

A good lesson to libraries is furnished in the experience of the Cleveland (Ohio) Public Library. In 1878, out of 16,000 volumes in that library, no less than 6,000 were novels. The governing board, on the plea of giving people what they wanted, bought nearly all new books of fiction, and went so far, even, as to buy of Pinkerton's Detective stories, fifteen copies each, fifteen of all Mrs. Southworth's novels, etc. But a change took place in the board, and the librarian was permitted to stop the growing flood of worthless fiction, and as fast as the books were worn out, they were replaced by useful reading. It resulted that four years later, with 40,000 volumes in the library, only 7,000 were novels, or less than one-fifth, instead of more than one-third of the whole collection, as formerly. In the same time, the percentage of fiction drawn out was reduced from 69 per cent. of the aggregate books read, to 50 per cent.

Libraries are always complaining that they cannot buy many valuable books from lack of funds. Yet some of them buy a great many that are valueless in spite of this lack. Can any thing be conceived more valueless than a set of Sylvanus Cobb's novels, reprinted to the number of thirty-five to forty, from the New York Ledger? Yet these have been bought for scores of libraries, which could not afford the latest books in science and art, or biography, history, or travel. There are libraries in which the latest books on electricity, or sewerage, or sanitary plumbing, might have saved many lives, but which must go without them, because the money has been squandered on vapid and pernicious literature.

In almost every library, while some branches of knowledge are fairly represented, others are not represented at all. Nearly all present glaring deficiencies, and these are often caused by want of systematic plan in building up the collection. Boards of managers are frequently changed, and the policy of the library with them. All the more important is it that the librarian should be so well equipped with a definite aim, and with knowledge and skill competent to urge that aim consistently, as to preserve some unity of plan.

I need not add that a librarian should be always wide awake to the needs of his library in every direction. It should be taken for granted that its general aim is to include the best books in the whole range of human knowledge. With the vast area of book production before him, he should strengthen every year some department, taking them in order of importance.

Some scholarly writers tell us that very few books are essential to a good education. James Russell Lowell named five, which in his view embraced all the essentials; namely, Homer, Dante, Shakespeare, Cervantes, and Goethe's Faust. Prof. Charles E. Norton of Harvard remarked that this list might even be abridged so as to embrace only Homer, Dante and Shakespeare. I can only regard such exclusiveness as misleading, though conceding the many-sidedness of these great writers. To extend the list is the function of all public libraries, as well as of most of the private ones. Next after the really essential books, that library will be doing its public good service which acquires all the important works that record the history of man. This will include biography, travels and voyages, science, and much besides, as well as history.

Special pains should be taken in every library to have every thing produced in its own town, county, and State. Not only books, but all pamphlets, periodicals, newspapers, and even broadsides or circulars, should be sought for and stored up as memorials of the present age, tending in large part rapidly to disappear.

In selecting editions of standard authors, one should always discriminate, so as to secure for the library, if not the best, at least good, clear type, sound, thick paper, and

mendations, at its discretion; but expensive works are referred to the whole board for determination.

In the New York Mercantile Library, which must keep continually up to date in its supply of new books, the announcements in all the morning papers are daily scanned, and books just out secured by immediate order. Many publishers send in books on approval, which are frequently bought. An agent in London is required to send on the day of publication all new books on certain subjects.

The library boards of management meet weekly in New York and Philadelphia, but monthly in most country libraries. The selection of books made by committees introduces often an element of chance, not quite favorable to the unity of plan in developing the resources of the library. But with a librarian of large information, discretion, and skill, there need seldom be any difficulty in securing approval of his selections, or of most of them. In some libraries the librarian is authorized to buy at discretion additions of books in certain lines, to be reported at the next meeting of the board; and to fill up all deficiencies in periodicals that are taken. This is an important concession to his judgment, made in the interest of completeness in the library, saving a delay of days and sometimes weeks in waiting for the board of directors.

All orders sent out for accessions should previously be compared with the alphabeted order-card list, as well as with the general catalogue of the library, to avoid duplication. After this the titles are to be incorporated in the alphabet of all outstanding orders, to be withdrawn only on receipt of the books.

The library should invite suggestions from all frequenting it, of books recommended and not found in the collection. A blank record-book for this purpose, or an equivalent in order-cards, should be always kept on the counter of the library.

CHAPTER 2.

BOOK BUYING.

The buying of books is to some men a pastime; to others it is a passion; but to the librarian and the intelligent book collector it is both a business and a pleasure. The man who is endowed with a zeal for knowledge is eager to be continually adding to the stores which will enable him to acquire and to dispense that knowledge. Hence the perusal of catalogues is to him an ever fresh and fascinating pursuit. However hampered he may be by the lack of funds, the zest of being continually in quest of some coveted volumes gives him an interest in every sale catalogue, whether of bookseller or of auctioneer. He is led on by the perennial hope that he may find one or more of the long-wished for and waited-for *desiderata* in the thin pamphlet whose solid columns bristle with book-titles in every variety of abbreviation and arrangement. It is a good plan, if one can possibly command the time, to read every catalogue of the book auctions, and of the second-hand book dealers, which comes to hand. You will thus find a world of books chronicled and offered which you do not want, because you have got them already: you will find many, also, which you want, but which you know you cannot have; and you may find some of the very volumes which you have sought through many years in vain. In any case, you will have acquired valuable information—whether you acquire any books or not; since there is hardly a priced catalogue, of any considerable extent, from which you cannot reap knowledge of some kind—knowledge of editions, knowledge of prices, and knowledge of the comparative scarcity or full supply of many books, with a glimpse of titles which you may never have met before. The value of the study of catalogues as an education in bibliography can never be over-estimated.

The large number of active and discriminating book-buyers from America has for years past awakened the interest and jealousy of collectors abroad, where it has very largely enhanced the price of all first-class editions, and rare works.

No longer, as in the early days of Dibdin and Heber, is the competition for the curiosities of old English literature confined to a half-score of native amateurs. True, we have no such omnivorous gatherers of literary rubbish as that magnificent *helluo librorum*, Richard Heber, who amassed what was claimed to be the largest collection of books ever formed by a single individual. Endowed with a princely fortune, and an undying passion for the possession of books, he spent nearly a million dollars in their acquisition. His library, variously stated at from 105,000 volumes (by Dr. Dibdin) to 146,000 volumes (by Dr. Allibone) was brought to the hammer in 1834. The catalogue filled 13 octavo volumes, and the sale occupied 216 days. The insatiable owner (who was a brother of Reginald Heber, Bishop of Calcutta) died while still collecting, at the age of sixty, leaving his enormous library, which no single house of ordinary size could hold, scattered in half a dozen mansions in London, Oxford, Paris, Antwerp, Brussels and Ghent.

Yet the owner of this vast mass of mingled nonsense and erudition, this library of the curiosities of literature, was as generous in imparting as in acquiring his literary treasures. No English scholar but was freely welcome to the loan of his volumes; and his own taste and critical knowledge are said to have been of the first order.

From this, probably the most extensive private library ever gathered, let us turn to the largest single purchase, in number of volumes, made at one time for a public library. When Dr. J. G. Cogswell went abroad in 1848, to lay the foundations of the Astor Library, he took with him credentials for the expenditure of $100,000; and, what was of even greater importance, a thoroughly digested catalogue of *desiderata*, embracing the most important books in every department of literature and science. No such opportunity of buying the finest books at the lowest prices is likely ever to occur again, as the fortuitous concourse of events brought to Dr. Cogswell. It was the year of revolutions—the year when the thrones were tottering or falling all over Europe, when the wealthy and privileged classes were trembling for their possessions, and anxious to turn them into ready money. In every time of panic, political or financial, the prices of books, as well as of all articles of luxury, are the first to fall. Many of the choicest collections came to the hammer; multitudes were eager to sell—but there were few buyers except the book merchants, who were all ready to sell again. The result was that some 80,-000 volumes were gathered for the Astor Library, embracing a very large share of the best editions and the most expensive works, with many books strictly denominated rare, and nearly all bound in superior style, at an average cost of about $1.40 per volume. This extraordinary good fortune enabled the Astor Library to be opened on a very small endowment, more splendidly equipped for a library of reference than any new institution could be today with four or five times the money.

Compared with such opportunities as these, you may consider the experiences of the little libraries, and the narrow means of recruitment generally found, as very literally the day of small things. But a wise apportionment of small funds, combined with a good knowledge of the commercial value of books, and perpetual vigilance in using opportunities, will go very far toward enlarging any collection in the most desirable directions.

Compare for a moment with the results stated of the Astor Library's early purchases, the average prices paid by British Libraries for books purchased from 1826 to 1854, as published in a parliamentary return. The average cost per volume varied from 16s or about $4 a volume, for the University Library of Edinburg, to 4s 6d, or $1.10 a volume for the Manchester Free Library. The latter, however, were chiefly popular new books, published at low prices, while the former included many costly old works, law books, etc. The British Museum Library's average was 8s 5d or about $2.00 per volume. Those figures represent cloth binding, while the Astor's purchases were mostly in permanent leather bindings.

Averages are very uncertain standards of comparison, as a single book rarity often costs more than a hundred volumes of the new books of the day; but in a library filled with the best editions of classical and scientific works, and reference books, I presume that two dollars a volume is not too high an estimate of average cost, in these days represented by the last twenty years. For a circulating library, on the other hand, composed chiefly of what the public most seek to read, half that average would perhaps express the full commercial value of the collection. Of its intrinsic value I will not here pause to speak.

There are many methods of book buying, of which we may indicate the principal as follows:

1. By direct orders from book dealers.
2. By competition on select lists of wants.
3. By order from priced catalogues.
4. By purchase at auction sales.

5. By personal research among book stocks.

6. By lists and samples of books sent on approval.

Each of these methods has its advantages—and, I may add, its disadvantages likewise. The collector who combines them, as opportunity presents, is most likely to make his funds go the farthest, and to enrich his collection the most. Direct orders for purchase are necessary for most new books wanted, except in the case of the one government library, which in most countries, receives them under copyright provision. An advantageous arrangement can usually be made with one or more book-dealers, to supply all new books at a fairly liberal discount from retail prices. And it is wise management to distribute purchases where good terms are made, as thereby the trade will feel an interest in the library, and a mutuality of interest will secure more opportunities and better bargains.

The submission of lists of books wanted, to houses having large stocks or good facilities, helps to make funds go as far as possible through competition. By the typewriter such lists can now be manifolded much more cheaply than they can be written or printed.

Selection from priced catalogues presents a constantly recurring opportunity of buying volumes of the greatest consequence, to fill gaps in any collection, and often at surprisingly low prices. Much as book values have been enhanced of late years, there are yet catalogues issued by American, English and continental dealers which quote books both of the standard and secondary class at very cheap rates. Even now English books are sold by the Mudie and the W. H. Smith lending libraries in London, after a very few months, at one-half to one-fourth their original publishing price. These must usually be rebound, but by instructing your agent to select copies which are clean within, all the soil of the edges will disappear with the light trimming of the binder.

Purchase at auction supplies a means of recruiting libraries both public and private with many rare works, and with the best editions of the standard authors, often finely bound. The choice private libraries of the country, as well as the poor ones, tend to pour themselves sooner or later into public auctions. The collectors of books, whose early avidity to amass libraries of fine editions was phenomenal, rarely persist in cultivating the passion through life. Sometimes they are overtaken by misfortune—sometimes by indifference—the bibliomania not being a perennial inspiration, but often an acute and fiery attack, which in a few years burns out. Even if the library gathered with so much money and pains descends to the heirs of the collector, the passion for books is very seldom an inherited one. Thus the public libraries are constantly recruited by the opportunities of selection furnished by the forced sale of the private ones. Here, public competition frequently runs up the price of certain books to an exorbitant degree, while those not wanted often sell for the merest trifle. One should have a pretty clear idea of the approximate commercial value of books, before competing for them at public sale. He may, however, if well persuaded in his own mind as to the importance or the relative unimportance to his own collection of any work, regulate his bids by that standard, regardless of commercial value, except as a limit beyond which he will not go. Few librarians can personally attend auction sales—nor is it needful, when limits can so easily be set to orders. It is never safe to send an unlimited bid, as there may be others without limit, in which case the book is commonly awarded to the most remote bidder.

There are many curiosities of the auction room, one of

them being the frequent re-appearance of book rarities which have been through several auctions, sometimes at intervals of years, keenly competed for by rival bibliophiles, and carried off in triumph by some ardent collector, who little thought at the time how soon his own collection would come to the hammer.

There are also many curiosities of compilation in auction catalogues. Not to name errors of commission, like giving the authorship of books to the wrong name, and errors of omission, like giving no author's name at all, some catalogues are thickly strewn with the epithets *rare*—and *very rare*, when the books are sufficiently common in one or the other market. Do not be misled by these surface indications. Books are often attributed in catalogues to their editor or translator, and the unwary buyer may thus find himself saddled with a duplicate already in his own collection. There has been much improvement in late years in the care with which auction catalogues are edited, and no important collection at least is offered, without having first passed through the hands of an expert, familiar with bibliography. It is the minor book sales where the catalogues receive no careful editing, and where the dates and editions are frequently omitted, that it is necessary to guard against. It is well to refrain from sending any bids out of such lists, because they furnish no certain identification of the books, and if all would do the same, thus diminishing the competition and the profit of the auctioneer, he might learn never to print a catalogue without date, place of publication, and full name of author of every book offered.

Never be too eager to acquire an auction book, unless you are very thoroughly assured that it is one of the kind truly designated *rarissimus*. An eminent and thoroughly informed book collector, with an experience of forty years

devoted to book auctions and book catalogues, assured me
that it was his experience that almost every book would
turn up on the average about every seven years.   Of course
there are notable exceptions—and especially among the
class of books known as *incunabula*, (or cradle-books
printed in the infancy of printing) and of early Americana:
but it is not these which the majority of libraries are
most in search of.   Remember always, if you lose a coveted
volume, that there will be another chance—perhaps many
of them.   The private collector, who carries it off against
you, has had no former opportunity to get the rare volume,
and may never have another.   He is therefore justified in
paying what is to ordinary judgment an extraordinary
price.   Individual collectors die, but public libraries are
immortal.

If you become thoroughly conversant with priced catalogues, you will make fewer mistakes than most private
buyers.   Not only catalogues of notable collections, with
the prices obtained at auction, but the large and very
copious catalogues of such London book-dealers as Quaritch and Sotheran, are accessible in the great city libraries.   These are of the highest use in suggesting the proxi-
mate prices at which important books have been or may
be acquired.   Since 1895, annual volumes entitled "American Book Prices Current" have been issued, giving the
figures at which books have been sold at all the principal
auction sales of the year.

There is no word so much abused as the term *rare*, when
applied to books.   Librarians know well the unsophisti-
cated citizen who wants to sell at a high price a "rare"
volume of divinity "a hundred and fifty years old" (worth
possibly twenty-five cents to half a dollar,) and the persistent woman who has the rarest old bible in the country,
which she values anywhere from fifty to five hundred dol-

lars, and which turns out on inspection to be an imperfect copy of one of Barker's multitudinous editions of 1612 to '18, which may be picked up at five to eight shillings in any old London book-shop. The confident assertions so often paraded, even in catalogues, "only three copies known," and the like, are to be received with absolute incredulity, and the claims of ignorant owners of books who fancy that their little pet goose is a fine swan, because they never saw another, are as ridiculous as the laudation bestowed by a sapient collector upon two of his most valued nuggets. "This, sir, is unique, but not so unique as the other."

Buying books by actual inspection at the book-shops is even more fascinating employment than buying them through catalogues. You thus come upon the most unexpected volumes unawares. You open the covers, scan the title-pages, get a glimpse of the plates, and flit from book to book, like a bee gathering honey for its hive. It is a good way to recruit your library economically, to run through the stock of a book-dealer systematically—neglecting no shelf, but selecting throughout the whole stock, and laying aside what you think you may want. When this is done, you will have quite a pile of literature upon which to negotiate with the proprietor. It is cheaper to buy thus at wholesale than by piecemeal, because the bookseller will make you a larger discount on a round lot of which you relieve his shelves.

Another method of recruiting your library is the examination of books "on approval." Most book-dealers will be so obliging as to send in parcels of books for the inspection of a librarian or collector, who can thus examine them leisurely and with more thoroughness than in a book store, without leaving his business.

All books, by whatever course they may be purchased,

are indispensably to be collated before they are accepted
and paid for.　Neglect of this will fill any library with imperfections, since second-hand books are liable to have
missing leaves, or plates, or maps, while new books may
lack signatures or plates, or be wrongly bound together.
In the case of new books, or books still in print, the publisher is bound to make good an imperfection.

In old books, this is usually impossible, and the only
remedy is to return the imperfect books upon the seller's
hands, unless there may be a reason, such as the rarity of
the volume, or its comparative little cost, or the trifling
nature of the imperfection, for retaining it.　The equi-
ties in these cases are in favor of the buyer, who is presumed to have purchased a perfect copy.　But the right of
reclamation must be exercised promptly, or it may be for-
feited by lapse of time.　If an imperfection in any book
you order is noted in the catalogue, it is not subject to return.　I have ever found the book auctioneers most courteous and considerate in their dealings—and the same can
be said of the book trade generally, among whom instances
of liberality to libraries are by no means rare.

One of the choicest pleasures of the book collector,
whether private student or librarian, is to visit the second-
hand book-shops of any city, and examine the stock with
care.　While he may find but few notable treasures in one
collection, a search through several shops will be almost
sure to reward him.　Here are found many of the out-
pourings of the private libraries, formed by specialists or
amateurs, and either purchased by the second-hand dealer
en bloc, or bid off by him at some auction sale.　Even rare
books are picked up in this way, no copies of which can be
had by order, because long since "out of print."　The
stock in these shops is constantly changing, thus adding a
piquant and sometimes exciting element to the book-

hunter, who is wise in proportion as he seizes quickly upon all opportunities of new "finds" by frequent visits. To mourn over a lost chance in rare books is often more grievous to the zealous collector, than to lose a large share out of his fortune; while to exult over a literary nugget long sought and at length found is a pleasure to which few others can be compared.

Of the many *bouquinistes* whose open-air shops line the quays of Paris along the Seine, numbering once as many as a hundred and fifty dealers in second-hand books, I have no room to treat; books have been written about them, and the *littérateurs* of France, of Europe, and of America have profited by countless bargains in their learned wares. Nor can I dwell upon the literary wealth of London bookshops, dark and dingy, but ever attractive to the hungry scholar, or the devotee of bibliomania.

Of the many second-hand booksellers (or rather sellers of second-hand books) in American cities, the more notable have passed from the stage of action in the last quarter of a century. Old William Gowans, a quaint, intelligent Scotchman, in shabby clothes and a strong face deeply marked with small pox, was for many years the dean of this fraternity in New York. His extensive book-shop in Nassau street, with its dark cellar, was crowded and packed with books on shelves, on stairways and on the floors, heaped and piled in enormous masses, amid which the visitor could hardly find room to move. On one of the piles you might find the proprietor seated—

> Books to the right of him,
> Books to the left of him,
> Books behind him,
> Volleyed and tumbled,

while he answered inquiries for books from clergymen and students, or gruffly bargained with a boy or an old woman for a dilapidated lot of old books. He had a curious quiz-zical way with strangers, who at once set him down as an oddity, and his impatience with ignoramuses and bores gave him the repute of crustiness, which was redeemed by suavity enough whenever he met with people of intelligence.

Gowans issued scores of catalogues of his stock, in which titles were often illustrated by notes, always curious and often amusing, credited to "Western Memorabilia," a work which no bookseller or man of letters had ever heard of, but which was shrewdly suspected to have been a projected scrap-book of the observations and opinions of William Gowans.

There was another eccentric book-dealer's shop in Nassau street kept by one John Doyle, who aimed so high in his profession as to post over his door a sign reading "The Moral Centre of the Intellectual Universe." This establishment was notably full of old editions of books of English history and controversial theology.

The most famous second-hand book-shop in Boston was Burnham's, whose fore-name was Thomas Oliver Hazard Perry, shortened into "Perry Burnham" by his familiars. He was a little, pale-faced, wiry, nervous man, with piercing black eyes and very brusque manners. In old and musty books he lived and moved and had his being, for more than a generation. He exchanged a stuffy, narrow shop in Cornhill for more spacious quarters in Washington street, near School street, where he bought and sold books with an assiduous devotion to business, never trusting to others what he could do himself. He was proud of his collection and its extent. He bought books and pamphlets at auction literally by the cart-load, every thing that nobody else wanted being bid off to Burnham at an insignificant price, almost nominal. He got a wide reputation for selling cheaply, but he always knew when to charge a stiff price for a book, and to stick to it. Once when I was pricing a lot of miscellaneous books picked out for purchase, mostly under a dollar a volume, we came to a copy of "The Constitutions of the Several Independent States of America," 1st edition, Philadelphia, 1781, of which two hundred copies only were printed, by order of Congress. This copy was in the original boards, uncut, and with the autograph of Timothy Pickering on the title page. "If the Congress Library wants that book," said Mr. Burnham, "it will have to pay eight dollars for it." I took it, well pleased to secure what years of search had failed to bring. The next year my satisfaction was enhanced when an inferior copy of the same book was offered at twenty dollars.

Burnham died a wealthy man, having amassed a million dollars in trade and by rise in real estate, as he owned the land on which the Parker House stands in Boston.

Among Philadelphia dealers in second-hand books, one John Penington was recognized as most intelligent and honorable. He was a book-lover and a scholar, and one instinctively ranked him not as a bookseller, but as a gentleman who dealt in books. On his shelves one always found books of science and volumes in foreign languages.

Another notable dealer was John Campbell, a jolly, hearty Irish-American, with a taste for good books, and an antipathy to negroes, as keen as the proverbial hatred of the devil for holy water. Campbell wrote a book entitled "Negromania," published in 1851, in which his creed was set forth in strong language. He was a regular bidder at book auctions, where his burly form and loud voice made him a prominent figure.

Of notable auction sales of books, and of the extravagant prices obtained for certain editions by ambitious and eager competition, there is little room to treat. The oft-told

story of the Valdarfer Boccaccio of 1471, carried off at the
Roxburghe sale in 1812, at £2,260 from Earl Spencer by
the Marquis of Blandford, and re-purchased seven years
after at another auction for £918, has been far surpassed in
modern bibliomania. "The sound of that hammer," wrote
the melodramatic Dibdin, "echoed through Europe:" but
what would he have said of the Mazarin Bible of Gutenberg and Fust (1450-55) sold in 1897, at the Ashburnham
sale, for four thousand pounds, or of the Latin Psalter of
Fust and Schoeffer, 2d ed. 1459, which brought £4,950 at
the Syston Park sale in 1884? This last sum (about twenty-four thousand dollars) is the largest price ever yet recorded as received for a single volume. Among books of
less rarity, though always eagerly sought, is the first folio
Shakespeare of 1623, a very fine and perfect copy of which
brought £716.2 at Daniel's sale in 1864. Copies warranted
perfect have since been sold in London for £415 to £470.
In New York, a perfect but not "tall" copy brought $4,-
200 in 1891 at auction. Walton's "Compleat Angler,"
London, 1st ed. 1653, a little book of only 250 pages, sold
for £310 in 1891. It was published for one shilling and
sixpence. The first edition of Robinson Crusoe brought
£75 at the Crampton sale in 1896.

The rage for first editions of very modern books reached
what might be called high-water mark some time since,
and has been on the decline. Shelley's "Queen Mab," 1st
ed. 1813, was sold at London for £22.10, and his "Refuta-
tion of Deism," 1814, was sold at £33, at a London sale in
1887. In New York, many first editions of Shelley's
poems brought the following enormous prices in 1897.

Shelley's Adonais, 1st ed. Pisa, Italy, 1821, $335.

Alastor, London, 1816, $130.

The Cenci, Italy, 1819, $65.

Hellas, London, 1822, $13.

But these were purely adventitious prices, as was clearly shown in the sale at the same auction rooms, a year or two earlier, of the following:

Shelley's Adonais, 1st ed. Pisa, 1821, $19.

Alastor, London, 1816, $32.

The Cenci, Italy, 1819, $21.

Hellas, London, 1822, $2.

The sales occasionally made at auction of certain books at extraordinary prices, prove nothing whatever as to the real market value, for these reasons: (1) The auctioneer often has an unlimited bid, and the price is carried up to an inordinate height. (2) Two or more bidders present, infatuated by the idea of extreme rarity, bid against one another until all but one succumb, when the price has reached a figure which it is a mild use of terms to call absurd. (3) Descriptions in sale catalogues, though often entirely unfounded, characterising a book as "excessively rare;" "only — copies known," "very scarce," "never before offered at our sales," etc., may carry the bidding on a book up to an unheard-of price.

The appeal always lies to the years against the hours; and many a poor book-mad enthusiast has had to rue his too easy credulity in giving an extravagant sum for books which he discovers later that he could have bought for as many shillings as he has paid dollars. Not that the *rarissimi* of early printed books can ever be purchased for a trifle; but it should ever be remembered that even at the sales where a few—a very few—bring the enormous prices that are bruited abroad, the mass of the books offered are knocked down at very moderate figures, or are even sacrificed at rates very far below their cost. The possessor of one of the books so advertised as sold at some auction for a hundred dollars or upwards, if he expects to realise a tithe

of the figure quoted, will speedily find himself in the voca-
tive.

While there are almost priceless rarities not to be found
in the market by any buyer, let the book collector be con-
soled by the knowledge that good books, in good editions,
were never so easy to come by as now. A fine library can
be gathered by any one with very moderate means, supplemented by a fair amount of sagacity and common sense.
The buyer with a carefully digested list of books wanted
will find that to buy them wisely takes more time and less
money than he had anticipated. The time is required to
acquaint himself with the many competing editions, with
their respective merits and demerits. This involves a comparison of type, paper, and binding, as well as the comparative prices of various dealers for the same books. No one
who is himself gifted with good perceptions and good taste,
should trust to other hands the selection of his library.
His enjoyment of it will be proportioned to the extent to
which it is his own creation. The passion for nobly written books, handsomely printed, and clothed in a fitting
garb, when it has once dawned, is not to be defrauded of its
satisfaction by hiring a commission merchant to appease
it. What we do for ourselves, in the acquirement of any
knowledge, is apt to be well done: what is done for us by
others is of little value.

We have heard of some uninformed *parvenus*, grown
suddenly rich, who have first ordered a magnificent library
room fitted with rose-wood, marble and gilded trappings,
and then ordered it to be filled with splendidly bound volumes at so much per volume. And it is an authentic fact,
that a bookseller to the Czar of Russia one Klostermann,
actually sold books at fifty to one hundred roubles by the
yard, according to the binding. The force of folly could

no farther go, to debase the aims and degrade the intellect of man.

In the chapter upon rare books, the reader will find instances in great variety of the causes that contribute to the scarcity and enhancement of prices of certain books, without at all affecting their intrinsic value, which may be of the smallest.

CHAPTER 3.

The Art of Book Binding.

In these suggestions upon the important question of the binding of books, I shall have nothing to say of the history of the art, and very little of its aesthetics. The plainest and most practical hints will be aimed at, and if my experience shall prove of value to any, I shall be well rewarded for giving it here. For other matters readers will naturally consult some of the numerous manuals of book-binding in English, French and German. The sumptuous bindings executed in the sixteenth century, under the patronage and the eyes of Grolier, the famous tooled masterpieces of Derome, Le Gascon, Padeloup, Trautz and other French artists, and the beautiful gems of the binder's art from the hands of Roger Payne, Lewis, Mackenzie, Hayday and Bedford, are they not celebrated in the pages of Dibdin, Lacroix, Fournier, Wheatley, and Robert Hoe?

There are some professed lovers of books who affect either indifference or contempt for the style in which their favorites are dressed. A well known epigram of Burns is sometimes quoted against the fondness for fine bindings which widely prevails in the present day, as it did in that of the Scottish Poet. A certain Scottish nobleman, endowed with more wealth than brains, was vain of his splendidly bound Shakespeare, which, however, he never read. Burns, on opening the folio, found the leaves sadly worm-eaten, and wrote these lines on the fly-leaf:

"Through and through th' inspired leaves,
Ye maggots make your windings;
But O respect his lordship's taste,
And spare the golden bindings!"

(50)

Yet no real book-lover fails to appreciate the neatness
and beauty of a tasteful binding, any more than he is indifferent to the same qualities in literary style. Slovenly
binding is almost as offensive to a cultivated eye as slovenly
composition. No doubt both are "mere externals," as we
are told, and so are the splendors of scenery, the beauty of
flowers, and the comeliness of the human form, or features,
or costume. Talk as men will of the insignificance of
dress, it constitutes a large share of the attractiveness of
the world in which we live.

The two prime requisites of good binding for libraries
are neatness and solidity. It is pleasant to note the steady
improvement in American bindings of late years. As the
old style of "Half cloth boards," of half a century ago, with
paper titles pasted on the backs, has given way to the neat,
embossed, full muslin gilt, so the clumsy and homely sheep-
skin binding has been supplanted by the half-roan or morocco, with marble or muslin sides. Few books are issued, however, either here or abroad, in what may be
called permanent bindings. The cheapness demanded by
buyers of popular books forbids this, while it leaves to the
taste and fancy of every one the selection of the "library
style" in which he will have his collection permanently
dressed.

What is the best style of binding for a select or a public
library? is a question often discussed, with wide discrepancies of opinion. The so universally prevalent cloth
binding is too flimsy for books subjected to much use—as
most volumes in public collections and many in private libraries are likely to be. The choice of the more substantial bindings lies between calf and morocco, and between
half or full bindings of either. For nearly all books, half
binding, if well executed, and with cloth sides, is quite as
elegant, and very nearly as solid and lasting as full leather;

for if a book is so worn as to need rebinding, it is generally
in a part where the full binding wears out quite as fast as
the other.   That is, it gets worn at the hinges and on the
back, whether full or half-bound.   The exceptions are the
heavy dictionaries, encyclopaedias, and other works of reference, which are subjected to much wear and tear at the
sides, as well as at the back and corners.   Full leather is
much more expensive than half binding, though not
doubly so.

Every librarian or book collector should understand
something of book-binding and its terms, so that he may
be able to give clear directions as to every item involved in
binding, repairing, or re-lettering, and to detect imperfect
or slighted work.

The qualities that we always expect to find in a well-
bound book are solidity, flexibility, and elegance.   Special
examination should be directed toward each of these points
in revising any lot of books returned from a binder.   Look
at each book with regard to:—

1. Flexibility in opening.

2. Evenness of the cover, which should lie flat and
smooth—each edge being just parallel with the others
throughout.

3. Compactness—see that the volumes are thoroughly
pressed—solid, and not loose or spongy.

4. Correct and even lettering of titles, and other tooling.

5. Good wide margins.

A well-bound book always opens out flat, and stays open.
It also shuts up completely, and when closed stays shut.
But how many books do we see always bulging open at the
sides, or stiffly resisting being opened by too great tight-
ness in the back?   If the books you have had bound do not
meet all these requirements, it is time to look for another
binder.

The different styles of dressing books may all be summed up in the following materials: Boards, cloth, vellum, sheep, bock, pig-skin, calf, Russia, and morocco—to which may be added of recent years, buckram, duck, linoleum, and the imitations of leather, such as leatherette and morocco paper, and of parchment. I take no account here of obsolete styles—as ivory, wood, brass, silver and other metals, nor of velvet, satin, and other occasional luxuries of the binder's art. These belong to the domain of the amateur, the antiquary, or the book-fancier—not to that of the librarian or the ordinary book-collector.

Roan leather is nothing but sheep-skin, stained or colored; basil or basan is sheepskin tanned in bark, while roan is tanned in sumac, and most of the so called moroccos are also sheep, ingeniously grained by a mechanical process. As all the manufactures in the world are full of "shoddy," or sham materials, the bookbinder's art affords no exception. But if the librarian or collector patronises shams, he should at least do it with his eyes open, and with due counting of the cost.

Now as to the relative merits and demerits of materials for binding. No one will choose boards covered with paper for any book which is to be subjected to perusal, and cloth is too flimsy and shaky in its attachment to the book, however cheap, for any library volumes which are to be constantly in use. It is true that since the bulk of the new books coming into any library are bound in cloth, they may be safely left in it until well worn; and by this rule, all the books which nobody ever reads may be expected to last many years, if not for generations. Cloth is a very durable material, and will outlast some of the leathers, but any wetting destroys its beauty, and all colors but the darkest soon become soiled and repulsive, if in constant use. In most libraries, I hold that every cloth-bound book which is read, must sooner or later come to have a stout leather jacket. It may go for years, especially if the book is well sewed, but to rebinding it must come at last; and the larger the volume, the sooner it becomes shaky, or broken at some weak spot.

The many beautiful new forms of cloth binding should have a word of praise, but the many more which we see of gaudy, fantastic, and meretricious bindings, and frightful combinations of colors must be viewed with a shudder.

Vellum, formerly much used for book-bindings, is the modern name for parchment. Parchment was the only known writing material up to the 12th century, when paper was first invented. There are two kinds—animal and vegetable. The vegetable is made from cotton fibre or paper, by dipping it in a solution of sulphuric acid and [sometimes] gelatine, then removing the acid by a weak solution of ammonia, and smooth finishing by rolling the sheets over a heated cylinder. Vegetable parchment is used to bind many booklets which it is desired to dress in an elegant or dainty style, but is highly unsuitable for library books. Vellum proper is a much thicker material, made from the skins of calves, sheep, or lambs, soaked in lime-water, and smoothed and hardened by burnishing with a hard instrument, or pumice-stone. The common vellum is made from sheep-skin splits, or skivers, but the best from whole calf-skins. The hard, strong texture of vellum is in its favor, but its white color and tendency to warp are fatal objections to it as a binding material.

Vellum is wholly unfit for the shelves of a library; the elegant white binding soils with dust, or the use of the hands, more quickly than any other; and the vellum warps in a dry climate, or curls up in a heated room, so as to be unmanageable upon the shelves, and a nuisance in the eyes of librarian and reader alike. The thin vegetable parchment lately in vogue for some books and booklets is too unsubstantial for anything but a lady's boudoir, where it may have its little day—"a thing of beauty," but by no means "a joy forever."

Sheepskin—once the full binding for most school-books, and for a large share of law and miscellaneous works for libraries, is now but little used, except in its disguised forms. It is too soft a leather for hard wear and tear, and what with abrasion and breaking at the hinges (termed by binders the joints), it will give little satisfaction in the long run. Under the effect of gas and heated atmospheres sheep crumbles and turns to powder. Its cheapness is about its only merit, and even this is doubtful economy, since no binding can be called cheap that has to be rebound or repaired every few years. In the form of half-roan or bock, colored sheep presents a handsome appearance on the shelf, and in volumes or sets which are reasonably secure from frequent handling, one is sometimes justified in adopting it, as it is far less expensive than morocco. Pigskin has been recently revived as a binding material, but though extremely hard and durable, it is found to warp badly on the shelves.

Calf bindings have always been great favorites with book-lovers, and there are few things more beautiful—*prima facie*, than a volume daintily bound in light French calf, as smooth as glass, as fine as silk, with elegant gold tooling without and within, gilt edges, and fly-leaves of finest satin. I said beautiful, *prima facie*—and this calls to mind the definition of that law term by a learned Vermont jurist, who said: "Gentlemen of the jury, I must explain to you that a *prima facie* case is a case that is very good in front, but may be very bad in the rear." So of our so much lauded and really lovely calf bindings: they develop qualities in use which give us pause. Calf is the most brittle of the leathers—hence it is always breaking at the hinges; it is a very smooth leather—hence it shows every scratch instantly; it is a light and delicate leather—hence it shows soils and stains more quickly than any other. Out of every hundred calf-bound volumes in any well-used library, there will not remain ten which have not had to be re-bound or repaired at the end of twenty or thirty years. Heavy volumes bound in calf or half-calf leather will break by their own weight on the shelves, without any use at all; and smaller volumes are sure to have their brittle joints snapped asunder by handling sooner or later—it is only a question of time.

Next comes Russia leather, which is very thick and strong, being made of the hides of cattle, colored, and perfumed by the oil of birch, and made chiefly in Russia. The objections to this leather are its great cost, its stiffness and want of elasticity, and its tendency to desiccate and lose all its tenacity in the dry or heated atmosphere of our libraries. It will break at the hinges—though not so readily as calf.

Lastly, we have the morocco leather, so called because it was brought from Morocco, in Africa, and still we get the best from thence, and from the Mediterranean ports of the Levant—whence comes another name for the best of this favorite leather, "Levant morocco," which is the skin of the mountain goat, and reckoned superior to all other leathers. The characteristics of the genuine morocco, sometimes called Turkey morocco, having a pebbled grain, distinguishing it from the smooth morocco, are its toughness and durability, combined with softness and flexibility. It has a very tenacious fibre, and I have never found a real morocco binding broken at the hinges. The old proverb —"there is nothing like leather"—is pregnant with meaning, and especially applies to the best morocco. As no material yet discovered in so many ages can take the place of leather for foot-wear and for harness, such is its tenacity and elasticity—so for book coverings, to withstand wear and tear, good leather is indispensable. There are thoroughly-bound books existing which are five centuries old —representing about the time when leather began to replace wood and metals for binding. The three great enemies of books are too great heat, too much moisture, and coal gas, which produces a sulphurous acid very destructive to bindings, and should never be used in libraries. From the dangers which destroy calf and Russia leather, morocco is measurably free.

As to color, I usually choose red for books which come to binding or rebinding, for these reasons. The bulk of every library is of dark and sombre color, being composed of the old-fashioned calf bindings, which grow darker with age, mingled with the cloth bindings of our own day, in which dark colors predominate. Now the intermixture of red morocco, in all or most of the newly bound books, relieves the monotony of so much blackness, lights up the shelves, and gives a more cheerful aspect to the whole library. Some there are who insist upon varying the colors of bindings with the subjects of the books—and the British Museum Library actually once bound all works on botany in green, poetry in yellow, history in red, and theology in blue; but this is more fanciful than important. A second reason for preferring red in moroccos is that, being dyed with cochineal, it holds its color more permanently than any other—the moroccos not colored red turning to a dingy, disagreeable brown after forty or fifty years, while the red are found to be fast colors. This was first discovered in the National Library of France, and ever since most books in that great collection have been bound in red. A celebrated binder having recommended this color to a connoisseur who was having fine morocco binding done, instanced the example of the Paris Library, whose books, said he, are "mostly red," to which the amateur replied that he hoped they were.

Add to the merits of morocco leather the fact that it is not easily scratched nor stained, that it is very tough in wear, and resists better than any other the moisture and soiling of the hands—and we have a material worthy of all acceptance.

In half-binding chosen for the great majority of books because it is much cheaper than full leather, the sides are covered with muslin or with some kind of colored paper— usually marble. The four corners of every book, however, should always be protected by leather or, better still, by vellum, which is a firmer material—otherwise they will rapidly wear off, and the boards will break easily at their corners. As to the relative merits of cloth and paper for the sides of books, cloth is far more durable, though it costs more. Paper becomes quickly frayed at the edges, or is liable to peel where pasted on, though it may be renewed at small expense, and may properly be used except upon the much-read portion of the library. The cloth or paper should always harmonize in color with the leather to which it is attached. They need not be the same, but they should be of similar shade.

One more reason for preferring morocco to other leathers is that you can always dispense with lettering-pieces or patches in gilding the titles on the back. All light-colored bindings (including law calf) are open to the objection that gold lettering is hardly legible upon them. Hence the necessity of stamping the titles upon darker pieces of leather, which are fastened to the backs. These lettering-pieces become loose in over-heated libraries, and tend continually to peel off, entailing the expense of re-

pairing or re-lettering. Every morocco bound book can
be lettered directly upon the leather. Bock is made of the
skin of the Persian sheep, and is called Persian in London.
It is a partially unsuccessful-imitation of morocco, becoming easily abraded, like all the sheep-skin leathers, and although it is to be had in all colors, and looks fairly handsome for a time, and is tougher than skiver (or split sheep-
skin), the books that are bound in it will sooner or later
become an eyesore upon the shelves. A skin of Persian
leather costs about one-third the price of genuine morocco,
or goat. But the actual saving in binding is in a far less
ratio—the difference being only six to eight cents per volume. It is really much cheaper to use morocco in the first
place, than to undergo all the risks of deterioration and
re-binding.

Of the various imitations of leather, or substitutes for it,
we have leatherette, leather-cloth, duck, fibrette, feltine,
and buckram. Buckram and duck are strong cotton or
linen fabricks, made of different colors, and sometimes figured or embossed to give them somewhat the look of
leather. Hitherto, they are made mostly in England, and
I have learned of no American experience in their favor
except the use of stout duck for covering blank books and
binding newspapers. The use of buckram has been mostly
abandoned by the libraries. Morocco cloth is American,
but has no advantage over plain muslin or book cloth, that
I am aware of. Leatherette, made principally of paper,
colored and embossed to simulate morocco leather, appears
to have dropped out of use almost as fast as it came in, having no quality of permanence, elegance, or even of great
cheapness to commend it. Leatherette tears easily, and
lacks both tenacity and smoothness.

Both feltine and fibrette are made of paper—tear quickly, and are unfit for use on any book that is ever likely to

be read.   All these imitations of leather are made of paper
as their basis, and hence can never be proper substitutes
for leather.

All torn leaves or plates in books should be at once
mended by pasting a very thin onion-skin paper on both
sides of the torn leaf, and pressing gently between leaves
of sized paper until dry.

Corners made of vellum or parchment are more durable
than any leather.   When dry, the parchment becomes as
hard almost as iron and resists falls or abrasion.   To use
it on books where the backs are of leather is a departure
from the uniformity or harmony of style insisted upon by
many, but in binding books that are to be greatly worn, use
should come before beauty.

In rebinding, all maps or folded plates should be mounted on thin canvas, linen, or muslin, strong and fine, to protect them from inevitable tearing by long use.   If a coarse
or thick cloth is used, the maps will not fold or open easily
and smoothly.

The cutting or trimming of the edges of books needs to
be watched with jealous care.   Few have reflected that the
more margin a binder cuts off, the greater his profit on any
job, white paper shavings having a very appreciable price
by the pound.   A strictly uncut book is in many American
libraries a rarity.   And of the books which go a second
time to the binder, although at first uncut, how many retain their fair proportions of margin when they come back?
You have all seen books in which the text has been cut
into by the ruthless knife-machine of the binder.   This is
called "bleeding" a book, and there are no words strong
enough to denounce this murderous and cold-blooded atrocity.   The trimming of all books should be held within
the narrowest limits—for the life of a book depends largely
upon its preserving a good margin.   Its only chance of be-

ing able to stand a second rebinding may depend upon its being very little trimmed at its first. If it must be cut at all, charge your binder to take off the merest shaving from either edge.

Every new book or magazine added to the library, if uncut, should be carefully cut with a paper-knife before it goes into the hands of any reader. Spoiled or torn or ragged edges will be the penalty of neglecting this. You have seen people tear open the leaves of books and magazines with their fingers—a barbarism which renders him who would be guilty of it worthy of banishment from the resorts of civilization. In cutting books, the leaves should always be held firmly down—and the knife pressed evenly through the uncut leaves to the farthest verge of the back. Books which are cut in the loose fashion which many use are left with rough or ragged edges always, and often a slice is gouged out of the margin by the mis-directed knife. Never trust a book to a novice to be cut, without showing him how to do it, and how not to do it.

The collation of new books in cloth or *broché* should be done before cutting, provided they are issued to readers untrimmed. In collating books in two or more volumes double watchfulness is needed to guard against a missing signature, which may have its place filled by the same pages belonging to another volume—a mixture sometimes made in binderies, in "gathering" the sheets, and which makes it necessary to see that the signatures are right as well as the pages. The collator should check off all plates and maps called for by the table of contents to make sure that the copy is perfect. Books without pagination are of course to have their leaves counted, which is done first in detail, one by one, and then verified by a rapid counting in sections, in the manner used by printers and binders in counting paper by the quire.

The binding of books may be divided into two styles or methods, namely, machine-made book-bindings, and hand-made bindings. Binding by machinery is wholly a modern art, and is applied to all or nearly all new books coming from the press. As these are, in more than nine cases out of ten, bound in cloth covers, and these covers, or cases, are cut out and stamped by machinery, such books are called "case-made." The distinction between this method of binding and the hand method is that in the former the case is made separately from the book, which is then put into it. After the sheets of any book come pressed and dried from the printing office, the first step is to fold them from the large flat sheets into book form. This is sometimes done by hand-folders of bone or some other hard material, but in large establishments for making books, it is done by a folding machine. This will fold ten thousand or more sheets in a day. The folded sheets are next placed in piles or rows, in their numerical sequence, and "gathered" by hand, i. e: a bindery hand picks up the sheets one by one, with great rapidity, until one whole book is gathered and collated, and the process is repeated so long as any sheets remain. Next, the books are thoroughly pressed or "smashed" as it is called, in a powerful smashing-machine, giving solidity to the book, which before pressing was loose and spongy. Then the books are sawed or grooved in the back by another machine, operating a swiftly moving saw, and sewed on cords by still another machine, at about half the cost of hand-sewing. Next, they are cut or trimmed on the three edges in a cutting-machine. The backs of the books are made round by a rounding-machine, leaving the back convex and the front concave in form, as seen in all finished books. The books are now ready for the covers. These consist of binders' board or mill-board, cut out of large sheets into proper size, with lightning-like rapidity, by another machine called a rotary board-cutter. The cloth which is to form the back and sides of the book is cut out, of proper size for the boards, from great rolls of stamped or ribbed or embossed muslin, by another machine. The use of cloth, now so universal for book-binding, dates back little more than half a century. About 1825, Mr. Leighton, of London, introduced it as a substitute for the drab-colored paper then used on the sides, and for the printed titles on the backs. The boards are firmly glued to the cloth, the edges of which are turned over the boards, and fastened on the inside of the covers. The ornamental stamps or figures seen on the covers, both at the back and sides are stamped in with a heated die of brass, or other metal, worked by machinery. The lettering of the title is done in the same way, only that gold-leaf is applied before the die falls. Lastly, the book is pasted by its fly leaves or end-leaves, (sometimes with the addition of a cloth guard) to the inside of the cloth case or cover, and the book is done, after a final pressing. By these rapid machine methods a single book-manufacturing house can turn out ten thousand volumes in a day, with a rapidity which almost takes the breath away from the beholder.

There is a kind of binding which dispenses entirely with sewing the sheets of a book. The backs are soaked with a solution of india-rubber, and each sheet must be thoroughly agglutinated to the backs, so as to adhere firmly to its fellows. This requires that all the sheets shall be folded as single leaves or folios, otherwise the inner leaves of the sheets, having no sewing, would drop out. This method is employed on volumes of plates, music, or any books made up of large separate sheets.

In notable contrast to these rapid methods of binding

what are termed case-made books, comes the hand-made process, where only partial use of machinery is possible.

The rebinding process is divided into three branches: preparing, forwarding, and finishing. The most vital distinction between a machine-made and a hand-made binding, is that the cloth or case-made book is not fastened into its cover in a firm and permanent way, as in leather-backed books. It is simply pasted or glued to its boards—not interlaced by the cords or bands on which it is sewed. Hence one can easily tear off the whole cover of a cloth-bound book, by a slight effort, and such volumes tend to come to pieces early, under constant wear and tear of library service.

Let us now turn to the practical steps pursued in the treatment of books for library use. In re-binding a book, the first step is to take the book apart, or, as it is sometimes called, to take it to pieces. This is done by first stripping off its cover, if it has one. Cloth covers easily come off, as their boards are not tied to the cords on which the book is sewed, but are simply fastened by paste or glue to the boards by a muslin guard, or else the cloth is glued to the back of the book. If the book is leather-covered, or half-bound, i. e.: with a leather back and (usually) leather on its four corners, taking it to pieces is a somewhat slower process. The binder's knife is used to cut the leather at the joints or hinges of the volume, so that the boards may be removed. The cords that tie the boards to the volume are cut at the same time. If the book has a loose or flexible back, the whole cover comes easily off: if bound with a tight back, the glued leather back must be soaked with a sponge full of water, till it is soft enough to peel off, and let the sheets be easily separated.

The book is now stripped of its former binding, and the next step is to take it apart, signature by signature. A signature is that number of leaves which make up one sheet of the book in hand. Thus, an octavo volume, or a volume printed in eights, as it is called, has eight leaves, or sixteen pages to a signature; a quarto four leaves; a duodecimo, or 12 mo. twelve leaves. The term signature (from Lat. *signare*, a sign) is also applied to a letter or figure printed at the foot of the first page of each sheet or section of the book. If the letters are used, the signatures begin with A. and follow in regular sequence of the alphabet. If the book is a very thick one, (or more than twenty-six signatures) then after signature Z, it is customary to duplicate the letters—A. A.—etc., for the remaining signatures. If figures are used instead of letters, the signatures run on to the last, in order of numbers. These letters, indicating signatures are an aid to the binder, in folding, "gathering," and collating the consecutive sheets of any book, saving constant reference to the "pagination," as it is termed, or the paging of the volume, which would take much more time. In many books, you find the signature repeated in the "inset," or the inner leaves of the sheet, with a star or a figure to mark the sequence. Many books, however, are now printed without any signature marks whatever.

To return: in taking apart the sheets or signatures, where they are stuck together at the back by adhesive glue or paste, the knife is first used to cut the thread in the grooves, where the book is sewed on cords or tape. Then the back is again soaked, the sheets are carefully separated, and the adhering substance removed by the knife or fingers. Care has to be taken to lay the signatures in strict order or sequence of pages, or the book may be bound up wrongly. The threads are next to be removed from the inside of every sheet. The sheets being all separated, the book is next pressed, to render all the leaves smooth, and the book solid for binding. Formerly, books were beaten by a powerful hammer, to accomplish this, but it is much more quickly and effectively done in most binderies by the ordinary screw press. Every pressing of books should leave them under pressure at least eight hours.

After pressing, the next step is to sew the sheets on to cords or twine, set vertically at proper distances in a frame, called a "sewing bench," for this purpose. No book can be thoroughly well bound if the sewing is slighted in any degree. Insist upon strong, honest linen thread—if it breaks with a slight pull it is not fit to be used in a book. The book is prepared for the sewer by sawing several grooves across the back with a common saw. The two end grooves are light and narrow, the central ones wider and deeper. Into these inner grooves, the cords fit easily, and the book being taken, sheet by sheet, is firmly sewed around the cords, by alternate movements of the needle and thread, always along the middle of the sheet, the thread making a firm knot at each end (called the "kettle-stitch") as it is returned for sewing on the next sheet. Sometimes the backs are not sawed at all, but the sheets of the book are sewed around the cords, which thus project a little from the back, and form the "bands," seen in raised form on the backs of some books. Books should be sewed on three to six cords, according to their size. This raised-band sewing is reckoned by some a feature of excellent binding. The sunken-band style is apt to give a stiff back, while the raised bands are usually treated with a flexible back. When sewed, the book is detached from its fellows, which may have been sewed on the same bench, by slipping it along the cords, then cutting them apart, so as to leave some two inches of each cord projecting, as ends to be fastened later to the board. In careful binding, the thread is sewed "all along," *i. e.:* each sheet by itself, instead of "two on," as it is called.

The next process is termed "lining up," and consists of
putting on the proper fly-leaves or end-leaves, at the beginning and end of the volume. These usually consist of
four leaves of ordinary white printing paper at each end,
sometimes finished out with two leaves of colored or marbled paper, to add a touch of beauty to the book when
opened. Marbled paper is more durable in color than the
tinted, and does not stain so easily. One of these end-
leaves is pasted down to the inside cover, while the other is
left flying—whence "fly-leaf."

After this comes the cutting of the book at the edges.
This is done by screwing it firmly in a cutting-machine,
which works a sharp knife rapidly, shaving off the edges
successively of the head, front and end, or "tail" as it is
called in book-binding parlance. This trimming used to
be done by hand, with a sharp cutting knife called by binders a "plough." Now, there are many forms of cutting
machines, some of which are called "guillotines" for an
obvious reason. In binding some books, which it is desired
to preserve with wide margins, only a mere shaving is
taken off the head, so as to leave it smooth at the top, letting the front and tail leaves remain uncut. But in case
of re-binding much-used books, the edges are commonly so
much soiled that trimming all around may be required, in
order that they may present a decent appearance. Yet in
no case should the binder be allowed to cut any book
deeply, so as to destroy a good, fair margin. Care must
also be taken to cut the margins evenly, at right angles,
avoiding any crooked lines.

After cutting the book comes "rounding," or giving the
back of the book a curved instead of its flat shape. This
process is done with the hand, by a hammer, or in a rounding press, with a metallic roller. Before rounding, the
back of the book is glued up, that is, receives a coating

of melted glue with a glueing brush, to hold the sections
together, and render the back firm, and a thorough rubbing of the back with hot glue between the sections gives
strength to the volume.

Next comes the treatment of the edges of the book,
hitherto all white, in order to protect them from showing
soil in long use. Sometimes (and this is the cheaper process) the books are simply sprinkled at the edges with a
brush dipped in a dark fluid made of burnt umber or red
ochre, and shaken with a quick concussion near the edges
until they receive a sprinkle of color from the brush.
Other books receive what is called a solid color on the
edges, the books being screwed into a press, and the color
applied with a sponge or brush.

But a marbled edge presents a far more handsome appearance, and should harmonize in color and figure with
the marbled paper of the end leaves. Marbling, so called
from its imitation of richly veined colored marble, is stain-
ing paper or book edges with variegated colors. The process of marbling is highly curious, both chemically and aes-
thetically, and may be briefly described. A large shallow
trough or vat is filled with prepared gum water (gum-trag-
acanth being used); on the surface of this gum-water bright
colors, mixed with a little ox-gall, to be used in producing
the composite effect aimed at in the marbling are thrown
or sprinkled in liquid form. Then they are deftly stirred
or agitated on the surface of the water, with an implement
shaped to produce a certain pattern. The most commonly
used one is a long metallic comb, which is drawn across the
surface of the combined liquids, leaving its pattern impressed upon the ductile fluid. The edges of the book to
be marbled are then touched or dipped on the top of the
water, on which the coloring matter floats, and at once
withdrawn, exhibiting on the edge the precise pattern of

"combed marble" desired, since the various colors—red, yellow, blue, white, etc., have adhered to the surface of the book-edges. The serrated and diversified effect of most comb-marbling is due to stroking the comb in waved lines over the surface. The spotted effect so much admired in other forms, is produced by throwing the colors on with a brush, at the fancy of the skilled workman, or artist, as you may call him. Marbled paper is made in the same way, by dipping one surface of the white sheet, held in a curved form, with great care on the surface of the coloring vat. This is termed shell and wave marbling, as distinguished from comb-marbling. The paper or the book edges are next finished by sizing and burnishing, which gives them a bright glistening appearance.

A still more ornate effect in a book is attained by gilding the edges. Frequently the head of a book is gilt, leaving the front and tail of an uncut book without ornament, and this is esteemed a very elegant style by book connoisseurs, who are, or should be solicitous of wide margins. The gilding of the top edge is a partial protection from dust falling inside, to which the other edges are not so liable. To gild a book edge, it is placed in a press, the edges scraped or smoothed, and coated with a red-colored fluid, which serves to heighten the effect of the gold. Then a sizing is applied by a camel's-hair brush, being a sticky substance, usually the white of an egg, mixed with water (termed by binders "glaire") and the gold-leaf is laid smoothly over it. When the sizing is dry, the gold is burnished with a tool, tipped with an agate or blood-stone, drawn forcibly over the edge until it assumes a glistening appearance.

After the edges have been treated by whatever process, there follows what is termed the "backing" of the book. The volume is pressed between iron clamps, and the back is hammered or rolled where it joins the sides, so as to form a groove to hold the boards forming the solid portion of the cover of every book.   A backing-machine is sometimes used for this process, making by pressure the joint or groove for the boards.   Then the "head-band" is glued on, being a silk braid or colored muslin, fastened around a cord, which projects a little above the head and the tail, at the back of the book, giving it a more finished appearance. At the same time, a book-mark for keeping the place is sometimes inserted and fastened like the head-band.   This is often a narrow ribbon of colored silk, or satin, and helps to give a finish to the book, as well as to furnish the reader a trustworthy guide to keep a place—as it will not fall out like bits of paper inserted for that purpose.

Next, the mill-boards are applied, cut so as to project about an eighth to a quarter of an inch from the edges of the book on three sides.   The book is held to the boards by the ends of its cords being interlaced, *i. e.*: passed twice through holes pierced in the boards, the loose ends of the cords being then wet with paste and hammered down flat to the surface of the boards.   The best tar-boards should be used, which are made of old rope; no board made of straw is fit to be used on any book.   Straw boards are an abomination—a cheap expedient which costs dearly in the end.   The binder should use heavy boards on the larger and thicker volumes, but thin ones on all duodecimos and smaller sizes.

Next, the books are subjected to a second pressing, after which the lining of the back is in order.   Good thick brown paper is generally used for this, cut to the length of the book, and is firmly glued to the back, and rubbed down closely with a bone folder.   A cloth "joint," or piece of linen (termed "muslin super,") is often glued to the back, with two narrow flaps to be pasted to the boards, on each side, thus giving greater tenacity to the covering. If the book is to be backed so as to open freely, that is, to have a spring back or elastic back, two thicknesses of a firm, strong paper, or thin card-board are used, one thickness of the paper being glued to the back of the book, while the other—open in the middle, but fastened at the edges, is to be glued to the leather of which the back is to be made.

After this, comes putting the book in leather. If full bound a piece of leather cut full size of the volume, with about half an inch over, is firmly glued or pasted to the boards and the back, the leather being turned over the edges of the boards, and nicely glued on their inside margin. It is of great importance that the edges of the leather should be smoothly pared down with a sharp knife, so as to present an even edge where the leather joins the boards, not a protuberance—which makes an ugly and clumsy piece of work, instead of a neat one.

For half-binding, a piece of leather is taken large enough to cover the back lengthwise, and turn in at the head and tail, while the width should be such as to allow from one to one and a half inches of the leather to be firmly glued to the boards next the back. The four corners of the boards are next to be leathered, the edges of the leather being carefully pared down, to give a smooth surface, even with the boards, when turned in. The leather is usually wet, preparatory to being manipulated thus, which renders it more flexible and ductile than in its dry state. The cloth or marbled paper is afterwards pasted or glued to the sides of the book, and turned neatly over the edge of the boards.

It may be added, that the edges of the boards, in binding nice books, are sometimes ground off on a swiftly revolving emery-wheel, giving the book a beveled edge, which is regarded as handsomer and more finished than a straight rectangular edge.

All the processes hitherto described are called "forward-ing" the book: we now come to what is denominated "fin-ishing." This includes the lettering of the title, and the embellishing of the back and sides, with or without gild-ing, as the case may be. Before this is taken in hand, the leather of the book must be perfectly dry. For the letter-ing, copper-faced types are used to set up the desired se-quence of letters and words, and care and taste should be exercised to have (1) Types neither too large, which pre-sent a clumsy appearance, nor too small, which are diffi-cult to read. (2) Proper spacing of the words and lines, and "balancing" the component parts of the lettering on the back, so as to present a neat and harmonious effect to the eye. A word should never be divided or hyphenated in lettering, when it can be avoided. In the case of quite thin volumes, the title may be lettered lengthwise along the back, in plain, legible type, instead of in very small letters across the back, which are often illegible. The method of applying gold lettering is as follows: the back of the book where the title is to go, is first moistened with a sticky substance, as albumen or glaire, heretofore men-tioned, laid on with a camel's hair brush. The type (or the die as the case may be) is heated in a binder's charcoal fur-nace, or gas stove, to insure the adhesion of the gold leaf. The thin gold leaf (which comes packed in little square "books," one sheet between every two leaves) is then cut the proper size by the broad thin knife of the "finisher," and carefully laid over the sized spot to receive the letter-ing. Usually, two thicknesses of gold leaf are laid one above another, which ensures a brighter and more decided effect in the lettering. The type metal or die is then pressed firmly and evenly down upon the gold-leaf, and the surplus shavings of the gold carefully brushed off and hus-banded, for this leaf is worth money. The gold leaf generally in use costs about $6.50 for 500 little squares or sheets. It is almost inconceivably thin, the thickness of one gold leaf being estimated at about ᵣᵣᵤᵥᵤᵥ of an inch.

Besides the lettering, many books receive gold orna-mentation on the back or side of a more or less elaborate character. Designs of great artistic beauty, and in count-less variety, have been devised for book ornaments, and French and English book-binders have vied with each other for generations in the production of decorative bor-ders, fillets, centre-pieces, rolls, and the most exquisite gold-tooling, of which the art is capable.

These varied patterns of book ornamentation are cut in brass or steel, and applied by the embossing press with a rapidity far exceeding that of the hand-work formerly ex-ecuted by the gilders of books. But for choice books and select jobs, only the hands are employed, with such fillets, stamps, pallets, rolls, and polishing irons as may aid in the nice execution of the work. If a book is to be bound in what is called "morocco antique," it is to be "blind-tooled," *i. e.:* the hot iron wheels which impress the fillets or rolls, are to be worked in blank, or without gold-leaf ornamenta-tion. This is a rich and tasteful binding, especially with carefully beveled boards, and gilded edges.

On some books, money has been lavished on the binding to an amount exceeding by many fold the cost of the book itself. Elegant book-binding has come to be reckoned as a fine art, and why should not "the art preservative of all other arts"—printing—be preserved in permanent and sumptuous, if not splendid style, in its environment? Specimens of French artistic binding from the library of Grolier, that celebrated and munificent patron of art, who died in 1565, have passed through the hands of many eager connoisseurs, always at advancing prices. The Grolier binding was notable for the elegant finish of its interlaced

look as brilliant as jewels in their rich, lustrous adornment,
the design sometimes powdered with gold points and stars.
Some gems of art are lined with rich colored leather in the
inside covers, which are stamped and figured in gold. This
is termed *"doublé"* by the French. Some have their edges
gilded over marbling, a refinement of beauty which adds
richness to the work, the marble design showing through
the brilliant gold, when the edge is turned. Others have
pictorial designs drawn on the edges, which are then gilded
over the pictures. This complex style of gilding, the
French term *gaufré*. It was formerly much in vogue, but
is latterly out of fashion. Many gems of binding are
adorned with fly-leaves of moire silk, or rich colored satin.
Color, interspersed with gold in the finish of a book covering, heightens the effect. The morocco of the side-cover
is sometimes cut, and inlaid with leather of a different
color. Inlaying with morocco or kid is the richest style of
decoration which the art has yet reached. Beautiful bindings have been in greater request during the past twenty
years than ever before. There was a renaissance of the
ancient styles of decoration in France, and the choice
Grolier and Maioli patterns were revived with the general
applause of the lovers of fine books.

In vivid contrast to these lovely specimens of the binder's art, are found innumerable bibliopegic horrors, on the
shelves of countless libraries, public and private. Among
these are to be reckoned most law books, clad in that dead
monotony of ugliness, which Charles Dickens has described as "that *under-done pie-crust* cover, which is tech-
nically known as law calf." There are other uncouth and
unwholesome specimens everywhere abroad, "whom Satan
hath bound", to borrow Mr. Henry Stevens's witty application of a well-known Scripture text. Such repellant bind-

ings are only fit to serve as models to be avoided by the librarian.

The binding that is executed by machinery is sometimes called "commercial binding". It is also known as "edition binding", because the whole edition of a book is bound in uniform style of cover. While the modern figured cloth binding originated in England, it has had its fullest development in the United States. Here, those ingenious and powerful machines which execute every branch of the folding and forwarding of a book, and even the finishing of the covers, with almost lightning speed, were mostly invented and applied. Very vivid is the contrast between the quiet, humdrum air of the old-fashioned bindery hand-work, and the ceaseless clang and roar of the machinery which turns out thousands of volumes in a day.

> "Not as ours the books of old,
> Things that steam can stamp and fold."

I believe that I failed to notice, among the varieties of material for book-bindings heretofore enumerated, some of the rarer and more singular styles. Thus, books have been bound in enamel, (richly variegated in color) in Persian silk, in seal-skin, in the skin of the rabbit, white-bear, crocodile, cat, dog, mole, tiger, otter, buffalo, wolf, and even rattle-snake. A favorite modern leather for purses and satchels, alligator-skin, has been also applied to the clothing of books. Many eccentric fancies have been exemplified in book-binding, but the acme of gruesome oddity has been reached by binding books in human skin, of which many examples are on record. It is perhaps three centuries old, but the first considerable instance of its use grew out of the horrors of the French Revolution. In England, the Bristol law library has several volumes bound in the skin of local criminals, flayed after execution, and

specially tanned for the purpose.   It is described as rather
darker than vellum.   A Russian poet is said to have bound
his sonnets in human leather—his own skin—taken from
a broken thigh—and the book he presented to the lady of
his affections!   Such ghoulish incidents as these afford
curious though repulsive glimpses of the endless vagaries
of human nature.

It is said that the invention of half-binding originated
among the economists of Germany; and some wealthy
bibliophiles have stigmatized this style of dressing books
as "genteel poverty."   But its utility and economy have
been demonstrated too long to admit of any doubt that
half-binding has come to stay; while, as we have seen, it
is also capable of attractive aesthetic features.   Mr. William Matthews, perhaps the foremost of American binders,
said that "a book when neatly forwarded, and cleanly
covered, is in a very satisfactory condition without any
finishing or decorating."   It was this same binder who exhibited at the New York World's Fair Exhibition of 1853,
a copy of Owen Jones's Alhambra, bound by him in full
Russia, inlaid with blue and red morocco, with gold tooling all executed by hand, taking six months to complete,
and costing the binder no less than five hundred dollars.

Book lettering, or stamping the proper title on the back
of the book, is a matter of the first importance.   As the
titles of most books are much too long to go on the back,
a careful selection of the most distinctive words becomes
necessary.   Here the taste and judgment of the librarian
come indispensably into play.   To select the lettering of
a book should never be left to the binder, because it is not
his business, and because, in most cases, he will make a mistake somewhere in the matter.   From want of care on this
point, many libraries are filled with wrongly lettered books,
misleading titles, and blunders as ludicrous as they are dis-

tressing. I have had to have thousands of volumes in the
Library of Congress re-lettered. A copy of Lord Bacon's
"Sylva Sylvarum", for example, was lettered "Verlum's
Sylva"—because the sapient binder read on the title-page
"By Baron Verulam", and it was not his business to find
out that this was the title of honor which Bacon bore; so,
by a compound blunder, he converted Verulam into Verlum, and gave the book to an unknown writer. This is
perhaps an extreme case, but you will find many to match
it. Another folio, Rochefort's History of the Caribby Islands, was lettered "Davies' Carriby Islands," because the
title bore the statement "Rendered into English by John
Davies." In another library, the great work of the naturalist, Buffon, was actually lettered "Buffoon's Natural
History." Neither of these blunders was as bad as that
of the owner of an elegant black-letter edition of a Latin
classic, which was printed without title-page, like most
fifteenth century books, and began at the top of the first
leaf, in large letters—"HOC INCIPIT," signifying "This
begins", followed by the title or subject of the book. The
wiseacre who owned it had the book richly bound, and directed it to be lettered on the back—"Works of Hoc Incipit, Rome, 1490." This is a true story, and the hero of it
might perhaps, on the strength of owning so many learned
works, have passed for a philosopher, if he had not taken
the pains to advertise himself as a blockhead.

Some of the commonest blunders are stamping on the
back the translator's or the editor's name, instead of that
of the author of the book; putting on adjectives instead
of substantives for titles; modernizing ancient and characteristic spelling, found in the title, (the exact orthography
of which should always be followed); mixing up the number and the case of Latin titles, and those in other foreign

languages; leaving off entirely the name of the writer; and lettering periodicals by putting on the volume without the year, or the year, without the number of the volume. "No one but an idiot", said Mr. C. Walford to the London Librarians' Conference, "would send his books to the binder, without indicating the lettering he desires on the backs." The only safe-guard is for the librarian or owner to prescribe on a written slip in each volume, a title for every book, before it goes to the binder, who will be only too glad to have his own time saved—since time is money to him. I would not underrate the book-binders, who are a most worthy and intelligent class, numbering in their ranks men who are scholars as well as artists; but they are concerned chiefly with the mechanics and not with the metaphysics of their art, and moreover, they are not bound by that rigid rule which should govern the librarian—namely—to have no ignoramus about the premises.

In writing letterings (for I take it that no one would be guilty of defacing his title-pages by marking them up with directions to the binder) you should definitely write out the parts of the title as they are to run on the back of the book, spaced line upon line, and not "run together." I think that the name of the author should always stand first at the head of the lettering, because it affords the quickest guide to the eye in finding any book, as well as in replacing it upon the shelves. Especially useful and time-saving is this, where classes of books are arranged in alphabetical sequence. Is not the name of the author commonly uppermost in the mind of the searcher? Then, let it be uppermost on the book sought also. Follow the name of the author by the briefest possible words selected from the title which will suffice to characterize the subject of the work. Thus, the title—"On the Origin of Species by means of Natural Selection", by Charles Darwin, should be abbreviated into

Darwin

———

Origin of Species.

Here are no superfluous words, to consume the binder's time and gold-leaf, and to be charged in the bill; or to consume the time of the book-searcher, in stopping to read a lot of surplusage on the back of the book, before seizing it for immediate use. Books in several volumes should have the number of each volume plainly marked in Arabic (not Roman) numerals on the back. The old-fashioned method of expressing numerals by letters, instead of figures, is too cumbrous and time-consuming to be tolerated. You want to letter, we will say, vol. 88 of Blackwood's Magazine. If you follow the title-page of that book, as printed, you have to write

"Volume LXXXVIII," eight letters, for the number of the volume, instead of two simple figures—thus—88.

Now can any one give a valid reason for the awkward and tedious method of notation exhibited in the Roman numerals? If it were only the lost time of the person who writes it, or the binder's finisher who letters it, it would be comparatively insignificant. But think of the time wasted by the whole world of readers, who must go through a more or less troublesome process of notation before they get a clear notion of what all this superfluous stuff stands for instead of the quick intuition with which they take in the Arabic figures; and who must moreover, by the antiquated method, take valuable time to write out LXXXVIII, eight figures instead of two, to say nothing of the added liability to error, which increases in the exact ratio of the number of figures to be written. Which of these two forms of expression is more quickly written, or stamped, or read? By which method of notation will the library messenger boys or girls soonest find the book? This leads me to say what cannot be too strongly insisted upon; all library methods should be time-saving methods, and so devised for the benefit alike of the librarian, the assistants, and the readers. Until one has learned the supreme value of moments, he will not be fit for a librarian. The same method by Arabic numerals only, should be used in all references to books; and it would be well if the legal fashion of citing authorities by volume and page, now adopted in most law books, were extended to all literature —thus:

"3 Macaulay's England, 481. N. Y. 1854," instead of "Macaulay's England, N. Y. ed. 1854. vol. 3, page 481." It is a matter of congratulation to all librarians, as well as to the reading public, that Poole's Indexes to Periodical Literature have wisely adopted Arabic figures only, both for volume and page. The valuable time thus saved to all is quite incalculable.

Every book which is leather-bound has its back divided off into panels or sections, by the band across the back or by the gold or plain fillet or roll forming part of the finish of the book. These panels are usually five or six in number, the former being the more common. Now it is the librarian's function to prescribe in which of these panels the lettering of the book—especially where there is double lettering—shall go. Thus

2nd panel	COUSIN — HISTORY OF MODERN PHILOSOPHY.	4th panel	WIGHT	End	NEW YORK, 1852.

Many books, especially dramatic works, and the collected works of authors require the contents of the various volumes to be briefed on the back. Here is a Shakespeare, for example, in 10 volumes, or a Swift in 19, or Carlyle in 33, and you want to find *King Lear*, or *Gulliver's Travels*, or *Heroes and Hero Worship*. The other volumes concern you not—but you want the shortest road to these. If the name of each play is briefed by the first word upon the different volumes of your Shakespeare, or the contents of each volume upon the Swift and the Carlyle,—as they should be—you find instantly what you want, with one glance of the eye along the backs. If put to the trouble of opening every volume to find the contents, or of hunting it in the index, or the library catalogue, you lose precious time, while readers wait, thus making the needless delay cumulative, and as it must be often repeated, indefinite.

Each volume should have its date and place of publication plainly lettered at the lower end, or what binders term the tail of the book. This often saves time, as you may not want an edition of old date, or *vice versa*, while the place and date enable readers' tickets to be filled out quickly without the book. The name of the library might well be lettered also on the back, being more obvious as a permanent means of identification than the book-plate or inside stamp.

Books should never be used when fresh from the binder's hands. The covers are then always damp, and warp on exposure to air and heat. Unless pressed firmly in shelves, or in piles, for at least two weeks, they may become incurably warped out of shape. Many an otherwise handsomely bound book is ruined by neglect of this caution, for once thoroughly dried in its warped condition, there is no remedy save the costly one of rebinding.

Books are frequently lettered so carelessly that the titles instead of aligning, or being in straight horizontal lines, run obliquely upward or downward, thus defacing the volume. Errors in spelling words are also liable to occur. All crooked lettering and all mistakes in spelling should at once be rejected, and the faulty books returned to the binder, to be corrected at his own expense. This severe revision of all books when newly bound, before they are placed upon the shelves, should be done by the librarian's or owner's own eye—not entrusted to subordinates, unless to one thoroughly skilled.

One should never receive back books from a binder without collating them, to see if all are perfect as to pages, and if all plates or maps are in place. If deficiencies are found, the binder, and not the library is responsible, provided the book was known to be perfect when sent for binding.

In the Congressional Library I had the periodicals which are analyzed in Poole's Index of Periodical Literature thoroughly compared and re-lettered, wherever necessary, to make the series of volumes correspond with the references in that invaluable and labor-saving index. For instance, the Eclectic Review, as published in London, had eight distinct and successive series (thus confusing reference by making eight different volumes called 1, 2, 3, etc.) each with a different numbering, "First series, 2d series," etc., which Poole's Index very properly consolidated into one, for convenient reference. By adding the figures as scheduled in that work—prefixed by the words *Poole's Index No.* —— or simply *Poole*, in small letters, followed by the figure of the volume as given in that index, you will find a saving of time in hunting and supplying references that is almost incalculable. If you cannot afford to have this re-numbering done by a binder in gilt letters, it will many times repay the cost and time of doing it on thin manila paper titles, written or printed by a numbering machine and pasted on the backs of the volumes.

In all periodicals,—magazines and serials of every kind, —the covers and their advertisements should be bound in their proper place, with each month or number of the periodical, though it may interrupt the continuity of the paging. Thus will be preserved valuable contemporary records respecting prices, bibliographical information, etc., which should never be destroyed, as it is illustrative of the life and history of the period. The covers of the magazines, too, frequently contain the table of contents of the number, which of course must be prefixed to it, in order to be of any use. If advertising pages are very numerous and bulky, (as in many popular periodicals of late years) they may well be bound at the end of the volume, or, if so many as to make the volume excessively thick, they might be bound in a supplementary volume. In all books, half-titles or bastard titles, as they are called, should be bound in, as they are a part of the book.

With each lot of books to be bound, there should always be sent a sample volume of good work as a pattern, that the binder may have no excuse for hasty or inferior workmanship.

The Grolier Club was founded in New York in 1884, having for its objects to promote the literary study and progress of the arts pertaining to the production of books. It has published more than twenty books in sumptuous style, and mostly in quarto form, the editions being limited to 150 copies at first, since increased to 300, under the rapidly enlarging membership of the Club. Most of these books relate to fine binding, fine printing, or fine illustration of books, or are intended to exemplify them, and by their means, by lectures, and exhibitions of fine book-work, this society has contributed much toward the diffusion of correct taste. More care has been bestowed upon fine binding in New York than in London itself. In fact, elegant book-binding is coming to be recognized as one of the foremost of the decorative arts.

The art of designing book-covers and patterns for gilding books has engaged the talents of many artists, among whom may be named Edwin A. Abbey, Howard Pyle, Stanford White, and Elihu Vedder. Nor have skilful designs been wanting among women, as witness Mrs. Whitman's elegant tea-leaf border for the cover of Dr. O. W. Holmes's "Over the Tea-cups," and Miss Alice Morse's arabesques and medallions for Lafcadio Hearn's "Two Years in the French West Indies." Miss May Morris designed many tasteful letters for the fine bindings executed by Mr. Cobden-Sanderson of London, and Kate Greenaway's many exquisite little books for little people have become widely known for their quaint and curious cover designs. A new field thus opens for skilled cultivators of the beautiful who have an eye for the art of drawing.

Mr. William Matthews, the accomplished New York binder, in an address before the Grolier Club in 1895, said: "I have been astonished that so few women—in America, I know none—are encouragers of the art; they certainly could not bestow their taste on anything that would do them more credit, or as a study, give them more satisfaction." It is but fair to add that since this judgment was put forth, its implied reproach is no longer applicable: a number of American women have interested themselves in the study of binding as a fine art; and some few in practical work as binders of books.

There is no question that readers take a greater interest in books that are neatly and attractively bound, than in volumes dressed in a mean garb. No book owner or librarian with any knowledge of the incurable defects of calf, sheep, or roan leather, if he has any regard for the usefulness or the economies of his library, will use them in binding books that are to possess permanent value in personal or public use. True economy lies in employing the best description of binding in the first instance.

When it is considered that the purposed object of book-binding is to preserve in a shape at once attractive and permanent, the best and noblest thoughts of man, it rises to a high rank among the arts. Side by side with printing, it strives after that perfection which shall ensure the perpetuity of human thought. Thus a book, clothed in morocco, is not a mere piece of mechanism, but a vehicle in which the intellectual life of writers no longer on earth is transmitted from age to age. And it is the art of book-binding which renders libraries possible. What the author, the printer, and the binder create, the library takes charge of and preserves. It is thus that the material and the practical link themselves indissolubly with the ideal. And the ideal of every true librarian should be so to care for the embodiments of intelligence entrusted to his guardianship, that they may become in the highest degree useful to mankind. In this sense, the care bestowed upon thorough and enduring binding can hardly be overrated, since the life of the book depends upon it.

CHAPTER 4.

Preparation for the Shelves: Book Plates, etc.

When any lot of books is acquired, whether by purchase from book-dealers or from auction, or by presentation, the first step to be taken, after seeing that they agree with the bill, and have been collated, in accordance with methods elsewhere given, should be to stamp and label each volume, as the property of the library. These two processes are quite distinct, and may be performed by one or two persons, according to convenience, or to the library force employed. The stamp may be the ordinary rubber one, inked by striking on a pad, and ink of any color may be used, although black or blue ink has the neatest appearance. The stamp should bear the name of the library, in clear, legible, plain type, with year of acquisition of the book in the centre, followed by the month and day if desired. A more permanent kind of stamp is the embossing stamp, which is a steel die, the letters cut in relief, but it is very expensive and slow, requiring the leaf to be inserted between the two parts of the stamp, though the impression, once made, is practically indelible.

The size of the stamp (which is preferably oval in shape) should not exceed $1\frac{1}{4}$ to $1\frac{1}{2}$ inches in diameter, as a large, coarse stamp never presents a neat appearance on a book. Indeed, many books are too small to admit any but a stamp of very moderate dimensions. The books should be stamped on the verso (reverse) of the title page, or if preferred, on the widest unprinted portion of the title-page, preferably on the right hand of the centre, or just below the centre on the right. This, because its impression is far more legible on the plain white surface than on any part of the printed title. In a circulating library, the stamps should be impressed on one or more pages in the body of the book, as well as on the last page, as a means of identification if the book is stolen or otherwise lost; as it is very easy to erase the impression of a rubber stamp from the title-page, and thereby commit a fraud by appropriating or selling the book. In such a case, the duplicate or triplicate impression of the stamp on some subsequent page (say page 5 or 16, many books having but few pages) as fixed upon by the librarian, is quite likely to escape notice of the thief, while it remains a safe-guard, enabling the librarian to reclaim the book, wherever found. The law will enforce this right of free reclamation in favor of a public library, in the case of stolen books, no matter in what hands found, and even though the last holder may be an innocent purchaser. All libraries are victimized at some time by unscrupulous or dishonest readers, who will appropriate books, thinking themselves safe from detection, and sometimes easing their consciences, (if they have any) by the plea that the book is in a measure public property.

In these cases, there is no absolute safe-guard, as it is easy to carry off a book under one's coat, and the librarian and his few aids are far too busy to act as detectives in watching readers. Still, a vigilant librarian will almost always find out, by some suspicious circumstance—such as the hiding of books away, or a certain furtive action observed in a reader—who are the persons that should be watched, and when it is advisable to call in the policeman.

The British Museum Library, which has no circulation or book lending, enforces a rule that no one making his exit can have a book with him, unless checked as his own property, all overcoats and other wraps being of course checked at the door.

It is a melancholy fact, duly recorded in a Massachusetts paper, that no less than two hundred and fifty volumes, duly labeled and stamped as public library books, were stolen from a single library in a single year, and sold to second-hand booksellers.

The impression of the stamp in the middle of a certain page, known to the librarian, renders it less liable to detection by others, while if stamped on the lower unprinted margin, it might be cut out by a designing person.

Next to the stamping, comes the labeling of the books to be added to the library. This is a mechanical process, and yet one of much importance. Upon its being done neatly and properly, depends the good or bad appearance of the library books, as labels with rough or ragged edges, or put on askew, or trimmed irregularly at their margins, present an ugly and unfinished aspect, offensive to the eye of good taste, and reflecting discredit on the management. A librarian should take pride in seeing all details of his work carefully and neatly carried out. If he cannot have perfection, from want of time, he should always aim at it, at least, and then only will he come near to achieving it.

The label, or book-plate (for they are one and the same thing) should be of convenient size to go into books both small and large; and a good size is approximately $2\frac{1}{4}$ inches wide by $1\frac{1}{2}$ inches high when trimmed. As comparatively few libraries care to go to the expense, which is about ten times that of printing, of an engraved label (although such work adds to the attractiveness of the books containing it) it should be printed in clear, not ornamental type, with the name of the library, that of the city or town in which it is located (unless forming a part of the title) and the abbreviation No. for number, with such other spaces for section marks or divisions, shelf-marks, etc., as the classification adopted may require. The whole should be enclosed in an ornamental border—not too ornate for good taste.

The labels, nicely trimmed to uniform size by a cutting machine, (if that is not in the library equipment, any binder will do it for you) are next to be pasted or gummed, as preferred. This process is a nice one, requiring patience, care, and practice. Most libraries are full of books imperfectly labelled, pasted on in crooked fashion, or perhaps damaging the end-leaves by an over-use of paste, causing the leaves to adhere to the page labelled—which should always be the inside left hand cover of the book. This slovenly work is unworthy of a skilled librarian, who should not suffer torn waste leaves, nor daubs of over-running paste in any of his books. To prevent both these blunders in library economy, it is only needful to instruct any intelligent assistant thoroughly, by practical example how to do it—accompanied by a counter-example how not to do it. The way to do it is to have your paste as thin as that used by binders in pasting their fly-leaves, or their leather, or about the consistency of porridge or pea soup. Then lay the label or book-plate face downward on a board or table covered with blotting paper, dip your paste brush (a half inch bristle brush is the best) in the paste, stroke it (to remove too much adhering matter) on the inner side of your paste cup, then apply it across the whole surface of the label, with light, even strokes of the brush, until you see that it is all moistened with paste. Next, take up the label and lay it evenly in the middle of the left inner cover page of the book to be labelled, and with a small piece of paper (not with the naked fingers) laid over it, stroke it down firmly in its place, by rubbing over a few times the incumbent paper. This being properly done (and it is done by an expert, once learned, very rapidly) your book-plate will be firmly and smoothly pasted in, with no exuding of paste at the edges, to spoil the fly-leaves, and no . curling up of edges because insufficiently pasted down.

So much for the book-plate—for the inside of the volumes; now let us turn attention to the outside label. This is necessarily very much smaller than the book-plate: in fact, it should not be larger than three-quarters or seven-eighths of an inch in diameter, and even smaller for the thinner volumes, while in the case of the very smallest, or thinnest of books, it becomes necessary to paste the labels on the side, instead of on the back. This label is to contain the section and shelf-mark of the book, marked by plain figures, according to the plan of classification adopted. When well done, it is an inexpressible comfort to any librarian,. because it shows at one glance of the eye, and without opening the book at all, just where in the wide range of the miscellaneous library it is to go. Thus the book service of every day is incalculably aided, and the books are both found when sought on the shelves, and replaced there, with no trouble of opening them.

This outer-label system once established, in strict correspondence with the catalogue, the only part of the librarian's work remaining to be prescribed in this field, concerns the kind of label to be selected, and the method of affixing them to the books. The adhesive gummed labels furnished by the Library Bureau, or those manufactured by the Dennison Company of New York have the requisite qualities for practical use. They may be purchased in sheets, or cut apart, as convenient handling may dictate. Having first written in ink in plain figures, as large as the labels will bear, the proper locality marks, take a label moistener (a hollow tube filled with water, provided with a bit of sponge at the end and sold by stationers) and wet the label throughout its surface, then fix it on the back of the book, on the smooth part of the binding near the lower end, and with a piece of paper (not the fingers) press it down firmly to its place by repeated rubbings. If thoroughly done, the labels will not peel off nor curl up at the edges for a long time. Under much usage of the volumes, however, they must occasionally be renewed.

When the books being prepared for the shelves have all been duly collated, labelled and stamped, processes which should precede cataloguing them, they are next ready for the cataloguer. His functions having been elsewhere described, it need only be said that the books when catalogued and handed over to the reviser, (or whoever is to scrutinize the titles and assign them their proper places in the library classification) are to have the shelf-marks of the card-titles written on the inside labels, as well as upon the outside.

When this is done, the title-cards can be withdrawn and alphabeted in the catalogue drawers. Next, all the books thus catalogued, labelled, and supposed to be ready for the shelves, should be examined with reference to three points:

1st. Whether any of the volumes need re-lettering.

2nd. Whether any of them require re-binding.

3rd. If any of the bindings are in need of repair.

In any lot of books purchased or presented, are almost always to be found some that are wrongly or imperfectly lettered on the back. Before these are ready for the shelves, they should be carefully gone through with, and all errors or shortcomings corrected. It is needful to send to the binder

1st. All books which lack the name of the author on the back. This should be stamped by the binder at the head, if there is room—if not, in the middle panel on the back of the book.

2nd. All books lettered with mis-spelled words.

3rd. All volumes in sets, embracing several distinct

works—to have the name of each book in the contents plainly stamped on the outside.

4th. All books wholly without titles on the back, of which many are published—the title being frequently given on the side only, or in the interior alone.

5th. All periodicals having the volume on the back, without the year, to have the year lettered; and periodicals having the year, but not the volume, are to have the number of the volume added.

If these things, all essential to good management and prompt library service, are not done before the books go to their shelves, the chances are that they will not be done at all.

The second requisite to be attended to is to examine whether any of the volumes catalogued require to be bound or re-bound. In any lot of books of considerable extent, there will always be some (especially if from auction sales) dilapidated and shaken, so as to unfit them for use. There will be others so soiled in the bindings or the edges as to be positively shabby, and they should be re-bound to render them presentable.

The third point demanding attention is to see what volumes need repair. It very often happens that books otherwise pretty well bound have torn corners, or rubbed or shop-worn backs, or shabby marbled paper frayed at the sides, or some other defect, which may be cured by mending or furbishing up, without re-binding. This a skilful binder is always competent to take in charge; and as in the other cases, it should have attention immediately upon the acquisition of the books.

All books coming into a library which contain autographs, book-plates of former owners, coats of arms, presentation inscriptions from the author, monograms, or other distinguishing features, should preserve them as of interest to the present or the future.

And all printed paper covers should be carefully preserved by binding them inside the new cover which the book receives, thus preserving authentic evidence of the form in which the book was first issued to the public, and often its original price. In like manner, when a cloth-bound book comes to re-binding, its side and back covers may be bound in at the end of the book, as showing the style in which it was originally issued, frequently displaying much artistic beauty.

Whoever receives back any books which have been out in circulation, whether it be the librarian or assistant, must examine each volume, to see if it is in apparent good order. If it is found (as frequently happens) that it is shaky and loose, or if leaves are ready to drop out, or if the cover is nearly off, it should never be allowed to go back to the shelves, but laid aside for re-binding or repair with the next lot sent to the binder. Only prompt vigilance on this point, combined with the requirement of speedy return by the binder, will save the loss or injury beyond repair of many books. It will also save the patrons of the library from the frequent inconvenience of having to do without books, which should be on the shelves for their use. How frequent this sending of books to repair should be, cannot be settled by any arbitrary rule; but it would be wise, in the interest of all, to do it as often as two or three dozen damaged books are accumulated.

If you find other injury to a book returned, than the natural wear and tear that the library must assume, if a book, for example, is blotched with ink, or soiled with grease, or has been so far wet as to be badly stained in the leaves, or if it is found torn in any part on a hasty inspection, or if a plate or a map is missing, or the binding is violently broken (as sometimes happens) then the damage should be borne by the reader, and not by the library. This will sometimes require the purchase of a fresh copy of the book, which no fair-minded reader can object to pay, who is favored with the privileges of free enjoyment of the treasures of a public library. Indeed, it will be found in the majority of cases that honest readers themselves call attention to such injuries as books have accidentally received while in their possession, with voluntary offer to make good the damage.

All unbound or paper covered volumes should be reserved from the shelves, and not supplied to readers until bound. This rule may be relaxed (as there is almost no rule without some valid exception) in the case of a popular new book, issued only in paper covers, if it is desired to give an opportunity of early perusal to readers frequenting the library. But such books should not be permitted to circulate, as they would soon be worn to pieces by handling. Only books dressed in a substantial covering are fit to be loaned out of any library. In preparing for the bindery any new books, or old ones to be re-bound or repaired, lists should be made of any convenient number set apart for the purpose, prompt return should be required, and all should be checked off on the list when returned.

No shelf in a well-regulated library should be unprovided with book-supports, in order to prevent the volumes from sagging and straining by falling against one another, in a long row of books. Numerous different devices are in the market for this purpose, from the solid brick to the light sheet-iron support; but it is important to protect the end of every row from strain on the bindings, and the cost of book supports is indefinitely less than that of the re-binding entailed by neglecting to use them.

Some libraries of circulation make it a rule to cover all

their books with paper or thin muslin covers, before they
are placed on the shelves for use. This method has its advantages and its drawbacks. It doubtless protects the
bindings from soiling, and where books circulate widely
and long, no one who has seen how foul with dirt they become, can doubt the expediency of at least trying the experiment of clean covers. They should be of the firmest
thin but tough Manila paper, and it is claimed that twenty
renewals of clean paper covers actually cost less than one
re-binding. On the other hand, it is not to be denied that
books thus covered look shabby, monotonous, and uninteresting. In the library used for reference and reading
only, without circulation, covers are quite out of place.

Book-plates having been briefly referred to above, a few
words as to their styles and uses may here be pertinent.
The name "book-plate" is a clumsy and misleading title,
suggesting to the uninitiated the illustrations or plates
which embellish the text of a book. The name *Ex libris*,
two latin words used for book-plate in all European languages, is clearer, but still not exact, as a definition of the
thing, signifying simply "out of books." A book-plate is
the owner's or the library's distinctive mark of ownership,
pasted upon the inside cover, whether it be a simple name-
label, or an elaborately engraved heraldic or pictorial device. The earliest known book-plates date back to the fifteenth century, and are of German origin, though English
plates are known as early as 1700. In France, specimens
appear for the first time between 1600 and 1650.

Foreign book-plates are, as a rule, heraldic in design, as
are also the early American plates, representing the coat of
arms or family crest of the owner of the books, with a
motto of some kind. The fashion of collecting these owners' marks, as such, irrespective of the books containing
them, is a recent and very possibly a passing mania. Still,

there is something of interest in early American plates, and in those used by distinguished men, aside from the collector's fad. Some of the first American engravers showed their skill in these designs, and a signed and dated plate engraved by Nathaniel Hurd, for example, of Boston, is of some historic value as an example of early American art. He engraved many plates about the middle of the last century, and died in 1777. Paul Revere, who was an engraver, designed and executed some few plates, which are rare, and highly prized, more for his name than for his skill, for, as generally known, he was a noted patriot of the Revolutionary period, belonging by his acts to the heroic age of American history.

A book of George Washington's containing his book-plate has an added interest, though the plate itself is an armorial design, not at all well executed. Its motto is *"exitus acta probat"*—the event justifies the deed. From its rarity and the high price it commands, it has probably been the only American book-plate ever counterfeited. At an auction sale of books in Washington in 1863, this counterfeit plate had been placed in many books to give a fictitious value, but the fraud was discovered and announced by the present writer, just before the books were sold. Yet the sale was attended by many attracted to bid upon books said to have been owned by Washington, and among them the late Dr. W. F. Poole, then librarian of the Boston Athenaeum, which possesses most of the library authentically known to have been at Mount Vernon.

John Adams and John Quincy Adams used book-plates. and James Monroe and John Tyler each had a plain name-label. These are all of our presidents known to have used them, except General Carfield, who had a printed book-plate of simple design, with the motto *"inter folia fructus."* Eleven of the signers of the Declaration of Independence are known to have had these signs of gentle birth—for in the early years of the American Colonies, it was only the families of aristocratic connection and scholarly tastes who indulged in what may be termed a superfluous luxury.

The plates used among the Southern settlers were generally ordered from England, and not at all American. The Northern plates were more frequently of native design and execution, and therefore of much greater value and interest, though far inferior in style of workmanship and elaboration of ornament to the best European ones.

The ordinary library label is also a book-plate, and some of the early libraries and small collections have elaborate designs. The early Harvard College library plate was a large and fine piece of engraving by Hurd. The Harvard Library had some few of this fine engraved label printed in red ink, and placed in the rarer books of the library— as a reminder that the works containing the rubricated book-plates were not to be drawn out by students.

The learned bibliophile and librarian of Florence, Magliabecchi, who died in 1714, devised for his library of thirty thousand volumes, which he bequeathed to the Grand Duke of Tuscany, a book-plate representing his own profile on a medal surrounded with books and oak boughs, with the inscription—"Antonius Magliabecchius Florentinus."

Some book-plates embody designs of great beauty. The late George Bancroft's, engraved on copper, represented a winged cherub (from Raphael) gazing sun-ward, holding a tablet with the inscription *"Eis phaos,"* toward the light.

Some French book-plates aim at humor or caricature. One familiar example represents an old book-worm mounted on a tall ladder in a library, profoundly absorbed in reading, and utterly unconscious that the room beneath him is on fire.

To those who ask of what possible utility it can be to cultivate so unfruitful a pursuit as the devising or the collecting of book-plates, it may be pertinent to state the claim made in behalf of the amateurs of this art, by a connoisseur, namely, "Book-plates foster the study of art, history, genealogy, and human character." On this theory, we may add, the coat of arms or family crest teaches heraldry; the mottoes or inscriptions chosen cultivate the taste for language and sententious literature; the engraving appeals to the sense of the artistic; the names of early or ancient families who are often thus commemorated teach biography, history, or genealogy; while the great variety of sentiments selected for the plates illustrate the character and taste of those selecting them.

On the other hand, it must be said that the coat of arms fails to indicate individual taste or genius, and might better be supplanted by original and characteristic designs, especially such as relate to books, libraries, and learning.

CHAPTER 5.

The Enemies of Books.

We have seen in former chapters how the books of a library are acquired, how they are prepared for the shelves, or for use, and how they are or should be bound. Let us now consider the important questions which involve the care, the protection, and the preservation of the books.

Every librarian or book owner should be something more than a custodian of the books in his collection. He should also exercise perpetual vigilance with regard to their safety and condition. The books of every library are beset by dangers and by enemies. Some of these are open and palpable; others are secret, illusive, little suspected, and liable to come unlooked for and without warning. Some of these enemies are impersonal and immaterial, but none the less deadly; others are personally human in form, but most inhuman in their careless and brutal treatment of books. How far and how fatally the books of many libraries have been injured by these ever active and persistent enemies can never be adequately told. But we may point out what the several dangers are which beset them, and how far the watchful care of the librarian and his assistants may forestall or prevent them.

One of the foremost of the inanimate enemies of books is dust. In some libraries the atmosphere is dust-laden, to a degree which seems incredible until you witness its results in the deposits upon books, which soil your fingers, and contaminate the air you breathe, as you brush or blow it away. Peculiarly liable to dust are library rooms located in populous towns, or in business streets, and built close to

(101)

the avenues of traffic. Here, the dust is driven in at the windows and doors by every breeze that blows. It is an omnipresent evil, that cannot be escaped or very largely remedied. As preventive measures, care should be taken not to build libraries too near the street, but to have ample front and side yards to isolate the books as far as may be consistent with convenient access. Where the library is already located immediately on the street, a subscription for sprinkling the thoroughfare with water, the year round, would be true economy.

In some cities, the evils of street dust are supplemented by the mischiefs of coal smoke, to an aggravated degree. Wherever soft coal is burned as the principal fuel, a black, fuliginous substance goes floating through the air, and soils every thing it touches. It penetrates into houses and public buildings, often intensified by their own interior use of the same generator of dirt, and covers the books of the library with its foul deposits. You may see, in the public libraries of some western cities, how this perpetual curse of coal smoke has penetrated the leaves of all the books, resisting all efforts to keep it out, and slowly but surely deteriorating both paper and bindings. Here, preventive measures are impossible, unless some device for consuming the coal smoke of chimneys and factories were made compulsory, or the evil somewhat mitigated by using a less dangerous fuel within the library.

But, aside from these afflictions of dust, in its most aggravated form, every library and every room in any building is subject to its persistent visitations. Wherever carpets or rugs cover the floors, there dust has an assured abiding-place, and it is diffused throughout the apartment in impalpable clouds, at every sweeping of the floors. Hence it would be wise to adopt in public libraries a floor-covering like linoleum, or some substance other than woolen, which would be measurably free from dust, while soft enough to deaden the sound of feet upon the floors. Even with this preventive precaution, there will always be dust enough, and too much for comfort, or for the health of the books. Only a thorough dusting, carried on if possible daily, can prevent an accumulation of dust, at once deleterious to the durability of the books, and to the comfort both of librarians and readers. Dust is an insidious foe, stealing on its march silently and unobserved, yet, however impalpable in the atmosphere of a library, it will settle upon the tops of every shelf of books, it will penetrate their inner leaves, it will lodge upon the bindings, soiling books and readers, and constituting a perpetual annoyance.

It is not enough to dust the tops of the books periodically; a more full and radical remedy is required, to render library books presentable. At no long intervals, there should be a thorough library cleaning, as drastic and complete as the house-cleaning which neat housewives institute twice a year, with such wholesome results. The books are to be taken down from the shelves, and subjected to a shaking-up process, which will remove more of the dust they have absorbed than any brush can reach. To do this effectually, take them, if of moderate thickness, by the half-dozen at a time from the shelf, hold them loosely on a table, their fronts downward, backs uppermost, then with a hand at either side of the little pile, strike them smartly together a few times, until the dust, which will fly from them in a very palpable cloud, ceases to fall. Then lay them on their ends, with the tops uppermost on the table, and repeat the concussion in that posture, when you will eliminate a fresh crop of dust, though not so thick as the first. After this, let each volume of the lot be brushed over at the sides and back with a soft (never stiff) brush, or else with a piece of cotton or woolen cloth, and so restored clean to the shelves. While this thorough method of cleansing will take time and pains, it will pay in the long run. It will not eliminate all the dust (which in a large collection is a physical impossibility) but it will reduce it to a minimum. Faithfully carried out, as a periodical supplement to a daily dusting of the books as they stand on the shelves, it will immensely relieve the librarian or book-owner, who can then, (and then only) feel that he has done his whole duty by his books.

Another dangerous enemy of the library book is damp, already briefly referred to. Books kept in any basement room, or near any wall, absorb moisture with avidity; both paper and bindings becoming mildewed, and often covered with blue mould. If long left in this perilous condition, sure destruction follows; the glue or paste which fastens the cover softens, the leather loses its tenacity, and the leaves slowly rot, until the worthless volumes smell to heaven. Books thus injured may be partially recovered, before the advanced stage of decomposition, by removal to a dry atmosphere, and by taking the volumes apart, drying the sheets, and rebinding—a very expensive, but necessary remedy, provided the books are deemed worth preserving.

But a true remedy is the preventive one. No library should ever be kept, even in part, in a basement story, nor should any books ever be located near the wall of a building. All walls absorb, retain, and give out moisture, and are dangerous and oft-times fatal neighbors to books. Let the shelves be located at right angles to every wall—with the end nearest to it at least twelve to eighteen inches removed, and the danger will be obviated.

A third enemy of the book is heat. Most libraries are unfortunately over-heated,—sometimes from defective means of controlling the temperature, and sometimes from carelessness or want of thought in the attendant. A high temperature is very destructive to books. It warps their covers, so that volumes unprotected by their fellows, or by a book support, tend to curl up, and stay warped until they become a nuisance. It also injures the paper of the volumes by over-heating, and weakening the tenacity of the leaves held together by the glue on the back, besides drying to an extreme the leather, till it cracks or crumbles under the heat. The upper shelves or galleries of any library are most seriously affected by over-heating, because the natural law causes the heat to rise toward the ceiling. If you put your hand on some books occupying the highest places in some library rooms, in mid-winter, when the fires are kept at their maximum, the heat of the volume will almost burn your fingers. If these books were sentient beings, and could speak, would they not say—"our sufferings are intolerable?"

The remedy is of course a preventive one; never to suffer the library to become over-heated, and to have proper ventilation on every floor, communicating with the air outside. Seventy degrees Fahrenheit is a safe and proper maximum temperature for books and librarian.

The mischief arising from gas exhalations is another serious source of danger to books. In many well-lighted libraries, the heat itself from the numerous gas-burners is sufficient to injure them, and there is besides a sulphuric acid escaping from the coal-gas fluid, in combustion, which is most deleterious to bindings. The only remedy appears to be, where libraries are open evenings, to furnish them with electric lights. This improved mode of illumination is now so perfected, and so widely diffused, that it may be reckoned a positive boon to public libraries, in saving their books from one of their worst and most destructive enemies.

Another of the potent enemies of books is fire. I refer, not to over-heating the rooms they occupy, but to the risk they continually run, in most libraries, of total destruction. The chronicle of burned libraries would make a long and melancholy record, on which there is no space here to enter. Irreparable losses of manuscripts and early printed books, and precious volumes printed in small editions, have arisen from men's neglect of building our book-repositories fire-proof. In all libraries not provided with iron or steel shelves, there is perpetual danger. Books do not burn easily, unless surrounded with combustibles, but these are furnished in nearly all libraries, by surrounding the books on three sides with wooden shelves, which need only to be ignited at any point to put the whole collection in a blaze. Then follows the usual abortive endeavor to save the library by the aid of fire engines, which flood the building, until the water spoils nearly all which the fire does not consume. The incalculable losses which the cause of learning has sustained from the burning of public, university and ecclesiastical libraries are far greater than the cost which the provision of fire-proof repositories would have entailed.

Of late years, there has been a partial reform in library construction. Some have been built fire-proof throughout, with only stone, brick, concrete and iron material, even to the floors and window casings. Many more have had iron shelves and iron stacks to hold the shelves constructed, and there are now several competing manufacturers of these invaluable safeguards to books. The first library interior constructed wholly of iron was that of the Library of Congress at Washington, which had been twice consumed, first when the Capitol was burned by the British army in 1814, and again in 1851, through a defective flue, when only 20,000 volumes were saved from the flames, out

of a total of 55,000. The example of iron construction
has been slowly followed, until now the large cities have
most of their newly-constructed libraries approximately
fire-proof, although many are exposed to fire in parts,
owing to a niggardly and false economy. The lesson that
what is worth doing at all is worth doing well, and that
every neglect of security brings sooner or later irreparable
loss, is very slowly learned. Whole hecatombs of books
have been sacrificed to the spirit of commercial greed,
blind or short-sighted enough not to see that secure protection to public property, though costlier at first, is far
cheaper in the end. You may speak of insurance against
library losses by fire, but what insurance could restore the
rare and costly Shakespearean treasures of the Birming-
ham Free Library, or the unique and priceless manuscripts
that went up in flames in the city library of Strasburg, in
1870, or the many precious and irreplaceable manuscript
archives of so many of our States, burned in the conflagration of their capitols?

One would think that the civilized world had had lessons
enough, ever since that seventh century burning of the
Alexandrian library by the Caliph Omar, with that famous
but apocryphal rhetorical dilemma, put in his mouth perhaps by some nimble-witted reporter:—"If these books
agree with the Koran, they are useless, and should be
burned: if not, they are pernicious, and must not be
spared." But the heedless world goes carelessly on, deaf
to the voice of reason, and the lessons of history, amid the
holocausts of literature and the wreck of blazing libraries,
uttering loud newspaper wails at each new instance of destruction, forgotten in a week, then cheerfully renewing
the business of building libraries that invite the flames.

Nothing here said should be interpreted as advice not to
insure any library, in all cases where it is not provided with

iron cases for the books, or a fire-proof building. On the contrary, the menaced destruction of books or manuscripts that cannot be replaced should lead to securing means in advance for replacing all the rest in case of loss by fire. And the experience of the past points the wisdom of locating every library in an isolated building, where risks of fire from other buildings are reduced to a minimum, instead of in a block whose buildings (as in most commercial structures) are lined with wood.

You will perhaps attach but small importance at first thought, to the next insidious foe to library books that I shall name—that is, wetting by rain. Yet most buildings leak at the roof, sometime, and some old buildings are subject to leaks all the time. Even under the roof of the Capitol at Washington, at every melting of a heavy snow-fall, and on occasion of violent and protracted rains, there have been leaks pouring down water into the libraries located in the old part of the building. Each of these saturated and injured its quota of books, some of which could only be restored to available use by re-binding, and even then the leaves were left water-stained in part. See to it that your library roof is water-tight, or the contents of your library will be constantly exposed to damage against which there is no insurance.

Another besetting danger to the books of our libraries arises from insects and vermin. These animated foes appear chiefly in the form of book-worms, cockroaches, and mice. The first-named is rare in American libraries, though its ravages have extended far and wide among the old European ones. This minute little insect, whose scientific name is the *anobium paniceum*, bores through the leaves of old volumes, making sometimes holes which deface and mutilate the text. All our public libraries, doubtless, have on their shelves old folios in vellum or leather bindings, which present upon opening the disagreeable vision of leaves eaten through (usually before they crossed the sea) by these pernicious little borers. It is comforting to add, that I have never known of any book-worm in the Congressional Library—except the human variety, which is frequently in evidence. Georgetown College library once sent me a specimen of the insect, which was found alive in one of its volumes, but the united testimony of librarians is that this pest is rare in the United States. As to remedies, the preventive one of sprinkling the shelves twice a year with a mixture of powdered camphor and snuff, or the vapor of benzine or carbolic acid, or other repellant chemicals, is resorted to abroad, but I have not heard of any similar practice in this country. I may remark in passing, that the term "book-worm" is a misnomer, since it is not a worm at all, but an insect. A more serious insect menace is the cockroach, a hungry, unclean little beast, which frequents a good many libraries, and devours bindings (especially fresh ones) to get at the paste or savory parts of the binding. The remedy for this evil, when once found to exist, is to scatter the most effective roach poison that can be found, which may arrest further ravages.

Another insect pest is the Croton bug, *(Blatta Germanica)* which eats into cloth bindings to get at the sizing or albumen. The late eminent entomologist, Dr. C. V. Riley, pronounced them the worst pest known in libraries, but observed that they do not attack books bound in leather, and confine their ravages to the outside of cloth-bound books, never troubling the leaves. The remedy prescribed is a powder in which pyrethrum is the chief ingredient, sprinkled about the shelves.

Among the rodents, mice are apt to be busy and mischievous infesters of libraries. They are extremely fond of paste, and being in a chronic state of hunger, they watch opportunities of getting at any library receptacle of it. They will gnaw any fresh binding, whether of cloth, board, or leather, to get at the coveted food.   They will also gnaw some books, and even pamphlets, without any apparent temptation of a succulent nature.   A good library cat or a series of mouse traps, skilfully baited, may rid you of this evil.

The injury that comes to library books from insufficient care in protecting them on the shelves is great and incalculable.   There are to be seen in every library, volumes all twisted out of shape by the sagging or leaning, to which the end-book is subjected, and which is often shared by all its neighbors on the shelf.   The inevitable result is that the book is not only spoiled in its good looks, but (which is vastly more important) it is injured in its binding, which is strained and weakened just in proportion to the length of .time in which it is subjected to such risks.   The plain remedy is to take care that every volume is supported upright upon the shelf, in some way.   When the shelf is full, the books will support one another.   But when volumes are withdrawn, or when a shelf is only partly filled with books, the unsupported volumes tumble by force of gravitation, and those next them sag and lean, or fall like a row of bricks, pushing one another over.   No shelf of books can safely be left in this condition.   Some one of the numerous book-supports that have been contrived should be always ready, to hold up the volumes which are liable to lean and fall.

We come now to the active human enemies of books, and these are unhappily found among some of the readers who frequent our libraries.   These abuses are manifold and far-reaching.   Most of them are committed through ignorance, and can be corrected by the courteous but firm interposition of the librarian, instructing the delinquent how to treat a book in hand. Others are wilful and unpardonable offences against property rights and public morals, even if not made penal offences by law. One of these is book mutilation, very widely practiced, but rarely detected until the mischief is done, and the culprit gone. I have found whole pages torn out of translations, in the volumes of Bohn's Classical Library, doubtless by students wanting the translated text as a "crib" in their study of the original tongue. Some readers will watch their opportunity, and mutilate a book by cutting out plates or a map, to please their fancy, or perhaps to make up a defective copy of the same work. Those consulting bound files of newspapers will ruthlessly despoil them by cutting out articles or correspondence, or advertisements, and carrying off the stolen extracts, to save themselves the trouble of copying. Others, bolder still, if not more unscrupulous, will deliberately carry off a library book under a coat, or in a pocket, perhaps signing a false name to a reader's ticket to hide the theft, or escape detection. Against these scandalous practices, there is no absolute safeguard in any library. Even where a police watch is kept, thefts are perpetrated, and in most libraries where no watchman is employed, the librarian and his assistants are commonly far too busy to exercise close scrutiny of all readers. As one safeguard, no rare or specially costly book should be entrusted to a reader except under the immediate eye of the librarian or assistant. Ordinary books can be replaced if carried off, and by watching the rarities, risk of theft can be reduced to a minimum.

When newspapers are given out to readers, it should always be in a part of the library where those using them are conscious of a surveillance exercised over their movements. The penalty of neglecting this may at any time be the mu-

tilation of an important file, and it must be remembered
that such damage, once done, cannot be repaired. You
can replace a mutilated book usually by buying a new one,
but a newspaper can almost never be replaced. Even in
the city of Boston, the librarian of the Athenaeum library
records the disgraceful fact, that "the temptation to avoid
the trouble of copying, by cutting out articles from newspapers is too strong for the honesty of a considerable part
of the public." And it was recorded by the custodian of
a public library in Albany that all the plates were missing
from certain books, that the poetry and best illustrations
were cut from magazines before they had lain on the tables
a week, and strange to say, that many of these depredations
were committed by women.

It is a difficult problem how to prevent such outrages to
decency, and such irreparable depredations on the books in
our libraries as destroy, in great part, their value. A
posted notice, reminding readers that mutilation of books
or periodicals is a penal offence, will warn off many, if not
all, from such acts of vandalism. If there is no law pun-
ishing the offence, agitate until you get one. Expose
through the press such thefts and mutilations as are discovered. Interest readers whom you know, to be watchful
of those you do not know, and to quietly report any observed violation of rules. When a culprit is detected, push
the case to prompt legal hearing, and let the penalty of
the law be enforced. Let it be known that the public
property in books is too sacred a right to be violated with
impunity. Inculcate by every means and on every opportunity the sentiment that readers who freely benefit by the
books supplied should themselves feel personal concern in
their cleanliness and preservation, and that the interest of
the library is really the interest of all.

A daily abuse practiced by many readers in libraries,

though without wrongful intent, is the piling of one book
on top of another while open. This is inexcusable ill-
treatment, for it subjects the open book thus burdened, to
injury, besides probably soiling its pages with dust. Especially harmful is such careless treatment of large volumes of newspapers or illustrated works.

Careless use of ink is the cause of much injury to library
books. As a rule (to which the very fewest exceptions
should be made) pencils only should be allowed to readers,
who must forego the use of ink, with the inevitable risk of
dropping it upon the book to its irreparable injury. The
use of ink in fountain pens is less objectionable. Tracing
of maps or plates should not be allowed, unless with a soft
pencil. Under no circumstances should tracing with a
pen or other hard instrument be permitted to any reader.
Failure to enforce this rule may result in ruin of valuable
engravings or maps.

There is one class of books which demand special and
watchful care at the hands of the librarian. These are the
fine illustrated works, mostly in large folio, which include
the engravings of the art galleries of Europe, and many
other specially rare or costly publications. These should
be carefully shelved in cases where they can lie on their
sides, not placed upright, as in some collections, to lean
over, and, sooner or later to break their backs, and necessitate rebinding. When supplied to readers, there should
not be more than one volume at a time given out, to avoid
the risk, always threatening, of careless handling or of
opening one volume on top of another that is open. There
should also be a printed notice or label affixed to the side
cover of every illustrated work reading, "Never touch an
engraving," or an equivalent warning. This will go far,
by its plain reminder, to prevent soiling the pages by the
fingers, a practice which rapidly deteriorates fine books,

and if long continued, renders them unfit to be exhibited to clean-handed readers.

All plates should be stamped at some portion of their surface (it is often done on the back) with the embossing stamp of the library, as a means of identification if abstracted from the volume to which they belong.

Such books should, moreover, be consulted on a large table, or better an adjustable stand (to avoid frequent lifting or shifting of the position of the volume when inspecting the plates) and always under the eye of the librarian or an assistant not far removed. These precautions will insure far more careful treatment, and will result in handing down to a new generation of readers many a rare and precious volume, which would otherwise be destroyed or irretrievably injured in a very few years. The library treasures which cost so much to bring together should never be permitted to suffer from want of care to preserve them.

All writing upon the margins of books should be prohibited—other than simple pencil corrections of the text, as to an erroneous date, name, etc., which corrections of errors should not only be permitted, but welcomed, upon due verification. The marking of passages for copying or citation should be tolerated only upon the rigid condition that every user of the book rubs out his own pencil marks before returning it. I have seen lawyers and others thoughtless enough of right and wrong to mark long passages in pen and ink in books belonging to public libraries. This is a practice to be sternly repressed, even at the cost of denying further library privileges to the offender.

Turning down leaves in a book to keep the place is one of the easily besetting sins of too many readers. Those who thus dogs-ear a volume should be taught that the vile practice weakens and wears out the leaves thus folded down, and makes the book a more easy prey to dust and disintegration. However busy I may be, I instinctively turn back every turned-down leaf I notice in any book, before using it, or handing it to another. A good safe-guard would be to provide a supply of little narrow strips of paper, in the ticket boxes at the library tables to serve as the book-markers so frequently needed by readers. For this purpose, no thick or smooth calendered paper should be used, which falls out of any loosely bound book too readily—but a thin soft paper un-sized, which will be apt to retain its place. I have lost valuable time (which I shall never see again) in trying to find the pages marked for me by a searcher who had thoughtlessly inserted bits of cardboard as markers—which kept falling out by their own weight. The book-marks should be at least two inches long, and not more than half an inch wide; and rough edges are better than smooth ones, for they will adhere better to the head of the volume where placed. Better still it is, to provide paper book-marks forked at the lower end by slitting, then doubled so that the mark will go on both sides of the leaf at once. This is the only sure safeguard against these bits of paper falling out, and thus losing the place. Never put cards, or letters, or documents, or any solid substance into a book. It weakens the binding, and if continued, often breaks the back. The fact that most of the injuries to which books are exposed are unintentional injuries does not alter the fact that they are none the less injuries to be guarded against. Wilful perpetration of the many abuses referred to may be rare, but the unconscious perpetrators should be instructed how to use books by a vigilant librarian. And they who have thus been taught to be careful of the books in a public library will learn to be more careful of their own, which is a great step in the education of any one.

It ought not to be needful to charge any one never to wet the finger to turn over the leaves of a book—a childish habit, akin to running out the tongue when writing, or moving the lips when reading to one's self. The only proper way to turn the leaf is at the upper right-hand corner, and the index-finger of the right hand will always be found competent to that duty.

Still less should it be needful to insist upon the importance to every reader of books, of coming to their perusal clean-handed. When you reflect that nine-tenths of the soiling and spoiling which books undergo comes from the dirty hands of many readers, this becomes a vital point. Fouquet, a learned book collector of France, used to keep a pile of white gloves in the ante-room of his library, and no visitor was allowed to cross the threshold, or to handle a book without putting on a pair, lest he should soil the precious volumes with naked hands. Such a refinement of care to keep books immaculate is not to be expected in this age of the world; and yet, a librarian who respects his calling is often tempted to wish that there were some means of compelling people to be more careful about books than they are.

It ought not ever to be true that an enemy to the welfare of library books is found in the librarian himself, or in any of his assistants, yet there have been those employed in the care of books who have abused their positions and the volumes entrusted to their charge, not only by neglect of care, (which is a negative injury) but by positive and continual ill treatment. This may arise from ignorance of better methods, but ignorance is a poor excuse for one credited with the intelligence of a librarian. In some libraries, books are treated with positive indignity, and are permanently injured by tightly wedging them together. Never crowd books by main force into shelves too short or too small for them. It strains the backs, and seriously injures the bindings. Every book should slip easily past its fellows on the shelf. If a volume is too tall to go in its place, it should be relegated to lower shelves for larger books, never letting its head be crowded against the shelf above it.

One should never pull books out from the shelf by their head-bands, or by pulling at the binding, but place the finger firmly on the top of the book, next to the binding, and press down while drawing out the volume. From failure to observe this simple precaution, you will find in all libraries multitudes of torn or broken bindings at the top —a wholly needless defacement and waste.

Never permit a book to be turned down on its face to keep the place. This easily besetting habit weakens the book, and frequently soils its leaves by contact with a dusty table. For the same reason, one volume should not be placed within the leaves of another to keep the place where a book-mark of paper, so easily supplied, should always be used. Books should not be turned down on the fore-edges or fronts on the library tables, as practiced in most book-stores, in order to better display the stock. The same habit prevails in many libraries, from careless inattention. When necessary, in order to better read the titles, they should never be left long in such position. This treatment weakens the back infallibly, and if long continued breaks it. Librarians, of all persons in the world, should learn, and should lead others to learn, never to treat a book with indignity, and how truly the life of a book depends upon proper treatment, as well as that of an animated being.

These things, and others of my suggestions, may seem trifles to some; but to those who consider how much success in life depends upon attention to what are called trifles—nay, how much both human taste and human happiness are promoted by care regarding trifles, they will not appear unimportant. The existence of schools to teach library science, and of manuals devoted to similar laudable aims, is an auspicious omen of the new reign of refined taste in those nobler arts of life which connect themselves with literature, and are to be hailed as authentic evidences of the onward progress of civilization.

CHAPTER 6.

The Restoration and Reclamation of Books.

We are now to consider carefully the restoration and the reclamation of the books of a library, whether public or private.

Nothing can be more important than the means of restoring or reclaiming library books that are lost or injured, since every such restoration will save the funds of the library or collector from replacing them with fresh or newly bought copies, and will enable it to furnish its stores with as many new books as the money thus saved represents. The cardinal thing to be kept always in view is a wise economy of means. An every-day prudence is the price of successful administration. A management which permits any of the enemies of books to destroy or damage them, thereby wasting the substance of the library without repair, is a fatally defective management, which should be changed as soon as possible.

This consideration assumes added importance when it is remembered that the means of nearly all our libraries are very limited and inadequate to the drafts upon them, year by year. A great many libraries are compelled to let their books needing rebinding accumulate, from the mere want of money to pay for reclothing the nearly worn-out volumes, thus depriving the readers for a considerable time, of the use of many coveted books. And even with those which have large means, I have never yet heard of a library that had enough, either to satisfy the eager desire of the librarian to fill up deficiencies, or to meet fully the manifold wants of readers. So much the more important, then, is it to husband every dollar that can be saved, to keep the books in such good condition that they will not need frequent rebinding, and to reduce to a minimum all the evils which beset them, menacing their safety, or injuring their condition.

To attain these great ends, the librarian who is qualified for his responsible position, must be both a preserver and a restorer of books. If not personally able to go through the mechanical processes which belong to the art of restoration, (and this is the case in all libraries except the smallest) he should at least learn all about them, so as to be able to teach them thoroughly and intelligently to an assistant. It is frequently made an excuse for the soiled and slovenly and even torn condition of books and bindings in a much used public library, that neither the librarian nor his aids have any time to look into the condition of the books, much less to repair any of the numerous damages they sustain. But it should be remembered that in most libraries, even the busiest, there are seasons of the day, or periods of very stormy weather, when the frequentation of readers is quite small. Those times should always be seized upon to take hold of volumes which have had to be laid aside as damaged, in the hurry of business. To arrest such damages at the threshold is the duty and the interest of the library. A torn leaf can be quickly mended, a slightly broken binding can be pasted or glued, turned-down leaves can be restored where they belong, a plate or map that is started can be fastened in, by devoting a few minutes at the proper time, and with the proper appliances ready at hand. Multitudes of volumes can be so treated in the course of the year, thus saving the heavy cost of rebinding. It is the proverbial stitch in time that saves nine. Never wait, in such matters, for the leisure day that never comes, but seize the golden moment as it flies, when no reader is interrupting you, and clear off at least one of the little jobs that are awaiting your attention. No one who does not know how to use the odd moments is qualified for the duties of a librarian. I have seen, in country libraries, the librarian and his lady assistant absorbed in reading newspapers, with no other readers in the room. This is a use of valuable time never to be indulged in during library hours. If they had given those moments to proper care of the books under their charge, their shelves would not have been found filled with neglected volumes, many of which had been plainly badly treated and injured, but not beyond reclamation by timely and provident care.

It is amazing how any one can expect long employment as a librarian, who takes no interest in the condition of the books under his charge. The way to build up a library, and to establish the reputation of a librarian at the same time, is to devote every energy and intelligence to the great work in hand. Convince the library directors, by incessant care of the condition of the books, that you are not only a fit, but an indispensable custodian of them. Let them see your methods of preserving and restoring, and they will be induced to give you every facility of which you stand in need. Show them how the cost of binding or re-buying many books can be saved by timely repair within the library, and then ask for another assistant to be always employed on such work at very moderate cost. Library directors and trustees are commonly intensely practical men, and quick to see into the heart of good management. They do not want a librarian who has a great reputation as a linguist, or an educator, or a book-worm, but one who knows and cares about making their funds go as far as possible, and can show them how he has saved by restoring

old books, enough money to pay for a great many new
ones.

Nothing is more common in public lending libraries
than to find torn leaves in some of the books. If the leaf
is simply broken, without being absolutely detached, or if
part is torn off, and remains on hand, the volume may be
restored by a very simple process. Keep always at hand
in some drawer, a few sheets of thin "onion-skin" paper,
or the transparent adhesive paper supplied by the Library
Bureau. Paste this on either side of the torn leaf, seeing
that it laps over all the points of juncture where the tear
occurred, and that the fitting of the text or reading matter
is complete and perfect. The paper being transparent,
there will be no difficulty in reading the torn page through
it.

This little piece of restoration should always be effected
immediately on discovery, both that the torn piece or frag-
ment may be saved, and that the volume may be restored
to use.

In case of absolute loss of a leaf or a part of a page,
there are only three remedies known to me.

1. The book may be condemned as imperfect, and a new
copy purchased.

2. The missing part may be restored from a perfect copy
of the same work, by copying the portions of the text wanting, and inserting them where they belong. This can be
done with a pen, and the written deficiency neatly inserted, in fac-simile of the type, or in ordinary script hand; or
else the part wanting may be photographed or heliotyped
by the best modern process from a duplicate copy of the
book.

3. If the book is of very recent issue, the publishers may
furnish a signature or sheet which would make good the

deficiency, from the "imperfections" left in the bindery, after making up the edition of the work.

In most cases, the last named means of replacement will not be found available. The first, or buying a fresh copy, may entail a greater expense than the library authorities would deem proper at the time, and it might be preferred to continue the book in use, with a slight imperfection.

The second method, more or less troublesome according to circumstances, or the extent of the matter to be copied is sometimes the most economical. Of course, it is subject to the drawback of not being, when done, a *bona fide* or genuine copy of the book as published. This diminishes the commercial value of even the rarest book, although so fully restored as to text that the reader has it all before him, so that it supplies every requisite of a perfect copy for the purposes of a public library, or a private owner who is not a connoisseur in books.

When the corners of a book are found to be broken (as often happens by falling to the floor or severe handling) the book may be restored by a treatment which will give it new leather corners. With paste or glue well rubbed in, apply thick brown paper on the corners, which, when dry, will be as hard as desired, and ready to receive the leather. Then the sides may be covered with marbled paper or cloth, and the volume is restored.

When the back of a book becomes loose, the remedy is to take it out of the cover, re-sew it, and glue it firmly into the former back. This will of course render the back of the volume more rigid, but, in compensation, it will be more durable.

In these cases of loose or broken backs, the study should be to save the leather cover and the boards or sides of the book intact, so as to diminish by more than one-half the cost of repair. As the volume cannot be restored to a solid and safe condition without being re-sewed, it may be carefully separated from the cover by cutting the cords or bands at their junction with the boards, then slowly stripping the book out of its cover, little by little, and treating the sheets when separated as already indicated in the chapter on rebinding.

One of the most common defacements which library books undergo is marking up the margins with comments or references in pencil. Of course no thoughtful reader would be guilty of this practice, but thoughtless readers are often in the majority, and the books they read or fancy that they read, get such silly commentaries on the margins as these: "beautiful," "very sad," "perfectly splendid," "I think Becky is horrid," or, "this book ends badly." Such vile practices or defacements are not always traceable to the true offender, especially in a circulating library, where the hours are so busy as to prevent the librarian from looking through the volumes as they come in from the readers. But if detected, as they may be after a few trials of suspected parties, by giving them out books known to be clean and free from pencil marks when issued to them, the reader should be required always to rub out his own marks, as a wholesome object-lesson for the future. The same course should be pursued with any reader detected in scribbling on the margin of any book which is being read within the library. Incorrigible cases, amounting to malicious marking up of books, should be visited by severe penalties —even to the denial of further library privileges to the offender.

Not long ago, I bought at an auction sale a copy of the first edition of Tennyson's "In Memoriam," which was found on receipt to be defaced by marking dozens of verses in the margin with black lines drawn along them, absolutely with pen and ink! The owner of that book, who did the ruthless deed, never reflected that it might fall into hands where his indelible folly would be sharply denounced.

The librarian or assistant librarian who will instinctively rub out all pencil marks observed in a library book deserves well of his countrymen. It is time well spent.

The writing on book-margins is so common a practice, and so destructive of the comfort and satisfaction which readers of taste should find in their perusal of books, that no legitimate means of arresting it or repairing it should be neglected. In a public library in Massachusetts, a young woman of eighteen who was detected as having marked a library copy of "Middlemarch" with gushing effusions, was required to read the statute prescribing fine and imprisonment for such offenses, with very tearful effect, and undoubtedly with a wholesome and permanent improvement in her relations to books and libraries.

In some libraries, a warning notice is posted up like this: "Readers finding a book injured or defaced, are required to report it at once to the librarian, otherwise they will be held responsible for the damage done." This rule, while its object is highly commendable, may lead in practice to injustice to some readers. So long as the reader uses the book inside of the library walls, he should of course report such defects as meet his eye in reading, whether missing pages, plates, or maps, or serious internal soiling, torn leaves, etc. But in the case of drawing out books for home reading, the rule might embarrass any reader, however well disposed, if too strictly construed. A reader finding any serious defect in a library volume used at home, should simply place a mark or slip in the proper place with the word "damaged," or "defective" written on it. Then, on returning the book to the library, his simple statement of finding it damaged or defective when he came to read it should be accepted by the librarian as exonerating him from blame for any damage. And this gives point to the importance of examining every book, at least by cursory inspection, before it is handed out for use. A volume can be run through quickly by a practiced hand, so as to show in a moment or two any leaves started or torn, or, usually, any other important injury. If any such is found, the volume should under no circumstances be given out, but at once subjected to repair or restoration. This degree of care will not only save the books of the library from rapid deterioration, but will also save the feelings of readers, who might be anxious lest they be unjustly charged with damaging while in their hands.

The treatment of their imperfect books (which tend perpetually to accumulate) is very different in different libraries. Some libraries, where funds are ample enough to enable them to do it, condemn any book that has so much as a sentence torn out, and replace it on the shelves with a new copy. The imperfect volumes are sold for waste paper, or put into some sale of duplicate books, marked as imperfect, with note of the damage upon a slip inserted at the proper place in the book, and also in the catalogue, if sold at auction or in a printed list of duplicates offered by the library. This notice of what imperfection exists is necessary, so that no incautious purchaser may think that he is securing a perfect copy of the work.

Other libraries not blessed with means to pursue this course, do as best they can afford, supplying what is deficient when possible without much cost of time or money, or else continuing the damaged book in use "with all its imperfections on its head."

The loss of a single plate does not destroy the value of the book for readers, however to be regretted as diminishing the satisfaction to be derived from the volume. And one can sometimes pardon the loss of a part of a page in a mutilated book, especially when he is made aware of the fact that the library which welcomes him to the free enjoyment of its treasures cannot well afford to buy another.

It is disheartening to read, in an annual report of a public library of circulation in Massachusetts, that many of its popular books are so soiled and defaced, after a few readings, as to be unfit for further service; that books of poetry are despoiled by the scissors to save trouble of copying verses wanted; that plates are often abstracted, and that many magazines "seem to be taken from the library for no other reason than that private scrap-books may be enriched or restless children amused." The only remedy suggested is to examine each book before again giving it out, and, if returned defaced, to hold the borrower responsible.

The art of cleaning books that are stained or dirty, is a matter not widely known, and in this country there are few experts at it. Some of these keep closely guarded the methods they use to cleanse a book. Comparatively few libraries avail themselves of the practice of washing their soiled volumes, as the process is too expensive for most of them, and so they are accustomed to let the library books remain in use and re-issue them again and again, until they become so filthy as to be quite unfit to be seen—much less handled by any reader.

But there are often valuable or rare works which have sustained interior injury, and which it is desired to restore to a clean condition. The best method is to take the book apart as the first step. When separated into sheets, those leaves which are merely dirty should be placed in a bath composed of about four ounces of chloride of lime, dissolved in a quart of water. They should soak until all stains are removed, and the paper is restored to its proper color. Then the pages should be washed in cold water—

running water is preferable—and allowed to soak about six hours. This removes all traces of the lime, which would otherwise tend to rot or injure the book. After this, the sheets are to be "sized," *i. e.*, dipped in a bath of size and water, and laid out to dry. This process gives firmness and consistency to the paper, which would otherwise remain too soft to handle. The sheets should be pressed a few hours between glazed paste-boards, as used in printing offices. A cheap and simple size for this purpose may be made by mixing white gelatine with water, and this may be kept in a bottle, so as to be always conveniently at hand. The art of restoring and rendering fit for handling books and rare early pamphlets by sizing all the leaves is in constant use in Europe. By this means, and by piecing out margins, the most rotten paper, ready to drop apart in turning the leaves, may be restored to use, if not quite to its pristine condition.

Ink-spots or mildew stains may be wholly removed, when freshly made, by applying a solution of oxalic or citric acid, and then washing the leaf with a wet sponge. It is more effectual to follow the bath of oxalic acid by applying a solution of one part hydrochloric acid to six parts of water, after which bathe in cold water, and dry slowly. Or an infusion of hypochlorite of potash in twice its volume of water may be used instead of the preceding.

If a leather-bound book has grease on its cover, it can be removed by scraping French chalk or magnesia over the place, and ironing with a warm (not hot) iron. A simpler method is to apply benzine to the grease spots, (which dissolves the fatty material) and then dry the spot quickly with a fine cloth. This operation may be repeated, if not effectual at the first trial. The same method of applying benzine to oily spots upon plates or engravings, will remove the stains.

Ink-stains may also be taken off from the leather covers of books bound in calf or morocco by the use of oxalic acid. Care should be taken first to try the acid on a piece of similar leather or on a discarded book of the same color. If the leather is discolored after removing the black spot, one may apply, after taking out the traces of oxalic acid by some alkali, a coloring matter similar to the tint of the leather.

Spots or stains of grease or oil are often found in books. They may be wholly removed by applying carbonate of magnesia on both sides of the leaf stained, backed by paper, and pressing with a hot iron, after which the sheets should be washed and left under pressure over night. Another method is to dilute spirits of salts with five times its bulk of water, then let the stained leaves lie in the liquid four minutes, after which they are to be washed. Still another method is to make a mixture of one pound of soap, half a pound of clay and two ounces of lime, dissolved in water to a proper consistency; apply it to the spots; fifteen minutes after, dip the leaf in a bath of warm water for half an hour, after which dry and press until smooth.

Stains left by mud on the leaves of a book (a not uncommon fate of volumes falling in a wet street) can be removed thus: spread over the spots a jelly composed of white soap and water, letting it remain about half an hour. Then dip the leaf in clear water, and remove the soap with a fine sponge dipped in warm water; all the mud stains will disappear at the same time. To remove the last traces of the soap, dip a second time in clear water, place the leaf between two sheets of blotting paper, and dry slowly in a cool and shady place.

The same process, of washing in soap and water, will remove what are doubtless the most common of all the soil-ings that library books undergo, namely, the soil that comes from the dirty hands and fingers of readers.

It is sometimes necessary to color the sheets that have been washed white, so as to correspond in tint with the rest of the volume, which has not needed that treatment. An infusion of cheap tobacco leaves, or a bath of brown stout will effect this.

In all these methods of removing soil from the pages of books, it is absolutely necessary to give attention to thorough washing after the chemicals are used. Otherwise there will remain an element of destruction which will sooner or later spoil the book, to restore which so much pains may have been expended.

And one can readily learn how to restore a valuable book by these methods. He should, however, first practice on the restoration of a volume of little worth—and venture upon the treatment of a precious volume only after practice has made him an expert.

To restore a fresher look to volumes whose bindings are much rubbed or "scuffed" as it is sometimes called, one may spread over their surface a little wet starch pretty thick, with a little alum added, applied with an old leather glove. With this the back of the book, and the sides and edges of the boards should be smartly rubbed, after which, with a fine rag rub off the thicker part of the starch, and the book will present a much brighter appearance, besides being rid of dust and soil.

There will remain on the volume a very slight deposit of gelatine or gluten; before it dries completely, the palm of the hand may be passed over it at all points, and the leather, which may have assumed a dull color from the starch, will resume a bright brown or other tint. If this fails to appear, a bit of flannel, impregnated with a few drops of varnish, should be rubbed over the leather, and when nearly dry, rub with a white rag slightly touched with olive oil, and a brilliant appearance will be given to the binding.

When leaves are started, or a signature becomes loose in any volume, it should be at once withdrawn from circulation, or the loss of an important part of the book may result. The remedy commonly resorted to, of patching up the book by pasting in the loose leaves, is a mere make-shift which will not last. The cause of a loose signature is generally to be found in a broken thread in the sewing, and the only permanent cure is to take the book out of its cover, and re-sew it, when it may usually be re-inserted in the same binding. This is for cloth-bound books. When bound in leather, it is best to take out the loose sheet, "overcast" it, that is, secure all the leaves by sewing, then carefully lay some paste along the outer edge or back of the sheet, insert the sheet in its place, pressing it firmly with a paper knife along the middle of the sheet, and the volume will be restored ready for use after a few days drying under weight.

On occasion of a fire next to the Mercantile Library rooms in Philadelphia, in 1877, great damage was done, from water thrown by the fire-engines, to many thousands of books. The library authorities tried various methods of restoring the volumes, and among others, drying them in ovens was resorted to. This was found, however, to dry the books so rapidly, that the bindings cracked, and in many cases came off, while many volumes were much warped. The most advantageous method that was adopted was to prepare a large number of frames on which many wires were strung horizontally across a large room. The wet books (many of which were soaked through) were suspended on these wires in such a way as to dry them by degrees, the temperature of the room being raised considerably by furnace heat.

The condition in which the books were found after the wetting varied greatly. Nearly all that were printed on soft paper were wet through, while those next to them printed on thick paper, and with solid leather bindings, were scarcely damaged at all. The water stains constituted the most serious injury to the volumes, and multitudes of fine books that were wet will always bear the marks of the stain. Some of the more costly books were restored by taking them apart, washing them thoroughly, then placing them in a heated press, and drying them, so that the water-stains were removed. All the books, however different the degree of damage from the water, retained their legibility, and were put to the same uses in the library as before the fire occurred. None were burned, the actual fire being confined to the neighboring buildings of the block in the midst of which the library was unfortunately located.

The whole number of volumes damaged was about 55,-000, and the insurance, which was assessed by referees at the amount of $42,000, would nearly have replaced the books by new ones. Many of the volumes had to be re-bound as the damage by wetting the glue and paste which are such important elements in binding securely, led to the falling apart of the covers.

There are multitudes of books restored by some one of the processes which have been ingeniously contrived to make an old book as good as new, or an imperfect volume perfect. The art of reproducing in facsimile, by mere manual dexterity with the pen, letters, words, and whole pages, has been carried to a high degree of perfection, notably in London. A celebrated book restorer named Harris, gained a great reputation among book lovers and librarians by his consummate skill in the reproduction of the text of black-letter rarities and early-printed books of every kind. To such perfection did he carry the art of imitating an original that in many cases one could not distinguish the original from the imitation, and even experts have announced a Harris facsimile in a Shakespeare folio to be the printed original. The art has even been extended to engravings, with such success that the famous Droeshout portrait of Shakespeare, which illustrates the title-page of the first folio of 1623, has been multiplied in pen-made facsimile, so as to deceive the most careful scrutiny.

This nice and difficult art is not widely pursued in this country, though there are some experts among New York and Philadelphia book-binders, who practice it. The British Museum Library has a corps of workers engaged in the restoration both of books and of manuscripts (as well as engravings) who are men of the highest training and skill.

The process is necessarily quite expensive, because of the time required and of the small number of competing artists in this field. It is chiefly confined to the restoration of imperfect copies of early printed and rare books, which are so frequently found in imperfect condition, often wanting title-pages or the final leaves, or parts of pages in any part of the volume.

So costly, indeed, is this skilful hand-restoration of imperfect books, that it has been a great boon to the collectors of libraries and rare works, to see the arts of photography so developed in recent years, as to reproduce with almost exact fidelity printed matter of any kind from the pages of books. The cost of such facsimiles of course varies with the locality, the work, the skill, or the competition involved. But it may be said in general that the average cost of book-page facsimiles by photographic process need not exceed one dollar a page.

An entire edition of the Encyclopaedia Britannica has

"Any person who steals, defaces, injures, mutilates, tears, or destroys any book, pamphlet, work of art, or manuscript, belonging to any public library, or to the United States, in the District of Columbia, shall be fined ten dollars to one hundred dollars, and punished by imprisonment from one to twelve months, for every such offense."

This act will be found in the United States Statutes at Large, Vol. 20, p. 171. It would be well if the term "periodical" were added to the list of objects to be protected, to avoid all risk of a failure to punish the mutilation of newspapers and magazines, by pleading technical points, of which lawyers are prone to avail themselves in aiding offenders to escape conviction.

It will be observed, that the word "deface," employed in this statute, actually covers the marking of margins by any reader, all such marking constituting a defacement within the meaning of the law.

While the great multitude of readers who frequent our public libraries are honest and trustworthy, there are always some who are conspicuously the reverse. It is rarely safe in a large public library to admit readers to the shelves, without the company or the surveillance of an attendant. And it is not alone the uncultivated reader who cannot be trusted; the experience of librarians is almost uniform to the effect that literary men, and special scholars, as well as the collectors of rare books, are among those who watch the opportunity to purloin what they wish to save themselves the cost of buying. Sometimes, you may find your most valuable work on coins mutilated by the abstraction of a plate, carried off by some student of numismatics. Sometimes, you may discover a fine picture or portrait abstracted from a book by some lover of art or collector of portraits. Again, you may be horrified by finding a whole sermon torn out of a volume of theology by a theological student or even a clergyman. All these things have happened, and are liable to happen again. No library is safe that is not closely watched and guarded. In the Astor library a literary man actually tore out sixty pages of the *Revue de Paris*, and added to the theft the fraud of plagiarism, by translating from the stolen leaves an article which he sold to Appleton's Journal as an original production!

In this case, the culprit, though detected, could not be punished, the law of New York requiring the posting in the library of the statute prohibiting mutilation or other injury to the books, and this posting had not been done. The law has since been amended, to make the penalties absolute and unconditional.

In the Astor Library, over six hundred volumes were discovered to have been mutilated, including art works, Patent office reports, magazines, newspapers, and even encyclopaedias. The books stolen from that library had been many, until several exposures and punishment of thieves inspired a wholesome dread of a similar fate.

At a meeting of the American Library Association, one member inquired whether there was any effectual way to prevent the abstraction of books. He was answered by another librarian (from Cincinnati) who replied that he knew of only one effectual method, and that was to keep a man standing over each book with a club. Of course this was a humorous paradox, not to be taken literally, but it points a moral.

Seriously, however, the evil may be greatly curtailed, (though we may be hopeless of absolute prevention) by adopting the precautions already referred to. In the Library of the British Museum, a great library of reference, from which no book is permitted to be taken under any circumstances, the evil of mutilation was much reduced by prosecuting and posting the offenders publicly. After a few years, the obnoxious practice had so far ceased, that the placards, having an unpleasant aspect, were taken down. But on renewal of such depredations and defacements of books by readers, the placards were renewed, and some of the mutilated books, suitably labelled, were posted in the great reading room before the eyes of all. The authorities of the British Museum are convinced of the salutary effects of such warnings, though books are sometimes stolen or mutilated under the liberal management which leaves several thousand volumes open for reference, without tickets.

The late Dr. Wm. F. Poole, the Chicago librarian, recorded his experience in dealing with some clergymen, who, said he, seem to have as regards books, an imperfect appreciation of the laws of *meum* and *tuum*. He had found ministers more remiss in returning books than any other class of men. He would by no means reflect on a noble and sacred profession by charging the derelictions of a few upon the many. But he had had unpleasant experiences with men of that profession, who had absolutely purloined books from the Public Library, removed the bookplates and library stamp, and covered the volumes with paper carefully pasted down inside of the covers.

A librarian in Massachusetts testified that it was common experience that clergymen and professional men gave the most trouble. Second-hand book-dealers in Boston had found a judge of the court purloining rare pamphlets, and ministers making away with pamphlet sermons under their coats. Without insisting here upon any such extenuations of such practices as the prevalence of kleptomania, it has been made abundantly manifest that theft and mutilation of books are sufficiently common to demonstrate the weakness of human nature, and the necessity of every safe-guard which public libraries can provide against such abuses of their treasures.

A Boston librarian stated that the thieves or mutilators of books included school-boys, clerks, students, teachers, soldiers, physicians, lawyers, clergymen, etc. In only one case was the crime committed through want or suffering. Yet, though the offenders had been proven guilty in every instance, only two cases were known in which the penalty of the law had been enforced. Does not this bespeak laxity of public morals in Boston in regard to such abuses of library property?

The Union Theological Seminary at New York recorded its experience with ministers and theological students, to the effect that its library had lost more than a thousand volumes, taken and not returned. This of course included what were charged out, but could not be recovered.

A librarian in Auburn, N. Y., returning from vacation, found that the American Architect, an important illustrated weekly, had been mutilated in seven different volumes, and that 130 pages in all had been stolen. Fortunately, she was able to trace the reader who had been using the work, and succeeded in recovering the abstracted plates. The offender was prosecuted to conviction, and had to pay a fine of fifty dollars.

It often happens that books which disappear mysteriously from a public library re-appear quite as mysteriously. Those taking them, finding that the rules do not allow certain books to leave the library, make a law unto themselves, carry off the book wanted, keep it until read, and then return it surreptitiously, by replacing it on some shelf or table, when no one is looking. This is where no intention of stealing the book exists, and the borrower wilfully makes his own convenience override the library regulations, in the belief that he will not be found out. The

Buffalo Young Men's Library reported in one year eighteen illustrated works on the fine arts, reserved from being taken out by its by-laws, as disappearing for weeks, but brought back in this underhanded manner. In other cases of such return, it is likely that the purpose was to keep the book, but that conscience or better thoughts, or fear of detection prevailed, and secured its return.

Some instances where leniency has been exercised to save book thieves from penalties may be instructive. One man who had carried off and sold two volumes from the Astor Library was traced and arrested, when he pleaded that absolute want had driven him to the act. He had a wife ill and starving at his home, and this on investigation proving true, he was pardoned and saved further misery.

In another case, a poor German had stolen a volume of the classics which he pawned for a small sum to get bread for himself, being long out of work, and in a condition bordering closely upon starvation. He was released, the book reclaimed, and the offender turned over to the agencies of public charity.

A librarian of New York gave it as his experience that some ministers are not to be trusted any more than other people. Some of them like to write their opinions on the margins of the books. He found one of the library books written on in thirty pages, recognized the hand-writing, and wrote to the reverend gentleman asking an interview. He came, admitted the fact, and said that his notes made the book more valuable. This ingenious excuse did not satisfy the librarian, who said, "others do not think so, sir; so if you will get us a new book, you may keep the more valuable one." He soon brought in a new copy, and the matter ended.

At the New York Mercantile Library, a young lady, amply able to buy all the books she could want, was discovered going out of the library with one book in her hand which she was entitled to, it being charged, and with five others hidden under her cloak, without permission.

Mr. Melvil Dewey has truly said that it is very hard to tell a library thief at sight. Well-dressed, gentlemanly, even sanctimonious looking men are among them, and the wife of a well-known college professor, detected in purloining books, begged so hard not to be exposed, that she was reluctantly pardoned, and even restored to library privileges.

A prominent lawyer of Brooklyn, of distinguished appearance and fine manners, did not steal books, but his specialty was magazines and newspapers, which he carried off frequently. Being caught at it one day, and accused by the librarian, he put on an air of dignity, declared he was insulted, and walked out. The librarian found the periodical he had taken thrown down in the entry, and he never after frequented that library.

It is curious and instructive to know the experience of some libraries regarding the theft or mutilation of books. Thus, in the public library of Woburn, Mass., a case of mutilation occurred by the cutting out of a picture from "Drake's Historic Fields and Mansions of Middlesex County." On discovery of the loss, a reward of $10 was offered for information leading to detection of the culprit. This was published in the town paper, and an article was printed calling attention to these library thefts and abuses, followed by citing the State law making such depredations a penal offense. Within a week the missing plate came back to the librarian through the mail—anonymously of course, the person who had abstracted it finding that it was rather an unsafe picture to keep or exhibit, and so choosing to make his best policy honesty, though rather tardy in coming to that wise conclusion.

This experience, and others here cited, may serve as a hint what course to pursue under similar circumstances, in the reclamation of library books.

In the Library of the London Institution, continuous thefts of valuable editions of the classics had occurred. Putting a detective in the library, a young man of suspicious demeanor was soon identified as the thief, and was followed and arrested in the very act of selling a library book. He proved to be a young man of good family, education and previous good character; but the library had suffered such losses from his depredations, that no mercy was shown, and he received and underwent the sentence to two months imprisonment.

It may be added as an instance of methods availed of in London to trace missing books, that the librarian, knowing from the vacancies on the shelves what books had been abstracted, printed a list of them, sent it to every second-hand book-dealer in London, at the same time supplying it to the police, who circulate daily a list of missing property among all the pawn-brokers' shops in the city, and recovered all the books within twenty-four hours.

The Mercantile Library of Philadelphia missed a number of valuable books from its shelves, and on a watch being set, a physician in the most respectable rank in society was detected as the purloiner, and more than fifty volumes recovered from him.

A library at Lancaster, Pa., reported the almost incredible incident of a thief having hidden under his coat, and carried off, a Webster's Unabridged Dictionary!

In most cases of detected theft or mutilation of books, strong appeals are made by the culprit or his friends to save exposure by public prosecution. These are commonly, in the case of persons in very respectable circumstances in life, not so much to avoid paying fines imposed

by law as to avoid the disgrace attached to publicity, and
the consequent damage done to the character of the individual.   It is probably true that in a majority of cases,
such influences have been strong enough to overcome the
determination of the librarian or library authorities to let
the law take its course.   Now, while it must be admitted
that there is no rule without some valid exception that may
be made, it is nevertheless to be insisted upon that due protection to public property in libraries demands the enforcement of the laws enacted to that end.   The consequence
of leniency to the majority of book thieves would be not
only an indirect encouragement to the culprits to continue
their depredations, but it would also lead to a lax and dangerous notion of the obligations of readers, and the sacred-
ness of such property, in the public mind.   Enforcement
of the penalties of wrong-doing, on the other hand, tends
unquestionably to deter others, both by the fear of publicity which must follow detection, and by terror of the
penalty which is or may be imprisonment for a considerable term, besides the imposing of a fine.

At the Worcester, Mass., Public Library, a young man
of twenty-two was detected in stealing a book, obliged to
confess, and prosecuted.   Much pressure was brought to
bear by his family and friends, very respectable people, to
save him from the penalty.   The Court, however, imposed
a fine of thirty dollars, and it being represented that his
relatives would have to pay the amount, though innocent
parties, the judge suspended the sentence until the young
man should pay it in instalments from his own earnings,
one of the family giving bail.   The valuable lesson was in
this way not lost, either to the offender or to the community; the law was enforced, and the young man perhaps
saved from a life of wrong-doing, while if he had been let

off scot-free, in deference to the influence exerted to that end, he might have gone from bad to worse.

At the Pratt Institute Free Library in Brooklyn, books had been disappearing from the reference department at intervals of about a week, and a watch was instituted. After some weeks' fruitless watching, a young man who came frequently to consult books was singled out as the probable offender, and the eyes of the library staff were centered upon him. The janitor watched his movements for some days, from a concealed post of observation, as the young man walked back and forth between the book stacks, and one day caught him in the act of slipping a book into his pocket, and arrested him as he was leaving the building. He had stolen a dozen books from the library, all but three of which were recovered. He claimed to be a theological student, and that he had taken the books merely for the purposes of study. Much sympathy was expressed for him by people who believed that this was his motive, and that it was some partial atonement for his offense. The grief of his relatives at his disgrace was intense. The Court sentenced him to eight years in the penitentiary, but suspended the sentence in view of the fact that it was a first offense, by a youth of twenty-one years. He was put under police surveillance for his good behavior (equivalent to being paroled) but the sentence becomes active upon any further transgression of the law on his part.

It may be gathered from these many cases of library depredations, that they are very common, that perpetual vigilance is the price of safety, that punishment in nearly all cases is wiser than pardon, and that the few exceptions made should be mostly confined to offenders who steal books under desperate necessity or actual want.

CHAPTER 7.

Pamphlet Literature.

What is a pamphlet? is a question which is by no means capable of being scientifically answered. Yet, to the librarian dealing continually with a mass of pamphlets, books, and periodicals, it becomes important to define somewhere, the boundary line between the pamphlet and the book. The dictionaries will not aid us, for they all call the pamphlet "a few sheets of printed paper stitched together, but not bound." Suppose (as often happens) that you bind your pamphlet, does it then cease to be a pamphlet, and become a book? Again, most pamphlets now published are not stitched at all, but stabbed and wired to fasten the leaves together. The origin of the word "pamphlet," is in great doubt. A plausible derivation is from two French words, "*paume,*" and "*feuillet*," literally a hand-leaf; and another derives the word from a corruption of Latin—"*papyrus,*" paper, into *pampilus,* or *panfletus,* whence pamphlet. The word is in Shakespeare:

> "Comest thou with deep premeditated lines,
> With written pamphlets studiously devised?"

But we also find "pamphlets and bookys," in a work printed by Caxton in 1490, a hundred years before Shakespeare.

Whatever the origin, the common acceptation of the word is plain, signifying a little book, though where the pamphlet ends, and the book begins, is uncertain. The rule of the British Museum Library calls every printed publication of one hundred pages or less, a pamphlet. This is arbitrary, and so would any other rule be. As

that library binds its pamphlets separately, and counts
them in its aggregate of volumes, the reason for any distinction in the matter is not plain. Some of the government libraries in Europe are greatly overrated numerically
by reckoning pamphlets as volumes. Thus, the Royal Library at Munich, in Bavaria, has been ranked fourth among
the libraries of the world, claiming over a million volumes,
but as it reckons every university thesis, or discussion of
some special topic by candidates for degrees, as a volume,
and has perhaps 400,000 of this prolific class of publications, it is actually not so large as some American libraries,
which count their pamphlets as distinct from books in
their returns.

The pamphlet, or thin book, or tract (as some prefer to
call it) is reckoned by some librarians as a nuisance, and
by others as a treasure. That it forms rather a troublesome asset in the wealth of a library cannot be doubted.
Pamphlets taken singly, will not stand upon the shelves;
they will curl up, become dogs-eared, accumulate dust, and
get in the way of the books. If kept in piles, as is most
frequent, it is very hard to get at any one that is wanted
in the mass. Then it is objected to them, that the majority of them are worthless, that they cost altogether too
much money, and time, and pains, to catalogue them, and
that they are useless if not catalogued; that if kept bound,
they cost the library a sum out of all proportion to their
value; that they accumulate so rapidly (much faster, in
fact, than books) as to outrun the means at the disposal of
any library to deal with them; in short, that they cost more
than they come to, if bound, and if unbound, they vex the
soul of the librarian day by day.

This is one side of the pamphlet question; and it may
be candidly admitted, that in most libraries, the accumulation of uncatalogued and unbound pamphlets is one of the

chief among those arrears which form the skeleton in the closet of the librarian. But there is another side to the matter. It is always possible to divide your pamphlets into two classes—the important, and the insignificant. Some of them have great historical, or economic, or intellectual value; others are as nearly worthless as it is possible for any printed matter to be. Why should you treat a pamphlet upon Pears's soap, or a quack medicine, or advertising the Columbia bicycle, with the same attention which you would naturally give to an essay on international politics by Gladstone, or a review of the Cuban question by a prominent Spaniard, or a tract on Chinese immigration by Minister Seward, or the pamphlet genealogy of an American family? Take out of the mass of pamphlets, as they come in, what appear to you the more valuable, or the more liable to be called for; catalogue and bind them, or file them away, according to the use which they are likely to have: relegate the rest, assorted always by subject-matters or classes, to marked piles, or to pamphlet cases, according to your means; and the problem is approximately solved.

To condemn any pamphlet to "innocuous desuetude," or to permanent banishment from among the intellectual stores of a library, merely because it is innocent of a stiff cover, is to despoil the temple of learning and reject the good things of Providence. What great and influential publications have appeared in the world in the guise of pamphlets! Milton's immortal "Areopagitica, or Plea for Unlicenced Printing," was a pamphlet of only forty pages; Webster's speech for the Union, in reply to Hayne, was a pamphlet; every play of Shakespeare, that was printed in his life-time, was a pamphlet; Charles Sumner's discourse on "The True Grandeur of Nations" was a pamphlet; the "Crisis" and "Common Sense" of Thomas Paine, which fired the American heart in the Revolution, were pamphlets. Strike out of literature, ancient and modern, what was first published in pamphlets, and you would leave it the poorer and weaker to an incalculable degree.

Pamphlets are not only vehicles of thought and opinion, and propagandists of new ideas; they are often also storehouses of facts, repositories of history, annals of biography, records of genealogy, treasuries of statistics, chronicles of invention and discovery. They sometimes throw an unexpected light upon obscure questions where all books are silent. Being published for the most part upon some subject that was interesting the public mind when written, they reflect, as in a mirror, the social, political, and religious spirit and life of the time. As much as newspapers, they illustrate the civilization (or want of it) of an epoch, and multitudes of them, preserved in great libraries, exhibit this at those early periods when no newspapers existed as vehicles of public opinion. Many of the government libraries of Europe have been buying up for many years past, the rare, early-printed pamphlets of their respective countries, paying enormous prices for what, a century ago, they would have slighted, even as a gift.

When Thomas Carlyle undertook to write the life of Oliver Cromwell, and to resurrect from the dust-bins of two centuries, the letters and speeches of the great Protector, he found his richest quarry in a collection of pamphlets in the British Museum Library. An indefatigable patriot and bookseller, named Thomason, had carefully gathered and kept every pamphlet, book, periodical, or broadside that appeared from the British press, during the whole time from A. D. 1649 to 1660, the period of the interregnum in the English monarchy, represented by Cromwell and the Commonwealth. This vast collection, numbering over 20,000 pamphlets, bound in 2,000 volumes, after escaping the perils of fire, and of both hostile armies, was finally purchased by the King, and afterward presented to the British Museum Library. Its completeness is one great source of its value, furnishing, as it does, to the historical student of that exceedingly interesting revolution, the most precious memorials of the spirit of the times, many of which have been utterly lost, except the single copy preserved in this collection.

Several great European libraries number as many pamphlets as books in their collections. The printed catalogue of the British Museum Library is widely sought by historical students, because of the enormous amount of pamphlet literature it contains, that is described nowhere else. And the Librarian of the Boston Athenaeum said that some readers found the great interest in his catalogue of that collection lay in its early American pamphlets.

As another instance of the value to the historical stores of a public library of this ephemeral literature, it may be noted that the great collection of printed matter, mostly of a fugitive character, relating to the French Revolutionary period, gathered by the late M. de La Bedoyère, amounted to 15,000 volumes and pamphlets. Fifty years of the life of the wealthy and enthusiastic collector, besides a very large sum of money, were spent in amassing this collection. With an avidity almost incredible, he ransacked every book-store, quay, and private shelf that might contribute a fresh morsel to his stores; and when Paris was exhausted, had his agents and purveyors busy in executing his orders all over Europe. Rival collectors, and particularly M. Deschiens, who had been a contemporary in the Revolution, and had laid aside everything that appeared in his day, only contributed at their decease, to swell the precious stores of M. de La Bedoyère. This vast collection, so precious for the history of France at its most memorable period, contained several thousands of volumes of newspapers and ephemeral journals, and was acquired in the year 1863, for the National Library of France, where it will ever remain a monument to the enlightened and far-sighted spirit of its projector.

In like manner, the late Peter Force, Mayor of Washington City, and historiographer of the "American Archives," devoted forty years to amassing an extensive collection of *Americana,* or books, pamphlets, newspapers, manuscripts, and maps, relating to the discovery, history, topography, natural history, and biography of America. He carried off at auction sales, from all competitors, six great collections of early American pamphlets, formed by Ebenezer Hazard, William Duane, Oliver Wolcott, etc., representing the copious literature of all schools of political opinion. He sedulously laid aside and preserved every pamphlet that appeared at the capital or elsewhere, on which he could lay hands, and his rich historical collection, purchased by the government in 1866, thirty-three years ago, now forms an invaluable portion of the Congressional Library.

Of the multitudinous literature of pamphlets it is not necessary to speak at length. Suffice it to say that the library which neglects the acquisition and proper preservation and binding of these publications is far behind its duty, both to those of its own generation, and to those which are to follow. The pamphlet literature of every period often furnishes the most precious material to illustrate the history and development of that period. The new ideas, the critical sagacity, the political controversies, the mechanical and industrial development, the religious thought, and the social character of many epochs, find their best expression in the pamphlets that swarmed from the press while those agencies were operating. The fact that multitudes of these productions are anonymous, does not detract from their value as materials for students.

Pamphlets, from their peculiar style of publication, and the difficulty of preserving them, tend to disappear more quickly than any class of publications except newspapers, and broad-sides, and hand-bills. They are far less likely to be preserved in the hands of private holders than even reviews and magazines. It is the common experience of librarians that a pamphlet is far more difficult to procure than a book. Multitudes of pamphlets are annually lost to the world, from the want of any preserving hand to gather them and deposit them permanently in some library. So much the more important is it that the custodians of all our public libraries should form as complete collections as possible of all pamphlets, at least, that appear in their own city or neighborhood. How to do this is a problem not unattended with difficulty. Pamphlets are rarely furnished for sale in the same manner as books, and when they are, book-sellers treat them with such indignity that they are commonly thrust aside as waste paper, almost as soon as they have appeared from the press. If all the writers of pamphlets would take pains to present them to the public libraries of the country, and especially to those in their own neighborhood, they would at once enrich these collections, and provide for the perpetuity of their own thought. A vigilant librarian should invite and collect from private libraries all the pamphlets which their owners will part with. It would also be a wise practice to engage the printing-offices where these fugitive leaves of literature are put in type, to lay aside one copy of each for the library making the collection.

Our local libraries should each and all make it a settled object to preserve not only full sets of the reports of all societies, corporations, charity organizations, churches, railroads, etc., in their own neighborhood, but all catalogues of educational institutions, all sermons or memorial addresses, and in short, every fugitive publication which helps to a knowledge of the people or the region in which the library is situated.

The binding of pamphlets is a mooted point in all libraries. While the British Museum and the Library of Congress treat the pamphlets as a book, binding all separately, this is deemed in some quarters too vexatious and troublesome, as well as needlessly expensive. It must be considered, however, that the crowding together of a heterogenous mass of a dozen or twenty pamphlets, by different authors, and on various subjects, into a single cover, is just as objectionable as binding books on unrelated subjects together. Much time is consumed in finding the pamphlet wanted, among the dozen or more that precede or follow it, and, if valuable or much sought-for pamphlets are thus bound, many readers may be kept waiting for some of them, while one reader engrosses the volume containing all. Besides, if separately bound, a single pamphlet can be far more easily replaced in case of loss than can a whole volume of them. Pamphlets may be lightly bound in paste-board, stitched, with cloth backs, at a small cost; and the compensating advantage of being able to classify them like books upon the shelves, should weigh materially in the decision of the question. If many are bound together, they should invariably be assorted into classes, and those only on the same general topic should be embraced in the same cover. The long series of annual reports of societies and institutions, corporations, annual catalogues, etc., need not be bound separately, but should be bound in chronological series, with five to ten years in a volume, according to thickness. So may several pamphlets, by the same writer, if preferred, be bound together. Libraries which acquire many bound volumes of pamphlets should divide them into series, and number them throughout with strict reference to the catalogue. There will thus be accumulated a constantly increasing series of theological, political, agricultural, medical, educational, scientific, and other pamphlets, while the remaining mass, which cannot be thus classified, may be designated in a consecutive series of volumes, as "Miscellaneous Pamphlets." When catalogued, the title-page or beginning of each pamphlet in the volume, should be marked by a thin slip of unsized paper, projected above the top of the book, to faciliate quick reference in finding each one without turning many leaves to get at the titles. In all cases, the contents of each volume of pamphlets should be briefed in numerical order upon the fly-leaf of the volume, and its corresponding number, or sequence in the volumes written in pencil on the title page of each pamphlet, to correspond with the figures of this brief list. Then the catalogue of each should indicate its exact location, thus: Wilkeson (Samuel) How our National Debt may become a National Blessing, 21 pp. 8vo. Phila., 1863 [Miscellaneous pamphlets, v. 347:3], meaning that this is the third pamphlet bound in vol. 347.

The only objection to separate binding of each pamphlet, is the increased expense. The advantage of distinct treatment may or may not outweigh this, according to the importance of the pamphlet, the circumstances of the library, and the funds at its command. If bound substantially in good half-leather, with leather corners, the cost is reckoned at 1 *s.* 4 *d.* each, in London. Here, they cost about thirty cents with cloth sides, which may be reduced by the use of marble or Manila paper, to twenty cents each. Black roan is perhaps the best leather for pamphlets, as it brings out the lettering on the backs more distinctly—always a cardinal point in a library.

But there is a more economical method, which dispenses with leather entirely. As no patent is claimed for the invention, or rather the modification of well-known methods, it may be briefly described. The thinnest tar-board is used for the sides, which, *i. e.*, the boards, are cut down to nearly the size of the pamphlet to be bound. The latter is prepared for the boards by adding two or more waste leaves to the front and back, and backing it with a strip of common muslin, which is firmly pasted the full length of the back, and overlaps the sides to the width of an inch or more. The pamphlet has to be stitched through, or stabbed and fastened with wire, in the manner commonly practiced with thin books; after which it is ready to receive the boards. These are glued to a strip of book muslin, which constitutes the ultimate back of the book, being turned in neatly at each end, so as to form, with the boards, a skeleton cover, into which the pamphlet is inserted, and held in its place by the inner strip of muslin before described, which is pasted or glued to the inside of the boards. The boards are then covered with marbled paper, turned in at each edge, and the waste leaves pasted smoothly down to the boards on the inside. The only remaining process is the lettering, which is done by printing the titles in bronze upon glazed colored paper, which is pasted lengthwise on the back. A small font of type, with a hand-press, will suffice for this, and a stabbing machine, with a small pair of binding shears, constitutes the only other apparatus required. The cost of binding pamphlets in this style varies from seven to twelve cents each, according to the material employed, and the amount of labor paid for. The advantages of the method are too obvious to all acquainted with books to require exemplification.

Two still cheaper methods of binding may be named. What is known as the Harvard binder, employed in that library at Cambridge, Mass., consists simply of thin board sides with muslin back, and stubs also of cloth on the inside. The pamphlet is inserted and held in place by paste or glue. The cost of each binding is stated at six cents.

The cheapest style of separate treatment for pamphlets yet suggested is of stiff Manila paper, with cloth back, costing about three cents each.

I think that the rule of never mixing incongruous subjects within the same cover should be adhered to. The expense, by the cheaper method of binding referred to, is but slightly greater than must be incurred by binding several in a volume, in solid half morocco style. But, whenever pamphlets are bound together, the original printed paper covers should never be destroyed, but should be bound in.

Another method of preserving pamphlets is to file them away in selected lots, placed inside of cloth covers, of considerable thickness. These may be had from any bookbinder, being the rejected covers in which books sent for re-binding were originally bound. If kept in this way, each volume, or case of pamphlets, should be firmly tied with cord (or better with tape) fastened to the front edge of the cloth cover. Never use rubber or elastic bands for this, or any other purpose where time and security of fastening are involved, because the rubber will surely rot in a few weeks or months, and be useless as a means of holding together any objects whatever.

Still another means of assorting and keeping pamphlets is to use Woodruff's file-holders, one of which holds from ten to thirty pamphlets according to their thickness. They should be arranged in classes, placing in each file case only pamphlets on similar subjects, in order of the authors' names, arranged alphabetically. Each pamphlet should be plainly numbered at its head by colored pencil, with the figure of its place in the volume, and the number of the case, containing it, which should also be volumed, and assigned to shelves containing books on related subjects. I need not add that all these numbers should correspond with the catalogue-title of each pamphlet. Then, when any one pamphlet is wanted, send for the case containing it, find it and withdraw it at once by its number, place it in one of the Koch spring-back binders, and give it to the reader precisely like any book that is served at the library counter.

A more economical plan still, for libraries which cannot afford the expense of the Woodruff file-holders, is to cut out cases for the pamphlets, of suitable size, from tough Manila board, which need not cost more than about three cents each case.

In whatever way the unbound pamphlets are treated, you should always mark them as such on the left-hand margin of each catalogue-card, by the designation "ub." (unbound) in pencil. If you decide later, to bind any of them, this pencil-mark should be erased from the cards, on the return of the pamphlets from the bindery.

CHAPTER 8.

Periodical Literature.

The librarian who desires to make the management of his library in the highest degree successful, must give special attention to the important field of periodical literature. More and more, as the years roll on, the periodical becomes the successful rival of the book in the claim for public attention. Indeed, we hear now and then, denunciations of the ever-swelling flood of magazines and newspapers, as tending to drive out the book. Readers, we are told, are seduced from solid and improving reading, by the mass of daily, weekly, and monthly periodicals which lie in wait for them on every hand. But no indiscriminate censure of periodicals or of their reading, can blind us to the fact of their great value. Because some persons devote an inordinate amount of time to them, is no reason why we should fail to use them judiciously ourselves, or to aid others in doing so. And because many periodicals (and even the vast majority) are of little importance, and are filled with trifling and ephemeral matter, that fact does not discredit the meritorious ones. Counterfeit currency does not diminish the value of the true coin; it is very sure to find its own just level at last; and so the wretched or the sensational periodical, however pretentious, will fall into inevitable neglect and failure in the long run.

It is true that the figures as to the relative issues of books and periodicals in the publishing world are startling enough to give us pause. It has been computed that of the annual product of the American press, eighty-two per cent consists of newspapers, ten per cent of magazines and reviews, and only eight per cent of books. Yet this vast redundancy of periodical literature is by no means such a menace to our permanent literature as it appears at first sight;—and that for three reasons: (1) a large share of the books actually published, appear in the first instance in the periodicals in serial or casual form; (2) the periodicals contain very much matter of permanent value; (3) the steady increase of carefully prepared books in the publishing world, while it may not keep pace with the rapid increase of periodicals, evinces a growth in the right direction. It is no longer so easy to get a crude or a poor book published, as it was a generation ago. The standard of critical taste has risen, and far more readers are judges of what constitutes a really good book than ever before. While it is true that our periodical product has so grown, that whereas there were twenty years ago, in 1878, only 7,958 different newspapers and magazines published in the United States, there are now, in 1899, over 20,500 issued, it can also be stated that the annual product of books has increased in the same twenty years from less than two thousand to more than five thousand volumes of new issues in a year. Whatever may be the future of our American literature, it can hardly be doubted that the tendency is steadily toward the production of more books, and better ones.

Whether a public library be large or small, its value to students will depend greatly upon the care and completeness with which its selection of periodical works is made, and kept up from year to year. Nothing is more common in all libraries, public and private, than imperfect and partially bound sets of serials, whether newspapers, reviews, magazines or the proceedings and reports of scientific and other societies. Nothing can be more annoying than to find the sets of such publications broken at the very point where the reference or the wants of those consulting them require satisfaction. In these matters, perpetual vigilance is the price of completeness; and the librarian who is not willing or able to devote the time and means requisite to complete the files of periodical publications under his charge is to be censured or commiserated, according to the causes of the failure. The first essential in keeping up the completeness of files of ephemeral publications, next to vigilance on the part of their custodian, is room for the arrangement of the various parts, and means for binding with promptitude. Some libraries, and among them a few of the largest, are so hampered for want of room, that their serials are piled in heaps without order or arrangement, and are thus comparatively useless until bound. In the more fortunate institutions, which possess adequate space for the orderly arrangement of all their stores, there can be no excuse for failing to supply any periodical, whether bound or unbound, at the moment it is called for. It is simply necessary to devote sufficient time each day to the systematic arrangement of all receipts: to keep each file together in chronological order; to supply them for the perusal of readers, with a proper check or receipt, and to make sure of binding each new volume as fast as the publication of titles and index enables it to be done properly. While some libraries receive several thousands of serials, the periodical publications taken by others amount to a very small number; but in either case, the importance of prompt collation and immediate supply of missing parts or numbers is equally imperative. While deficiencies in daily newspapers can rarely be made up after the week, and sometimes not after the day of their appearance, the missing parts of official and other publications, as well as of reviews and magazines appearing at less frequent intervals, can usually be supplied within the year, although a more prompt securing of them is often necessary. In these publications, as in the acquisition of books for any library, the collation of each part or number is imperative, in order to avoid imperfections which may be irreparable.

First in the ranks of these ephemeral publications, in order of number, if not of importance, come the journals of all classes, daily and weekly, political, illustrated, literary, scientific, mechanical, professional, agricultural, financial, etc. From the obscure and fugitive beginnings of journalism in the sixteenth century to the establishment of the first continuous newspaper—the London Weekly News, in 1622, and Renaudot's Gazette (afterwards the *Gazette de France*) in 1631, followed by the issue of the first daily newspaper, the London Daily Courant, in 1702, and the Boston Weekly News-letter in 1704, (the first American journal)—to the wonderful fecundity of the modern periodical press, which scatters the leaves of more than thirty thousand different journals broadcast over the world, there is a long and interesting history of the trials and triumphs of a free press. In whatever respect American libraries may fall behind those of older lands (and their deficiencies are vast, and, in many directions permanent) it may be said with confidence, that in the United States the newspaper has received its widest and most complete development. Numerically, the fullest approximate return of the newspaper and periodical press gives a total number of 21,500 periodical publications, regularly appearing within the limits of the United States.

While no one library, however large and comprehensive, has either the space or the means to accumulate a tithe of the periodicals that swarm from a productive press, there are valid reasons why more attention should be paid by the librarian to a careful preservation of a wise selection of the best of all this current literature. The modern newspaper and other periodical publications afford the fullest and truest, and on the whole, the most impartial image of the age we live in, that can be derived from a single source. Taken together, they afford the richest material for the historian, or the student of politics, of society, of literature, and of civilization in all its varied aspects. What precious memorials of the day, even the advertisements and brief paragraphs of the newspapers of a century ago afford us! While in a field so vast, it is impossible for any one library to be more than a gleaner, no such institution can afford to neglect the collection and preservation of at least some of the more important newspapers from year to year. A public library is not for one generation only, but it is for all time. Opportunities once neglected of securing the current periodicals of any age in continuous and complete form seldom or never recur. The principle of selection will of course vary in different libraries and localities. While the safest general rule is to secure the best and most representative of all the journals, reviews, and magazines within the limit of the funds which can be devoted to that purpose, there is another principle which should largely guide the selection. In each locality, it should be one leading object of the principal library to gather within its walls the fullest representation possible, of the literature relating to its own State and neighborhood. In every city and large town, the local journals and other periodicals should form an indispensable part of a public library collection. Where the means are wanting to purchase these, the proprietors will frequently furnish them free of expense, for public use; but no occasion should be lost of securing, immediately on its issue from the press, every publication, large or small, which relates to the local history or interests of the place where the library is maintained.

While the files of the journals of any period furnish unquestionably the best instruments for the history of that epoch, it is lamentable to reflect that so little care has ever been taken to preserve a fair representation of those of any age.   The destiny of nearly all newspapers is swift destruction; and even those which are preserved, commonly survive in a lamentably fragmentary state.   The obvious causes of the rapid disappearance of periodical literature, are its great volume, necessarily increasing with every year, the difficulty of lodging the files of any long period in our narrow apartments, and the continual demand for paper for the uses of trade.   To these must be added the great cost of binding files of journals, increasing in the direct ratio of the size of the volume.   As so formidable an expense can be incurred by very few private subscribers to periodicals, so much the more important is it that the public libraries should not neglect a duty which they owe to their generation, as well as to those that are to follow. These poor journals of to-day, which everybody is willing to stigmatize as trash, not worth the room to store or the money to bind, are the very materials which the man of the future will search for with eagerness, and for some of which he will be ready to pay their weight in gold.   These representatives of the commercial, industrial, inventive, social, literary, political, moral and religious life of the times, should be preserved and handed down to posterity with sedulous care.   No historian or other writer on any subject who would write conscientiously or with full information, can afford to neglect this fruitful mine of the journals, where his richest materials are frequently to be found.

In the absence of any great library of journals, or of that universal library which every nation should possess, it becomes the more important to assemble in the various local libraries all those ephemeral publications, which, if not thus preserved contemporaneously with their issue, will disappear utterly, and elude the search of future historical inquirers. And that library which shall most sedulously gather and preserve such fugitive memorials of the life of the people among which it is situated will be found to have best subserved its purpose to the succeeding generations of men.

Not less important than the preservation of newspapers is that of reviews and magazines. In fact, the latter are almost universally recognized as far more important than the more fugitive literature of the daily and weekly press. Though inferior to the journals as historical and statistical materials, reviews and magazines supply the largest fund of discussion concerning such topics of scientific, social, literary, and religious interest as occupy the public mind during the time in which they appear. More and more the best thought of the times gets reflected in the pages of this portion of the periodical press. No investigator in any department can afford to overlook the rich stores contributed to thought in reviews and magazines. These articles are commonly more condensed and full of matter than the average books of the period. While every library, therefore, should possess for the current use and ultimate reference of its readers a selection of the best, as large as its means will permit, a great and comprehensive library, in order to be representative of the national literature, should possess them all.

The salient fact that the periodical press absorbs, year by year, more of the talent which might otherwise be expended upon literature of more permanent form is abundantly obvious. This tendency has both its good and its evil results. On the one hand, the best writing ability is often drawn out by magazines and journals, which are keen competitors for attractive matter, and for known reputations, and sometimes they secure both in combination. On the other hand, it is a notable fact that writers capable of excellent work often do great injustice to their reputations by producing too hastily articles written to order, instead of the well-considered, ripe fruits of their literary skill. Whether the brief article answering the limits of a magazine or a review is apt to be more or less superficial than a book treating the same topic, is a question admitting of different views. If the writer is capable of skilful condensation, without loss of grace of composition, or of graphic power, then the article, measured by its influence upon the public mind, must be preferred to the more diffuse treatise of the book. It has the immense advantage of demanding far less of the reader's time; and whenever its conclusions are stated in a masterly way, its impression should be quite as lasting as that of any book treating a similar theme. Such is doubtless the effect of the abler articles written for periodicals, which are more condensed and full of matter in speedily available form, than the average book of the period. In this sense it is a misuse of terms to call the review article ephemeral, or to treat the periodicals containing them as perishable literary commodities, which serve their term with the month or year that produced them. On the contrary, the experience of librarians shows that the most sought-for, and the most useful contributions to any subject are frequently found, not in the books written upon it, but in the files of current periodicals, or in those of former years. It is especially to be noted that the book may frequently lose its adaptation and usefulness by lapse of time, and the onward march of science, while the article is apt to reflect the latest light which can help to illustrate the subject.

While, therefore, there is always a liability of finding many crude and sketchy contributions in the literature of the periodical press, its conductors are ever on the alert to reduce to a minimum the weak or unworthy offerings, and to secure a maximum of articles embodying mature thought and fit expression. The pronounced tendency toward short methods in every channel of human activity, is reflected in the constantly multiplying series of periodical publications.

The publishing activities of the times are taking on a certain coöperative element, which was not formerly known. Thus, the "literary syndicate" has been developed by degrees into one of the most far-reaching agencies for popular entertainment. The taste for short stories, in place of the ancient three volume novel, has been cultivated even in conservative England, and has become so wide-spread in the United States, that very few periodicals which deal in fiction at all, are without their stories begun and finished in a single issue. The talent required to produce a fascinating and successful fiction in this narrow compass is a peculiar one, and while there are numerous failures, there are also a surprising number of successes. Well written descriptive articles, too, are in demand, and special cravings for personal gossip and lively sketches of notable living characters are manifest. That perennial interest which mankind and womankind evince in every individual whose name, for whatever reason, has become familiar, supplies a basis for an inexhaustible series of light paragraphic articles. Another fruitful field for the syndicate composition is brief essays upon any topic of the times, the fashions, notable events, or new inventions, public charities, education, governmental doings, current political movements, etc. These appear almost simultaneously, in many different periodicals, scattered throughout the country, under the copyright *imprimatur*, which warns off all journals from republishing, which have not subscribed to the special "syndicate" engaging them. Thus each periodical secures, at extremely moderate rates, contributions which are frequently written by the most noted and popular living writers, who, in their turn, are much better remunerated for their work than they would be for the same amount of writing if published in book form. Whether this now popular method of attaining a wide and remunerative circulation for their productions will prove permanent, is less certain than that many authors now find it the surest road to profitable employment of their pens. The fact that it rarely serves to introduce unknown writers of talent to the reading world, may be laid to the account of the eagerness of the syndicates to secure names that already enjoy notoriety.

The best method for filing newspapers for current reading is a vexed question in libraries. In the large ones, where room enough exists, large reading-stands with sloping sides furnish the most convenient access, provided with movable metal rods to keep the papers in place. Where no room exists for these stands, some of the numerous portable newspaper-file inventions, or racks, may be substituted, allowing one to each paper received at the library.

For filing current magazines, reviews, and the smaller newspapers, like the literary and technical journals, various plans are in use. All of these have advantages, while none is free from objection. Some libraries use the ordinary pamphlet case, in which the successive numbers are kept until a volume is accumulated for binding. This requires a separate case for each periodical, and where many are taken, is expensive, though by this method the magazines are kept neat and in order. Others use small newspaper files or tapes for periodicals. Others still arrange them alphabetically on shelves, in which case the latest is-sues are found on top, if the chronology is preserved. In serving periodicals to readers, tickets should be required (as for books) with title and date, as a precaution against loss, or careless leaving upon tables.

Whether current periodicals are ever allowed to be drawn out, must depend upon several weighty considera-tions. When only one copy is taken, no circulation should be permitted, so that the magazines and journals may be always in, at the service of readers frequenting the library. But in some large public libraries, where several copies of each of the more popular serials are subscribed to, it is the custom to keep one copy (sometimes two) always in, and to allow the duplicate copies to be drawn out. This circula-tion should be limited to a period much shorter than is al-lowed for keeping books.

In no case, should the bound volumes of magazines, re-views, and journals of whatever kind be allowed to leave the library. This is a rule which should be enforced for the common benefit of all the readers, since to lend to one reader any periodical or work of general reference is to de-prive all the rest of its use just so long as it is out of the library. This has become all the more important since the publication of Poole's Indexes to periodical literature has put the whole reading community on the quest for infor-mation to be found only (in condensed form, or in the latest treatment) in the volumes of the periodical press. And it is really no hardship to any quick, intelligent reader, to require that these valuable serials should be used within the library only. An article is not like a book;— a long and perhaps serious study, requiring many hours or days to master it. The magazine or review article, what-ever other virtues it may lack, has the supreme merit of brevity.

The only valid exception which will justify loaning the serial volumes of periodicals outside the library, is when there are duplicate sets of any of them. Some large libraries having a wide popular circulation are able to buy two or more sets of the magazines most in demand, and so to lend one out, while another is kept constantly in for use and reference. And even a library of small means might secure for its shelves duplicate sets of many periodicals, by simply making known that it would be glad to receive from any families or other owners, all the numbers of their magazines, etc., which they no longer need for use. This would bring in, in any large town or city, a copious supply of periodicals which house-keepers, tired of keeping, storing and dusting such unsightly property, would be glad to bestow where they would do the most good.

Whatever periodicals are taken, it is essential to watch over their completeness by keeping a faithfully revised check-list. This should be ruled to furnish blank spaces for each issue of all serials taken, whether quarterly, monthly, weekly, or daily, and no week should elapse without complete scrutiny of the list, and ordering all missing numbers from the publishers. Mail failures are common, and unceasing vigilance is the price that must be paid for completeness. The same check-list, by other spaces, should show the time of expiration of subscriptions, and the price paid per year. And where a large number of periodicals are received, covering many parts of the country, they should be listed, not only by an alphabet of titles, but by another alphabet of places where published, as well.

If a new library is to be formed, having no sets of periodicals on which to build, effort should be made to secure full sets from the beginning of as many of the prominent magazines and reviews, American and foreign, as the funds will permit. It is expedient to wait a little, rather than to take up with incomplete sets, as full ones are pretty sure to turn up, and competition between the many dealers should bring down prices to a fair medium. In fact, many old sets of magazines are offered surprisingly cheap, and usually well-bound. But vigilant care must be exercised to secure perfect sets, as numbers are often mutilated, or deficient in some pages or illustrations. This object can only be secured by collation of every volume, page by page, with due attention to the list of illustrations, if any are published.

In the absence of British bibliographical enterprise (a want much to be deplored) it has fallen to the lot of American librarians to produce the only general index of subjects to English periodical literature which exists. Poole's Index to Periodical Literature is called by the name of its senior editor, the late Dr. Wm. F. Poole, and was contributed to by many librarians on a coöperative division of labor, in indexing, under direction of Mr. Wm. I. Fletcher, librarian of Amherst College. This index to leading periodicals is literally invaluable, and indispensable as an aid to research. Its first volume indexes in one alphabet the periodicals embraced, from their first issues up to 1882. The second volume runs from 1882 to 1887, and the third covers the period from 1887 to 1891, while a fourth volume indexes the periodicals from 1892 to 1896, inclusive. For 1897, and each year after, an annual index to the publications of the year is issued.

Besides this, the *Review of Reviews* publishes monthly an index to one month's leading periodicals, and also an annual index, very full, in a single alphabet. And the "Cumulative Index," issued both monthly and quarterly, by W. H. Brett, the Cleveland, Ohio, librarian, is an admirably full means of keeping our keys to periodical literature up to date. There are other indexes to periodicals, published monthly or quarterly, too numerous to be noticed here. The annual *New York Tribune* Index (the only daily journal, except the *London Times*, which prints an index) is highly useful, and may be used for other newspapers as well, for the most important events or discussions, enabling one to search the dailies for himself, the date once being fixed by aid of the index.

Mention should also be made here of the admirably comprehensive annual *"Rowell's Newspaper Directory,"* which should rather be called the "American Periodical Directory," since it has a classified catalogue of all periodicals published in the United States and Canada.

CHAPTER 9.

The Art of Reading.

"The true University of these days," says a great scholar of our century, Thomas Carlyle, "is a collection of books, and all education is to teach us how to read."

If there were any volume, out of the multitude of books about books that have been written, which could illuminate the pathway of the unskilled reader, so as to guide him into all knowledge by the shortest road, what a boon that book would be!

When we survey the vast and rapidly growing product of the modern press,—when we see these hosts of poets without imagination, historians without accuracy, critics without discernment, and novelists without invention or style, in short, the whole prolific brood of writers who do not know how to write,—we are tempted to echo the sentiment of Wordsworth:—

"The intellectual power, through words and things,
    Goes sounding on a dim and perilous way."

The most that any one can hope to do for others is to suggest to them a clue which, however feeble, has helped to guide his uncertain footsteps through the labyrinthian maze of folly and wisdom which we call literature.

The knowledge acquired by a Librarian, while it may be very wide and very varied, runs much risk of being as superficial as it is diversified. There is a very prevalent, but very erroneous notion which conceives of a librarian as a kind of animated encyclopaedia, who, if you tap him in any direction, from A to Z, will straightway pour forth a flood of knowledge upon any subject in history, science, or

(171)

literature.   This popular ideal, however fine in theory, has
to undergo what commercial men call a heavy discount
when reduced to practice.   The librarian is a constant
and busy worker in far other fields than exploring the contents of books.   His day is filled with cataloguing, arranging and classifying them, searching catalogues, selecting
new books, correspondence, directing assistants, keeping
library records, adjusting accounts, etc., in the midst of
which he is constantly at the call of the public for books
and information.   What time has he, wearied by the day's
multifarious and exacting labors, for any thorough study
of books?   So, when anyone begins an inquiry with, "You
know everything; can you tell me,"—I say: "Stop a moment; omniscience is not a human quality; I really know
very few things, and am not quite sure of some of them."
There are many men, and women, too, in almost every
community, whose range of knowledge is more extended
than that of most librarians.

The idea, then, that because one lives perpetually among
books, he absorbs all the learning that they contain, must
be abandoned as a popular delusion.   To know a little
upon many subjects is quite compatible with not knowing
much about any one.   "Beware of the man of one book,"
is an ancient proverb, pregnant with meaning.   The man
of one book, if it is wisely chosen, and if he knows it all,
can sometimes confound a whole assembly of scholars.   An
American poet once declared to me that all leisure time is
lost that is not spent in reading Shakespeare.   And we remember Emerson's panegyric upon Plato's writings, borrowing from the Caliph Omar his famous (but apocryphal)
sentence against all books but the Koran: "Burn all the
libraries, for their value is in this book."   So Sheffield,
duke of Buckingham:

"Read Homer once, and you can read no more,
  For all books else appear so tame, so poor,
  Verse will seem prose, but still persist to read,
  And Homer will be all the books you need."

Of course I am far from designing to say anything
against the widest study, which great libraries exist to
supply and to encourage; and all utterances of a half-
truth, like the maxim I have quoted, are exaggerations.
But the saying points a moral—and that is, the supreme
importance of thoroughness in all that we undertake. The
poetical wiseacre who endowed the world with the maxim,
"A little learning is a dangerous thing," does not appear
to have reflected upon the logical sequence of the dictum,
namely: that if a little learning upon any subject is dangerous, then less must be still more dangerous.

The art of reading to the best advantage implies the
command of adequate time to read. The art of having
time to read depends upon knowing how to make the best
use of our days. Days are short, and time is fleeting, but
no one's day ever holds less than 24 hours. Engrossing
as one's occupation may be, it need never consume all
the time remaining from sleep, refreshment and social intercourse. The half hour before breakfast, the fifteen
minutes waiting for dinner, given to the book you wish to
read, will soon finish it, and make room for another. The
busiest men I have known have often been the most intelligent, and the widest readers. The idle person never
knows how to make use of odd moments; the busy one
always knows how. Yet the vast majority of people go
through life without ever learning the great lesson of the
supreme value of moments.

Let us suppose that you determine to devote two hours
every day to reading. That is equivalent to more than
seven hundred hours a year, or to three months of work-

ing time of eight hours a day. What could you not do in
three months, if you had all the time to yourself? You
could almost learn a new language, or master a new science; yet this two hours a day, which would give you three
months of free time every year, is frittered away, you
scarcely know how, in aimless matters that lead to nothing.

A famous writer of our century, some of whose books
you have read,—Edward Bulwer Lytton,—devoted only
four hours a day to writing; yet he produced more than
sixty volumes of fiction, poetry, drama and criticism, of
singular literary merit. The great naturalist, Darwin, a
chronic sufferer from a depressing malady, counted two
hours a fortunate day's work for him; yet he accomplished
results in the world of science which render his name immortal.

Be not over particular as to hours, or the time of day,
and you will soon find that all hours are good for the muse.
Have a purpose, and adhere to it with good-humored per-
tinacity. Be independent of the advice and opinions of
others; the world of books, like the world of nature, was
made for you; possess it in your own way. If you find no
good in ancient history or in metaphysics, let them alone
and read books of art, or poetry, or biography, or voyages
and travels. The wide domain of knowledge and the
world of books are so related, that all roads cross and con-
verge, like the paths that carry us over the surface of the
globe on which we live. Many a reader has learned more
of past times from good biographies, than from any formal
history; and it is a fact that many owe to the plays of
Shakespeare and the novels of Walter Scott nearly all the
knowledge which they possess of the history of England
and Scotland.

It is unhappily true that books do not teach the use of
books. The art of extracting what is important or in-

structive in any book, from the mass of verbiage that commonly overlays it, cannot be learned by theory. Invaluable as the art of reading is, as a means of enlightenment, its highest uses can only be obtained by a certain method of reading, which will separate the wheat from the chaff. Different readers will, of course, possess different capacities for doing this. Young or undisciplined minds can read only in one way,—and that way is, to mentally pronounce every word, and dwell equally upon all the parts of every sentence. This comes naturally in the first instance, from the mere method of learning to read, in which every word is a spoken symbol, and has to be sounded, whether it is essential to the sense, or not. This habit of reading, which may be termed the literal method, goes with most persons through life. Once learned, it is very hard to unlearn. There are multitudes who cannot read a newspaper, even, without dwelling upon every word, and coming to a full stop at the end of every sentence. Now this method of reading, while it may be indispensable to all readers at some time, and to some readers at all times, is too slow and fruitless for the student who aims to absorb the largest amount of knowledge in the briefest space of time. Life is too short to be wasted over the rhetoric or the periods of an author whose knowledge we want as all that concerns us.

Doubtless there are classes of literature in which form or expression predominates, and we cannot read poetry, for example, or the drama, or even the higher class of fiction, without lingering upon the finer passages, to get the full impression of their beauty. In reading works of the imagination, we read not for ideas alone, but for expression also, and to enjoy the rhythm and melody of the verse, if it be poetry, or, if prose, the finished rhetoric, and the pleasing cadence of the style. It is here that the literary skill of an accomplished writer, and all that we understand by rhetoric, becomes important, while in reading for information only, we may either ignore words and phrases entirely, or subordinate them to the ideas which they convey. In reading any book for the knowledge it contains, I should as soon think of spelling out all the words, as of reading out all the sentences. Just as, in listening to a slow speaker, you divine the whole meaning of what he is about to say, before he has got half through his sentence, so, in reading, you can gather the full sense of the ideas which any sentence contains, without stopping to accentuate the words.

Leaving aside the purely literary works, in which form or style is a predominant element, let us come to books of science, history, biography, voyages, travels, etc. In these, the primal aim is to convey information, and thus the style of expression is little or nothing—the thought or the fact is all. Yet most writers envelop the thought or the fact in so much verbiage, complicate it with so many episodes, beat it out thin, by so much iteration and reiteration, that the student must needs learn the art of skipping, in self-defense. To one in zealous pursuit of knowledge, to read most books through is paying them too extravagant a compliment. He has to read between the lines, as it were, to note down a fact here, or a thought there, or an illustration elsewhere, and leaves alone all that contributes nothing to his special purpose. As the quick, practiced eye glances over the visible signs of thought, page after page is rapidly absorbed, and a book which would occupy an ordinary reader many days in reading, is mastered in a few hours.

The habit of reading which I have outlined, and which may be termed the intuitive method, or, if you prefer it, the short-hand method, will more than double the working power of the reader. It is not difficult to practice, especially to a busy man, who does with all his might what he has got to do. But it should be learned early in life, when the faculties are fresh, the mind full of zeal for knowledge, and the mental habits are ductile, not fixed. With it one's capacity for acquiring knowledge, and consequently his accomplishment, whether as writer, teacher, librarian, or private student, will be immeasureably increased.

Doubtless it is true that some native or intuitive gifts must be conjoined with much mental discipline and perseverance, in order to reach the highest result, in this method of reading, as in any other study. *"Non omnia possumus omnes,"* Virgil says; and there are intellects who could no more master such a method, than they could understand the binomial theorem, or calculate the orbit of Uranus. If it be true, as has been epigramatically said, that "a great book is a great evil," let it be reduced to a small one by the skilful use of the art of skipping. Then, "he that runs may read" as he runs—while, without this refuge, he that reads will often assuredly be tempted to run.

What I said, just now, in deprecation of set courses of reading, was designed for private students only, who so often find a stereotyped sequence of books barren or uninteresting. It was not intended to discourage the pursuit of a special course of study in the school, or the society, or the reading class. This is, in fact, one of the best means of intellectual progress. Here, there is the opportunity to discuss the style, the merits, and the characteristics of the author in hand, and by the attrition of mind with mind, to inform and entertain the whole circle of readers. In an association of this kind, embracing one or two acute minds, the excellent practice of reading aloud finds its best

results. Here, too, the art of expression becomes important, how to adapt the sound to the sense, by a just empha-
sis, intonation, and modulation of the voice. In short, the
value of a book thus read and discussed, in an appreciative
circle, may be more than doubled to each reader.

It is almost literally true that no book, undertaken
merely as task work, ever helped the reader to knowledge
of permanent or material value. How many persons,
struck by Mr. Emerson's exalted praise of the writings of
Plato, have undertaken to go through the Dialogues.
Alas! for the vain ambition to be or to seem learned! After trying to understand the Phaedo, or falling asleep over
the Gorgias, the book has been dropped as hastily as it was
taken up. It was not perceived that in order to enjoy or
comprehend a philosopher, one must have a capacity for
ideas. It requires almost as much intelligence to appreciate an idea as to conceive one. One will bring nothing
home from the most persistent cruise after knowledge, unless he carries something out. In the realm of learning,
we recognize the full meaning of that Scripture, that to
him that hath, shall be given; and he that hath not,
though never so anxious to read and understand Plato, will
quickly return to the perusal of his daily newspaper.

It were easier, perhaps, in one sense, to tell what not
to read, than to recommend what is best worth reading.
In the publishing world, this is the age of compilation,
not of creation. If we seek for great original works, if
we must go to the wholesale merchants to buy knowledge,
since retail geniuses are worth but little, one must go
back many years for his main selection of books. It would
not be a bad rule for those who can read but little, to read
no book until it has been published at least a year or two.
This fever for the newest books is not a wholesome condition of the mind. And since a selection must indispensa-

bly be made, and that selection must be, for the great mass of readers, so rigid and so small, why should precious time be wasted upon the ephemeral productions of the hour? What business, for example, has one to be reading Rider Haggard, or Amélie Rives, or Ian Maclaren, who has never read Homer, or Dante, or even so much as half-a-dozen plays of Shakespeare?

One hears with dismay that about three-fourths of the books drawn from our popular libraries are novels. Now, while such aimless reading, merely to be amused, is doubtless better than no reading at all, it is unquestionably true that over-much reading of fiction, especially at an early age, enervates the mind, weakens the will, makes dreamers instead of thinkers and workers, and fills the imagination with morbid and unreal views of life. Yet the vast consumption of novels is due more to the cheapness and wide diffusion of such works, and the want of wise direction in other fields, than to any original tendency on the part of the young. People will always read the most, that which is most put before them, if only the style be attractive. The mischief that is done by improper books is literally immeasureable. The superabundance of cheap fictions in the markets creates and supplies an appetite which should be directed by wise guidance into more improving fields. A two-fold evil follows upon the reading of every unworthy book; in the first place, it absorbs the time which should be bestowed upon a worthy one; and secondly, it leaves the mind and heart unimproved, instead of conducing to the benefit of both. As there are few books more elevating than a really good novel, so there are none more fruitful of evil than a bad one.

And what of the newspaper? it may be asked. When I consider for how much really good literature we are beholden to the daily and weekly press, how indispensable is its function as purveyor of the news of the world, how widely it has been improved in recent years, I cannot advise quarreling with the bridge that brings so many across the gulf of ignorance. Yet the newspaper, like the book, is to be read sparingly, and with judgment. It is to be used, not abused. I call that an abuse which squanders the precious and unreturning hours over long chronicles of depravity. The murders, the suicides, the executions, the divorces, the criminal trials, are each and all so like one another that it is only a wanton waste of time to read them. The morbid style in which social disorders of all kinds are written up in the sensational press, with staring headlines to attract attention, ought to warn off every healthy mind from their perusal. Every scandal in society that can be brought to the surface is eagerly caught up and paraded, while the millions of people who lead blameless lives of course go unnoticed and unchronicled. Such journals thus inculcate the vilest pessimism, instead of a wholesome and honest belief in the average decency of human nature. The prolixity of the narrative, too, is always in monstrous disproportion to its importance. "Does not the burning of a metropolitan theatre," says a great writer, "take above a million times as much telling as the creation of a world?" Here is where the art of skipping is to be rigorously applied. Read the newspaper by headlines only,—skipping all the murders, all the fires, all the executions, all the crimes, all the news, except the most important and immediately interesting,—and you will spend perhaps fifteen or twenty minutes upon what would otherwise occupy hours. It is no exaggeration to say that most persons have spent time enough over the newspapers, to have given them a liberal education.

As all readers cannot have the same gifts, so all cannot

enjoy the same books. There are those who can see no greatness in Shakespeare, but who think Tupper's Proverbial Philosophy sublime. Some will eagerly devour every novel of Miss Braddon's, or "The Duchess," or the woman calling herself "Ouida," but they cannot appreciate the masterly fictions of Thackeray. I have known very good people who could not, for the life of them, find any humor in Dickens, but who actually enjoyed the strained wit of Mrs. Partington and Bill Nye. Readers who could not get through a volume of Gibbon will read with admiration a so-called History of Napoleon by Abbott. And I fear that you will find many a young lady of to-day, who is content to be ignorant of Homer and Shakespeare, but who is ravished by the charms of "Trilby" or the "Heavenly Twins." But taste in literature, as in art, or in anything else, can be cultivated. Lay down the rule, and adhere to it, to read none but the best books, and you will soon lose all relish for the poor ones. You can educate readers into good judges, in no long time, by feeding them on the masterpieces of English prose and poetry. Surely, we all have cause to deprecate the remorseless flood of fictitious literature in which better books are drowned.

Be not dismayed at the vast multitude of books, nor fear that, with your small leisure, you will never be able to master any appreciable share of them. Few and far between are the great books of the world. The works which it is necessary to know, may be comprised in a comparatively small compass. The rest are to be preserved in the great literary conservatories, some as records of the past, others as chronicles of the times, and not a few as models to be avoided. The Congressional Library at Washington is our great National conservatory of books. As the library of the government—that is, of the whole people,—it is inclusive of all the literature which the country produces, while all the other libraries are and must be more or less exclusive. No National Library can ever be too large. In order that the completeness of the collection shall not fail, and to preserve the whole of our literature, it is put into the Statute of Copyright, as a condition precedent of the exclusive right to multiply copies of any book, that it shall be deposited in the Library of Congress. Apprehension is sometimes expressed that our National Library will become overloaded with trash, and so fail of its usefulness. 'Tis a lost fear. There is no act of Congress requiring all the books to be read. The public sense is continually winnowing and sifting the literature of every period, and to books and their authors, every day is the day of judgment. Nowhere in the world is the inexorable law of the survival of the fittest more rigidly applied than in the world of books. The works which are the most frequently re-printed in successive ages are the ones which it is safe to stand by.

Books may be divided into three classes: 1st, acquaintances; 2d, friends; and 3d, intimates.

It is well enough to have an acquaintance with a multitude of books, as with many people; though in either case much time should not be given to merely pleasant intercourse, that leads to no result. With our literary friends, we can spend more time, for they awaken keen interest, and are to be read with zest, and consequently with profit. But for our chosen intimates, our heart-companions, we reserve our highest regard, and our best hours. Choice and sacred is the book that makes an era in the life of the reader; the book which first rouses his higher nature, and awakens the reason or the imagination. Such a volume will many a one remember; the book which first excited his own thought, made him conscious of untried powers, and opened to his charmed vision a new world.

Such a book has Carlyle's Sartor Resartus been to many; or the play of Hamlet, read for the first time; or the Faust of Goethe; or the Confessions of St. Augustine; or an essay of Emerson; or John Ruskin; or the Divine Comedy of Dante; or even an exquisite work of fiction, like John Halifax, or Henry Esmond. What the book is that works such miracles is never of so much importance as the epoch in the mind of the reader which it signalizes. It were vain to single out any one writer, and say to all readers—"Here is the book that must indispensably be read;" for the same book will have totally different effects upon different minds, or even upon the same mind, at different stages of development.

When I have been asked to contribute to the once popular *symposia* upon "Books which have helped me,"—I have declined, for such catalogues of intellectual aids are liable to be very misleading. Thus, if I were to name the book which did more than most others for my own mind, I should say that it was the Emile of Rousseau, read at about the age of seventeen. This work, written with that marvellous eloquence which characterises all the best productions of Jean Jacques, first brought me acquainted with those advanced ideas of education which have penetrated the whole modern world. Yet the Emile would probably appear to most of my readers trite and common-place, as it would now to me, for the reason that we have long passed the period of development when its ideas were new to us.

But the formative power of books can never be overrated: their subtle mastery to stimulate all the germs of intellectual and moral life that lie enfolded in the mind. As the poet sings—

"Books are not seldom talismans and spells."

Why should they not be so? They furnish us the means,

and the only means, whereby we may hold communion with the master-spirits of all ages. They bring us acquainted with the best thoughts which the human mind has produced, expressed in the noblest language. Books create for us the many-sided world, carry us abroad, out of our narrow provincial horizons, and reveal to us new scenery, new men, new languages, and new modes of life. As we read, the mind expands with the horizon, and becomes broad as the blue heaven above us. With Homer, we breathe the fresh air of the pristine world, when the light of poetry gilded every mountain top, and peopled the earth with heroes and demigods. With Plutarch, we walk in company with sages, warriors, and statesmen, and kindle with admiration of their virtues, or are roused to indignation at their crimes. With Sophocles, we sound the depths of human passion, and learn the sublime lesson of endurance. We are charmed with an ode of Horace, perfect in rhythm, perfect in sentiment, perfect in diction, and perfect in moral; the condensed essence of volumes in a single page. We walk with Dante through the nether world, awed by the tremendous power with which he depicts for us the secrets of the prison house. With Milton, we mount heaven-ward, and in the immortal verse of his minor poems, finer even than the stately march of Paradise Lost, we hear celestial music, and breathe diviner air. With that sovereign artist, Shakespeare, full equally of delight and of majesty, we sweep the horizon of this complex human life, and become comprehensive scholars and citizens of the world. The masters of fiction enthrall us with their fascinating pages, one moment shaking us with uncontrollable laughter, and the next, dissolving us in tears. In the presence of all these emanations of genius, the wise reader may feed on nectar and ambrosia, and forget the petty cares and vexations of to-day.

There are some books that charm us by their wit or their sweetness, others that surprise and captivate us by their strength: books that refresh us when weary: books that comfort us when afflicted: books that stimulate us by their robust health: books that exalt and refine our natures, as it were, to a finer mould: books that rouse us like the sound of a trumpet: books that illumine the darkest hours, and fill all our day with delight.

It is books that record the advance and the decline of nations, the experience of the world, the achievements and the possibilities of mankind. It is books that reveal to us ideas and images almost above ourselves, and go far to open for us the gates of the invisible. "A river of thought," says Emerson, "is continually flowing out of the invisible world into the mind of man:" and we may add that books contain the most fruitful and permanent of the currents of that mighty river.

I am not disposed to celebrate the praises of all books, nor to recommend to readers of any age a habit of indiscriminate reading: but for the books which are true helpers and teachers, the thoughts of the best poets, historians, publicists, philosophers, orators,—if their value is not real, then there are no realities in the world.

Very true is it, nevertheless, that the many-sided man cannot be cultivated by books alone. One may learn by heart whole libraries, and yet be profoundly unacquainted with the face of nature, or the life of man. The pale student who gives himself wholly to books pays the penalty by losing that robust energy of character, that sympathy with his kind, that keen sense of the charms of earth and sky, that are essential to complete development. "The world's great men," says Oliver Wendell Holmes, "have not commonly been great scholars, nor its scholars great men." To know what other men have said about things is not always the most important part of knowledge. There is nothing that can dispense us from the independent use of our own faculties. Meditation and observation are more valuable than mere absorption; and knowledge itself is not wisdom. The true way to use books is to make them our servants—not our masters. Very helpful, cheering, and profitable will they become, when they fall naturally into our daily life and growth—when they tally with the moods of the mind.

The habits and methods of readers are as various as those of authors. Thus, there are some readers who gobble a book, as Boswell tells us Dr. Johnson used to gobble his dinner—eagerly, and with a furious appetite, suggestive of dyspepsia, and the non-assimilation of food. Then there are slow readers, who plod along through a book, sentence by sentence, putting in a mark conscientiously where they left off to-day, so as to begin at the self-same spot to-morrow; fast readers, who gallop through a book, as you would ride a flying bicycle on a race; drowsy readers, to whom a book is only a covert apology for a nap, and who pretend to be reading Macaulay or Herbert Spencer only to dream between the leaves; sensitive readers, who cannot abide the least noise or interruption when reading, and to whose nerves a foot-fall or a conversation is an exquisite torture; absorbed readers, who are so pre-occupied with their pursuit that they forget all their surroundings—the time of day, the presence or the voices of others, the hour for dinner, and even their own existence; credulous readers, who believe everything they read because it is printed in a book, and swallow without winking the most colossal lying; critical and captious readers, who quarrel with the blunders or the beliefs of their author, and who cannot refrain from calling him an idiot or an ass—and perhaps even writing him down so on his own pages; admiring and receptive readers, who find fresh beauties in a favorite author every time they peruse him, and even discover beautiful swans in the stupidest geese that ever cackled along the flowery meads of literature; reverent readers, who treat a book as they would treat a great and good man, considerately and politely, carefully brushing the dust from a beloved volume with the sleeve, or tenderly lifting a book fallen to the floor, as if they thought it suffered, or felt harm; careless and rough readers, who will turn down books on their faces to keep the place, tumble them over in heaps, cram them into shelves never meant for them, scribble upon the margins, dogs-ear the leaves, or even cut them with their fingers—all brutal and intolerable practices, totally unworthy of any one pretending to civilization.

To those who have well learned the art of reading, what inexhaustible delights does the world of books contain! With Milton, "to behold the bright countenance of truth, in the quiet and still air of delightful studies;" to journey through far countries with Marco Polo; to steer across an unknown sea with Columbus, or to brave the dangers of the frozen ocean with Nansen or Dr. Kane; to study the manners of ancient nations with Herodotus; to live over again the life of Greece and Rome with Plutarch's heroes; to trace the decline of empires with Gibbon and Mommsen; to pursue the story of the modern world in the pages of Hume, Macaulay, Thiers and Sismondi, and our own Prescott, Motley, and Bancroft; to enjoy afresh the eloquence of Demosthenes, and the polished and splendid diction of Cicero; to drink in the wisdom of philosophers, and to walk with Socrates, Plato and the stoics through the groves of Academia; to be kindled by the saintly utterances of prophets and apostles, St. Paul's high reasoning of immortality, or the seraphic visions of St. John; to study

the laws that govern communities with the great publicists, or the economy of nations with Adam Smith and
Stuart Mill; with the naturalists, to sound the depths of
the argument as to the origin of species and the genesis of
man; with the astronomers, to leave the narrow bounds of
earth, and explore the illimitable spaces of the universe,
in which our solar system is but a speck; with the mathe-
maticians, to quit the uncertain realm of speculation and
assumption, and plant our feet firmly on the rock of exact
science:—to come back anon to lighter themes, and to
revel in the grotesque humor of Dickens, the philosophic
page of Bulwer, the chivalric romances of Walter Scott,
the ideal creations of Hawthorne, the finished life-pictures
of George Eliot, the powerful imagination of Victor Hugo,
and the masterly delineations of Thackeray; to hang over
the absorbing biographies of Dr. Franklin, Walter Scott
and Dr. Johnson; to peruse with fresh delight the master-
pieces of Irving and Goldsmith, and the best essays of Haz-
litt, De Quincey, Charles Lamb, and Montaigne; to feel
the inspiration of the great poets of all ages, from Homer
down to Tennyson; to read Shakespeare—a book that is in
itself almost a university:—is not all this satisfaction
enough for human appetite, however craving, solace
enough for trouble, however bitter, occupation enough for
life, however long?

There are pleasures that perish in the using; but the
pleasure which the art of reading carries with it is perennial. He who can feast on the intellectual spoils of centuries need fear neither poverty nor hunger. In the society of those immortals who still rule our spirits from
their urns, we become assured that though heaven and
earth may pass away, no true thought shall ever pass away.

The great orator, on whose lips once hung multitudes,
dies and is forgotten; the great actor passes swiftly off the

stage, and is seen no more; the great singer, whose voice charmed listening crowds by its melody, is hushed in the grave; the great preacher survives but a single generation in the memory of men; all we who now live and act must be, in a little while, with yesterday's seven thousand years: —but the book of the great writer lives on and on, inspiring age after age of readers, and has in it more of the seeds of immortality than anything upon earth.

CHAPTER 10.

AIDS TO READERS.

There is one venerable Latin proverb which deserves a wider recognition than it has yet received. It is to the effect that "the best part of learning is to know where to find things." From lack of this knowledge, an unskilled reader will often spend hours in vainly searching for what a skilled reader can find in less than five minutes. Now, librarians are presumed to be skilled readers, although it would not be quite safe to apply this designation to all of that profession, since there are those among librarians, or their assistants, who are mere novices in the art of reading to advantage. Manifestly, one cannot teach what he does not know: and so the librarian who has not previously travelled the same road, will not be able to guide the inquiring reader who asks him to point out the way. But if the way has once been found, the librarian, with only a fairly good memory, kept in constant exercise by his vocation, can find it again. Still more surely, if he has been through it many times, will he know it intuitively, the moment any question is asked about it.

It is true of the great majority of readers resorting to a library, that they have a most imperfect idea, both of what they want, and of the proper way to find it. The world of knowledge, they know, is vast, and they are quite bewildered by the many paths that lead to some part or other of it, crossing each other in all directions. And among the would-be readers may be found every shade of intelligence, and every degree of ignorance. There is the timid variety, too modest or diffident to ask for any help at all, and so feeling about among the catalogues or other reference-books in a baffled search for information. There is the sciolist variety, who knows it all, or imagines that he does, and who asks for proof of impossible facts, with an assurance born of the profoundest ignorance. Then, too, there is the half-informed reader, who is in search of a book he once read, but has clean forgotten, which had a remarkable description of a tornado in the West, or a storm and ship-wreck at sea, or a wonderful tropical garden, or a thrilling escape from prison, or a descent into the bowels of the earth, or a tremendous snow-storm, or a swarming flight of migratory birds, or a mausoleum of departed kings, or a haunted chamber hung with tapestry, or the fatal caving-in of a coal-mine, or a widely destructive flood, or a hair-breadth escape from cannibals, or a race for life, pursued by wolves, or a wondrous sub-marine grotto, or a terrible forest fire, or any one of a hundred scenes or descriptions, all of which the librarian is presumed, not only to have read, but to have retained in his memory the author, the title, and the very chapter of the book which contained it.

To give some idea of the extent and variety of information which a librarian is supposed to possess, I have been asked, almost at the same time, to refer a reader to the origin of Candlemas day, to define the Pragmatic Sanction, to give, out of hand, the aggregate wealth of Great Britain, compared with that of half-a-dozen other nations, to define the limits of neutrality or belligerent rights, to explain what is meant by the Gresham law, to tell what ship has made the quickest voyage to Europe, when she made it, and what the time was, to elucidate the meaning of the Carolina doctrine, to explain the character and objects of the Knights of the Golden Circle, to tell how large are the endowments of the British Universities, to give the origin

of the custom of egg-rolling, to tell the meaning of the
cipher dispatches, to explain who was "Extra Billy Smith,"
to tell the aggregate number killed on all sides during the
Napoleonic wars, to certify who wrote the "Vestiges of
Creation," or, finally, to give the author of one of those
innumerable ancient proverbs, which float about the world
without a father.

The great number and variety of such inquiries as are
propounded by readers should not appal one. Nor should
one too readily take refuge from a troublesome reader by
the plea, however convenient, that the library contains
nothing on that subject. While this may unquestionably
be true, especially as regards a small public library, it
should never be put forward as a certainty, until one has
looked. Most inquiring readers are very patient, and
being fully sensible how much they owe to the free enjoyment of the library treasures, and to the aid of the superintendent of them, they are willing to wait for information. However busy you may be at the moment, the reader
can be asked to wait, or to call at a less busy time, when
you will be prepared with a more satisfactory answer than
can be given on the spur of the moment. What cannot
be done to-day, may often be done to-morrow. Remember
always, that readers are entitled to the best and most careful service, for a librarian is not only the keeper, but the
interpreter of the intellectual stores of the library. It
is a good and a safe rule to let no opportunity of aiding a
reader escape. One should be particularly careful to
volunteer help to those who are too new or too timid to
ask: and it is they who will be most grateful for any assistance. The librarian has only to put himself in their
place—(the golden rule for a librarian, as for all the world
besides), and to consider how often, in his own searches in
libraries, in the continual, never-ending quest of knowl-

edge, he would have been thankful for a hint from some one who knew, or had been over the ground of his search before; and then he will feel the full value to the novice, of such knowledge as he can impart.

He is not to forget that his superior opportunities for learning all about things, with a whole library at command, and within elbow-reach every hour of the day, should impose upon him a higher standard of attainment than most readers are supposed to have reached. In the intervals of library work, I am accustomed to consider the looking up of subjects or authorities as one of my very best recreations. It is as interesting as a game of whist, and much more profitable. It is more welcome than routine labor, for it rests or diverts the mind, by its very variety, while, to note the different views or expressions of writers on the same subject, affords almost endless entertainment. In tracing down a quotation also, or the half-remembered line of some verse in poetry, you encounter a host of parallel poetic images or expressions, which contribute to aid the memory, or to feed the imagination. Or, in pursuing a sought-for fact in history, through many volumes, you learn collaterally much that may never have met your eye before. Full, as all libraries are, of what we call trash, there is almost no book which will not give us something,—even though it be only the negative virtue of a model to be avoided. One may not, indeed, always find what he seeks, because it may not exist at all, or it may not be found in the limited range of his small library, but he is almost sure to find something which gives food for thought, or for memory to note. And this is one of the foremost attractions, let me add, of the librarian's calling; it is more full of intellectual variety, of wide-open avenues to knowledge, than any other vocation whatever. His daily quests in pursuit of information to lay before others, bring him acquainted with passages that are full of endless suggestion for himself.   He may not be able to pursue any of these avenues at the moment; but he should make a mental or a written note of them, for future benefit.   His daily business being learning, why should he not in time, become learned?   There are, of course, among the infinitude of questions, that come before the librarian, some that are really insoluble problems.   One of these is to be found among the topics of inquiry I just now suggested; namely: what is the aggregate wealth of Great Britain, or that of other nations?   This is a question frequently asked by inquiring Congressmen, who imagine that an answer may readily be had from one of those gifted librarians who is invested with that apocryphal attribute, commonly called omniscience.   But the inquirer is suddenly confronted by the fact (and a very stubborn fact it is) that not a single foreign nation has ever taken any census of wealth whatever.   In Great Britain (about which country inquiry as to the national resources more largely centres) the government wisely lets alone the attempt to tabulate the value of private wealth, knowing that such an object is utterly impracticable.

But, while the British census makes no attempt at estimating the property of the people, the independent estimates of statistical writers vary hopelessly and irreconcilably.   Mr. J. R. McCulloch, one of the foremost accredited writers on economic science, lays it down as a dictum, that "sixty years is the shortest time in which the capital of an old and densely-peopled country can be expected to be doubled."   Yet Joseph Lowe assumes the wealth of the United Kingdom to have doubled in eighteen years, from 1823 to 1841; while George R. Porter, in his widely-accredited book on the "Progress of the Nation," and Leoni Levi, a publicist of high reputation, make out, (by combining their estimates) that the private wealth of England increased fifty per cent. in seventeen years, at which rate it would double in about twenty-nine years, instead of sixty, as laid down by Mr. McCulloch. Mr. Levi calculates the aggregate private wealth of Great Britain in 1858, at $29,178,000,000, being a fraction less than the guesses of the census enumerators at the national wealth of the United States, twelve years later, in 1870. Can one guess be said to be any nearer the fact than the other? May we not be pardoned for treating all estimates as utterly fallacious that are not based upon known facts and figures? Why do we hear so much of the "approximate correctness" of so many statistical tables, when, in point of fact, the primary data are incapable of proof, and the averages and conclusions built upon them are all assumed? "Statisticians," says one of the fraternity, "are generally held to be eminently practical people; on the contrary, they are more given to theorizing than any other class of writers; and are generally less expert in it."

In the presence of such gross discrepancies as these, by statisticians of the highest repute, and among such a practical people as the English, what value can be attached to the mere estimates of wealth which have been attempted in the census of the United States? The careful Superintendent of the Census of 1870 and 1880, the late Francis A. Walker, writes concerning it:

"At the best, these figures represent but the opinion of one man, or of a body of men, in the collection of material, and in the calculation of the several elements of the public wealth." And in the last Census Report for 1890, the results of the so-called "census of wealth," are cautiously submitted, "as showing in a general way a continuous increase in the wealth of the nation, the exact proportions of which cannot be measured."

Now, what are we to conclude regarding the attempt to
elevate to a rank in statistical science, mere estimates of
private wealth, for a large portion of which, by the statements of those who make them, no actual statistical data
exist?   And when this is confessedly the case in our own
country, the only one attempting the impossible task of
tabulating the wealth of the people, what shall we say of
the demand that is made upon our credulity of accepting
the guesses of Mr. Giffen, or Mr. Mulhall, as to British
wealth?   Are we not justified in applying the old Latin
maxim—"*De non apparentibus, et de non existentibus,
eadem est ratio,*" and replying to those who demand of us
to know how much any nation is worth, that it is sometimes an important part of knowledge to know that nothing can be known?

Among the literally innumerable inquiries liable to be
made of a librarian, here is one which may give him more
than a moment's pause, unless he is uncommonly well
versed in American political history—namely, "What was
the Ostend Manifesto?"   To a mind not previously instructed these two words "Ostend Manifesto", convey
absolutely no meaning.   You turn to the standard encyclopaedias, Appleton's, Johnson's Universal, and the Britannica, and you find an account of Ostend, a little Bel-
gian city, its locality, commerce, and population, but absolutely nothing about an Ostend manifesto.   But in J. N.
Larned's "History for Ready Reference", a useful book
in five volumes, arranged in alphabetical order, you get
a clue.   It refers you from Ostend, under letter O, to
Cuba, where you learn that this formidable Ostend manifesto was nothing more nor less than a paper drawn up and
signed by Messrs. Buchanan, Mason, and Slidell, Ministers of the United States to Great Britain, France, and
Spain, respectively, when at the watering-place of Ostend,

in 1854, importing that the island of Cuba ought to, and under certain circumstances, must belong to the United States. Looking a little farther, as the manifesto is not published in Larned, you find the text of the document itself in Cluskey's "Political Text-Book", of 1860, and in some of the American newspapers of 1854. This is a case of pursuing a once notorious, but more recently obscure topic, through many works of reference until found.

In many searches for names of persons, it becomes highly important to know before-hand where to look, and equally important where not to look, for certain biographies. Thus, if you seek for the name of any living character, it is necessary to know that it would be useless to look in the Encyclopædia Britannica, because the rule of compilation of that work purposely confined its sketches of notable persons to those who were already deceased when its volumes appeared. So you save the time of hunting in at least one conspicuous work of reference, before you begin, by simply knowing its plan.

In like manner, you should know that it is useless to search for two classes of names in the "Dictionary of National Biography," the most copious biographical dictionary of British personages ever published, begun in 1885, under Leslie Stephen, and reaching its sixty-first volume, and letter W in 1899, under the editorship of Sidney Lee. These two classes of names are first, all persons not British, that is, not either English, Scottish or Irish; and secondly, names of British persons now living. This is because this great work, like the Britannica, purposely confines itself to the names of notables deceased; and, unlike the Britannica, it further limits its biographies to persons connected by birth or long residence with the British kingdom. Knowing this fact before-hand, will save any time wasted in searching the Dictionary of National Biography for any persons now living, or for any American or European names.

Another caveat may properly be interposed as regards searches for information in that most widely advertised and circulated of all works of reference,—the Encyclopaedia Britannica. The plan of that work was to furnish the reading public with the very best treatises upon leading topics in science, history, and literature, by eminent scholars and specialists in various fields. Pursuant to this general scheme, each great subject has a most elaborate, and sometimes almost exhaustive article—as, for example, chemistry, geology, etc., while the minor divisions of each topic do not appear in the alphabet at all, or appear only by cross-reference to the generic name under which they are treated. It results, that while you find, for example, a most extensive article upon "Anatomy", filling a large part of a volume of the Britannica, you look in vain in the alphabet for such subjects as "blood, brain, cartilage, sinew, tissue," etc., which are described only in the article "Anatomy." This method has to be well comprehended in order for any reader to make use of this great Cyclopaedia understandingly. Even by the aid of the English index to the work, issued by its foreign publishers, the reader who is in hasty quest of information in the Britannica, will most frequently be baffled by not finding any minor subject in the index. The English nation, judged by most of the productions of its literary and scientific men in that field, has small genius for indexing. It was reserved to an American to prepare and print a thorough index, at once alphabetical and analytical, to this great English thesaurus of information—an index ten times more copious, and therefore more useful to the student, than the meagre one issued in England. This index fills 3,900 closely printed columns, forming the whole of volume 25 of the Philadelphia edition of the work. By its aid, every name and every topic, treated anywhere in this vast repository of human knowledge can be traced out and appropriated; while without it, the Encyclopaedia Britannica, with all its great merits, must remain very much in the nature of a sealed book to the reader who stands in need of immediate use and reference. We have to take it for what it is—a collection of masterly treatises, rather than a handy dictionary of knowledge.

The usefulness and success of any library will depend very largely upon the sympathy, so to speak, between the readers and the librarian. When this is well established, the rest is very easy. The librarian should not seclude himself so as to be practically inaccessible to readers, nor trust wholly to assistants to answer their inquiries. This may be necessary in some large libraries, where great and diversified interests connected with the building up of the collection, the catalogue system, and the library management and administration are all concerned. In the British Museum Library, no one ever sees the Principal Librarian; even the next officer, who is called the keeper of the printed books, is not usually visible in the reading-room at all.

A librarian who is really desirous of doing the greatest good to the greatest number of people, will be not only willing, but anxious to answer inquiries, even though they may appear to him trivial and unimportant. Still, he should also economise time by cultivating the habit of putting his answers into the fewest and plainest words.

How far the librarian should place himself in direct communication with readers, must depend largely upon the extent of the library, the labor required in managing its various departments, the amount and value of assistance at his command, and upon various other circumstances, depending upon the different conditions with different librarians. But it may be laid down as a safe general rule, that the librarian should hold himself perpetually as a public servant, ready and anxious to answer in some way, all inquiries that may come to him. Thus, and thus only, can he make himself, and the collection of books under his charge, useful in the highest degree to the public. He will not indeed, in any extensive library, find it convenient, or even possible, to answer all inquiries in person; but he should always be ready to enable his assistants to answer them, by his superior knowledge as to the best sources of information, whenever they fail to trace out what is wanted. In any small library, he should be always accessible, at or near the place where people are accustomed to have their wants for books or information supplied: and the public resorting to the library will thus come not only to rely upon him for aid in their intellectual researches, but to appreciate and respect him for the wide extent of his knowledge, and to consider him, in time, an indispensable guide, if not leader, in the community. His reputation, in fact, will depend upon the extent to which he has been able to help others, as well as upon the number of people whom he has thus aided.

In a very high sense, the true librarian is an educator; his school is as large as the town in which his library is situated. Very few people in that town know what he is always presumed to know,—namely—to what books to go to get answers to the questions they want answered. In supplying continually the means of answering these countless questions, the library becomes actually a popular university, in which the librarian is the professor, the tuition is free, and the course is optional, both as to study and as to time.

Most persons who come to make any investigation in a

public library require a good deal of assistance. For example, a reader is in need of the latest information as to the amount of steel and iron made in this country, and what State produces these important manufactures. He has not the faintest idea where to look for the information, except that it may be in the census, but the census is nine years old, and he wants recent facts. It is vain to turn him over to the cyclopaedias, for there is not one whose information upon such statistics comes anywhere near up to date. You have to put before him a pamphlet annual, published by the American Iron and Steel Association, which contains exactly what he wants; and no other source of information does contain it.

Another inquirer seeks to know how to treat some disease. In such cases, of course, the librarian should not go farther than to put before the reader a work on domestic medicine, for it is not his function to deal in recommendations of this, that, or the other method of treatment, any more than it is to give legal opinions, if asked— although he may have studied law. So, if the reader wants to know about the religious tenets of the Presbyterians, or the Mormons, or the Buddhists, or the doctrines of the Catholic Church, and asks the librarian's opinion about any controverted question of belief, he is to be answered only by the statement that the library is there to supply information, not opinions, and then pointed to the religious cyclopaedias, which give full summaries of all the sects.

He may frequently be asked for information on a subject which he knows nothing about; and I have heard a librarian declare, that he often found himself able to give fuller and better information on a subject of which he was previously ignorant, than upon one he had long been familiar with. The reason was that in the one case he had freshly looked up all the authorities, and put them before the reader, while in the other, giving the references from a memory, more or less imperfect, he had overlooked some of the most important means of information.

The constant exercise of the habit of supplying helps to readers is a splendid intellectual school for the librarian himself. Through it, his memory is quickened and consequently improved, (as every faculty is by use) his habits of mental classification and analysis are formed or strengthened, and his mind is kept on the alert to utilize the whole arsenal of the knowledge he has already acquired, or to acquire new knowledge.

Another very important benefit derived by the librarian from his constantly recurring attention to the calls of readers for aid, is the suggestion thereby furnished of the deficiencies in the collection in his charge. This will be a continual reminder to him, of what he most needs, namely, how to equip the library with the best and most recent sources of information in every field of inquiry. Whether the library be a large or a small one, its deficiencies in some directions are sure to be very considerable: and these gaps are more conspiciously revealed in trying to supply readers with the means of making what may be termed an exhaustive research upon a given subject, than in any other way. You find, for example, in looking up your authorities in what has come to be called Egyptology, that while you have Wilkinson's Ancient Egypt, and Lane's Modern Egyptians, both of which are very valuable works, you have not the more modern books of Brugsch-Bey, or of A. H. Sayce, or of Maspero. You may also find out, by mingling freely with a good part of the readers, what subjects are most frequently looked into or inquired about, and you can thus secure valuable information as to the directions in which the library most needs strengthening. Thus, in a community largely made up of people connected with manufacturing interests, the inquiries are liable to be much concerned with the mechanic arts; and you would therefore naturally seek to acquire a liberal selection of the best and latest works in technical science, or the useful arts. If you have, on the other hand, very few inquiries, indeed, for theological works, you take it as some evidence that that department of the collection needs little enlargement, and you may devote your funds in other directions. Then too, the great value of popularising the library by the hearty interest shown by the librarian in the wants of the people can hardly be over-rated. This interest, being a perennial one, and continued through a series of years, the number of citizens and their families assisted will be constantly on the increase, and the public opinion of the town will come in time, to regard the library as a great popular necessity. Hence, if it is an institution supported in whole or in part by town or municipal funds, its claims to liberal consideration will be immeasurably strengthened. If an enlargement of room for the books, or even a new library building comes to be needed, its chances for securing the funds requisite will be excellent. If a more liberal supply of new books, or an extended range of older ones of great value is reported by the librarian as wanted to increase the usefulness of the library, the authorities will more cheerfully consider the claim. And if it is proposed that additional and competent assistance shall be given to the librarian, or that he should be more liberally compensated for his highly useful and important labors, that, too, may be accomplished—especially if it has come to be recognized that by his wide knowledge, and skilful management, and helpful devotion to the service of the reading public, he has rendered himself indispensable.

In the supply of information desired by readers, it is better to leave them to their own search, once you have put

before them the proper authorities, than to spend your
time in turning for them to the volume and page. This,
for two reasons—first, it leaves your own time free to help
other readers, or to attend to the ever-waiting library
work; and, secondly, it induces habits of research and
self-help on the part of the reader. It is enough for the
librarian to act as an intelligent guide-post, to point the
way; to travel the road is the business of the reader himself. Therefore, let the visitor in quest of a quotation,
look it out in the index of the volumes you put before him.
If he fails to find it, it will then be time for you to intervene, and lend the aid of your more practiced eye, and
superior knowledge of how to search; or else, let the
reader look for it in some more copious anthology, which
you may put before him. There are multitudes of inquiries for the authors of poems, which are in no sense
"familiar quotations," nor even select quotations, but
which are merely common-place sentiments expressed in
language quite unpoetic,—and not the work of any notable
writer at all. They are either the production of some
utterly obscure author of a volume of verse, quite unknown
to fame, or, still more probably, the half-remembered
verses of some anonymous contributor to the poet's corner
of the newspaper or magazine. In such cases, where you
see no poetic beauty or imaginative power in the lines, it
is well to inform the inquirer at once that you do not
think them the production of any noted writer, and thus
end the fruitless search for memorizing what is not at all
memorable. What may strike uncultivated readers as
beautiful, may be set down as trash, by a mind that has
been fed upon the masterpieces of poetry. Not that the
librarian is to assume the air of an oracle or a censor,
(something to be in all circumstances avoided) or to pronounce positive judgment upon what is submitted: he

should inform any admiring reader of a passage not
referred to in any of the anthologies, and not possessing
apparent poetic merit, that he believes the author is unknown to fame. That should be sufficient for any reasonably disposed reader, who, after search duly completed,
will go away answered, if not satisfied.

I gave some instances of the singular variety of questions asked of a librarian. Let me add one, reported by
Mr. Robert Harrison, of the London Library, as asked of
him by William M. Thackeray. The distinguished author
of Esmond and The Virginians wanted a book that would
tell of General Wolfe, the hero of Quebec. "I don't want to
know about his battles", said the novelist. "I can get
all that from the histories. I want something that will
tell me the color of the breeches he wore." After due
search, the librarian was obliged to confess that there was
no such book.

A librarian is likely to be constantly in a position to aid
the uninformed reader how to use the books of reference
which every public library contains. The young person
who is new to the habit of investigation, or the adult who
has never learned the method of finding things, needs to
be shown how to use even so simple a thing as an index.
Do not be impatient with his ignorance, although you may
find him fumbling over the pages in the body of the book
in vain, to find what you, with your acquired knowledge
of indexes and their use, can find in half a minute or less.
Practice alone can make one perfect in the art of search
and speedy finding. The tyro who tries your patience this
year, will very likely become an expert reader the next.
Wide as is the domain of ignorance, there are few among
those intelligent enough to resort to a library at all, who
cannot learn. You will find some who come to the library
so unskilled, that they will turn over the leaves even of

an index, in a blind, hap-hazard way, evidently at a loss
how to use it.   These must be instructed first, that the index is arranged just like a dictionary, in the alphabetical
order of the names or subjects treated, and secondly, that
after finding the word they seek in it, they must turn to
the page indicated by the figure attached to that word.
This is the very primer of learning in the use of a library,
but the library in any town, used as it is by many boys
and girls of all ages, has to be a primary school for beginners, as well as a university for advanced students.
Despise not the day of small things, however you may find
it more agreeable to be occupied with great ones.

On the other hand, you will find at the other extreme
of intelligence, among your clientage of readers, those who
are completely familiar with books and their uses.   There
are some readers frequenting public libraries, who not only
do not need assistance themselves, but who are fully competent to instruct the librarian.   In meeting the calls of
such skilled readers, who always know what they require,
it is never good policy to obtrude advice or suggestion,
but simply to supply what they call for.   You will readily
recognize and discriminate such experts from the mass of
readers, if you have good discernment.   Sometimes they
are quite as sensitive as they are intelligent, and it may
annoy them to have offered them books they do not want,
in the absence of what they require.   An officious, or
super-serviceable librarian or assistant, may sometimes
prejudice such a reader by proffering help which he does
not want, instead of waiting for his own call or occasion.

Let us look at a few examples of the numerous calls at
a popular library.   For example, a reader asks to see a
book, giving an account of the marriage of the Adriatic.
You know that this concerns the history of Venice and its
Doges, and you turn to various books on Venice, and its

history, until you find a description of the strange festival. It may be, and probably is the case, that the books, like most descriptive works and narratives of travellers, are without index. This is a disability in the use of books which you must continually encounter, since multitudes of volumes, old and new, are sent out without a vestige of an index to their contents. Some writers have urged that a law should be made refusing copyright to the author of any book who failed to provide it with an index; a requirement highly desirable, but also highly impracticable. Yet you will find in most books, a division of the contents into chapters, and in the beginning of the volume a table of the contents of each chapter, giving its leading topics. This is a substitute for an index, although (not being arranged in alphabetical order) it is far less useful than that time-saving aid to research. But you have to learn to take advantage of even poor and inferior helps, when you cannot have the best, (as a poor guide is better than no guide at all, unless it misguides,) and so you run your eye quickly through the table of contents to find what you seek. In the case supposed, of the ceremony at Venice, you will be aided in the search by having in mind that the catch-words involved are "Adriatic," and "Doge," and as these begin with capital letters, which stand out, as it were, from the monotonous "lower case" type (as printers call all the letters that are not capitals) your search will be much abridged by omitting to read through all the sentences of your table of contents, and seizing only the passage or passages where "Doge," or "Adriatic," may occur.

This remark will apply as well to numerous other searches which you will have to make in books. The table of contents will commonly take note of all the more salient topics that are treated in the book, whether of persons, of places, of notable scenes, historic events, etc., and so will aid you in finding what you seek. In the last resort only, in the books whose table of contents fails you, will you have to turn the leaves page by page, which, while not equivalent to reading the book through, is a time-consuming business.

Of course no librarian can devote hours of his precious time to searches in such detail for readers. They are to be supplied with the books likely to contain what they are in search of, and left to seek it in their own way, with such hints and cautions as to saving time by taking the shortest road, as the experience of the librarian enables him to supply. The suggestions here given are not needed by scholarly readers, but are the fruits of long experience in searching books for what they contain.

Again, let us take the case of a call by a reader who happens to be a decorative painter, for patterns which may furnish him hints in finishing an interior of a house. Of course he wants color—that is, not theory only, but illustration, or practical examples. So you put before him Owen Jones's *Grammar of Ornament*, or Racinet's *L'Ornement polychrome*, both illustrated with many beautiful designs in color, which he is delighted to find.

Another reader is anxious to see a picture of "St. George and the Dragon." If you have the "Museum of Painting and Sculpture," in 17 volumes, or Champlin's "Cyclopaedia of Painters and Painting," a dictionary of art in four volumes, you find it in either work, in the alphabet, under "St. George," and his want is satisfied.

A youngster wants to know how to build a boat, and you find him Folkard on Boats, or Frazar's Sail-boats, which describe and figure various styles of water-craft.

Perhaps an inquisitive reader wants to find out all about the families of the various languages, and what is known

of their origin, and you supply him with W. D. Whitney's
"Life and Growth of Language," or Max Müller's "Science
of Language," either of which furnishes full information.

Another inquirer seeks for information about the aggregate debts of nations. You give him the great quarto
volume of the last Census on Wealth and Indebtedness, or
for still later information the Statesman's Year Book for
1899, or the Almanach de Gotha for the current year, both
of which contain the comparative debts of nations at the
latest dates.

The inquirer who seeks to know the rates of wages paid
for all kinds of labor in a series of several years, can be
supplied with the elaborate Report on Labor and Wages
for fifty-two years, published by the U. S. Government in
1893, in four volumes.

Another reader wishes, we will suppose, to hunt up the
drawings of all patents that have been issued on type-
writers, and type-writing inventions. You put before
him the many indexes to the Patent Specifications and
Patent Office Gazette; he makes out from these his list of
volumes wanted, which are at once supplied, and he falls
to work on his long, but to him interesting job.

A reader who has seen in the library or elsewhere a book
he would much like to own, but cannot find a copy in town,
wants to know what it will cost: you turn to your American or foreign catalogue, covering the year of publication,
and give him not only the price, but the publisher's name
from whom he can order it, and he goes on his way re-
joicing.

An artist engaged upon a painting in which he wishes
to introduce a deer, or a group of rabbits, or an American
eagle, or a peacock, asks for an accurate picture of the
bird or animal wanted. You put before him J. S. Kings-

ley's Riverside Natural History, in six volumes, and his desire is satisfied.

In dealing with books of reference, there will often be found very important discrepancies of statement, different works giving different dates, for example, for the same event in history or biography.

Next to a bible and a dictionary of language, there is no book, perhaps, more common than a biographical dictionary. Our interest in our fellow-men is perennial; and we seek to know not only their characteristics, and the distinguishing events of their lives, but also the time of their birth into the world and their exit from it. This is a species of statistics upon which one naturally expects certainty, since no person eminent enough to be recorded at all is likely to have the epoch of his death, at least, unremarked. Yet the seeker after exact information in the biographical dictionaries will find, if he extends his quest among various authorities, that he is afloat on a sea of uncertainties. Not only can he not find out the date of decease of some famous navigators, like Sir John Franklin and La Perouse, who sailed into unexplored regions of the globe, and were never heard of more, but the men who died at home, in the midst of friends and families, are frequently recorded as deceased at dates so discrepant that no ingenuity can reconcile them.

In Haydn's Dictionary of Dates, Sir Henry Havelock was said to have died November 25th, 1857, while Maunder's Treasury of Biography gives November 21st, the London Almanac, November 27th, and the Life of Havelock, by his brother-in-law, November 24th. Here are four distinct dates of death given, by authorities apparently equally accredited, to a celebrated general, who died within forty years of our own time. Of the death of the notorious Robespierre, guillotined in 1794, we find in Chalmers'

Biographical Dictionary that he died July 10th, in Rees's Cyclopaedia, July 28th, and in Alison's History of Europe, July 29th. Doubtless it is some comfort to reflect, in view of his many crimes, that the bloody tyrant of the Jacobins is really dead, irrespective of the date, about which biographers may dispute. Of the English mechanician Joseph Bramah, inventor of the Bramah lock, we learn from the English Cyclopaedia, that he died in 1814, and from Rose's Biographical Dictionary, that he died in 1815.

Now, although a large share of the errors and discrepancies that abound in biographical dictionaries and other books of reference may be accounted for by misprints, others by reckoning old style instead of new, and many more by carelessness of writers and transcribers, it is plain that all the variations cannot be thus accounted for. Nothing is more common in printing offices than to find a figure 6 inverted serving as a 9, a 5 for a 3, or a 3 for an 8, while 8, 9, and 0, are frequently interchanged. In such cases, a keen-eyed proof-reader may not always be present to prevent the falsification of history; and it is a fact, not sufficiently recognized, that to the untiring vigilance, intelligence, and hard, conscientious labors of proof-readers, the world owes a deeper debt of gratitude than it does to many a famous maker of books. It is easy enough to make books, Heaven knows, but to make them correct, "*Hic labor, hoc opus est.*"

A high authority in encyclopaedical lore tells us that the best accredited authorities are at odds with regard to the birth or death of individuals in the enormous ratio of from twenty to twenty-five per cent. of the whole number in the biographical dictionaries. The Portuguese poet Camoens is said by some authorities to have been born in 1517, and by others in 1525; a discrepancy of eight years.

Chateaubriand is declared by the English Cyclopaedia to have been born September 4th, 1768; September 14th, 1768, by the Nouvelle Biographie générale of Dr. Hoefer; and September 4th, 1769, by the Conversations-Lexicon. Of course it is clear that all these authorities cannot be right; but which of the three is so, is matter of extreme doubt, leaving the student of facts perplexed and uncertain at the very point where certainty is not only most important, but most confidently expected.

Of another kind are the errors that sometimes creep into works of reference of high credit, by accepting too confidently statements publicly made. In one edition of the Dictionary of Congress a certain honorable member from Pennsylvania, in uncommonly robust health, was astonished to find himself recorded as having died of the National Hotel disease, contracted at Washington in 1856. In this case, the editor of the work was a victim of too much confidence in the newspapers. In the Congressional Directory, where brief biographies of Congressmen are given, one distinguished member was printed as having been elected to Congress at a time which, taken in connection with his birth-date in the same paragraph, made him precisely one year old when he took his seat in Congress.

Even in reporting the contents of public and private libraries, exaggeration holds sway. The library of George the Fourth, inherited by that graceless ignoramus from a book-collecting father, and presented to the British nation with ostentatious liberality only after he had failed to sell it to Russia, was said in the publications of those times to contain about 120,000 volumes. But an actual enumeration when the books were lodged in the King's library at the British Museum, where they have ever since remained, showed that there were only 65,250 volumes, being but little more than half the reported number. Many libraries, public and private, are equally over-estimated. It is so much easier to guess than to count, and the stern test of arithmetic is too seldom applied, notwithstanding the fact that 100,000 volumes can easily be counted in a day by a single person, and so on in the same proportion. Here, as in the statistics of population, the same proverb holds good, that the unknown is always the magnificent, and on the surface of the globe we inhabit, the unexplored country is always the most marvellous, since the world began.

These discrepancies in authorities, and exaggerations of writers, are not referred to for the purpose of casting doubt upon all published history, but only to point out that we cannot trust implicitly to what we find in books. Bearing in mind always, that accuracy is perhaps the rarest of human qualities, we should hold our judgment in reserve upon controverted statements, trusting no writer implicitly, unless sustained by original authorities. When asked to recommend the best book upon any subject, do not too confidently assert the merits of the one you may think the best, but say simply that it is well accredited, or very popular. It is not always safe to recommend books, and the librarian does well to speak with proper reservations as to most of them, and to recommend only what are well known to him to be good, by his own intimate acquaintance with them, or, which is the surest test of all, by the verdicts of critical reviews, or by the constant reprinting of them in many successive years.

It was the well-nigh unanimous report at a Conference of American librarians, upon the subject of "aids to readers", that "nothing can take the place of an intelligent and obliging assistant at the desk." This was after a thorough canvass of the relative merits of the various reference books and helps to readers in book form. Not only the casual reader, and the reader with a purpose may be constantly aided by the librarian's knowledge, and larger experience in the art of finding things, but teachers in the schools, clergymen preparing discourses, and every one seeking to know anything, should find the librarian a living catalogue. There is nothing so effective in the world as individual effort.

CHAPTER 11.

Access to Library Shelves.

The matter of free or unrestricted access to the books on the shelves is a vexed question in libraries. Open and unprotected shelves, either in alcoves or the main reading room, while they appear to be a boon to readers, who can thus browse at will through the literary pastures, and turn over volumes at their pleasure, furnish by no means good security for the books. Some of the smaller public libraries protect their books from access by glass doors in front of the shelves, which form also a partial protection against dust. Others again, use wire screen doors, opened, like the others, by lock and key when books are wanted. Both of these arrangements give to readers the advantage of reading the titles on the backs of most of the books in the library, while protecting them from being handled, disarranged, or removed. But they are also open to the objection that they obstruct the prompt service of the books, by just the amount of time it takes to open the doors or screens, and close them again. This trouble and delay may overbalance the supposed advantages. Certainly they must do so in all large libraries, where the frequentation is great, and where every moment's delay in the book service works disadvantage to numerous readers. While private libraries, or quite small public ones, can indulge in the luxury of glass cases, no extensive collection can be managed with the requisite promptitude under their obstructions.

But how to avoid the indiscriminate and usually careless handling of the books on shelves, by the people fre-

quenting the library, and still extend to readers prompt
and full service of all the books they wish to consult on any
subject, is a problem. In a few of the great libraries,
where that modern improvement, the stack system, prevails, the difficulty is solved by the storing of the books in
the outside repositories, or iron book-stacks to which readers are not admitted. In this case the reading room is
only for books in use by those frequenting it, or is supplied
with a selection of reference books simply, the stacks being
drawn upon for all the rest. This of course secures the
books both from misplacement and from pillage.

In smaller libraries which have no stack system (and
this includes by far the greater number) a variety of treatment prevails. Most of them are unprovided with any effective means of guarding the books on the shelves from
handling. The result is great insecurity, and inevitable
misplacement of books, amounting often to confusion and
chaos on the shelves, unless corrected by much daily re-
arrangement by the librarian or assistants. This con-
sumes much valuable time, which ought to be devoted to
other pressing duties.

One remedy is to guard the shelves by a railing of some
kind, which cannot be passed, except at the gates or pas-
sage-ways provided for the attendants. This simple provision will protect the orderly arrangement as well as the
safety of the library—two objects both of cardinal importance. Absolutely free access to all the shelves means,
sooner or later, loss to the library. And the books most
certain to be taken or mutilated are those which it is costly, or difficult, or in some cases, impossible to replace.
The chances of abstracting engravings from books are
much greater in the shadow of the shelves, than in the
open reading-room, under the eyes of many. In any library but the smaller ones, the difficulties and dangers of

unrestricted handling of all the books by the public will be developed in the direct ratio of the size of the library. Nor will it do to admit one class of readers to the shelves, and exclude others. It often happens that persons claiming to have special literary or scientific objects, and who profess that they cannot get along at all by having books brought to them, are favored in their wish to go to the shelves, while others are disfavored. This raises at once the just complaint that invidious distinctions are made. The only safe rule to follow is that of universal free access, or impartial and uniform exclusion from the shelves. In the latter case, no one can complain, especially when made aware that he can have all the works on a given subject brought to his seat in a brief time, and can work upon them to much greater comfort and advantage, seated where there is good light and ample room, than if standing up in the shadow of the shelves to pursue his researches.

It is also to be considered that such disarrangement of books as inevitably follows free admission to the shelves deprives the very persons who claim this privilege, of finding what they seek, until a complete replacement takes place, throughout the library, and this is necessarily a work of time. That it involves much more time and consequent delay than is occasioned by the re-shelving of books used in a day, is apparent when we consider that in the latter case, only the number of volumes actually withdrawn from shelves by the library attendants have to be replaced, and that these are in conveniently assorted piles all ready to go to their respective shelves; while in the other case, the displacement is made by many hands, most of them careless of any convenience but their own, and moreover, the disarranged books are, or are liable to be, scattered on the wrong shelves, thus throwing the entire library into dis-

order, requiring great pains, knowledge, and time to repair.

In any well-regulated library, the absence of any book
from its place can almost always be accounted for. Thus
it is either—1. In the reading room, in use; or 2. Charged
out to a borrower; or 3. Sent to the binder for rebinding,
or repair; or 4. Reserved for some reader's use; or 5. In
temporary use by a cataloguer, or some other library assistant; or 6. Among the books not yet re-shelved from
recent use.

Now each of these is a legitimate reason for the absence
of any book not found in its place. By search under each
of these heads, *seriatim*, aided by the memory of librarian
and assistants, the missing volume should be readily located, and soon availed of for use.

But in the case of books misplaced by readers, no such
tracing out of the whereabouts of any volume is effectual,
for the reason that the book may have been (and probably
is) put on some shelf where it does not belong. And the
question, where in an extensive collection, a book-hunter
admitted to freely range over all the shelves, and a
stranger to the minute classification of books, has misplaced the missing volumes, is an insoluble problem, except by hunting over or handling the entire library.

In this close practical view of the case we have to add to
the long list of the enemies of books, formerly enumerated,
those who demand a right to browse (as they term it)
among the shelves of a public library, and who displace the
books they take down to gratify, it may be, only an idle
curiosity. Their offence consists, not in being anxious to
see the books, but in preventing others from seeing them,
by segregating them where neither librarian nor assistants
may be able to find them, when called for. The whole
question is summed up in the statement that the ability to

produce library books when called for, depends strictly upon keeping them in their proper place: and this is quite incompatible with promiscuous handling upon the shelves.

The preservation of order is alike in the interest of the reading public, of the librarian and his assistants, and of the very persons who complain of it as depriving them of library facilities. If library facilities consist in rendering the books in it unfindable, and therefore unavailable to any reader, then the argument for free range of the shelves arrives at a *reductio ad absurdum*. The true library facilities consist in a classification and a catalogue which arrange the books in systematic order, and keep them there, save when called into use. Thus, and thus only, can those who resort to a public library for actual research, be assured of finding what they want, just when they want it. The time saved to all readers by the sure and steady preservation of an orderly arrangement of the books, is simply incalculable. Multiply the number of volumes out of place by the number of readers who call for them, and you have some idea of the mischief that may be done through the carelessness of a few favored readers, to the whole community of scholars. Of course the considerations here set forth pre-suppose an active and intelligent librarian, and zealous and willing attendants, all ever ready to aid the researches of readers by the most prompt and helpful suggestions, and by dispatch in placing before them what they most need. The one cardinal design of a library—to supply the largest amount of information in the shortest time, is subverted by any disorganizing scheme. If the library be administered on the just principle of "the greatest good to the greatest number," then such individual favoritism should never be allowed.

It may, indeed, be claimed that there is no rule without some valid exceptions; but these exceptions should never be permitted to defeat the cardinal object of the rule—which is to keep every book strictly in its own place. Let the exception be confined to allowing an occasional inspection of the shelves in the company of a library attendant, and there will be no trouble.

But there is another danger, aside from the misplacement of books. Experience has shown that thefts or mutilations of books have been numerous, in direct proportion to the extension of freedom and opportunity to those frequenting the library. Literary men and book-lovers are frequently book-collectors also; and the temptation to take what is often too loosely considered public property is sometimes yielded to by persons whose character and standing may render them the least suspected. In one of the largest lending libraries in this country, the purloining of books had been carried so far, that the authorities had to provide a wire fence all around the reading room, to keep the readers from access to the shelves. The result was soon seen in the reduction of the number of books stolen from 700 volumes to 300 volumes a year.

After several years' experience of the Astor Library in opening its alcoves to readers (amounting to practical free admission to the shelves to all calling themselves special students) the losses and mutilations of books became so serious, that alcove admissions have been greatly curtailed.

At the Conference of Librarians in London, in 1877, the subject of admission or non-admission to the shelves was discussed with the result that opinions were preponderantly adverse to the free range of the library by readers. It was pointed out that libraries are established and maintained at great cost for serious purposes of reading and study, and that these ends are best subserved by systematic service at a common centre—not by letting the readers scatter themselves about the library shelves. To one

speaker who held that every one in a free public library
had the right to go to the shelves, and choose his books for
himself, it was answered that this was equivalent to saying that it is the idler's right to stroll about in every place
devoted to a special business, and interrupt that business
at his pleasure.

At the International Conference of 1897, an able defence of open shelves was presented, claiming that it saves
much librarians' time in finding books, if readers are allowed to find them for themselves; that thefts and mutilations are inconsiderable; that it makes an appeal to the
honor of people to respect the books; that the open shelf
system does better educational work; that it is economical
by requiring fewer library attendants; that it has grown
steadily in favor in America, and that it gives the people
the same right in the library which is their own, as the
individual has in his own.

On the other hand, it was urged that the arguments for
open shelves were all arguments for anarchy; that the
readers who want to rummage about for what they want
lack proper discipline of the mind; that the number of
books lost under it has been very large; that librarians are
custodians and conservers, as well as dispensers of books;
that all books misplaced are practically lost to the library
for the time being; that the open shelf system requires far
more space, and is more expensive; and that, however desirable, its general adoption is utterly impracticable.

The practice of libraries in this particular of administration differs widely, as do the opinions of librarians regarding it. In most colleges and universities free access
is allowed; and in some public free libraries, both east and
west, the readers are allowed to handle the books on the
shelves. This is comparatively safe in the smaller town
libraries, where the books are in compact shape, and the

unavoidable misplacement can be corrected daily in no long time. The experience of "open shelves" in such collections has been so favorable that their librarians have testified that the losses were insignificant when compared with the great public convenience resulting. But the difficulty and confusion arising from free handling of the books on shelves increases in the direct ratio of the size of the library, until, in an extensive collection, it reaches an intolerable result.

What is encountered continually in enforcing the rule of exclusion from shelves is the almost universal conceit that some reader is entitled to exemption from such a rule. Explain to him never so courteously that experience has proved that a library is thrown into confusion by such admission; that while he may be careful to replace every book handled in the same spot, nearly all readers are careless, and he will insist that he is the exception, and that he is always careful. That is human nature, the world over— to believe that one can do things better than any one else. But if such importunities prevail, the chances are that books will be misplaced by the very literary expert who has solemnly asserted his infallibility.

On the whole, open shelves may be viewed as an open question. It may be best for small libraries, as to all the books, and for all libraries as to some classes of books. But make it general, and order and arrangement are at an end, while chaos takes the place of cosmos. The real student is better served by the knowledge and aid of the librarian, thus saving his time for study, than he can be by ranging about dark shelves to find, among multitudes of books he does not want, the ones that he actually does want. The business of the librarian, and his highest use, is to bring the resources of the library to the reader. If this takes a hundred or more volumes a day, he is to have them; but to give him the right to throw a library into confusion by "browsing around," is to sacrifice the rights of the public to prompt service, to the whim of one man. Those who think that "browsing" is an education should reflect that it is like any other wandering employment, fatal to fixity of purpose. Like desultory reading of infinite periodicals, it tends rather to dissipate the time and the attention than to inform and strengthen the mind.

In libraries of wide circulation in America, many have open shelves, and many more free access to certain classes of books. The Newark Free Library opens all departments except fiction; others open fiction and current literature only. Some libraries, notably in England, have a "safe-guarded" open-shelf system, by which the public are given free range inside the library, while the librarians take post at the outside railing, to charge books drawn, and check off depredations. This method may be styled "every one his own librarian," and is claimed by its originators to work well.

At the Conference of the American Library Association in 1899, after discussion, votes were taken, showing 50 librarians in favor of free access to shelves for small libraries, as against only 10 for unrestricted access in large libraries.

The debate brought out curious and instructive facts as to losses of books where free range is allowed. The Denver Public Library lost in one year 955 volumes; the Buffalo Public Library 700 books in seventeen months; the Minneapolis, 300 in a year; and the St. Louis Public Library 1,062 volumes in two years, out of "a very limited open shelf collection." One librarian, estimating the loss of books at $1,000 worth in two years, said the library board were perfectly satisfied, and that "unless we lose $2,500 worth of books a year, the open-shelf system pays in its

saving of the expenses of attendance." It does not appear
to have occurred to them that a public library owes anything to the public morality, nor that a library losing its
books by the thousand, to save the cost of proper management, may be holding out a premium to wholesale robbery.

There is another precaution essential to be observed regarding the more costly and rare possessions of the library.
Such books should not be placed upon the shelves with the
ordinary books of the collection, but provided for in a repository under lock and key. In a large library, where
many hundred volumes of books of especial rarity and
value are to be found, a separate room should always exist
for this class of books. They will properly include (1) Incunabula, or early printed books; (2) Manuscripts, or
unique specimens, such as collections of autographs of notable people; (3) Illuminated books, usually written on
vellum, or printed in color; (4) Early and rare Americana,
or books of American discovery, history, etc., which are
scarce and difficult to replace; (5) Any books known to be
out of print; and (6) Many costly illustrated works which
should be kept apart for only occasional inspection by readers. Where no separate room exists for safe custody of
such treasures, they should be provided with a locked book-
case or cases, according to their number. When any of
these reserved books are called for, they should be supplied to readers under special injunctions of careful handling. Neglect of precaution may at any time be the means
of losing to the library a precious volume. It is easy for
an unknown reader who calls for such a rare or costly
work, to sign his ticket with a false name, and slip the book
under his coat when unobserved, and so leave the library
unchallenged. But the librarian or assistant who supplies
the book, if put on his guard by having to fetch it from a
locked repository, should keep the reader under observa-

tion, unless well known, until the volume is safely returned. Designing and dishonest persons are ever hovering about public libraries, and some of the most dangerous among them are men who know the value of books.

This class of reserved books should not be given out in circulation, under any circumstances. Not only are they subject to injury by being handled in households where there are children or careless persons, who soil or deface them, but they are exposed to the continual peril of fire, and consequent loss to the library. There are often books among these rarities, which money cannot replace, because no copies can be found when wanted. In the Library of Congress, there is a very salutary safe-guard thrown around the most valuable books in the form of a library regulation which provides that no manuscript whatever, and no printed book of special rarity and value shall be taken out of the library by any person. This restriction of course applies to Members of Congress, as well as to those officials who have the legal right to draw books from the library.

CHAPTER 12.

THE FACULTY OF MEMORY.

To every reader nothing can be more important than that faculty of the mind which we call memory. The retentive memory instinctively stores up the facts, ideas, imagery, and often the very language found in books, so clearly that they become available at any moment in after life. The tenacity of this hold upon the intellectual treasures which books contain depends largely upon the strength of the impression made upon the mind when reading. And this, in turn, depends much upon the force, clearness and beauty of the author's style or expression. A crude, or feeble, or wordy, redundant statement makes little impression, while a terse, clear, well-balanced sentence fixes the attention, and so fastens itself in the memory. Hence the books which are best remembered will be those which are the best written. Great as is the power of thought, we are often obliged to confess that the power of expression is greater still. When the substance and the style of any writing concur to make a harmonious and strong impression on the reader's mind, the writer has achieved success. All our study of literature tends to confirm the conviction of the supreme importance of an effective style.

We must set down a good memory as a cardinal qualification of the librarian. This faculty of the mind, in fact, is more important to him than to the members of any other profession whatever, because it is more incessantly drawn upon. Every hour in the day, and sometimes every minute in the hour, he has to recall the names of certain books, the authors of the same, including both their surnames and Christian or forenames, the subjects principally treated in them, the words of some proverb or quotation, or elegant extract in poetry or prose, the period of time of an author or other noted person, the standard measurements and weights in use, with their equivalents, the moneys of foreign nations and their American values, the time of certain notable events in history, whether foreign or American, ancient or modern, the names and succession of rulers, the prices of many books, the rules observed in the catalogue, both of authors and subjects, the names and schools of great artists, with their period, the meaning in various foreign languages of certain words, the geographical location of any place on the earth's surface, the region of the library in which any book is located—and, in short, an infinitude of items of information which he wants to know out of hand, for his own use, or in aid of Library readers or assistants. The immense variety of these drafts upon his memory seldom perplexes one who is well endowed with a natural gift in that direction. In fact, it seems actually true of such minds, that the more numerous the calls upon the memory, the more ready is the response.

The metaphysicians have spent many words in attempting to define the various qualities of the mind, and to account for a strong or a weak memory; but after all is said, we find that the surprising difference between different memories is unaccounted for; as unaccountable, indeed, as what differences the man of genius from the mere plodder. The principle of association of ideas is doubtless the leading element in a memory which is not merely verbal. We associate in our minds, almost instinctively, ideas of time, or space, or persons, or events, and these connect or compare one with another, so that

what we want is called up or recalled in memory, by a train
of endless suggestion.   We all have this kind of memory,
which may be termed the rational or ideal, as distinguished
from the verbal and the local memory.   The verbal memory is that which retains in the mind, and reproduces at
will what has been said in our hearing by others, or what
we have read which has made a marked impression upon
us.   Thus, some persons can repeat with almost exact
accuracy, every word of a long conversation held with
another.   Others can repeat whole poems, or long passages
in prose from favorite authors, after reading them over
two or three times, and can retain them perfectly in memory for half a century or more.   There have even been
persons to whom one single reading of any production was
sufficient to enable them to repeat it *verbatim*.   These instances of a great verbal memory are by no means rare,
although some of them appear almost incredible.   John
Locke tells us of the French philosopher Pascal, that he
never forgot anything of what he had done, said, or
thought, in any part of his natural life.   And the same
thing is recorded of that great scholar of Holland, Hugo
Grotius.

The mathematician Euler could repeat the Aeneid of
Virgil from beginning to end, containing nearly nine
thousand lines.   Mozart, upon hearing the *Miserere* of
Allegri played in the Sistine Chapel at Rome, only once,
went to his hotel, and wrote it all down from memory, note
for note.

Cardinal Mezzofanti both wrote and spoke thirty languages, and was quite familiar with more than a hundred.
He said that if he once heard the meaning of a word in any
language, he never forgot it.   Yet he was of the opinion,
that although he had twenty words for one idea, it was
better to have twenty ideas for one word; which is no

doubt true, so far as real intellectual culture is concerned. Lord Macaulay, who had a phenomenal memory, said that if all the copies of Milton's Paradise Lost were to be destroyed, he could reproduce the book complete, from memory. In early life he was a great admirer of Walter Scott's poetry, and especially the "Lay of the Last Minstrel", and could repeat the whole of that long poem, more than six hundred lines, from memory. And at the age of fifty-seven he records—"I walked in the portico, and learned by heart the noble fourth act of the Merchant of Venice. There are four hundred lines. I made myself perfect master of the whole in two hours." It was said of him that every incident he heard of, and every page he read, "assumed in his mind a concrete spectral form."

But the memory for names and words has been sometimes called the lowest form of memory. Persons of defective or impaired intellect frequently have strong and retentive verbal memories. Mrs. Somerville records the case of an idiot who could repeat a whole sermon *verbatim*, after once hearing it, but who was stupid and ignorant as to every thing else. And there are many instances in the books to the same effect.

Another kind of memory may be called, for want of a better name, the local memory. A person who has this strongly developed, if he once goes to a place, whether a room, or a street in a city, or a road in any part of the country, knows the way again, and can find it by instinct ever after. In the same way any one gifted with this almost unerring sense of locality, can find any book on any shelf in any part of a library where he has once been. He knows, in like manner, on which side of the page he saw any given passage in a book, which impressed him at the time, although he may never have had the volume in his hand more than once. He may not remember the number of the page, but he is sure of his recollection that it was the left or the right hand one, as the case may be, and this knowledge will abridge his labor and time in finding it again by just one half.   This local memory is invaluable to a librarian or an assistant in shortening the labor of finding things.   If you have a good local memory, you can, in no long time, come to dispense with the catalogue and its shelf-marks or classification marks, almost entirely, in finding your books.   Although this special gift of memory—the sense of locality—is unquestionably a lower faculty of the mind than some others named, and although there are illiterate persons who can readily find and produce any books in a library which have often passed through their hands, yet it is a faculty by no means to be despised.   It is one of the labor-saving, time-saving gifts, which should be welcomed by every librarian.   The time saved from searching the catalogues for location-marks of the outside of books, will enable him to make many a research in their inside.   This faculty, of course, is indefinitely strengthened and improved by use—and the same is true of the other branches of the sense which we call memory.   The oftener you have been to any place, the better you know the way.   The more frequently you have found and produced a given book from its proper receptacle, the easier and the quicker will be your finding it again.

Another faculty or phase of memory is found in the ability to call up the impression made by any object once seen by the eye, so as to reproduce it accurately in speech or writing.   This may be termed the intuitive memory. There are many applications or illustrations of this faculty. Thus, for example, you see a book on some shelf in your library.   You take in its size, its binding, both the material and the color, and its title as lettered on the back. All this you absorb with one glance of the eye.   You remember it by the principle of association—that is, you associate with that particular book, in connection with its title, a certain dimension, color, and style of binding. Now, when you have occasion to look up that special volume again, you not only go, aided by your memory of locality, to the very section and shelf of the library where it belongs, but you take with you instinctively, your memory or mental image of the book's appearance. Thus, you perhaps distinctly remember (1) that it was an octavo, and your eye in glancing along the shelf where it belongs, rejects intuitively all the duodecimos or books of lesser size, to come to the octavos. (2) Then you also remember that it was bound in leather, consequently you pass quickly by all the cloth bound volumes on the shelf. (3) in the third place you know that its color was red; and you pay no attention whatever to books of any other color, but quickly seize your red leather-bound octavo, and bear it off to the reading-room in triumph. Of course there are circumstances where this quick operation of the faculties of memory and intuition combined, would not be so easy. For example, all the books (or nearly all) on a given shelf might be octavos; or they might all be leather-bound; or a majority of them with red backs; and the presence of one or more of these conditions would eliminate one or more of the facilities for most rapidly picking out the book wanted. But take a pile of books, we will say returned by many readers, on the library counter. You are searching among them for a particular volume that is again wanted. There is no order or arrangement of the volumes, but you distinctly remember, from having handled it, its size both as to height and thickness, its color, and how it was bound. You know it was a thin 12mo. in green cloth binding. Do you, in your search, take up every book in that mass, to scrutinize its title, and see if it is the one you seek? By no means. You quickly thrust aside, one by one, or by the half-dozen, all the volumes which are not green, cloth-bound, thin duodecimos, without so much as glancing at them. Your special volume is quickly found among hundreds of volumes, and your faculty of memory and intuition has saved you perhaps a quarter of an hour of valuable time, which, without that faculty, might have been wasted in search.

Again, another circumstance which might intervene to diminish the frequency of application of the memory referred to, as to the physical features or appearance of a book sought for, is where the shelf-arrangement is alphabetical, by authors' names, or by the names of the subjects of the books, if it is an alphabet of biographies. Here, the surest and the quickest guide to the book is of course the alphabetical order, in which it must necessarily be found.

This memory of the aspect of any object once looked at, is further well illustrated in the very varied facilities for the spelling of words found in different persons. Thus, there are people who, when they once see any word (we will say a proper name) written or printed, can always afterwards spell that word unerringly, no matter how uncommon it may be. The mental retina, so to speak, receives so clear and exact an impression of the form of that word from the eye, that it retains and reproduces it at will.

But there are others, (and among them persons of much learning in some directions) upon whom the form or orthography of a word makes little or no impression, however frequently it meets the eye in reading. I have known several fine scholars, and among them the head of an institution of learning, who could not for the life of them spell correctly; and this infirmity extended even to some of the commonest words in the language. Why this inaptitude on the part of many, and this extraordinary facility on the part of others, in the memorizing faculty, is a phenomenon which may be noted down, but not solved. That vivid mental picture which is seen by the inward eye of the person favored with a good memory, is wholly wanting, or seen only dimly and rarely in the case of one who easily forgets.

So vital and important is memory, that it has been justly denominated by the German philosopher, Kant, "the most wonderful of our faculties." Without it, the words of a book would be unintelligible to us, since it is memory alone which furnishes us with the several meanings to be attached to them.

Some writers on the science of mind assert that there is no such thing with any of us as absolutely forgetting anything that has once been in the mind. All mental activities, all knowledge which ever existed, persists. We never wholly lose them, but they become faint and obscure. One mental image effaces another. But those which have thus disappeared may be recalled by an act of reminiscence. While it may sometimes be impossible to recover one of them at the moment when wanted, by an act of voluntary recollection, some association may bring it unexpectedly and vividly before us. Memory plays us many strange tricks, both when we wake and when we dream. It revives, by an involuntary process, an infinite variety of past scenes, faces, events, ideas, emotions, passions, conversations, and written or printed pages, all of which we may have fancied had passed forever from our consciousness.

The aids to memory supposed to be furnished by the various mnemonic systems may now be briefly considered. These methods of supplying the defects of a naturally weak memory, or of strengthening a fairly good one, are one and all artificial. This might not be a conclusive objection to them, were they really effective and permanent helps, enabling one who has learned them to recall with certainty ideas, names, dates, and events which he is unable to recall by other means. Theory apart, it is conceded that a system of memorizing which had proved widely or generally successful in making a good memory out of a poor one, would deserve much credit. But experience with these systems has as yet failed to show, by the stern test of practical utility, that they can give substantial (and still less permanent) aid in curing the defects of memory. Most of the systems of mnemonics that have been invented are constructed on the principle of locality, or of utilizing objects which appeal to the sight. There is nothing new in these methods, for the principle is as old as Simonides, who lived in the fifth century before Christ, and who devised a system of memorizing by locality. One of the most prevalent systems now taught is to select a number of rooms in a house (in the mind's eye, of course) and divide the walls and the floors of each room into nine equal parts or squares, three in a row. Then

"On the front wall—that opposite the entrance of the first room—are the units, on the right-hand wall the tens, on the left hand the twenties, on the fourth wall the thirties, and on the floor the forties. Numbers 10, 20, 30, and 40, each find a place on the roof above their respective walls. One room will thus furnish 50 places, and ten rooms as many as 500, while 50 occupies the centre of the roof. Having fixed these clearly in the mind, so as to be able readily and at once to tell the exact position of each place or number, it is then necessary to associate with each of them some familiar object (or symbol) so that the object being suggested, its place may be instantly remembered, or when the place is before the mind, its object may immediately spring up. When this has been done thoroughly, the objects can be run over in any order from beginning to end, or from end to beginning, or the place of any particular one can at once be given. All that is further necessary is to associate the ideas we wish to remember with the objects in the various places, by which means they are readily remembered, and can be gone over in any order. In this way, one may learn to repeat several hundred disconnected words or ideas in any order, after hearing them only once."

This rather complicated machinery for aiding the memory is quite too mechanical to commend itself to any one accustomed to reflect or to take note of his own mental processes. Such an elaborate system crowds the mind with a lot of useless furniture, and hinders rather than helps a rational and straightforward habit of memorizing. It too much resembles the feat of trying to jump over a wall by running back a hundred or more yards to acquire a good start or momentum. The very complication of the system is fitted to puzzle rather than to aid the memory. It is based on mechanical or arithmetical associations—not founded on nature, and is of very small practical utility. It does not strengthen or improve the habit of memorizing, which should always be based upon close attention, and a logical method of classifying, associating, and analyzing facts or ideas.

Lord Bacon, more than two centuries ago, wisely characterized mnemonic systems as "barren and useless." He wrote, "For immediately to repeat a multitude of names or words once repeated before, I esteem no more than rope-dancing, antic postures, and feats of activity; and, indeed, they are nearly the same thing, the one being the abuse of the bodily, as the other is of mental powers; and though they may cause admiration, they cannot be highly esteemed."

In fact, these mnemonical systems are only a kind of crutches, sometimes useful to people who cannot walk, but actual impediments to those having the use of their limbs, and who by proper exercise can maintain their healthy and natural use indefinitely.

I have given you an account of one of these artificial systems of memory, or systems of artificial memory, as you may choose to call them. There have been invented more than one hundred different systems of mnemonics, all professing to be invaluable, and some claiming to be infallible. It appears to be a fatal objection to these memory-systems that they substitute a wholly artificial association of ideas for a natural one. The habit of looking for accidental or arbitrary relations of names and things is cultivated, and the power of logical, spontaneous thought is injured by neglecting essential for unessential relations. These artificial associations of ideas work endless mischief by crowding out the natural ones.

How then, you may ask, is a weak memory to be strengthened, or a fairly good memory to be cultivated into a better one? The answer is, by constant practice, and for this the vocation of a librarian furnishes far more opportunities than any other. At the basis of this practice of the memory, lies the habit of attention. All memory depends upon the strength or vividness of the impression made upon the mind, by the object, the name, the word, the date, which is sought to be remembered. And this, in turn, depends on the degree of attention with which it was first regarded. If the attention was so fixed that a clear mental image was formed, there will be no difficulty in remembering it again. If, on the other hand, you were inattentive, or listless, or pre-occupied with other thoughts, when you encountered the object, your impression of it would be hazy and indistinct, and no effort of memory would be likely to recall it.

Attention has been defined as the fixing of the mind

intently upon one particular object, to the exclusion for a time, of all other objects soliciting notice. It is essential to those who would have a good memory, to cultivate assiduously the habit of concentration of thought. As the scattering shot hits no mark, so the scattering and random thoughts that sweep through an unoccupied brain lead to no memorable result, simply from want of attention or of fixation upon some one mental vision or idea. With your attention fastened upon any subject or object, you see it more clearly, and it impresses itself more vividly in the memory, as a natural consequence. Not only so, but its related objects or ideas are brought up by the principle of association, and they too make a deeper impression and are more closely remembered. In fact, one thing carefully observed and memorized, leads almost insensibly to another that is related to it, and thus the faculty of association is strengthened, the memory is stimulated, and the seeds of knowledge are deeply planted in that complex organism which we call the mind. This power of attention, of keeping an object or a subject steadily in view until it is absorbed or mastered, is held by some to be the most distinctive element in genius. Most people have not this habit of concentration of the mind, but allow it to wander aimlessly on, flitting from subject to subject, without mastering any; but then, most people are not geniuses. The habit to be cultivated is that of thinking persistently of only one thing at a time, sternly preventing the attention from wandering.

It may be laid down as an axiom that the two cornerstones of memory are attention and association. And both of these must act in harmony, the habit of fixed attention being formed or guided by the will, before a normal or retentive memory becomes possible. What is called cultivating the memory, therefore, does not mean anything more than close attention to whatever we wish to remember, with whatever associations naturally cling to it, until it is actually mastered. If one has not an instinctive or naturally strong memory, he should not rest satisfied with letting the days go by until he has improved it. The way to improve it, is to begin at the foundation, and by the constant exercise of the will-power, to take up every subject with fixed attention, and one at a time, excluding every other for the time being. There is no doubt whatever that the memory is capable of indefinite improvement; and though one's first efforts in that direction may prove a disappointment, because only partially successful, he should try, and try again, until he is rewarded with the full fruits of earnest intellectual effort, in whatever field. He may have, at the start, instead of a fine memory, what a learned professor called, "a fine forgettery," but let him persevere to the end. None of us were made to sit down in despair because we are not endowed with an all-embracing memory, or because we cannot "speak with the tongues of men and of angels," and do not know "all mysteries and all knowledge." It rather becomes us to make the best and highest use, day by day, of the talents that are bestowed upon us, remembering that however short of perfection they may be, we are yet far more gifted than myriads of our fellow-creatures in this very imperfect world.

There is no question that the proper cultivation of the memory is, or ought to be, the chief aim of education. All else is so dependent upon this, that it may be truly affirmed that, without memory, knowledge itself would be impossible. By giving up oneself with fixed attention to what one seeks to remember, and trusting the memory, though it may often fail, any person can increase his powers of memory and consequently of learning, to an indefinite degree. To improve and strengthen the memory, it must be constantly exercised. Let it be supplied with new knowledge frequently, and called on daily to reproduce it. If remembered only imperfectly or in part, refresh it by reference to the source whence the knowledge came; and repeat this carefully and thoroughly, until memory becomes actually the store-house of what you know on that subject. If there are certain kinds of facts and ideas which you more easily forget than others, it is a good way to practice upon them, taking up a few daily, and adding to them by degrees. Dr. W. T. Harris, the United States Commissioner of Education, gave his personal experience to the effect that he always found it hard to remember dates. He resolved to improve a feeble memory in this respect by learning the succession of English Kings, from William the Conqueror, down to Victoria. With his characteristic thoroughness, he began by learning three or four dates of accession only, the first day; two new ones were added the second day; then one new king added the third day; and thereafter even less frequency was observed in learning the chronology. By this method he had the whole table of thirty-six sovereigns learned, and made familiar by constant review. It had to be learned anew one year after, and once again after years of neglect. But his memory for dates steadily grew, and without conscious effort, dates and numbers soon came to be seized with a firmer grasp than before. This kind of memory, he adds, now improves or increases with him from year to year. Here is an instance of cultivation of memory by a notable scholar, who adds a monition to learners with weak memories, not to undertake to memorize too much at once. Learning a succession of fifty names slowly, he says, will so discipline the memory for names, as to partially or even permanently remove all embarrassment from that source. I may add that a long table of names or dates, or any prolonged extract in verse or prose, if learned by repeating it over and over as a whole, will be less tenaciously retained in memory, than if committed in parts.

The highest form of memory is actually unconscious, *i. e.*, that in which what we would recall comes to us spontaneously, without effort or lapse of time in thinking about it. It is this kind of memory that has been possessed by all the notable persons who have been credited with knowing everything, or with never forgetting anything. It is not to be reckoned to their credit, so much as to their good fortune. What merit is there in having a good memory, when one cannot help remembering?

There is one caution to be given to those who are learning to improve a memory naturally weak. When such a one tries to recall a date, or name, or place, or idea, or book, it frequently happens that the endeavor fails utterly. The more he tries, the more obstinately the desired object fails to respond. As the poet Pope wrote about the witless author:

> "You beat your pate, and fancy wit will come;
> Knock as you please, there's nobody at home."

In these cases, no attempt to force the memory should be made, nor should the attention be kept long on the subject, for this course only injures the faculty, and leads to confusion of mind. To persist in a constantly baffled effort to recover a word, or other forgotten link in memory, is a laborious attempt which is itself likely to cause failure, and induce a distrust of the memory which is far from rational. The forgotten object will probably recur in no long time after, when least expected.

Much discursive reading is not only injurious to the faculty of memory, but may be positively destructive of it. The vast extent of our modern world of reviews, magazines and newspapers, with their immense variety of subjects, dissipates the attention instead of concentrating it, and becomes fatal to systematic thought, tenacious memory, and the acquirement of real knowledge. The mind that is fed upon a diet of morning and evening newspapers, mainly or solely, will become flabby, uncertain, illogical, frivolous, and, in fact, little better than a scatterbrains. As one who listens to an endless dribble of small talk lays up nothing out of all the palaver, which, to use a common phrase, "goes in at one ear, and out at the other," so the reader who continuously absorbs all the stuff which the daily press, under the pretext of "printing the news," inflicts upon us, is nothing benefited in intellectual gifts or permanent knowledge. What does he learn by his assiduous pursuit of these ephemeral will o' the wisps, that only "lead to bewilder, and dazzle to blind?" He absorbs an incredible amount of empty gossip, doubtful assertions, trifling descriptions, apocryphal news, and some useful, but more useless knowledge. The only visible object of spending valuable time over these papers appears to be to satisfy a momentary curiosity, and then the mass of material read passes almost wholly out of the mind, and is never more thought of. Says Coleridge, one of the foremost of English thinkers: "I believe the habit of perusing periodical works may be properly added to the catalogue of anti-mnemonics, or weakeners of the memory."

If read sparingly, and for actual events, newspapers have a value which is all their own; but to spend hours upon them, as many do, is mere mental dissipation.

CHAPTER 18.

Qualifications of a Librarian.

In directing attention to some of the more important elements which should enter into the character and acquirements of a librarian, I shall perhaps not treat them in the order of their relative importance. Thus, some persons might consider the foremost qualification for one aspiring to the position of a librarian to be wide knowledge in literature and science: others would say that the possession of sound common sense is above all things essential; others an excellent and retentive memory; still others might insist that business habits and administrative faculty are all-important; and others again, a zeal for learning and for communicating it to others.

I shall not venture to pronounce what, among the multitude of talents that are requisite to constitute a good librarian is the most requisite. Suffice it to say, that all of them which I shall notice are important, and that the order of their treatment determines nothing as to which are more and which are less important. So much is expected of librarians that it actually appears as if a large portion of the public were of the opinion that it is the duty of him who has a library in charge to possess himself, in some occult or mysterious way, unknown to the common mind, of all the knowledge which all the books combine.

The Librarian of the British Museum, speaking to a conference of librarians in London, quoted a remark of Pattison, in his "Life of Casaubon," that "the librarian who reads is lost." This was certainly true of that great scholar Casaubon, who in his love for the contents of the

(242)

books under his charge, forgot his duties as a librarian. And it is to a large degree true of librarians in general, that those who pursue their own personal reading or study during library hours do it at the expense of their usefulness as librarians. They must be content with such snatches of reading as come in the definite pursuit of some object of research incident to their library work, supplemented by such reading time as unoccupied evenings, Sundays, and annual vacations may give them.

Yet nothing is more common than for applicants for the position of librarians or assistant librarians to base their aspiration upon the foolish plea that they are "so fond of reading", or that they "have always been in love with books." So far from this being a qualification, it may become a disqualification. Unless combined with habits of practical, serious, unremitting application to labor, the taste for reading may seduce its possessor into spending the minutes and the hours which belong to the public, in his own private gratification. The conscientious, the useful librarian, living amid the rich intellectual treasures of centuries, the vast majority of which he has never read, must be content daily to enact the part of Tantalus, in the presence of a tempting and appetizing banquet which is virtually beyond his reach.

But he may console himself by the reflection that comparatively few of the books upon his shelves are so far worth reading as to be essential. "If I had read as many books as other men," said Hobbes of Malmesbury, "I should have been as ignorant as they."

If the librarian, in the precious time which is indisputably his, reads a wise selection of the best books, the masterpieces of the literature of all lands, which have been consecrated by time and the suffrages of successive generations of readers, he can well afford to apply to the rest, the

short-hand method recommended in a former chapter, and
skim them in the intervals of his daily work, instead of
reading them.   Thus he will become sufficiently familiar
with the new books of the day (together with the information about their contents and merits furnished by the literary reviews, which he must read, however sparingly, in
order to keep up with his profession) to be able to furnish
readers with some word of comment as to most books coming into the Library.   This course, or as close an approximation to it as his multifarious duties will permit, will go
far to solve the problem that confronts every librarian who
is expected to be an exponent of universal knowledge.
Always refraining from unqualified praise of books (especially of new ones) always maintaining that impartial attitude toward men and opinions which becomes the librarian, he should act the part of a liberal, eclectic, catholic guide to inquirers of every kind.

And here let me emphasize the great importance to every
librarian or assistant of early learning to make the most
of his working faculties.   He cannot afford to plod along
through a book, sentence by sentence, like an ordinary
reader.   He must learn to read a sentence at a glance.
The moment his eye lights upon a title-page he should be
able to take it all in by a comprehensive and intuitive
mental process.   Too much stress cannot be laid upon the
every-day habit or method of reading.   It makes all the
difference between time saved, and time wasted; between
efficiency and inefficiency; between rapid progress and
standing still, in one's daily work.   No pains should be
spared, before entering upon the all-engrossing work of a
library, to acquire the habit of rapid reading.   An eminent
librarian of one of the largest libraries was asked whether
he did not find a great deal of time to read?   His reply
was—"I wish that I could ever get as much as one hour

a day for reading—but I have never been able to do it."
Of course every librarian must spend much time in special
researches; and in this way a good deal of some of his days
will be spent in acquainting himself with the resources of
his library; but this is incidental and not systematic reading.

In viewing the essential qualifications of a librarian, it
is necessary to say at the outset that a library is no place
for uneducated people. The requirements of the position
are such as to demand not only native talent above the
average, but also intellectual acquirements above the average. The more a librarian knows, the more he is worth,
and the converse of the proposition is equally true, that the
less he knows the less he is worth. Before undertaking
the arduous task of guiding others in their intellectual pursuits, one should make sure that he is himself so well-
grounded in learning that he can find the way in which to
guide them. To do this, he must indispensably have something more than a smattering of the knowledge that lies at
the foundation of his profession. He must be, if not widely
read, at least carefully grounded in history, science, literature, and art. While he may not, like Lord Bacon, take
all knowledge to be his province, because he is not a Lord
Bacon, nor if he were, could he begin to grasp the illimitable domain of books of science and literature which have
been added to human knowledge in the two centuries and
a half since Bacon wrote, he can at least, by wise selection,
master enough of the leading works in each field, to make
him a well-informed scholar. That great treasury of information on the whole circle of the sciences, and the
entire range of literature, the Encyclopaedia Britannica,
judiciously studied, will alone give what would appear to
the average mind, a very liberal education.

One of the most common and most inconsiderate questions propounded to a librarian is this: "Do you ever expect to read all these books through?" and it is well answered by propounding another question, namely—"Did *you* ever read your dictionary through?" A great library is the scholar's dictionary—not to be read through, but to enable him to put his finger on the fact he wants, just when it is wanted.

A knowledge of some at least of the foreign languages is indispensable to the skilled librarian. In fact, any one aspiring to become an assistant in any large library, or the head of any small one, should first acquire at least an elementary knowledge of French and Latin. Aside from books in other languages than English which necessarily form part of every considerable library, there are innumerable quotations or words in foreign tongues scattered through books and periodicals in English, which a librarian, appealed to by readers who are not scholars, would be mortified if found unable to interpret them. The librarian who does not understand several languages will be continually at a loss in his daily work. A great many important catalogues, and bibliographies, essential parts of the equipment of a library, will be lost to him as aids, and he can neither select foreign books intelligently nor catalogue them properly. If he depends upon the aid of others more expert, his position will be far from agreeable or satisfactory. How many and what foreign languages should be learned may be matter for wide difference of opinion. But so far-reaching is the prevalence of the Latin, as one of the principal sources of our own language, and of other modern tongues, that a knowledge of it is most important. And so rich is the literature of France, to say nothing of the vast number of French words constantly found in current English and American books and periodicals, that at least a fairly thorough mastery of that language should be acquired. The same may be said of the German, which is even more important in some parts of the United States, and which has a literature most copious and valuable in every varied department of knowledge. With these three tongues once familiar, the Italian, Spanish, Portuguese, Dutch, and Scandinavian languages may be, through the aid of dictionaries, so far utilized as to enable one to read titles and catalogue books in any of them, although a knowledge of all, so as to be able to read books in them, is highly desirable.

In the Boston Public Library, the assistants are required to possess an adequate knowledge of Latin, French, and German. And all candidates for positions in the reading-room of the British Museum Library must undergo a thorough test examination as to their knowledge of the Latin language. Opportunities for acquiring foreign languages are now so abundant that there is small excuse for any one who wants to know French, Latin or German, and yet goes through life without learning them. There are even ways of learning these languages with sufficient thoroughness for reading purposes without a teacher, and sometimes without a text-book. Two assistant librarians taught themselves French and German in their evenings, by setting out to read familiar works of English fiction in translations into those languages, and soon acquired a good working knowledge of both, so as to be able to read any work in either, with only occasional aid from the dictionary for the less common words. It is surprising how soon one can acquire a sufficient vocabulary in any language, by reading any of its great writers. A good way for a beginner to learn French without a master is to take a French New Testament, and read the four Gospels through. After doing this three or four times, almost any one who is at all familiar with the Scriptures, will be able

to read most books in the French language with facility.
In the great art of learning, all doors are easily unlocked—
by those who have the key.

It should go without saying that the librarian should
possess a wide knowledge of books. This knowledge should
include (1) an acquaintance with ancient and modern literature, so as to be able to characterize the notable writers
in each of the leading languages of the world; (2) a knowledge of history extensive enough to enable him to locate
all the great characters, including authors, in their proper
century and country; (3) a knowledge of editions, so as to
discriminate between the old and the new, the full and
the abridged, the best edited, best printed, etc.; (4) an
acquaintance with the intrinsic value or the subject and
scope of most of the great books of the world; (5) a knowledge of commercial values, so as to be able to bid or to buy
understandingly, and with proper economy; (6) a familiar-
ity with what constitutes condition in library books, and
with binding and repairing processes, for the restoration
of imperfect volumes for use.

The librarian should be one who has had the benefit of
thorough preliminary training, for no novice is qualified to
undertake the role of an expert, and any attempt to do so
can result only in disappointment and failure. No one
who has read little or nothing but novels since leaving
school need ever hope to succeed.

No librarian can know too much, since his work brings
him into relation with the boundless domain of human
knowledge. He should not be a specialist in science (except in the one science of bibliography) but must be content with knowing a little about a great many things, rather
than knowing everything about one thing. Much converse
with books must fill him with a sense of his own ignorance.
The more he comes to know, the wider will open before

him the illimitable realm of what is yet to be known.   In the lowest deep which research the most profound can reach, there is a lower deep still unattained—perhaps, even, unattainable.   But the fact that he cannot by any possibility master all human knowledge should not deter the student from making ever advancing inroads upon that domain.   The vast extent of the world of books only emphasizes the need of making a wise selection from the mass. We are brought inevitably back to that precept by every excursion that we make into whatever field of literature.

The librarian should possess, besides a wide acquaintance with books, a faculty of administration, and this rests upon careful business habits.   He should have a system in all the library work.   Every assistant should have a prescribed task, and be required to learn and to practice all the methods peculiar to library economy, including the economy of time.   Each day's business should be so organized as to show an advance at the end.   The library must of course have rules, and every rule should be so simple and so reasonable that it will commend itself to every considerate reader or library assistant.   All questions of doubt or dispute as to the observance of any regulation, should be decided at once, courteously but firmly, and in a few words.   Nothing can be more unseemly than a wrangle in a public library over some rule or its application, disturbing readers who are entitled to silence, and consuming time that should be given to the service of the public.

When Thomas Carlyle, one of the great scholars of modern times, testified in 1848 before a Parliamentary Commission upon the British Museum Library, he thus spoke of the qualifications of a librarian:

"All must depend upon the kind of management you get within the library itself.   You must get a good pilot to steer the ship, or you will never get into the harbor.   You must have a man to direct who knows well what the duty is that he has to do, and who is determined to go through that, in spite of all clamor raised against him; and who is not anxious to obtain approbation, but is satisfied that he will obtain it by and by, provided he acts ingenuously and faithfully."

Another quality most important in a librarian is an even temper. He should be always and unfailingly courteous, not only to scholars and visitors of high consideration, but to every reader, however humble or ignorant, and to every employee, however subordinate in position. There is nothing which more detracts from one's usefulness than a querulous temper. Its possessor is seldom happy himself, and is the frequent cause of unhappiness in others. Visitors and questions should never be met with a clouded brow. A cheerful "good-morning" goes a great way oftentimes. Many library visitors come in a complaining mood —it may be from long waiting to be served, or from mistake in supplying them with the wrong books, or from errors in charging their accounts, or from some fancied neglect or slight, or from any other cause. The way to meet such ill-humored or offended readers is to gently explain the matter, with that "soft answer which turneth away wrath." Many a foolish and useless altercation may thus be avoided, and the complainant restored to cheerfulness, if not to courtesy; whereas, if the librarian were to meet the case with a sharp or haughty answer, it would probably end without satisfaction on either side. Whatever you do, never permit yourself to be irritable, and resolve never to be irritated. It will make you unhappy, and will breed irritation in others. Cheerfulness under all circumstances, however difficult, is the duty and the interest of the librarian. Thus he will cultivate successfully an obliging disposition, which is a prime requisite to his success with the public and his usefulness as a librarian.

It ought not to be requisite to insist upon good health as a condition precedent for any one aspiring to be a librarian. So very much depends upon this, that it should form a part of the conscientious duty of every one to acquire and maintain a sound condition of physical health, as a most important adjunct of a thoroughly sound and healthy condition of the mind. This is easier than most persons are aware. If we except inherited constitutional weaknesses, or maladies of a serious character, there is almost no one who is not able by proper diet, regimen, and daily exercise, to maintain a degree of health which will enable him to use his brain to its full working capacity. It demands an intelligent and watchful care of the daily regimen, so that only simple and wholesome food and drink may be taken into the system, and what is equally important, adequate sleep, and habitual moderate exercise. No one can maintain perfect health without breathing good unadulterated air, and exercising in it with great frequency. One's walks to and from the library may be sufficient to give this, and it is well to have the motive of such a walk, since exercise taken for the mere purpose of it is of far less value. The habit of taking drugs, or going to a doctor for every little malady, is most pernicious. Every one, and especially a librarian, who is supposed (however erroneously) to know everything, should know more of his own constitution than any physician. With a few judicious experiments in daily regimen, and a little abstinence now and then, he can subdue head-aches, catarrhs and digestive troubles, and by exercising an intelligent will, can generally prevent their recurrence. If one finds himself in the morning in a state of languor and lassitude, be sure he has abused some physical function, and apply a remedy.

An invalid will make a poorly equipped librarian. How can a dyspeptic who dwells in the darkness of a disease, be a guiding light to the multitudes who beset him every hour? There are few callings demanding as much mental and physical soundness and alertness as the care of a public library.

Sound common sense is as essential to the librarian as sound health. He should always take the practical straightforward view of every item of library business and management, remembering that the straight road is always the shortest way between two points. While he may be full of ideas, he should be neither an idealist nor a dreamer. In library methods, the cardinal requisites to be aimed at, are utility and convenience. A person of the most perfect education, and the highest literary attainments, but destitute of common sense, will not succeed in the conduct of a library. That intuitive judgment, which sees the reason of everything at a glance, and applies the proper agencies to the case in hand, is wanting in his composition. Multitudes of emergencies arise in library service, where the prompt and practical sense of the librarian is required to settle a dispute, adjust a difficulty, or to direct what is to be done in some arrangement or re-arrangement of books, or some library appliance or repair. In such cases, the unpractical or impracticable man will be very likely to decide wrongly, choosing the inconvenient method instead of the convenient, the more costly instead of the more economical, the laborious in place of the obvious and easy; in short, some way of doing the work or settling the difficulty which will not permit it to stay settled, or will require the work to be done over again. The man of common-sense methods, on the other hand, will at once see the end from the beginning, anticipate every difficulty, and decide upon the proper course without trouble or hesitation, finding his judgment fully vindicated by the result.

The librarian in whom the quality of common sense is well developed will be ever ready to devise or to accept improvements in library methods. Never a slave to "red tape," he will promptly cut it wherever and whenever it stands in the way of the readiest service of books and information to all comers.

Another quality which every librarian or assistant in a library should possess is a thorough love of his work. He should cherish a noble enthusiasm for the success and usefulness of the institution with which he has chosen to be associated. Nor should this spirit be by any means limited to the literary and scientific aid which he is enabled to extend to others, nor to the acquisition of the knowledge requisite to meet the endless inquiries that are made of him. He should take as much interest in restoring a broken binding, or in seeing that a torn leaf is repaired, as in informing a great scholar what the library contains upon any subject.

No one who is listless or indifferent in the discharge of daily duties is fit for a place in a public library. There should be an *esprit de corps*, a zeal for his profession, which will lead him to make almost any sacrifice of outside interests to become proficient in it. Thus only will he render himself indispensable in his place, and do the greatest amount of service to the greatest number of readers. I have seen employees in libraries so utterly careless of what belongs to their vocation, as to let books, totally unfit for use, ragged or broken, or with plates loosened, ready to drop out and disappear, go back to the shelves unrepaired, to pursue the downward road toward destruction. And I have been in many libraries in which the books upon the shelves exhibited such utter want of care, such disarrangement, such tumbling about and upside-down chaos, and such want of cleanliness, as fairly to make one's heart ache. In some cases this may have been due in great part to unwise free admission of the public to the shelves, and consequent inevitable disorder; in others, it may be partially excused by the librarian's absolute want of the needful help or time, to keep the library in order; but in others, it was too apparent that the librarian in charge took no interest in the condition of the books. Too many librarians (at least of the past, however it may now be) have been of the class described by Dr. Poole, the Chicago librarian. He said that library trustees too often appeared to think that anybody almost would do for a librarian; men who have failed in everything else, broken-down clergymen, or unsuccessful teachers, and the like.

Passing now to other needful qualifications of librarians and library assistants, let me say that one of the foremost is accuracy. Perhaps I have before this remarked that exact accuracy is one of the rarest of human qualities. Even an approximation to it is rare, and absolute accuracy is still rarer. Beware of the person who is sure of every thing—who retails to you a conversation he has heard, affecting to give the exact words of a third person, or who quotes passages in verse or in prose, with glib assurance, as the production of some well-known writer. The chances are ten to one that the conversation is mainly manufactured in the brain of the narrator, and that the quotation is either not written by the author to whom it is attributed, or else is a travesty of his real language. It is Lord Byron who tells of that numerous class of sciolists whom one finds everywhere—

"With just enough of learning to misquote."

The books one reads abound in erroneous dates, mistaken names, garbled extracts, and blundering quotations.

So much the more important is it to the librarian, who is so continually drawn upon for correct information upon every subject, to make sure of his facts, before communicating them. When (as frequently happens) he has no way of verifying them, he should report them, not as his own conclusions, but on the authority of the book or periodical where found. This will relieve him of all responsibility, if they turn out to be erroneous. Whenever I find a wrong date or name in a printed book, or an erroneous reference in the index, or a mis-spelled word, I always pencil the correct date, or name, or page of reference in the margin. This I do as a matter of instinct, as well as of duty, for the benefit of future inquirers, so that they may not be misled. I speak here of errors which are palpable, or of the inaccuracy of which I have positive knowledge; if in doubt, I either let the matter go entirely, or write a query in pencil at the place, with the presumed correct substitute appended.

Never be too sure of what you find in books; but prove all things and hold fast to those only which you find to be beyond dispute. Thus will you save yourself from falling into many errors, and from recanting many opinions. It is the method of ordinary education to take everything for granted; it is the method of science to take nothing for granted.

I may refer here to another rule always to be observed, and pertaining to the theme of strict accuracy in your daily work. That is, the necessity of carefully examining every piece of work you may have done, before it leaves your hands, for the purpose of correcting errors. All of us are not only liable to make mistakes, but all of us do make them; and if any one has a conceit of his own accuracy, the surest way to take it out of him is to let him serve an ap-

prenticeship in some library, where there is competent revision of all the labor performed. There are multitudes of
assistants in libraries who cannot write a letter, even,
without making one or more errors. How often do
you leave out a word in your writing experience, which
may change the meaning of a whole sentence? So, in
writing titles, whether for the catalogue, or for a library order, or for the information of some inquirer, you
are liable to make errors of date, or edition, or place of
publication, or size, or to misplace or omit or substitute
some word in the description of the book. There is nothing in the world quite so easy as to be mistaken: and
the only remedy (and it is an all-essential one) is to go
over every line and every word of what you have written,
before it leaves your hands. As second thoughts are pro-
verbially best, so a second careful glance over a piece
of writing will almost always reveal some error or omission to be corrected. Think of the mortification you
must feel at finding an unverified piece of work returned
upon your hands, with several glaring mistakes marked
by the reviser! Think, on the other hand, of the inward satisfaction experienced when you have done your
best, written and revised your own work, and found it always passed as perfect. I have tried many persons by
many tests, and while I have found a great number who
were industrious, intelligent, zealous, conscientious, good-
tempered, and expeditious, I have found scarcely one who
was always accurate. One of the rarest things in a library
is to find an assistant who has an unerring sense of the
French accents. This knowledge, to one expert in that
language, even if he does not speak it, should be as intuitive as the art of spelling correctly, either in English
or French. He should write the proper accent over a

letter just as infallibly as he writes the proper letters in a word. But, strange to say, it is very common, even with good French scholars (in the book-sense or literary sense of scholarship) to find them putting the acute accent for the grave over a vowel, or the grave instead of the acute, or omitting the circumflex accent entirely, and so on.

Every one commits errors, but the wise man is he who learns by his mistakes, and applies the remedy. The best remedy (as I said in the case of memory in another chapter,) is to cultivate a habit of trained attention in whatever we do. Yet many people (and I am afraid we must say most people) go on through life, making the same blunders, and repeating them. It appears as if the habit of inaccuracy were innate in the human race, and only to be reformed by the utmost painstaking, and even with the aid of that, only by a few. I have had to observe and correct such numberless errors in the work of well-educated, adult, and otherwise accomplished persons, as filled me with despair. Yet there is no more doubt of the improvability of the average mind, however inaccurate at the start, than of the power of the will to correct other bad habits into which people unconsciously fall.

One of the requisites of a successful librarian is a faculty of order and system, applied throughout all the details of library administration. Without these, the work will be performed in a hap-hazard, slovenly manner, and the library itself will tend to become a chaos. Bear in mind the great extent and variety of the objects which come under the care of the librarian, all of which are to be classified and reduced to order. These include not only books upon every earthly subject (and very many upon unearthly ones) but a possibly wide range of newspapers and periodicals, a great mass of miscellaneous pamphlets, sometimes of maps and charts, of manuscripts and broadsides, and frequently

collections of engravings, photographs, and other pictures,
all of which come in to form a part of most libraries. This
great complexity of material, too, exhibits only the physical aspect of the librarian's labors. There are, besides, the
preparation, arrangement and continuation of the catalogue, in its three or more forms, the charging and credit-
ing of the books in circulation, the searching of many book
lists for purchases, the library bills and accounts, the supervision and revision of the work of assistants, the library
correspondence, often requiring wide researches to answer
inquiries, the continual aid to readers, and a multitude of
minor objects of attention quite too numerous to name.
Is it any over-statement of the case to say that the librarian
who has to organize and provide for all this physical and
intellectual labor, should be systematic and orderly in a
high degree?

That portion of his responsibile task which pertains to
the arrangement and classification of books has been elsewhere treated. But there is required in addition, a faculty of arranging his time, so as to meet seasonably the
multifarious drafts upon it. He should early learn not
only the supreme value of moments, but how to make all
the library hours fruitful of results. To this end the time
should be apportioned with careful reference to each department of library service. One hour may be set for revising one kind of work of assistants; another for a different one; another for perusing sale catalogues, and marking
desiderata to be looked up in the library catalogue; another
for researches in aid of readers or correspondents; still another for answering letters on the many subjects about
which librarians are constantly addressed; and still another
for a survey of all the varied interests of the library and its
frequenters, to see what features of the service need
strengthening, what improvements can be made, what

errors corrected, and how its general usefulness can be increased. So to apportion one's time as to get out of the day (which is all too short for what is to be done in it) the utmost of accomplishment is a problem requiring much skill, as well as the ability to profit by experience. One has always to be subject to interruptions—and these must be allowed for, and in some way made up for. Remember, when you have lost valuable time with some visitor whose claims to your attention are paramount, that when to-morrow comes one should take up early the arrears of work postponed, and make progress with them, even though unable to finish them.

Another suggestion; proper system in the management and control of one's time demands that none of it be absorbed by trifles or triflers; and so every librarian must indispensably know how to get rid of bores. One may almost always manage to effect this without giving offense, and at the same time without wasting any time upon them, which is the one thing needful. The bore is commonly one who, having little or nothing to do, inflicts himself upon the busy persons of his acquaintance, and especially upon the ones whom he credits with knowing the most—to wit, the librarians. Receive him courteously, but keep on steadily at the work you are doing when he enters. If you are skilful, you can easily do two things at once, for example, answer your idler friend or your bore, and revise title-cards, or mark a catalogue, or collate a book, or look up a quotation, or write a letter, at the same time. Never lose your good humor, never say that your time is valuable, or that you are very busy; never hint at his going away; but never quit your work, answer questions cheerfully, and keep on, allowing nothing to take your eyes off your business. By and by he will take the hint, if not wholly pachydermatous, and go away of his own accord. By pursuing this course I have saved infinite time, and got rid of infinite bores, by one and the same process.

The faculty of organizing one's work is essential, in order to efficiency and accomplishment. If you do not have a plan and adhere to it, if you let this, that, and the other person interrupt you with trifling gossip, or unnecessary requests, you will never get ahead of your work; on the contrary, your work will always get ahead of you. The same result will follow if you interrupt yourself, by yielding to the temptation of reading just a page or a paragraph of something that attracts your eye while at work. This dissipation of time, to say nothing of its unfair appropriation of what belongs to the library, defeats the prompt accomplishment of the work in hand, and fosters the evil habit of scattering your forces, in idleness and procrastination.

It ought not to be needful to urge habits of neatness and the love of order upon candidates for places in libraries. How much a neat and carefully arranged shelf of books appeals to one's taste, I need not say, nor urge the point how much an orderly and neatly kept room, or desk, or table adds to one's comfort. The librarian who has the proper spirit of his calling should take pains to make the whole library look neat and attractive, to have a place for everything, and everything in its place. This, with adequate space existing, will be found easier than to have the books and other material scattered about in confusion, thus requiring much more time to find them when wanted. A slovenly-kept library is certain to provoke public criticism, and this always tells to the disadvantage of the librarian; while a neatly kept, carefully arranged collection of books is not only pleasing to the eye, but elicits favorable judgment from all visitors.

Among the qualities that should enter into the composition of a successful librarian must be reckoned an inexhaustible patience. He will be sorely tried in his endeavors to satisfy his own ideals, and sometimes still more sorely in his efforts to satisfy the public. Against the mistakes and short-comings of assistants, the ignorance of many readers, and the unreasonable expectations of others, the hamperings of library authorities, and the frequently unfounded criticisms of the press, he should arm himself with a patience and equanimity that are unfailing. When he knows he is right, he should never be disturbed at complaint, nor suffer a too sensitive mood to ruffle his feelings. When there is any foundation for censure, however slight, he should learn by it and apply the remedy. The many and varied characters who come within the comprehensive sphere of the librarian necessarily include people of all tempers and dispositions, as well as of every degree of culture. To be gracious and courteous to all is his interest as well as his duty. With the ignorant he will often have to exercise a vast amount of patience, but he should never betray a supercilious air, as though looking down upon them from the height of his own superior intelligence. To be always amiable toward inferiors, superiors, and equals, is to conciliate the regard of all. Courtesy costs so little, and makes so large a return in proportion to the investment, that it is surprising not to find it universal. Yet it is so far from being so that we hear people praising one whose manners are always affable, as if he were deserving of special credit for it, as an exception to the general rule. It is frequently observed that a person of brusque address or crusty speech begets crustiness in others. There are subtle currents of feeling in human intercourse, not easy to define, but none the less potent in effect. A person of marked suavity of speech and bearing radiates about him an atmosphere of good humor, which insensibly influences the manners and the speech of others.

There will often come into a public library a man whose whole manner is aggressive and over-bearing, who acts and talks as if he had a right to the whole place, including the librarian. No doubt, being a citizen, he has every right, except the right to violate the rules—or to make himself disagreeable. The way to meet him is to be neither aggressive, nor submissive and deferential, but with a cool and pleasant courtesy, ignoring any idea of unpleasant feeling on your part. You will thus at least teach a lesson in good manners, which may or may not be learned, according to circumstances and the hopeful or hopeless character of the pupil.

Closely allied to the virtue of patience, is that of unfailing tact. This will be found an important adjunct in the administration of a public library. How to meet the innumerable inquiries made of him with just the proper answer, saying neither too much, nor too little, to be civil to all, without needless multiplication of words, this requires one to hold his faculties well in hand, never to forget himself, and to show that no demand whatever can vex or fluster him. The librarian should know how, or learn how to adapt himself to all readers, and how to aid their researches without devoting much time to each. This requires a fine quality of tact, of adapting one's self quickly to the varied circumstances of the case in hand. One who has it well developed will go through the manifold labors and interviews and annoyances of the day without friction, while one who is without tact will be worried and fretted until life seems to him a burden.

Need I mention, after all that has been said of the exacting labors that continually wait upon the librarian, that he should be possessed both of energy and untiring industry? By the very nature of the calling to which he is dedicated, he is pledged to earnest and thorough work in it. He cannot afford to be a trifler or a loiterer on the way, but must push on continually. He should find time for play, it is true, and for reading for his own recreation and instruction, but that time should be out of library hours. And a vigilant and determined economy of time in library hours will be found a prime necessity. I have dwelt elsewhere upon the importance of choosing the shortest methods in every piece of work to be accomplished. Equally important is it to cultivate economy of speech, or the habit of condensing instructions to assistants, and answers to inquiries into the fewest words. A library should never be a circumlocution office. The faculty of condensed expression, though somewhat rare, can be cultivated.

In the relations existing between librarian and assistants there should be mutual confidence and support. All are equally interested in the credit and success of the institution which engages their services, and all should labor harmoniously to that end. Loyalty to one's employers is both the duty and the interest of the employed: and the reciprocal duty of faithfulness to those employed, and interest in their improvement and success should mark the intercourse of the librarian with his assistants. He should never be too old nor too wise to learn, and should welcome suggestions from every intelligent aid. I have suggested the importance of an even temper in the relations between librarians and readers; and it is equally important as between all those associated in the administration of a library. Every one has faults and weaknesses; and those encountered in others will be viewed with the most charity by those who are duly conscious of their own. Every one makes mistakes, and these are often provoking or irritating to one who knows better; but a mild and pleasant explanation of the error is far more likely to lead to amendment, than a sharp reproof, leaving hard feeling or bitterness behind. Under no circumstances is peevishness or passion justifiable. Library assistants in their bearing toward each other, should suppress all feelings of censoriousness, fault-finding or jealousy, if they have them, in favor of civility and good manners, if not of good fellowship. They are all public servants engaged in a common cause, aiming at the enlightenment and improvement of the community; they should cherish a just pride in being selected for this great service, and to help one another in every step of the work, should be their golden rule. Everything should be done for the success and usefulness of the library, and all personal considerations should be merged in public ones.

Turning now to what remains of suggestion regarding the qualities which should enter into the character, or form a part of the equipment of a librarian, let me urge the importance of his possessing a truly liberal and impartial mind. It is due to all who frequent a public library to find all those in charge ready and willing to aid their researches in whatever direction they may lie. Their attitude should be one of constant and sincere open-mindedness. They are to remember that it is the function of the library to supply the writings of all kinds of authors, on all sides of all questions. In doing this, it is no part of a librarian's function to interpose any judgments of his own upon the authors asked for. He has no right as a librarian to be an advocate of any theories, or a propagandist of any opinions. His attitude should be one of strict and absolute impartiality. A public library is the one common property of all, the one neutral ground where all varieties of character, and all schools of opinion meet and mingle. Within its hallowed precincts, sacred to literature and science, the voice of controversy should be hushed. While the librarian may and should hold his own private opinions with firmness and entire independence, he should keep them private—as regards the frequenters of the library. He may, for example, be profoundly convinced of the truth of the Christian religion; and he is called on, we will suppose, for books attacking Christianity, like Thomas Paine's "Age of Reason," or Robert G. Ingersoll's lectures on "Myth and Miracle." It is his simple duty to supply the writers asked for, without comment, for in a public library, Christian and Jew, Mahometan and Agnostic, stand on the same level of absolute equality. The library has the Koran, and the Book of Mormon, as well as the Scriptures of the Old and New Testament, and one is to be as freely supplied as the other. A library is an institution of universal range— of encyclopaedic knowledge, which gathers in and dispenses to all comers, the various and conflicting opinions of all writers upon religion, science, politics, philosophy, and sociology. The librarian may chance to be an ardent Republican or a zealous Democrat; but in either case, he should show as much alacrity in furnishing readers with W. J. Bryan's book "The First Battle," as with McKinley's speeches, or the Republican Hand-Book. A library is no place for dogmatism; the librarian is pledged, by the very nature of his profession, which is that of a dispenser of all knowledge—not of a part of it—to entire liberality, and absolute impartiality. Remembering the axiom that all errors may be safely tolerated, while reason is left free to combat them, he should be ever ready to furnish out of the intellectual arsenal under his charge, the best and strongest weapons to either side in any conflict of opinion.

It will have been gathered from what has gone before, in recapitulation of the duties and responsibilities of the librarian's calling, that it is one demanding a high order of talent. The business of successfully conducting a public library is complex and difficult. It is full of never-ending detail, and the work accomplished does not show for what it is really worth, except in the eyes of the more thoughtful and discerning observers.

I may here bring into view some of the drawbacks and discouragements incident to the librarian's vocation, together with an outline of the advantages which belong to it.

In the first place, there is little money in it. No one who looks upon the acquisition of money as one of the chief aims of life, should think for a moment of entering on a librarian's career. The prizes in the profession are few—so few indeed, as to be quite out of the question for most aspirants. The salaries paid in subordinate positions are very low in most libraries, and even those of head-librarians are not such that one can lay up money on them. A lady assistant librarian in one city said she had found that one of a librarian's proper qualifications was to be able to live on two meals a day. This doubtless was a humorous exaggeration, but it is true that the average salaries hitherto paid in our public libraries, with few exceptions, do not quite come up to those of public school teachers, taking the various grades into account. Most of the newly formed libraries are poor, and have to be economical. But there is some reason to hope that as libraries multiply and their unspeakable advantages become more fully appreciated, the standard of compensation for all skilled librarians will rise. I say skilled, because training and experience are the leading elements which command the better salaries, in this, as in other professions.

Another drawback to be recognized in the librarian's calling, is that there are peculiar trials and vexations connected with it. There are almost no limits to the demands made upon the knowledge and the time of the librarian. In other professions, teaching for example, there are prescribed and well-defined routines of the instruction to be given, and the teacher who thoroughly masters this course, and brings the pupils through it creditably, has nothing to do beyond. The librarian, on the other hand, must be, as it were, a teacher of all sciences and literatures at once. The field to be covered by the wants of readers, and the inquiries that he is expected to answer, are literally illimitable. He cannot rest satisfied with what he has already learned, however expert or learned he may have become; but he must keep on learning forevermore. The new books that are continually flooding him, the new sciences or new developments of old ones that arise, must be so far assimilated that he can give some account of the scope of all of them to inquiring readers.

In the third place, there are special annoyances in the service of a public, which includes always some inconsiderate and many ignorant persons, and these will frequently try one's patience, however angelic and forbearing. So, too, the short-comings of library assistants or associates may often annoy him, but as all these trials have been before referred to, it may be added that they are not peculiar to library service, but are liable to occur in the profession of teaching or in any other.

In the next place, the peculiar variety and great number of the calls incessantly made upon the librarian's knowledge, constitute a formidable draft upon any but the strongest brain. There is no escape from these continual drafts upon his nervous energy for one who has deliberately chosen to serve in a public library. And he will sometimes find, wearied as he often must be with many cares and a perfect flood of questions, that the most welcome hour of the day is the hour of closing the library.

Another of the librarian's vexations is frequently the interference with his proper work by the library authorities. Committees or trustees to oversee the management and supervise expenditures are necessary to any public library. Sometimes they are quick-sighted and intelligent persons, and recognize the importance of letting the librarian work out everything in his own way, when once satisfied that they have got a competent head in charge. But there are sometimes men on a board of library control who are self-conceited and pragmatical, thinking that they know everything about how a library should be managed, when in fact, they are profoundly ignorant of the first rudiments of library science. Such men will sometimes overbear their fellows, who may be more intelligent, but not so self-asserting, and so manage as to overrule the best and wisest plans, or the most expedient methods, and vex the very soul of the librarian. In such cases the only remedy is patience and tact. Some day, what has been decided wrongly may be reversed, or what has been denied the librarian may be granted, through the conversion of a minority of the trustees into a majority, by the gentle suasion and skilful reasoning of the librarian.

There are other drawbacks and discomforts in the course of a librarian's duties which have been referred to in dealing with the daily work under his charge. There remains the fact that the profession is no bed of roses, but a laborious and exacting calling, the price of success in which is an unremitting industry, and energy inexhaustible. But these will not appear very formidable requisites to those who have a native love of work, and it is a fact not to be doubted that work of some kind is the only salvation of every human creature.

Upon the whole, if the calling of the librarian involves many trials and vexations, it has also many notable compensations. Foremost among these is to be reckoned the fact that it opens more and wider avenues to intellectual culture than any other profession whatever. This comes in a two-fold way: first, through the stimulus to research given by the incessant inquiries of readers, and by the very necessity of his being, as a librarian; and secondly, by the rare facilities for investigation and improvement supplied by the ample and varied stores of the library always immediately at hand. Other scholars can commonly command but few books, unless able to possess a large private library: their reasearches in the public one are hampered by the rule that no works of reference can be withdrawn, and that constitutes a very large and essential class, constantly needed by every scholar and writer. The librarian, on the other hand, has them all at his elbow.

In the next place, there are few professions which are in themselves so attractive as librarianship. Its tendency is both to absorb and to satisfy the intellectual faculties. No where else is the sense of continual growth so palpable; in no other field of labor is such an enlargement of the bounds of one's horizon likely to be found. Compare it with the profession of teaching. In that, the mind is chained down to a rigorous course of imparting instruction in a narrow and limited field. One must perforce go on rehearsing the same rudiments of learning, grinding over the same Latin gerunds, hearing the same monotonous recitations, month after month, and year after year. This continual threshing over of old straw has its uses, but to an ardent and active mind, it is liable to become very depressing. Such a mind would rather be kept on the *qui vive* of activity by a volley of questions fired at him every hour in a library, than to grind forever in an intellectual treadmill, with no hope of change and very little of relief. The very variety of the employments which fill up the library hours, the versatility required in the service, contributes to it a certain zest which other professions lack.

Again, the labors of the librarian bring him into an intimate knowledge of a wide range of books, or at least an acquaintance with authors and titles far more extensive than can be acquired by most persons. The reading of book catalogues is a great and never-ending fascination to one who has a love for books. The information thus acquired of the mighty range of the world's literature and science is of inestimable value. Most of it, if retained in a retentive memory, will enable its possessor to answer multitudes of the questions continually put to the librarian.

Then, too, the service of a public library is a valuable school for the study of human nature. One comes in contact with scholars, men of business, authors, bright young people, journalists, professional men and cultured women, to an extent unequaled by the opportunities of any other calling. This variety of intercourse tends to broaden one's sympathies, to strengthen his powers of observation, to cultivate habits of courtesy, to develop the faculty of adapting himself to all persons—qualities which contribute much to social interest and success. The discipline of such an intercourse may sometimes make out of a silent and bashful recluse, a ready and engaging adept in conversation, able to command the attention and conciliate the regard of all. Farther than this, one brought into so wide a circle of communication with others, cannot fail to learn something from at least some among them, and so to receive knowledge as well as to impart it. The curious and diverse elements of character brought out in such intercourse will make their impress, and may have their value. All these many facilities for intellectual intercourse both with books and with men, contribute directly to keep the librarian in contact with all the great objects of human interest. They supply an unfailing stimulus to his intellectual and moral nature. They give any active-minded person rare facilities, not only for the acquisition, but for the communication of ideas. And there is one avenue for such communication that is peculiarly open to one whose mind is stored with the ripe fruits of reading and observation. I mean the field of authorship—not necessarily the authorship of books, but of writing in the form of essays, reviews, lectures, stories or contributions to the periodical press. There are in every community literary societies, clubs, and evening gatherings, where such contributions are always in demand, and always welcomed, in exact proportion to their inherent interest and value. Such avenues for the communication of one's thought are of great and sometimes permanent advantage. The knowledge which we acquire is comparatively barren, until it is shared with others. And whether this be in an appreciative circle of listeners, or in the press, it gives a certain stimulus and reward to the thinker and writer, which nothing else can impart. To convey one's best thought to the world is one of the purest and highest of intellectual pleasures.

Let me add that there are two sides to the question of authorship, as concerns librarians. On the one hand, their advantages for entering that field are undoubtedly superior, both from the ready command of the most abundant material, and from experience in its use. On the other hand, while authorship may be said to be the most besetting temptation of the librarian, it is one that should be steadily resisted whenever it encroaches on the time and attention due to library duties. If he makes it a rule to write nothing and to study nothing for his own objects during library hours, he is safe. Some years since it was a common subject of reproach regarding the librarians of

several university libraries in England that they were so
engaged in writing books, that no scholar could get at them
for aid in his literary researches.   The librarians and assistants employed in the British Museum Library, where
the hours of service are short, have found time to produce
numerous contributions to literature.   Witness the works,
as authors and editors, of Sir Henry Ellis, Antonio Panizzi, Dr. Richard Garnett, Edward Edwards, J. Winter
Jones, Thomas Watts, George Smith, and others.   And
in America, the late Justin Winsor was one of the most
prolific and versatile of authors, while John Fiske, once
assistant librarian at Harvard, Reuben A. Guild, William
F. Poole, George H. Moore, J. N. Larned, Frederick Saun-
ders and others have been copious contributors to the
press.

In a retrospective view of what has been said in respect
to the qualifications of a librarian, it may appear that I
have insisted upon too high a standard, and have claimed
that he should be possessed of every virtue under heaven.
I freely admit that I have aimed to paint the portrait of
the ideal librarian; and I have done it in order to show
what might be accomplished, rather than what has been
accomplished.   To set one's mark high—higher even than
we are likely to reach, is the surest way to attain real excellence in any vocation.   It is very true that it is not
given to mortals to achieve perfection: but it is none the
less our business to aim at it, and the higher the ideal, the
nearer we are likely to come to a notable success in the
work we have chosen.

Librarianship furnishes one of the widest fields for the
most eminent attainments.   The librarian, more than any
other person whatever, is brought into contact with those
who are hungering and thirsting after knowledge.   He
should be able to satisfy those longings, to lead inquirers

in the way they should go, and to be to all who seek his assistance a guide, philosopher and friend. Of all the pleasures which a generous mind is capable of enjoying, that of aiding and enlightening others is one of the finest and most delightful. To learn continually for one's self is a noble ambition, but to learn for the sake of communicating to others, is a far nobler one. In fact, the librarian becomes most widely useful by effacing himself, as it were, in seeking to promote the intelligence of the community in which he lives. One of the best librarians in the country said that such were the privileges and opportunities of the profession, that one might well afford to live on bread and water for the sake of being a librarian, provided one had no family to support.

There is a new and signally marked advance in recent years, in the public idea of what constitutes a librarian. The old idea of a librarian was that of a guardian or keeper of books—not a diffuser of knowledge, but a mere custodian of it. This idea had its origin in ages when books were few, were printed chiefly in dead languages, and rendered still more dead by being chained to the shelves or tables of the library. The librarian might be a monk, or a professor, or a priest, or a doctor of law, or theology, or medicine, but in any case his function was to guard the books, and not to dispense them. Those who resorted to the library were kept at arm's length, as it were, and the fewer there were who came, the better the grim or studious custodian was pleased. Every inquiry which broke the profound silence of the cloistered library was a kind of rude interruption, and when it was answered, the perfunctory librarian resumed his reading or his studies. The institution appeared to exist, not for the benefit of the people, but for that of the librarian; or for the benefit, besides, of a few sequestered scholars, like himself, and any wide popular use of it would have been viewed as a kind of profanation.

We have changed all that in the modern world, and library service is now one of the busiest occupations in the whole range of human enterprise. One cannot succeed in the profession, if his main idea is that a public library is a nice and easy place where one may do one's own reading and writing to the best advantage. A library is an intellectual and material work-shop, in which there is no room for fossils nor for drones. My only conception of a useful library is a library that is used—and the same of a librarian. He should be a lover of books—but not a book-worm. If his tendencies toward idealism are strong, he should hold them in check by addicting himself to steady, practical, every-day work. While careful of all details, he should not be mastered by them. If I have sometimes seemed to dwell upon trifling or obvious suggestions as to temper, or conduct, or methods, let it be remembered that trifles make up perfection, and that perfection is no trifle.

I once quoted the saying that "the librarian who reads is lost"; but it would be far truer to say that the librarian who does not read is lost; only he should read wisely and with a purpose. He should make his reading helpful in giving him a wide knowledge of facts, of thoughts, and of illustrations, which will come perpetually in play in his daily intercourse with an inquiring public.

CHAPTER 14.

SOME OF THE USES OF LIBRARIES.

Let us now consider the subject of the uses of public libraries to schools and those connected with them. Most town and city libraries are supported, like the free schools, by the public money, drawn from the tax-payers, and supposed to be expended for the common benefit of all the people. It results that one leading object of the library should be to acquire such a collection of books as will be in the highest degree useful to all. And especially should the wants of the younger generation be cared for, since they are always not only nearly one half of the community, but they are also to become the future citizens of the republic. What we learn in youth is likely to make a more marked and lasting impression than what we may acquire in later years. And the public library should be viewed as the most important and necessary adjunct of the school, in the instruction and improvement of the young. Each is adapted to supply what the other lacks. The school supplies oral instruction and public exercises in various departments of learning; but it has few or no books, beyond the class text-books which are used in these instructions. The library, on the other hand, is a silent school of learning, free to all, and supplying a wide range of information, in books adapted to every age. It thus supplements, and in proportion to the extent and judicious choice of its collections, helps to complete that education, which the school falls short of. In this view, we see the great importance of making sure that the public library has not only a full supply of the best books in every field, avoiding (as previously urged) the bad or the inferior ones, but also that it has the best juvenile and elementary literature in ample supply. This subject of reading for the young has of late years come into unprecedented prominence. Formerly, and even up to the middle of our century, very slight attention was paid to it, either by authors or readers. Whole generations had been brought up on the New England Primer, with its grotesque wood-cuts, and antique theology in prose and verse, with a few moral narratives in addition, as solemn as a meeting-house, like the "Dairyman's Daughter," the "History of Sandford and Merton," or "The Shepherd of Salisbury Plain." Very dreary and melancholy do such books appear to the frequenters of our modern libraries, filled as they now are with thousands of volumes of lively and entertaining juvenile books.

The transition from the old to the new in this class of literature was through the Sunday-school and religious tract society books, professedly adapted to the young. While some of these had enough of interest to be fairly readable, if one had no other resource, the mass were irredeemably stale and poor. The mawkishness of the sentiment was only surpassed by the feebleness of the style. At last, weary of the goody-goody and artificial school of juvenile books, which had been produced for generations, until a surfeit of it led to something like a nausea in the public mind, there came a new type of writers for the young, who at least began to speak the language of reason. The dry bones took on some semblance of life and of human nature, and boys and girls were painted as real boys and genuine girls, instead of lifeless dolls and manikins. The reformation went on, until we now have a world of books for the young to choose from, very many of which are fresh and entertaining.

But the very wealth and redundancy of such literature

is a new embarrassment to the librarian, who must indispensably make a selection, since no library can have or ought to have it all. Recurring to the function of the public library as the coadjutor of the school, let us see what classes of books should form essential parts of its stores.

1. As geography, or an account of the earth on which we live, is a fundamental part of education, the library should possess a liberal selection of the best books in that science. The latest general gazetteer of the world, the best modern and a good ancient atlas, one or more of the great general collections of voyages, a set of Baedeker's admirable and inexpensive guide books, and descriptive works or travels in nearly all countries—those in America and Europe predominating—should be secured. The scholars of all grades will thus be able to supplement their studies by ready reference, and every part of the globe will lie open before them, as it were, by the aid of the library.

2. The best and latest text-books in all the sciences, as geology, chemistry, natural history, physics, botany, agriculture, mechanic arts, mathematics, mental and moral science, architecture, fine arts, music, sociology, political science, etc., should be accessible.

3. Every important history, with all the latest manuals or elementary books in general and national history should be found.

4. The great collections of biography, with separate lives of all noted characters, should be provided.

5. Dictionaries, cyclopaedias, statistical annuals, and other books of reference will be needed in abundance.

6. A small but select number of approved works in law, medicine, and theology should be embraced in the library.

7. I need not add that the poets and novelists should be well represented, as that goes without saying in all popular libraries.

And special attention should be paid to building up a collection of the best books for juvenile readers, such as have passed the ordeal of good critical judgment among the librarians, as eminently fit to be read.   There are several useful catalogues of such reading, as: Caroline M. Hewins' "Books for the Young," G. E. Hardy's "Five Hundred Books for the Young," and the admirable "List of Books for Girls and Women" by Augusta H. Leypoldt and Geo. Iles, contributed to by many experts, and copiously supplied with notes describing the scope and quality of the books.   The last two are published by the Library Bureau.

With this broad equipment of the best books in every field, and vigilance in constant exercise to add fresh stores from the constantly appearing and often improved text-books in every science, the library will be a treasury of knowledge both for teachers and pupils in the schools. And the fact should not be overlooked, that there will be found as much growth for teachers as for scholars in such a collection of books.   Very few teachers, save those of well-furnished minds and of much careful reading, are competent to guide their scholars into the highways and byways of knowledge, as the librarian should be able to do.

To establish a relation of confidence and aid with teachers is the preliminary step to be taken in order to make the library at once practically useful to them and to their scholars.   In case there are several public schools in charge of a general superintendent, that officer should be first consulted, and tendered the free aid of the library and its librarian for himself and the teachers.   In some public libraries, the school superintendent is made an *ex officio* member of the library board.   Then suitable regulations should be mutually agreed upon, fixing the number of books to be drawn on account of the schools at any one time, and the period of return to the library.   It is most usual to charge such books on teachers' cards, or account, to fix responsibility, although the teachers loan them to the scholars at their option.

In places where there are no school libraries proper, the public library will need to provide a goodly number of duplicates, in order to meet the special school demand. This, however, will usually be of low-priced rather than costly books, as the elementary text-books do not draw heavily upon library funds.

A very attractive feature in providing books for the young is the large number of illustrated books now available to all libraries. All the kingdoms of nature are depicted in these introductory manuals of science, rendering its pursuit more interesting, and cultivating the habits of observation of form and of proportion, in the minds of the young. Pupils who have never accomplished anything in school have been roused by interest in illustrated natural histories to take an eager interest in learning all about birds and animals. This always leads on and up to other study, since the mind that is once awakened to observation and to thought, needs only a slight guidance to develop an unappeasable hunger for finding out all about things.

The ancient maxim that "it is only the first step that costs" is especially true in the great art of education. It matters little what it is that first awakens the intellect— the great fact is that it is awakened, and sleeps no more thenceforward. A mottled bird's egg, found on the way to school, excites the little finder to ascertain the name of the bird that laid it. The school or the teacher supplies no means of finding out, but the public library has books upon birds, with colored plates of their eggs, and an eager search ensues, until the young student is rewarded by finding the very bird, with its name, plumage, habits, size, and season, all described. That child has taken an enormous step forward on the road to knowledge, which will never be forgotten.

Instances might be multiplied indefinitely of such valuable aids to research, afforded by libraries, all along the innumerable roads travelled by students of every age in search of information. One of the most profitable of school exercises is to take up successively the great men and notable women of the past, and, by the effective and practical aid of the libraries, to find out what is best worth knowing about Columbus, Franklin, Walter Scott, Irving, Prescott, Bancroft, Longfellow, Hawthorne, Whittier, Emerson, Lowell, Victor Hugo, or others too numerous to name. Reading Longfellow's Evangeline will lead one to search out the history and geography of Acadia, and so fix indelibly the practical facts concerned, as well as the imagery of a fine poem. So in the notable events of history, if a study is made of the English Commonwealth, or the French Revolution, or the war between the United States and England in 1812-15, the library will supply the student with copious materials for illustration.

Not alone in the fields of science, history, and biography, but in the attractive fields of literature, also, can the libraries aid and supplement the teachings of the school. A fine poem, or a simple, humorous, or pathetic story, told with artless grace or notable literary skill, when read aloud by a teacher in school, awakens a desire in many to have the same book at home to read, re-read, and perhaps commit to memory the finer passages. What more inspiring or pleasing reading than some of Longfellow's poems, or the Vicar of Wakefield, or Milton's L' Allegro and Il Penseroso, or Saintine's Picciola, or selections from the poems of Holmes, Whittier, Kipling, or Lowell? For all these and similar wants, the library has an unfailing supply.

As a practical illustration of the extensive use of books by schools in some advanced communities, I may note that Librarian Green, of the Worcester (Mass.) Public Library, said in 1891 that his average daily account of the books loaned to schools in two busy winter months showed over 1,600 volumes thus in daily use. This too, was in addition to all that were drawn out by pupils on their own independent cards as borrowers. Such a record speaks volumes.

In the same city, where the Massachusetts State Normal School is located, sixty-four per cent. of the scholars visited the library to look up subjects connected with their studies.

A forcible argument for librarians taking an interest in reading for schools is that both parents and teachers often neglect to see that the young get only proper books to read. The children are themselves quite ignorant what to choose, and if left to themselves, are likely to choose unwisely, and to read story papers or quite unimproving books. Their parents, busied as they are, commonly give no thought to the matter, and are quite destitute of that knowledge of the various classes of books which it is the province of the librarian to know and to discriminate. Teachers themselves do not possess this special knowledge, except in rare instances, and have to become far more conversant with libraries than is usual, in order to acquire it.

That the very young, left to themselves, will choose many bad or worthless books is shown in the account of a principal of a school in San Francisco, who found that sixty per cent of the books drawn from the public library by pupils had been dime novels, or other worthless literature. The wide prevalence of the dime novel evil appeared in the report of the reading of 1,000 boys in a western New York city. Out of this number, 472 (or nearly one-half) were in the habit of devouring this pernicious

trash, procured in most cases by purchase at the news
stands.   The matter was taken up by teachers, and, by wise
direction and by aid of the public library, the reading of
these youthful candidates for citizenship was led into more
improving fields.   To lead a mind in the formative stage
from the low to the high, from tales of wild adventure to
the best stories for the young, is by no means difficult.
Take a book that you know is wholesome and entertaining,
and it will be eagerly read by almost every one.   There is
an endless variety of good books adapted to the most rudi-
mentary capacity.   Even young minds can become interested in the works of standard writers, if the proper selection is made.   Wonderful is the stimulus which the reading of a purely written, fascinating book gives to the young
mind.   It opens the way for more books and for infinite
growth.   All that is needed is to set the youth in the right
direction, and he will go forward with rapid strides of his
own accord.   This teaching how to read is really the most
profitable part of any education.   To recite endless lessons
is not education: and one book eagerly read through, has
often proved more valuable than all the text-books that
ever were printed.

THE USES OF THE LIBRARY TO THE UNIVERSITY.

Closely allied to the benefits derived from the library by
the teachers and scholars in public schools are its uses to all
those engaged in the pursuit of higher education.   For our
colleges and universities and their researches, the library
must have all that we have suggested as important for the
schools, and a great deal more.   The term university implies an education as broad as the whole world of books
can supply: yet we must here meet with limitations that
are inevitable.   In this country we have to regret the application of the word "university" to institutions where

the training is only academical, or at the highest, collegiate. The university, properly speaking, is an institution for the most advanced scholars or graduates of our colleges. Just as the college takes up and carries forward the training of those who have been through the academy, the seminary, or the high school, so it is the function of the university to carry forward (we will not say complete) the education of the graduate of the college. No education is ever completed: the doctor who has received the highest honors at the university has only begun his education—for that is to go on through life—and who knows how far beyond?

Now the aid which a well equipped library can furnish to all these higher institutions of learning, the academy, the seminary, the college, and the university, is quite incalculable. Their students are constantly engaged upon themes which not only demand the text-books they study, but collateral illustrations almost without number. The professors, too, who impart instruction, perpetually need to be instructed themselves, with fuller knowledge upon the themes they are daily called upon to elucidate. There is no text-book that can teach all, or anywhere near all there is upon the subject it professes to cover. So the library, which has many books upon that subject, comes in to supply its deficiencies. And the librarian is useful to the professors and students just in proportion as he knows, not the contents, but the range of books upon each subject sought to be investigated. Here is where the subject catalogue, or the dictionary catalogue, combining the subjects and the authors under a single alphabet, comes into play. But, as no catalogue of subjects was ever yet up to date in any considerable library, the librarian should be able to supplement the catalogue by his own knowledge of later works in any line of inquiry.

The most profitable studies carried on in libraries are,

beyond all question, what we may term topical researches. To pursue one subject though many authorities is the true way to arrive at comprehensive knowledge. And in this kind of research, the librarian ought to be better equipped than any who frequent his library. Why? Simply because his business is bibliography; which is not the business of learned professors, or other scholars who visit the library.

The late Librarian Winsor said that he considered the librarian's instruction far more valuable than that of the specialist. And this may be owing largely to the point of view, as well as to the training, of each. The specialist, perhaps, is an enthusiast or a devotee to his science, and so apt to give undue importance to the details of it, or to magnify some one feature: the librarian, on the other hand, who is nothing if not comprehensive, takes the larger view of the wide field of literature on each subject, and his suggestions concerning sources of information are correspondingly valuable.

In those constantly arising questions which form the subjects of essays or discussions in all institutions of learning, the well-furnished library is an unfailing resource. The student who finds his unaided mind almost a blank upon the topic given out for treatment, resorts at once to the public library, searches catalogues, questions the librarian, and surrounds himself with books and periodicals which may throw light upon it. He is soon master of facts and reasonings which enable him to start upon a train of thought that bears fruit in an essay or discourse. In fact, it may be laid down as an axiom, that nearly every new book that is written is indebted to the library for most of its ideas, its facts, or its illustrations, so that libraries actually beget libraries.

Some of the endlessly diversified uses of a well-equipped

library, not only to scholars but to the general public, may here be referred to. Among the most sought for sources of information, the periodical press, both of the past and the current time, holds a prominent rank. When it is considered how far-reaching are the fields embraced in the wide range of these periodicals, literary, religious, scientific, political, technical, philosophical, social, medical, legal, educational, agricultural, bibliographical, commercial, financial, historical, mechanical, nautical, military, artistic, musical, dramatic, typographical, sanitary, sporting, economic, and miscellaneous, is it any wonder that specialists and writers for the press seek and find ready aid therein for their many-sided labors?

To the skeptical mind, accustomed to undervalue what does not happen to come within the range of his pet idols or pursuits, the observation of a single day's multifold research in a great library might be in the nature of a revelation. Hither flock the ever-present searchers into family history, laying under contribution all the genealogies and town and county histories which the country has produced. Here one finds an industrious compiler intent upon the history of American duels, for which the many files of Northern and Southern newspapers, reaching back to the beginning of the century, afford copious material. At another table sits a deputation from a government department, commissioned to make a record of all notable strikes and labor troubles for a series of years, to be gleaned from the columns of the journals of leading cities.

An absorbed reader of French romances sits side by side with a clergyman perusing homilies, or endeavoring to elucidate, through a mass of commentators, a special text. Here are to be found ladies in pursuit of costumes of every age; artists turning over the great folio galleries of Europe for models or suggestions; lawyers seeking precedents or leading cases; journalists verifying dates, speeches, conventions, or other forgotten facts; engineers studying the literature of railways or machinery; actors or amateurs in search of plays or works on the dramatic art; physicians looking up biographies of their profession or the history of epidemics; students of heraldry after coats of arms; inventors searching the specifications and drawings of patents; historical students pursuing some special field in American or foreign annals; scientists verifying facts or citations by original authorities; searchers tracing personal residences or deaths in old directories or newspapers; querists seeking for the words of some half-remembered passage in poetry or prose, or the original author of one of the myriad proverbs which have no father; architects or builders of houses comparing hundreds of designs and models; teachers perusing works on education or comparing text-books new or old; readers absorbing the great poems of the world; writers in pursuit of new or curious themes among books of antiquities or folk-lore; students of all the questions of finance and economic science; naturalists seeking to trace through many volumes descriptions of species; pursuers of military or naval history or science; enthusiasts venturing into the occult domains of spiritualism or thaumaturgy; explorers of voyages and travels in every region of the globe; fair readers, with dreamy eyes, devouring the last psychological novel; devotees of musical art perusing the lives or the scores of great composers; college and high-school students intent upon "booking up" on themes of study or composition or debate; and a host of other seekers after suggestion or information in a library of encyclopedic range.

CHAPTER 15.

The History of Libraries.

The Library, from very early times, has enlisted the enthusiasm of the learned, and the encomiums of the wise. The actual origin of the earliest collection of books (or rather of manuscripts) is lost in the mists of remote antiquity. Notwithstanding professed descriptions of several libraries found in Aulus Gellius, Athenaeus, and others, who wrote centuries after the alleged collections were made, we lack the convincing evidence of eye-witnesses and contemporaries. But so far as critical research has run, the earliest monuments of man which approached collections of written records are found not in Europe, but in Africa and Asia.

That land of wonders, Egypt, abounds in hieroglyphic inscriptions, going back, as is agreed by modern scholars, to the year 2000 before the Christian era. A Papyrus manuscript, too, exists, which is assigned to about 1600 B. C. And the earliest recorded collection of books in the world, though perhaps not the first that existed, was that of the Egyptian king Ramses I.—B. C. 1400, near Thebes, which Diodorus Siculus says bore the inscription "Dispensary of the soul." Thus early were books regarded as remedial agents of great force and virtue.

But before the library of Ramses the Egyptian king, there existed in Babylonia collections of books, written not on parchment, nor on the more perishable papyrus, but on clay. Whole poems, fables, laws, and hymns of the gods have been found, stamped in small characters upon baked bricks. These clay tablets or books were arranged in numerical order, and the library at Agane, which existed about 2000 B. C. even had a catalogue, in which each piece of literature was numbered, so that readers had only to write down the number of the tablet wanted, and the librarian would hand it over. Two of these curious poems in clay have been found intact, one on the deluge, the other on the descent of Istar into Hades.

The next ancient library in point of time yet known to us was gathered in Asia by an Assyrian King, and this collection has actually come down to us, *in propria persona*. Buried beneath the earth for centuries, the archaeologist Layard discovered in 1850 at Nineveh, an extensive collection of tablets or tiles of clay, covered with cuneiform characters, and representing some ten thousand distinct works or documents. The Assyrian monarch Sardanapalus, a great patron of letters, was the collector of this primitive and curious library of clay. He flourished about 1650 B. C.

In Greece, where a copious and magnificent literature had grown up centuries before Christ, Pisistratus collected a library at Athens, and died B. C. 527. When Xerxes captured Athens, this collection, which represents the earliest record of a library dedicated to the public, was carried off to Persia, but restored two centuries later. The renowned philosopher Aristotle gathered one of the largest Greek libraries, about 350 B. C. said to have embraced about 1400 volumes, or rather, rolls. Plato called Aristotle's residence "the house of the reader." This library, also, was carried off to Scepsis, and later by the victorious Sulla to Rome. History shows that the Greek collections were the earliest "travelling libraries" on record, though they went as the spoils of war, and not to spread abroad learning by the arts of peace.

Rome having conquered Athens, we hear no more of the Athenian libraries, but the seat of ancient learning was transferred to Alexandria, where were gathered under the liberal sway of the Ptolemies, more books than had ever been assembled together in any part of the world. Marc Antony presented to Cleopatra the library of the Kings of Pergamus, said to have contained 200,000 rolls. There is no space to sketch the ancient libraries, so scantily commemorated, of Greece. Through Aristotle's enthusiasm for learning, as it is believed, the Ptolemies were fired with the zeal of book-collecting, and their capital of Alexandria became the seat of extensive libraries, stored in the Brucheion and the Serapeum. Here, according to general belief, occurred the burning of the famous Alexandrian library of 700,000 volumes, by the Saracens under Omar, A. D. 640. If any one would have an object lesson in the uncertainties of history and of human testimony, let him read the various conflicting accounts of the writers who have treated upon this subject. The number of volumes varies from 700,000, as stated by Aulus Gellius, to 100,000 by Eusebius. The fact that in ancient times each book or division of an author's work written on a roll of papyrus was reckoned as a volume, may account for the exaggeration, since the nine books of Herodotus would thus make nine volumes, and the twenty-four of Homer's Iliad, twenty-four volumes, instead of one. So, by an arbitrary application of averages, the size of the Alexandrian Library might be brought within reasonable dimensions, though there is nothing more misleading than the doctrine of averages, unless indeed it be a false analogy. But that any library eight hundred years before the invention of printing contained 700,000 volumes in the modern sense of the word, when the largest collection in the world, three centuries after books began to be multiplied by types, held less than 100,000 volumes, is one of the wildest fictions which writers have imposed upon the credulity of ages.

I cannot even touch upon the libraries of the Romans, though we have very attractive accounts, among others, of the literary riches of Lucullus, of Atticus, and of Cicero. The first library in Rome was founded 167 B. C. and in the Augustan age they multiplied, until there were twenty-nine public libraries in Hadrian's time, 120 A. D. The emperor Julian, in the fourth century, was a founder of libraries, and is said to have placed over the doors this inscription: *"Alii quidem equos amant, alii oves, alii feros; mihi vero a puerulo mirandum acquirendi et possidendi libros insedit desiderium."*

The libraries of the middle ages were neither large nor numerous. The neglect of learning and of literature was wide-spread; only in the monasteries of Europe were to be found scholars who kept alive the sacred flame. In these were renewed those fruitful labors of the *scriptorium* which had preserved and multiplied so many precious books in classic times among the Romans. The monks, indeed, were not seldom creators as well as copyists, though the works which they composed were mainly theological (as became their sacred profession and ascetic life). The Latin, however, being the almost universal language for so many centuries, the love of learning conspired to widen the field of monastic study. Many zealous ecclesiastics were found who revived the classic authors, and copies of the works of poets, historians, philosophers and rhetoricians were multiplied. Then were gradually formed those monastic libraries to which so many thousands of mediaeval scholars owed a debt of gratitude. The order of Benedictines took a leading and effective part in this revival of learning. Taxes were levied on the inmates of monasteries expressly for furnishing the library with books, and the novices in many houses must contribute writing materials upon entering, and books at the close of their novitiate, for the enrichment of the library. Among notably valuable libraries, several of which still survive, were those of Monte Cassino in Italy, the Abbey of Fleury in France, St. Gall in Switzerland, and that of the illustrious congregation of St. Maur in France. The latter had at one time no less than one hundred and seven writers engaged in multiplying books.

The first library in England is recorded (in the Canterbury Chartulary) to have been given by Pope Gregory the Great, and brought by St. Augustine, first Archbishop of Canterbury, on his mission to England about A. D. 600. It consisted of nine precious volumes on vellum, being copies of parts of the Scriptures, with commentaries, and a volume of Lives of the Martyrs. The library of the Benedictine Monastery at Canterbury had grown in the 13th century to 3000 titles, being very rich in theology, but with many books also in history, poetry and science. At York had been founded, in the 8th century, a noble library by Archbishop Egbert, and the great scholar Alcuin here acquired, amidst that "infinite number of excellent books," his life-long devotion to literature. When he removed to Tours, in France, he lamented the loss of the literary treasures of York, in a poem composed of excellent hexameters. He begged of Charlemagne to send into Britain to procure books, "that the garden of paradise may not be confined to York."

Fine libraries were also gathered at the monasteries of Durham, of Glastonbury, and of Croyland, and at the Abbeys of Whitby and Peterborough.

Nor were the orders of Franciscans and Dominicans far behind as book-collectors, though they commonly preferred to buy rather than to transcribe manuscripts, like

the Benedictines. "In every convent of friars," wrote
Fitzralph to the Pope, in 1350, "there is a large and noble
library." And Richard de Bury, Bishop of Durham, and
Chancellor of England in 1334, whose "Philobiblon" is the
most eloquent treatise in praise of books ever written, said,
when visiting places where the mendicants had convents;
"there amid the deepest poverty, we found the most precious riches stored up." The Pope, it appears, relaxed for
these orders the rigor of their vows of poverty, in favor
of amassing books—mindful, doubtless, of that saying of
Solomon the wise—"Therefore get wisdom, because it is
better than gold."

Richard de Bury, the enthusiast of learning, wrote thus:

"The library, therefore, of wisdom is more precious than
all riches, and nothing that can be wished for is worthy to
be compared with it. Whosoever, therefore, acknowledges
himself to be a zealous follower of the truth, of happiness,
of wisdom, of science, or even of the faith, must of necessity make himself a lover of books."

And said Joseph Hall, Bishop of Norwich—"I can wonder at nothing more than how a man can be idle—but of
all others a scholar; in so many improvements of reason,
in such sweetness of knowledge, in such variety of studies,
in such importunity of thoughts. To find wit in poetry;
in philosophy profoundness; in history wonder of events;
in oratory, sweet eloquence; in divinity, supernatural light
and holy devotion—whom would it not ravish with delight?"

Charles the Fifth of France amassed a fine library, afterwards sold to an English nobleman. Lorenzo de Medici, of
Hungary, and Frederic Duke of Urbino, each gathered in
the 15th century a magnificent collection of books. All of
these became widely dispersed in later years, though the

manuscripts of the Duke of Urbino's collection are preserved in the library of the Vatican.

I may here note a very few of the most extensive library collections now existing in Europe and America.

1. Of the great public libraries of Europe, which owe much of their riches to the government privilege of the copy-tax, the national library of France is the oldest and the largest, now numbering two million six hundred thousand volumes. Founded in the 15th century, it has had four hundred years of opportunity for steady and large increase. Paris abounds in other public libraries also, in which respect it is far superior to London.

2. Next to the Bibliothèque nationale of France, comes the Library of the British Museum, with 2,000,000 volumes, very rich both in manuscripts and in printed books in all languages. A liberal Parliamentary grant of $60,000 a year for purchase of books and manuscripts keeps this great collection well up to date as to all important new works, besides enabling it constantly to fill up deficiencies in the literature of the past. Following this, among the great libraries having over half a million books, come in numerical order

	Volumes.
3. Russian Imperial Library, St. Petersburg,	1,200,000
4. Royal Library of Prussia, Berlin, ...	1,000,000
5. Royal Library of Bavaria, Munich, ...	980,000
6. Library of Congress, Washington City,...	840,000
7. Boston Public Library, ...	734,000
8. University Library, Strasburg, Germany,	700,000
9. Imperial Public Library, Vienna, ...	575,000
10. Bodleian Library, Oxford	530,000

It is a notable fact that among the richest monuments of learning that have been gathered by mankind, the University libraries hold a very high rank. Reckoned in **number** of volumes, there are many of them which **far outrank** the government libraries, except in six instances. **Out of** 174 libraries, all exceeding 100,000 volumes, as **reported** in the annual *Minerva*, in October, 1898, no less than **72** are the libraries of universities. Strasburg heads the **list**, with a noble collection of 700,000 volumes; then Oxford university, whose Bodleian library numbers 530,000; Leipzig university, 504,000; Cambridge university, England, Göttingen university, and Harvard university, 500,000 each; the university of Vienna, 475,000; the universities of Heidelberg and of Munich, 400,000 each; Ghent and Würzburg universities, 350,000 each; Christiania, Norway, university, and Tübingen, each 340,000; University of Chicago, 330,000; Copenhagen university, 305,000; Breslau, Cracow, Rostock and Upsala, 300,000 each; Yale university, New Haven, 280,000; St. Petersburg, 257,000; Bologna, 255,000; Freiburg and Bonn universities, 250,000 each; Prague, 245,000; Trinity, Dublin, 232,000; Königsberg, 231,000; Kiel, 229,000; Naples, 224,000; and Buda-Pest, 210,000. I need not detain you by enumerating those that fall below 200,000 volumes, but will say that the whole number of volumes in the 72 university libraries embraced in my table is more than fifteen millions, which would be much enlarged if smaller libraries were included. A noble exhibit is this, which the institutions of the highest education hold up before us.

We may now consider, somewhat more in detail as to particulars, the origin and growth of the libraries of the United States. The record will show an amazingly rapid development, chiefly accomplished during the last quarter of a century, contrasted with the lamentably slow growth of earlier years.

Thirty years ago the present year, I was invited to give to the American Social Science Association, then meeting at New York, a discourse upon Public Libraries in the United States. On recurring to this address, I have been agreeably surprised to find how completely its facts and figures belong to the domain of ancient history. For, while it may excite a smile to allude to anything belonging to a period only thirty years back as ancient history, yet, so rapid has been the accumulation, not only of books, but of libraries themselves in that brief period of three decades, as almost to justify the term employed.

Antiquarians must ever regard with interest the first efforts for the establishment of public libraries in the New World. The first record of books dedicated to a public purpose in that part of this country now occupied by the English-speaking race is, I believe, to be found in the following entry in the Records of the Virginia Company of London:

"November 15, 1620.—After the Acts of the former Courte were read, a straunger stept in presentinge a Mapp of Sʳ Walter Rawlighes contayinge a Descripcon of Guiana, and with the same fower great books as the Guifte of one unto the Company that desyred his name might not be made knowne, whereof one booke was a treatise of St. Augustine of the Citty of God translated into English, the other three greate Volumes wer the works of Mr. Perkins' newlie corrected and amended, wch books the Donor desyred they might be sent to the Colledge in Virginia there to remayne in saftie to the use of the collegiates thereafter, and not suffered at any time to be sent abroad or used in the meane while. For wch so worthy a guifte my Lord of Southampton desyred the p'tie that presented them to returne deserued thanks from himselfe and the rest of the Company to him that had so kindly bestowed them."[*]

The college here referred to was the first ever founded in America, and was seated at Henrico, at the confluence of the James River with the Chickahominy. It was designed not only for the education of the Virginia settlers, but to teach science and Christianity to the Indians. Large contributions were raised in England by Sir Edwin Sandys, and others of the Virginia Company, for its support. But this Virginia college and its incipient library were doomed to a speedy extinction. Like so many other brilliant "prospects for planting arts and learning in America," it did not survive the perils of the colonial epoch. It was brought to a period by the bloody Indian massacre of March 22, 1622, when three hundred and forty-seven of the Virginia settlers were slaughtered in a day, the new settlement broken up, and the expanding lines of civilization contracted to the neighborhood of Jamestown.

Harvard University Library was founded in 1638 by the endowment of John Harvard, who bequeathed to the new college his library and half of his estate. Soon afterwards enriched by the zealous contributions of English Puritans and philosophers, of Berkeley, and Baxter, and Lightfoot, and Sir Kenelm Digby, the first university library in America, after a century and a quarter of usefulness, was totally destroyed with the college edifice in the year 1764 by fire. When we contemplate the ravages of this element, which has consumed so many noble libraries, destroying not only printed books of priceless value, but often precious manuscripts which are unique and irreplaceable,

---

[*]MS. Records of the Virginia Company, in the Library of Congress.

a lively sense of regret comes over us that these creations of the intellect, which should be imperishable, are even yet at the mercy of an accident in all the libraries of the world save a very few. The destruction of books in private hands is natural and inevitable enough, and goes on continually. Whole editions of books, now sought with avidity as the rarest volumes known to literature, have been gradually destroyed in innumerable fires, worn out in the hands of readers, used for waste paper by grocers and petty tradesmen, swallowed up in the sack of towns, or consumed by dampness, mould, or, in rare instances, by the remorseless tooth of time. Yet there have always existed public libraries enough, had they been fire-proof, to have preserved many copies of every book bequeathed to the world, both before the invention of printing and since. But, when your insurance office is bankrupt, what becomes of the insured? When nearly all our public libraries are so constructed as to become an easy prey to the flames, the loss of so many books which have completely perished from the earth ceases to be wonderful.

The growth of Harvard University library, from its second foundation a century ago, has been steady, though at no time rapid. Select and valuable in its principal contents, it has received numerous benefactions from the friends of learning, and promises to become the best, as it already is much the largest, among the university libraries of the country. Its present strength is about 500,000 volumes.

The year 1700 witnessed the birth of the first New York library open to public use. The Rev. John Sharp, then chaplain of His Majesty's forces in that city (it was in the days of good King William of Orange), bequeathed his private collection of books to found a "public library" in

New York. The library thus organized was placed in charge of the corporation of the city, but the first city library of New York languished with little or no increase until 1754, when a society of gentlemen undertook to found a public library by subscription, and succeeded so well that the city authorities turned over to them what remained of the Public City Library. This was the beginning of the New York Society Library, one of the largest of the proprietary libraries of the country. It was then, and for a long time afterwards, commonly known as "The City Library." The Continental Congress profited by its stores, there being no other library open to their use; and the First Congress under the Constitution, which met in New York in 1789, received the free use of the books it contained. The library is conducted on the share system, the payment of twenty-five dollars, and an annual assessment of six dollars, giving any one the privilege of membership. It now contains about 100,000 volumes.

The same year, 1700, in which the New York Library was founded, ten Connecticut ministers met together at Lyme, each bringing a number of books, and saying, "I give these books for the founding of a college in this colony." Such was the foundation of Yale University, an institution that has done inestimable service to the cause of letters, having been fruitful of writers of books, as well as of living contributions to the ranks of every learned profession. Thirty years later, we find the good Bishop Berkeley pausing from the lofty speculations which absorbed him, to send over to Yale College what was called "the finest collection of books that ever came together at one time into America." For a century and a half the growth of this library was very slow, the college being oppressed with poverty. In 1869, the number of volumes had risen only to 50,000, but it is cheering to relate that the last thirty years have witnessed a growth so rapid that in 1899 Yale University Library had 285,000 volumes.

The fourth considerable library founded in the United States was due in a large degree to the industry and zeal for knowledge of the illustrous Franklin. As unquestionably the first established proprietary library in America, the Library Company of Philadelphia merits especial notice. Let us reverently take a leaf out of the autobiography of the printer-statesman of Pennsylvania:

"And now I set on foot my first project of a public nature, that for a subscription library. I drew up the proposals, got them put into form by our great scrivener, Brockden, and by the help of my friends in the Junto [the Junto was a club for mutual improvement, founded by Franklin] procured fifty subscribers at forty shillings each to begin with, and ten shillings a year for fifty years, the term our company was to continue. We afterwards obtained a charter, the company being increased to one hundred; this was the mother of all the North American subscription libraries now so numerous. It is become a great thing itself, and continually increasing. These libraries have improved the general conversation of the Americans, made the common tradesmen and farmers as intelligent as most gentlemen from other countries, and perhaps have contributed in some degree to the stand so generally made throughout the colonies in defence of their privileges."

When this Philadelphia Library was founded, in 1731, not a single city or town in England possessed a subscription library. Even the library of the British Museum, since become the greatest collection of books in the world, save one, was not opened until 1759, more than a quarter of a century afterwards. Although not designed as a public library of circulation, save to its own subscribers, the Philadelphia Library has been kept free to all for reference and consultation. The record of the gradual increase of the first Philadelphia Library from its first few hundred volumes, when Franklin was but twenty-five years of age, to its present rank as the largest proprietary library in America, with 195,000 volumes of books, is highly interesting. Its history, in fact, is to a large extent the history of intellectual culture in Philadelphia, which remained, until the second decade in the present century, the foremost city of the Union in population, and, from 1791 to 1800, the seat of government of the United States.

The Philadelphia Library Company, in 1774, voted that "the gentlemen who were to meet in Congress" in that city should be furnished with such books as they might have occasion for; and the same privilege was exercised on the return of the Government to that city, in 1791, and until the removal of Congress to Washington in 1800. During the nine months' occupation of Philadelphia by the British army, it is refreshing to read that the conquerors lifted no spear against the Muses' bower, but that "the officers, without exception, left deposits, and paid hire for the books borrowed by them." The collection, in respect of early printed books, is one of the largest and most valuable in America, embracing some books and files of newspapers which are to be found in no other public library. The selection of new books has been kept unusually free from the masses of novels and other ephemeral publications which overload most of our popular libraries, and the collection, although limited in extent in every field, and purposely leaving special topics, such as the medical and natural sciences, to the scientific libraries which abound in Philadelphia, affords to the man of letters a good working library.

The shares in the library cost forty dollars, with an annual assessment of four dollars to each stockholder.

In 1869, the great bequest of Doctor James Rush to the Philadelphia Library of his whole property, valued at over $1,000,000, was accepted by its stockholders, by the bare majority of five votes in a poll of over five hundred. This lack of harmony is attributable to the fact that the bequest, so generous in itself, was hampered by the donor with numerous conditions, deemed by many friends of the library to be highly onerous and vexatious. Not the least among these was the following, which is cited from the will itself:

"Let the library not keep cushioned seats for time-wasting and lounging readers, nor places for every-day novels, mind-tainting reviews, controversial politics, scribblings of poetry and prose, biographies of unknown names, nor for those teachers of disjointed thinking, the daily newspapers."

Here is one more melancholy instance of a broad and liberal bequest narrowly bestowed. The spirit which animated the respectable testator in attempting to exclude the larger part of modern literature from the library which his money was to benefit may have been unexceptionable enough. Doubtless there are evils connected with a public supply of frivolous and trifling literature; and perhaps our periodicals may be justly chargeable with devoting an undue proportion of their columns to topics of merely ephemeral interest. But it should never be forgotten that the literature of any period is and must be largely occupied with the questions of the day. Thus, and thus only, it becomes a representative literature, and it is precious to posterity in proportion as it accurately reflects the spirit, the prejudices, and the personalities of a time which has passed into history, leaving behind it no living representatives. If we admit that the development of the human intellect at any particular period is worth studying, then all books are, or may become, useful. It is amazing that a person with any pretensions to discernment should denounce newspapers as unfitted to form a part of a public library. The best newspapers of the time are sometimes the best books of the time. A first-class daily journal is an epitome of the world, recording the life and the deeds of men, their laws and their literature, their politics and religion, their social and criminal statistics, the progress of invention and of art, the revolutions of empires, and the latest results of science. Grant that newspapers are prejudiced, superficial, unfair; so also are books. Grant that the journals often give place to things scurrilous and base; but can there be anything baser or more scurrilous than are suffered to run riot in books? There is to be found hidden away in the pages of some books such filth as no man would dare to print in a newspaper, from fear of the instant wrath of the passers-by.

When I consider the debt which libraries and literature alike owe to the daily and weekly press, it is difficult to characterize with patience the Parthian arrow flung at it from the grave of a querulous millionaire, who will owe to these very newspapers the greater part of his success and his reputation. The father of the respectable testator, Doctor Benjamin Rush, has left on record many learned speculations concerning the signs and evidences of lunacy. We may now add to the number the vagaries of the author of a ponderous work on the human intellect, who gravely proposed to hand over to posterity an expurgated copy of the nineteenth century, with all its newspapers left out.

The Library of Congress, or, as it was called in its first general catalogue in 1815, "The Library of the United States," was founded in 1800, by the purchase of five thousand dollars' worth of books by act of Congress, upon the removal of the government to Washington. By the act of January 26, 1802, entitled "An act concerning the Library for the use of both Houses of Congress," this library was placed in charge of a joint committee of both Houses of Congress, consisting of three Senators and three Representatives, and a Librarian, to be appointed by the President of the United States. It had grown to the number of only 3,000 volumes in 1814, when the British army made a bonfire of our national Capitol, and the library was consumed in the ruins. The first library of Congress being thus destroyed, ex-President Jefferson, then living, involved in debt, and in his old age, at Monticello, offered his fine private library of 6,700 volumes to Congress, through friends in that body, the terms of payment to be made convenient to the public, and the price to be fixed by a committee. The proposition met with able advocacy and also with some warm opposition. It is illustrative of the crude conceptions regarding the uses of books which prevailed in the minds of some members, that the library was objected to on the somewhat incongruous grounds of embracing too many editions of the Bible, and a number of the French writers in skeptical philosophy. It was gravely proposed to pack up this portion of the library, and return it to the illustrious owner at Monticello, paying him for the remainder. More enlightened counsels, however, prevailed, and the nation became possessed, for about $23,000, of a good basis for a public library which might become worthy of the country. The collection thus formed grew by slow accretion until, in 1851, it had accumulated 55,000 volumes. On the 24th

of December in that year, a defective flue in the Capitol
set fire to the wood-work with which the whole library was
surrounded, and the result was a conflagration, from which
20,000 volumes only were saved.   Congress at once appropriated, with praiseworthy liberality, $75,000 for the pur-
chase of new books, and $92,500 for rebuilding the library
room in solid iron; the first instance of the employment of
that safe and permanent material, so capable of the light-
est and most beautiful architectural effects, in the entire
interior structure of any public building.   The appropriation of $75,000 was principally expended in the purchase
of standard English literature, including complete sets of
many important periodicals, and a selection of the more
costly works in science and the fine arts.   In 1866, two
wings, each as large as the central library, and constructed
of the same fire-proof material, were added to it, and quickly filled by the accession, the same year and the following,
of two large libraries, that of the Smithsonian Institution,
and the historical library of Peter Force, of Washington.
The latter was the largest private library ever then
brought together in the United States, but its chief value
consisted in its possession of a very great proportion of the
books relating to the settlement, history, topography, and
politics of America, its 45,000 pamphlets, its files of early
newspapers of the Revolution, its early printed books, and
its rich assemblage of maps and manuscripts, many of the
latter being original autographs of the highest historical
interest, including military letters and papers of the period
of the American Revolution.   The Smithsonian library,
the custody of which was accepted by Congress as a trust,
is rich in scientific works in all the languages of Europe,
and forms an extensive and appropriate supplement to the
Library of Congress, the chief strength of which lies in

jurisprudence, political science, history, and books relating
to America. Yet no department of literature or science
has been left unrepresented in its formation, and the fact
has been kept steadily in view that the Library of the
Government must become, sooner or later, a universal
one. As the only library which is entitled to the benefit
of the copyright law, by which copies of each publication
for which the Government grants an exclusive right must
be deposited in the National Library, this collection must
become annually more important as an exponent of the
growth of American literature. This wise provision of
law prevents the dispersion or destruction of books that
tend continually to disappear; a benefit to the cause of
letters, the full value of which it requires slight reflection
to estimate.

This National Library now embraces 840,000 volumes,
besides about 250,000 pamphlets. It is freely open, as a
library of reference and reading, to the whole people; but
the books are not permitted to be drawn out, except by
Senators and Representatives and a few officials for use at
the seat of government. Its new, commodious and beautiful building, which may fitly be called the book-palace of
the American people, open day and evening to all comers,
is a delight to the eye, and to the mind.

The library of the Boston Athenaeum originated, in the
year 1806, with a society of gentlemen of literary tastes,
who aimed at creating a reading-room for the best foreign
and American periodicals, together with a library of books.
To this a gallery of art was subsequently added. The undertaking proved at once successful, leaving us to wonder
why cultivated Boston, though abounding in special and
parish libraries, should so long have done without a good
general library; New York having anticipated her by fifty-

two years, and Philadelphia by three-quarters of a century. The Athenaeum Library is peculiarly rich in files of American newspapers, both old and new, and its collection of early pamphlets is one of the largest in the country. In literature and science it embraces a heavy proportion of the best books, its total number of volumes being reckoned at 190,000. Its collection of books, pamphlets, and newspapers relating to the recent civil war is among the completest known. The price of a share in the Athenaeum is three hundred dollars, a large sum when compared with that of other proprietary libraries; but it involves much more valuable property-rights than any other. The annual assessment is five dollars to shareholders, who alone possess the right to draw books. The proprietors have also the power to grant free admission to others, and the library and reading-room are thus thrown open for reference to a wide range of readers.

The history of the Astor Library, opened in 1854, has been made too familiar by repeated publication to need repetition here. The generous founder gave two per cent. out of his fortune of $20,000,000 to create a free public library for the city which had given him all his wealth. The gift was a splendid one, greater than had ever before been given in money to found a library. Moreover, the $400,000 of Mr. Astor, half a century ago, appeared to be, and perhaps was, a larger sum relatively than four millions in New York of to-day. Yet it remains true that the bequest was but one-fiftieth part of the fortune of the donor, and that the growth and even the proper accommodation of the library must have stopped, but for the spontaneous supplementary gifts of the principal inheritors of his vast wealth.

The growth of the Astor library has been very slow, the

annual income from what was left of Mr. Astor's $400,000 bequest, after defraying the cost of the library building, and the $100,000 expended for books at its foundation in 1848, having been so small as to necessitate a pinching economy, both in salaries of the library staff, and in the annual purchase of books. It was an example of a generous act performed in a niggardly way. But after the lapse of half a century, enlightened public policy, building upon the Astor foundation, and on the Lenox and Tilden bequests for founding public libraries in New York city, is about to equip that long neglected city with a library worthy of the name. There has already been gathered from these three united benefactions, a collection of no less than 450,000 volumes, making the New York Public Library take rank as the fourth, numerically, in the United States.

While no library in America has yet reached one million volumes, there are five libraries in Europe, which have passed the million mark. Some of these, it is true, are repositories of ancient and mediaeval literature, chiefly, with a considerable representation of the books of the last century, and but few accessions from the more modern press. Such, for the most part, are the numerous libraries of Italy, while others, like the Library of the British Museum, in London, and the National Library, at Paris, are about equally rich in ancient and modern literature. The one great advantage which European libraries possess over American consists in the stores of ancient literature which the accumulations of the past have given them. This advantage, so far as manuscripts and early printed books are concerned, can never be overcome. With one or two hundred thousand volumes as a basis, what but utter neglect can prevent a library from becoming a great and useful institution? The most moderate share of discrimination, applied to the selection of current literature, will keep up the character of the collection as a progressive one. But with nothing at all as a basis, as most of our large American libraries have started, it will take generations for us to overtake some of the vast collections of Europe—even numerically.

In the "American Almanac" for 1837 was published the earliest statistical account of American libraries which I have found. It is confined to a statement of the numerical contents of twenty public and university libraries, being all the American libraries which then (sixty years since) contained over 10,000 volumes each. The largest library in the United States at that date was that of the Philadelphia Library Company, which embraced 44,000 volumes. The first organized effort to collect the full statistics of libraries in the United States was made in 1849, by Professor C. C. Jewett, then librarian of the Smithsonian Institution, and the results were published in 1851, under the auspices of that institution, in a volume of 207 pages. It contains interesting notices of numerous libraries, only forty of which, however, contained as many as 10,000 volumes each. In 1859, Mr. W. J. Rhees, of the Smithsonian Institution, published "A Manual of Public Libraries, Institutions, and Societies in the United States," a large volume of 687 pages, filled with statistical information in great detail, and recording the number of volumes in 1338 libraries. This work was an expansion of that of Professor Jewett. The next publication of the statistics of American Libraries, of an official character, was published in "The National Almanac," Philadelphia, for the year 1864, pp. 58-62, and was prepared by the present writer. It gave the statistics of 104 libraries, each numbering 10,000 volumes or upwards, exhibiting a gratifying progress in all the larger collections, and commemorating the more advanced and vigorous of the new libraries which had sprung into life.

The work of collecting and publishing the statistics of American Libraries has for years past been admirably performed by the United States Bureau of Education. Begun in 1875, that institution has issued four tabular statements of all libraries responding to its circulars of inquiry, and having (as last reported in 1897) one thousand volumes or upwards. Besides these invaluable reports, costing much careful labor and great expense, the Bureau of Education published, in 1876, an extensive work wholly devoted to the subject of libraries, bearing the title "Special Report on Public Libraries in the United States." This publication (now wholly out of print) consisted of 1222 pages, replete with information upon the history, management, and condition of American Libraries, under the editorship of S. R. Warren and S. N. Clark, of the Bureau of Education. It embraced many original contributions upon topics connected with library science, by experienced librarians, viz: Messrs. W. F. Poole, Justin Winsor, C. A. Cutter, J. S. Billings, Theo. Gill, Melvil Dewey, O. H. Robinson, W. I. Fletcher, F. B. Perkins, H. A. Homes, A. R. Spofford, and others.

I have prepared a table of the numerical contents of the thirty-four largest libraries in this country in 1897, being all those having 100,000 volumes each or upwards:

Library of Congress, Washington, ...	840,000
Boston Public Library, Boston, ...	730,000
Harvard University Library, Cambridge, ...	510,000
New York Public Library, New York City, ...	450,000
University of Chicago Library, ...	335,000

New York State Library, Albany, ...	320,710
Yale University Library, New Haven, ...	285,000
New York Mercantile Library, New York, ...	270,000
Columbia University Library, New York, ...	260,000
Chicago Public Library, ...	235,385
Cincinnati Public Library, ...	223,043
Cornell University Library, Ithaca, N. Y.,.....	220,000
Sutro Library, San Francisco, ...	206,300
Newberry Library, Chicago, ...	203,108
Philadelphia Library Company, ...	200,000
Philadelphia Mercantile Library, ...	190,000
Boston Athenaeum Library, ...	190,000
Enoch Pratt Library, Baltimore, ...	185,902
Philadelphia Mercantile Library, ...	183,000
Detroit Public Library, Detroit, Mich.,........	148,198
University of Pennsylvania Library, Phila.,....	140,000
Princeton University Library, Princeton, N. J.,	135,000
Pennsylvania State Library, Harrisburg,......	134,000
Peabody Institute Library, Baltimore, ...	130,000
Cleveland Public Library, Cleveland, O., ...	129,000
St. Louis Public Library, ...	125,000
Mechanics and Tradesmen's Library, New York,	115,185
Free Public Library, Worcester, Mass.,........	115,000
San Francisco Public Library, ...	108,066
Philadelphia Free Library, ...	105,000
American Antiquarian Society Library ,Worcester, Mass., ...	105,000
California State Library, Sacramento, ...	100,032
Massachusetts State Library, Boston, ...	100,000
New York Society Library, New York, ...	100,000

Public libraries endowed by private munificence form already a large class, and these are constantly increasing. Of the public libraries founded by individual bequest, some of the principal are the Public Library of New York, the Watkinson Library, at Hartford, the Peabody Institute Libraries, of Baltimore, and at Danvers and Peabody, Mass., the Newberry Library and the John Crerar Library at Chicago, the Sutro Library, San Francisco, the Enoch Pratt Library, Baltimore, and the Carnegie Libraries at Pittsburgh and Allegheny City, Pa. Nearly all of them are the growth of the last quarter of a century. The more prominent, in point of well equipped buildings or collections of books, are here named, including all which number ten thousand volumes each, or upwards, among the public libraries associated with the founder's name.

New York Public Library (Astor Lenox and Tilden Foundations),	450,000
Newberry Library, Chicago,	203,100
Sutro Library, San Francisco,	206,300
Enoch Pratt Library, Baltimore,	185,900
Peabody Institute Library, Baltimore,	130,000
Davenport Library, Bath, N. Y.,	90,000
Silas Bronson Library, Waterbury, Conn.,	52,000
Pratt Institute Free Library, Brooklyn, N. Y.,	51,000
Watkinson Library, Hartford, Conn.,	47,000
Sage Library, New Brunswick, N. Y.,	43,000
Case Library, Cleveland, Ohio,	40,000
Grosvenor Library, Buffalo, N. Y.,	39,000
Forbes Library, Northampton, Mass.,	36,000
Cooper Union Library, New York,	34,000
Fisk Free Public Library, New Orleans,	33,000
Peabody Institute Library, Peabody, Mass.,	33,000
Reynolds Library, Rochester, N. Y.,	33,000
Carnegie Free Library, Allegheny, Pa.,	30,000
Fletcher Free Library, Burlington, Vt.,	30,000
Howard Memorial Library, New Orleans,	26,000
Carnegie Library, Pittsburgh, Pa.,	25,000

Sage Public Library, West Bay City, Mich.,.... **25,000**
Hoyt Public Library, Saginaw, Mich., ... **24,000**
Osterhout Free Library, Wilkesbarre, Pa.,.... **24,000**
Seymour Library, Auburn, N. Y., ... **24,000**
Hackley Public Library, Muskegon, Mich., ... **22,000**
Willard Library, Evansville, Ind., ... **22,000**
Otis Library, Norwich, Conn., ... **21,000**
Morrison-Reeves Library, Richmond, Ind.,.... **21,000**
Baxter Memorial Library, Rutland, Vt.,...... **20,000**
Cornell Library Association, Ithaca, N. Y., ... **20,000**
Thomas Crane Public Library, Quincy, Mass.,.. **19,000**
Dimmick Library, Mauch Chunk, Pa.,......... **18,000**
Gail Borden Public Library, Elgin, Ill., ... **17,000**
Peabody Institute Library, Danvers, Mass.,.... **17,000**
Tufts Library, Weymouth, Mass.,............ **17,000**
Warder Public Library, Springfield, Ohio, ... **17,000**
Withers Public Library, Bloomington, Ill.,.... **15,000**
Cary Library, Lexington, Mass., ... **15,000**
Fritz Public Library, Chelsea, Mass.,......... **15,000**
Turner Free Library, Randolph, Mass.,........ **15,000**
Ames Free Library, North Easton, Mass.,...... **14,000**
Bigelow Free Library, Clinton, Mass.,......... **14,000**
Clarke Public Library, Coldwater, Mich.,...... **14,000**
Harris Institute Library, Woonsocket, R. I.,.... **14,000**
Merrick Public Library, Brookfield, Mass.,..... **14,000**
Robbins Library, Arlington, Mass.,........... **14,000**
Nevins Memorial Library, Methuen, Mass.,.... **14,000**
Sturgis Library, Barnstable, Mass.,.......... **13,000**
Birchard Library, Fremont, Ohio,............ **12,500**
James Prendergast Library, Jamestown, N. Y., **12,500**
Rogers Free Library, Bristol, R. I., ... **12,300**
Abbott Public Library, Marblehead, Mass., ... **12,000**
Armour Institute, Chicago, Ill., ... **12,000**

Beebe Town Library, Wakefield, Mass.,....... 12,000
Carnegie Free Library, Braddock, Pa.,........ 12,000
Goodnow Library, South Sudbury, Mass.,...... 12,000
Millicent Library, Fairhaven, Mass.,......... 12,000
Thayer Public Library, South Braintree, Mass., 11,000
Dyer Library, Saco, Maine,................. 10,500
Cossit Library, Memphis, Tenn.,............ 10,000
Gloucester (Mass.) Sawyer Free Library, ... 10,000
Ferguson Library, Stamford, Conn., ... 10,000
Parlin Memorial Library, Everett, Mass.,...... 10,000
Jennie D. Haynes Library, Alton, Ill.,......... 10,000
Hornell Free Library, Hornellsville, N: Y., ... 10,000

Besides the preceding list, purposely confined to free libraries chiefly founded by individuals, which have reached the ten thousand volume mark, there are a multitude of others, too numerous to be named, having a less number of volumes. In fact, the public spirit which gives freely of private wealth to enlarge the intelligence of the community may be said to grow by emulation. Many men who have made fortunes have endowed their native places with libraries. It is yearly becoming more and more widely recognized that a man can build no monument to himself so honorable or so lasting as a free public library. Its influence is well nigh universal, and its benefits are perennial.

We now come to consider the city or town libraries, created or maintained by voluntary taxation. These, like the class of libraries founded by private munificence, are purely a modern growth. While the earliest movement in this direction in Great Britain dates back only to 1850, New Hampshire has the honor of adopting the first free public library law, in America, in the year 1849. Massachusetts followed in 1851, and the example was emulated by other States at various intervals, until there now remain but fifteen out of our forty-five States which have no public library law. The general provisions of these laws authorize any town or city to collect taxes by vote of the citizens for maintaining a public library, to be managed by trustees elected or appointed for the purpose.

But a more far-reaching provision for supplying the people with public libraries was adopted by New Hampshire (again the pioneer State), in 1895. This was nothing less than the passage of a State law making it compulsory on every town in New Hampshire to assess annually the sum of thirty dollars for every dollar of public taxes apportioned to such town, the amount to be appropriated to establish and maintain a free public library. Library trustees are to be elected, and in towns where no public library exists, the money is to be held by them, and to accumulate until the town is ready to establish a library.

This New Hampshire statute, making obligatory the supply of public information through books and periodicals in free libraries in every town, may fairly be termed the high-water mark of modern means for the diffusion of knowledge. This system of creating libraries proceeds upon the principle that intellectual enlightenment is as much a concern of the local government as sanitary regulations or public morality. Society has an interest that is common to all classes in the means that are provided for the education of the people. Among these means free town or city libraries are one of the most potent and useful. New Hampshire and Massachusetts, in nearly all of their towns and cities, have recognized the principle that public books are just as important to the general welfare as public lamps. What are everywhere needed are libraries open to the people as a matter of right, and not as a matter of favor.

The largest library in the country, save one (that at Washington), owes its origin and success to this principle, combined with some private munificence. The Boston Public Library is unquestionably one of the most widely useful collections of books open to the public in this country. Of all the greater collections, it is the only one which lends out books free of charge to all citizens. Instituted in 1852, its career has been one of rapid progress and ever widening usefulness. I shall not dwell upon it at length, as the facts regarding it have been more widely published than those relating to any other library.

Under the permissive library laws of thirty States, there had been formed up to 1896, when the last comprehensive statistics were gathered, about 1,200 free public libraries, supported by taxation, in the United States.

A still more widely successful means of securing a library foundation that shall be permanent is found in uniting private benefactions with public money to found or to maintain a library. Many public-spirited citizens, fortunately endowed with large means, have offered to erect library buildings in certain places, on condition that the local authorities would provide the books, and the means of maintaining a free library. Such generous offers, whether coupled with the condition of perpetuating the donor's name with that of the library, or leaving the gift unhampered, so that the library may bear the name of the town or city of its location, have generally been accepted by municipal bodies, or by popular vote. This secures, in most cases, a good working library of choice reading, as well as its steady annual growth and management, free of the heavy expense of building, of which the tax-payers are relieved. The many munificent gifts of library buildings by Mr. Andrew Carnegie, to American towns and cities, and to some in his native Scotland, are worthy of special note.

And the reader will see from the long list heretofore given
of the more considerable public libraries to be credited
wholly or in part to private munificence, that American
men of wealth have not been wanting as public benefactors.

In some cases, whole libraries have been given to a town
or village where a public library already existed, or liberal
gifts or bequests of money, to be expended in the enrichment of such libraries, have been bestowed. Very interesting lists of benefactions for the benefit of libraries may
be found in the volumes of the Library Journal, New York.
It is with regret that candor requires me to add, that
several proffers of fine library buildings to certain places,
coupled with the condition that the municipal authorities
would establish and maintain a free library, have remained without acceptance, thus forfeiting a liberal endowment. Where public education has been so neglected
as to render possible such a niggardly, penny-wise and
pound-foolish policy, there is manifestly signal need of
every means of enlightenment.

We now come to the various State libraries founded at
the public charge, and designed primarily for the use
of the respective legislatures of the States. The earliest
of these is the New Hampshire State Library, established
in 1790, and the largest is the New York State Library,
at Albany, founded in 1818, now embracing 325,000 volumes, and distinguished alike by the value of its stores and
the liberality of its management. The reason for being
of a State library is obviously and primarily to furnish the
legislative body and State courts with such ample books
of reference in jurisprudence, history, science, etc., as will
aid them in the intelligent discharge of their duties as
law-makers and judges of the law. The library thus existing at each State capital may well be opened to the

public for reading and reference, thus greatly enlarging
its usefulness.

Every State in the Union has now at least a legislative
library, although the most of them consist chiefly of laws
and legislative documents, with a few works of reference
superadded; and their direct usefulness to the public is
therefore very circumscribed. The New York State Library is a model of what a great public library should be
in the capital of a State. In it are gathered a great proportion of the best books in each department of literature
and science, while indefatigable efforts have been made to
enrich it in whatever relates to American history and pol-
ity. Its reading-room is freely opened to the public during
many hours daily. But a State library should never be
made a library of circulation, since its utility as a reference
library, having its books always in for those who seek them,
would thereby be destroyed. Even under the existing system, with the privilege of drawing books out confined to
the Legislature, some of the State libraries have been de-
pleted and despoiled of many of their most valuable books,
through loaning them freely on the orders of members.
The sense of responsibility is far less in the case of borrowed books which are government property, than in other
cases. The only safe rule for keeping a government library from being scattered, is strict refusal of orders for
loaning to any one not legally entitled to draw books, and
short terms of withdrawal to legislators, with enforcement
of a rule of replacement, at their expense, as to all books
not returned at the end of each session.

There is one class of libraries not yet touched upon,
namely, school district libraries. These originated for the
first time in a legally organized system, through an act of
the New York State Legislature in 1835, authorizing the

voters in each school district to levy a tax of twenty dollars with which to start a library, and ten dollars a year for adding to the same. These were not to be for the schools alone, but for all the people living in the district where the school was located. This was supplemented in 1838 by a State appropriation of $55,000 a year, from New York's share of the surplus revenue fund distributed by Congress to the States in 1837, and the income of which was devoted by New York to enlarging the school district libraries. After spending nearly two millions of dollars on these libraries in forty years, the system was found to have been so far a failure that the volumes in the libraries had decreased from 1,600,000 to 700,000 volumes.

This extraordinary and deplorable result was attributed to several distinct causes. 1st. No proper responsibility as to the use and return of books was enforced. 2d. The insignificance of the sum raised by taxation in each district prevented any considerable supply of books from being acquired. 3d. The funds were largely devoted to buying the same books in each school district, instead of being expended in building up a large and varied collection. Thus the system produced innumerable petty libraries of duplicates, enriching publishers and booksellers, while impoverishing the community. The school district library system, in short, while promising much in theory, in the way of public intelligence, broke down completely in practice. The people quickly lost interest in libraries which gave them so little variety in books, either of instruction or of recreation.

Although widely introduced in other States besides New York, from 1837 to 1877, it proved an admitted failure in all. Much public money, raised by taxation of the people, was squandered upon sets of books, selected by State authority, and often of inferior interest and utility. Finally, it was recognized that school district libraries were an evanescent dream, and that town libraries must take their place. This instructive chapter in Library history shows an experience by which much was learned, though the lesson was a costly one.

The Historical libraries of the country are numerous, and some of the larger ones are rich in printed Americana, and in historical manuscripts. The oldest is that of the Massachusetts Historical Society, founded in 1791, and among the most extensive are those of the New York Historical Society, American Antiquarian Society, the Historical Society of Pennsylvania, the New England Historic-genealogical Society, and the Wisconsin State Historical Society. There are no less than 230 historical societies in the U. S., some forty of which are State associations.

The Mercantile libraries are properly a branch of the proprietary, though depending mostly upon annual subscriptions. The earliest of these was the Boston Mercantile Library, founded in 1820, and followed closely by the New York Mercantile the same year, the Philadelphia in 1821, and the Cincinnati Mercantile in 1835.

Next we have the professional libraries, law, medical, scientific, and, in several cities, theological. These supply a want of each of these professions seldom met by the public collections, and are proportionately valuable.

The most recent plan for the wide diffusion of popular books is the travelling library. This originated in New York in 1893, when the Legislature empowered the Regents of the State University (a body of trustees having charge of all library interests in that State) to send out selections of books to any community without a library, on request of 25 resident taxpayers. The results were most beneficial, the sole expense being five dollars for each library.

Travelling libraries, (mostly of fifty volumes each) have been set on foot in Massachusetts, Michigan, Iowa, Wisconsin, Pennsylvania, and other States, and, as the system appears capable of indefinite expansion, great results are anticipated in the direction of the public intelligence. It is pointed out that while the State, by its free school system, trains all the people to read, it should not leave the quality of their reading to chance or to utter neglect, when a few cents *per capita* annually would help them to an education of inestimable value in after life.

Some objections, on the other hand, have been urged to the system, as introducing features of paternalism into State government, and taking out of the hands of individual generosity and local effort and enterprise what belongs properly to such agencies. The vexed question of the proper function and limitations of State control in the domain of education cannot here be entered upon.

In the volume last published of statistics of American libraries, that of 1897, great progress was shown in the five years since 1891. The record of libraries reported in 1896 embraced 4,026 collections, being all which contained over 1,000 volumes each. The increase in volumes in the five years was a little over seven millions, the aggregate of the 4,026 libraries being 33,051,872 volumes. This increase was over 27 per cent. in only five years.

If the good work so splendidly begun, in New England, New York, Pennsylvania, and some of the Western States, in establishing libraries through public taxation and private munificence, can only be extended in the Southern and Middle States, the century now about to dawn will witness an advance quite as remarkable as we have seen in the latter years of the century about to close.

CHAPTER 16.

LIBRARY BUILDINGS AND FURNISHINGS.

Proceeding now to the subject of library buildings, reading-rooms, and furnishings, it must be remarked at the outset that very few rules can be laid down which are of universal application. The architectural plans, exterior and interior, of such great institutions as the Library of Congress, or the Boston Public Library, with their costly marbles, splendid mural decorations, and electric book-serving machinery, afford no model for the library building in the country village. Where the government of a nation or a wealthy city has millions to devote for providing a magnificent book-palace for its library, the smaller cities or towns have only a few thousands. So much the more important is it, that a thoroughly well-considered plan for building should be marked out before beginning to build, that no dollars should be wasted, or costly alterations required, in order to fit the interior for all the uses of a library.

The need of this caution will be abundantly evident, in the light of the unfit and inconvenient constructions seen in so many public libraries, all over the country. So general has been the want of carefully planned and well-executed structures for books, that it may fairly be said that mistakes have been the rule, and fit adaptation the exception. For twenty years past, at every meeting of the American Library Association, the reports upon library buildings have deplored the waste of money in well-meant edifices designed to accommodate the library service, but successful only in obstructing it. Even in so recent a

construction as the Boston Public Library building, so
many defects and inconveniences were found after it was
supposed to have been finished, that rooms had to be torn
out and re-constructed on three floors, while the pneumatic
tube system had been found so noisy as to be a public
nuisance, and had to be replaced by a later improved construction.

One leading cause for the mistakes which are so patent
in our library buildings is that they are not planned by
librarians but mainly by architects. The library authorities commonly take it for granted that the able architect
is master of his profession, and entrust him with the whole
design, leaving out of account the librarian, as a mere subordinate, entitled only to secondary consideration. The
result is a plan which exhibits, in its prominent features,
the architect's skill in effective pilasters, pillars, archi-
traves, cornices, and balustrades, while the library apartments which these features ornament are planned, not for
convenient and rapid book-service, but mainly for show.
It is the interest of architects to magnify their profession:
and as none of them has ever been, or ever will be a librarian, they cannot be expected to carry into effect unaided, what they have never learned; namely, the interior
arrangements which will best meet the utilities of the library service. Here is where the librarian's practical experience, or his observation of the successes or failures in
the reading-room and delivery service of other libraries,
should imperatively be called in. Let him demonstrate to
the governing board that he knows what is needed for
prompt and economical administration, and they will heed
his judgment, if they are reasonable men. While it belongs to the architect to plan, according to his own ideas,
the outside of the building, the inside should be planned
by the architect in direct concert with the librarian, in
all save merely ornamental or finishing work.

We do not erect a building and then determine whether it is to be a school house or a church: it is planned from the start with strict reference to the utilities involved; and so should it always be with a library.

In treating this subject, I shall not occupy space in outlining the proper scheme of building and interior arrangement for a great library, with its many distinct departments, for such institutions are the exceptions, while most libraries come within the rule of very moderate size, and comparatively inexpensive equipment. The first requisite for a public library, then, is a good location. It is important that this should be central, but it is equally important that the building should be isolated—that is, with proper open space on all sides, and not located in a block with other buildings. Many libraries have been destroyed or seriously damaged by fire originating in neighboring buildings, or in other apartments in the same building; while fires in separate library buildings have been extremely rare. It would be a wise provision to secure a library lot sufficiently large in area to admit of further additions to the building, both in the rear and at the side; and with slight addition to the cost, the walls and their supports may be so planned as to admit of this. Committees are seldom willing to incur the expense of an edifice large enough to provide for very prolonged growth of their collection; and the result is that the country is full of overcrowded libraries, without money to build, and prevented from expanding on the spot because no foresight was exercised in the original construction or land purchase, to provide for ready increase of space by widening out, and removing an outer wall so as to connect the old building with the new addition. If a library has 10,000 volumes, it would be very short-sighted policy to plan an edifice to contain less than 40,000, which it is likely to reach in from ten to forty years.

The next requisite to a central and sufficient site is that the location must be dry and airy. Any low site, especially in river towns, will be damp, and among the enemies of books, moisture holds a foremost place. Next, the site should afford light on all sides, and if necessary to place it near any thoroughfare, it should be set back so as to afford ample light and ventilation in front.

It need hardly be said that every library building should be fire-proof, after the many costly lessons we have had of the burning of public libraries at home and abroad. The material for the outside walls may be brick or stone, according to taste or relative cost. Brick is good enough, and if of the best quality, and treated with stone trimmings, is capable of sufficiently ornate effects, and is quite as durable as any granite or marble. No temptation of cheapness should ever be allowed to introduce wood in any part of the construction: walls, floors, and roof should be only of brick, stone, iron, or slate. A wooden roof is nothing but a tinder-box that invites the flames.

In general, two stories is a sufficient height for library buildings, except in those of the largest class, and the upper floors may be amply lighted by sky-lights. The side-lights can hardly be too numerous: yet I have seen library buildings running back from a street fifty to seventy-five feet, without a single window in either of the side walls. The result was to throw all the books on shelves into a gloomy shade for many hours of each day.

The interior construction should be so managed as to effect the finding and delivery of books to readers with the greatest possible economy of time and space. No shelves should be placed higher than can be reached by hand without mounting upon any steps or ladders; *i. e.*, seven to seven and a half feet. The system of shelving should all be constructed of iron or steel, instead of surrounding the books on three sides with combustible wood, as is done in most libraries. Shelves of oxidized metal will be found smooth enough to prevent any abrasion of bindings. Shelves should be easily adjustable to any height, to accommodate the various sizes of books.

In calculating shelf capacity, one and a half inches thickness a volume is a fair average, so that each hundred volumes would require about thirteen feet of linear shelf measurement. The space between uprights, that is, the length of each shelf, should not exceed two and a half feet. All spaces between shelves should be $10\frac{1}{2}$ or 11 inches high, to accommodate large octavos indiscriminately with smaller sizes; and a base shelf for quartos and folios, at a proper height from the floor, will restrict the number of shelves to six in each tier.

In the arrangement of the cases or book-stacks, the most economical method is to place book-cases of double face, not less than three feet apart, approached by aisles on either side, so as to afford free passage for two persons meeting or passing one another. The cases may be about ten feet each in length. There should be electric lights between all cases, to be turned on only when books are sought. The cases should be set at right angles to the wall, two or three feet from it, with the light from abundant windows coming in between them. The width of shelves may be from 16 to 18 inches in these double cases, thus giving about eight to nine inches depth to each side. No partition is required between the two sides.

It should be stated that the light obtained from windows, when thrown more than twenty feet, among cases of books on shelves, becomes too feeble for effective use in finding books. This fact should be considered in advance, while plans of construction, lighting, and interior arrangement are being made. All experience has shown that too much light cannot be had in any public library.

Railings and stair-cases for the second or upper floors should be of perforated iron.

The reading-room should be distinct from the book delivery or charging-room, to secure quiet for readers at all hours, avoiding the pressure, hurry and noise of conversation inevitable in a lending library or department. In the reading-room should be shelved a liberal supply of books of reference, and bibliographies, open without tickets to the readers. Next the central desk there should be shelves for the deposit of books reserved day by day for the use of readers. The library chairs, of whatever pattern may be preferred, should always combine the two requisites of strength and lightness. The floor should be covered with linoleum, or some similar floor covering, to deaden sound. Woolen carpets, those perennial breeders of dust, are an abomination.

In a library reading-room of any considerable size, each reader should be provided with table or desk room, not flat but sloping at a moderate angle, and allowing about three feet of space for each reader. These appliances for study need not be single pieces of furniture, but made in sections to accommodate from three to six readers at each. About thirty inches from the floor is a proper height.

For large dictionaries, atlases, or other bulky volumes, the adjustable revolving case, mounted on a pedestal, should be used.

For moving any large number of volumes about the library, book-trucks or barrows, with noiseless rubber wheels, are required.

Every library will need one or more catalogue cases to hold the alphabetical card catalogue. These are made with a maximum of skill by the Library Bureau, Boston.

The location of the issue-counter or desk is of cardinal importance. It should be located near the centre of the system of book-cases, or near the entrance to the stack, so as to minimize the time consumed in collecting the books wanted. It should also have a full supply of light, and this may be secured by a location directly in front of a large side window. Readers are impatient of delay, and the farther the books are from the issue-counter the longer they will have to wait for them.

Among modern designs for libraries, that of Dr. W. F. Poole, adapted for the Newberry Library, Chicago, is notable for dividing the library into many departments or separate rooms, the book shelves occupying one half the height of each, or 7½ feet out of 15, the remaining space being occupied by windows. This construction, of course, does not furnish as compact storage for books as the stack system. It is claimed to possess the advantage of extraordinarily good light, and of aiding the researches of readers. But it has the disadvantage of requiring readers to visit widely separated rooms to pursue studies involving several subjects, and of mounting in elevators to reach some departments. A system which brings the books to the reader, instead of the readers travelling after the books, would appear to be more practically useful to the public, with whom time is of cardinal importance.

In all libraries, there should be a receiving or packing room, where boxes and parcels of books are opened and books mended, collated, and prepared for the shelves. This room may well be in a dry and well lighted basement. Two small cloak-rooms for wraps will be needed, one for each sex. Two toilet rooms or lavatories should be provided. A room for the library directors or trustees, and one for the librarian, are essential in libraries of much extent. A janitor's room or sleeping quarters sometimes needs to be provided. A storage room for blanks, stationery, catalogues, etc., will be necessary in libraries of much

extent. A periodical room is sometimes provided, distinct
from the reading-room or the delivery department. In
this case, if several hundred periodicals are taken, an attendant should be always present to serve them to readers,
from the shelves or cases where they should be kept in
alphabetical order. Without this, and a ticket system to
keep track of what are in use, no one can readily find what
is needed, nor ascertain whether it is in a reader's hands
when sought for. System and the alphabet alone will
solve all difficulties.

As to the space required for readers in a periodical
room, it may be assumed that about five hundred square
feet will accommodate twenty-five readers, and the same
proportion for a larger number at one time. A room
twenty-five by forty would seat fifty readers, while one
twenty-five by twenty would accommodate twenty-five
readers, with proper space for tables, &c. The files for
newspapers are referred to in another chapter on periodicals.

In a library building, the heating and ventilation are of
prime importance. Upon their proper regulation largely
depends the health and consequently the efficiency of all
employed, as well as the comfort of the reading public.
There is no space to enter upon specific descriptions, for
which the many conflicting systems, with experience of
their practical working, should be examined. Suffice it to
say in general, that a temperature not far below nor above
70 degrees Fahrenheit should be aimed at; that the fur-
nace, with its attendant nuisances of noise, dust, and odors,
should be outside the library building—not under it; and
that electric lighting alone should be used, gas being
highly injurious to the welfare of books.

In calculating the space required for books shelved as
has been heretofore suggested, it may be approximately

stated that every one thousand volumes will require at least eighty to one hundred square feet of floor measurement. Thus, a library of 10,000 volumes would occupy an area of nearly one thousand square feet. But it is necessary to provide also for the continual growth of the collection. To do this, experience shows that in any flourishing public library, space should be reserved for three or four times the number of volumes in actual possession. If rooms are hired for the books, because of inability to build, the library should be so arranged as to leave each alternate shelf vacant for additions, or, in the more rapidly growing divisions, a still greater space. This will permit accessions to be shelved with their related books, without the trouble of frequently moving and re-arranging large divisions of the library. This latter is a very laborious process, and should be resorted to only under compulsion. The preventive remedy, of making sure of space in advance, by leaving a sufficiency of unoccupied shelves in every division of the library, is the true one.

In some libraries, a separate reading-room for ladies is provided. Mr. W. F. Poole records that in Cincinnati such a room was opened at the instance of the library directors. The result was that the ladies made it a kind of social rendezvous, where they talked over society matters, and exhibited the bargains made in their shopping excursions. Ladies who came to study preferred the general reading room, where they found every comfort among well conducted gentlemen, and the "ladies' reading-room" was abandoned, as not fulfilling its object. The same experiment in the Chicago Public Library had the same result.

Some libraries in the larger towns provide a special reading-room for children; and this accomplishes a two-fold object, namely, to keep the public reading-room free from flocks of little people in pursuit of books under difficulties, and to furnish the boys and girls with accommodations of their own. It may be suggested as an objection, that the dividing line as to age is difficult to be drawn: but let each applicant be questioned, and if falling below twelve, or fifteen, or whatever the age limit may be, directed to the juvenile reading-room, and there need be no trouble. Of course there will be some quite young readers who are gifted with intelligence beyond their years, and who may dislike to be reckoned as children; but library rules are not made to suit exceptions, but for the average; and as no book need be refused to any applicant in the juvenile department, no just cause of complaint can arise.

In some libraries, and those usually of the larger size, an art room is provided, where students of works on painting, sculpture, and the decorative arts can go, and have about them whatever treasures the library may contain in that attractive field. The advantages of this provision are, first, to save the necessity of handling and carrying so many heavy volumes of galleries of art and illustrated books to the general reading-room, and back again, and secondly, to enable those in charge of the art department to exercise more strict supervision in enforcing careful and cleanly treatment of the finest books in the library, than can be maintained in the miscellaneous crowd of readers in the main reading-room. The objections to it concern the general want of room to set apart for this purpose, and the desirability of concentrating the use of books in one main hall or reading-room. Circumstances and experience should determine the question for each library.

Some public libraries, and especially those constructed in recent years, are provided with a lecture-hall, or a large room for public meetings, concerts, or occasionally, even an opera-house, in the same building with the library. There are some excellent arguments in favor of this; and especially where a public benefactor donates to a city a building which combines both uses. The building given by Mr. Andrew Carnegie to the Public Library of Washington will be provided with a small hall suited to meetings, &c. But in all cases, such a public hall should be so isolated from the library reading-room as not to annoy readers, to whom quiet is essential. This end can be effected by having the intervening walls and floors so constructed as completely to deaden sound. A wholly distinct entrance should also be provided, not communicating with the doors and passages leading to the library.

Comparisons are sometimes made as to the relative cost of library buildings to the number of volumes they are designed to accommodate; but such estimates are misleading. The cost of an edifice in which architectural beauty and interior decoration concur to make it a permanent ornament to a city or town, need not be charged up at so much per volume. Buildings for libraries have cost all the way from twenty-five cents up to $4. for each volume stored. The Library of Congress, which cost six million dollars, and will ultimately accommodate 4,500,000 volumes, cost about $1.36 per volume. But it contains besides books, some half a million musical compositions, works of graphic art, maps and charts, etc.

The comparative cost of some library buildings erected in recent years, with ultimate capacity of each, may be of interest. Kansas City Public Library, 132+144, 125,000 vols., $200,000. Newark, N. J. Free Library, 138+216, 400,000 vols., $188,000. Forbes Library, Northampton, Mass. (granite), 107+137, 250,000 vols., $134,000. Fall River, Ms. Library, 80+130, 250,000 vols., $100,000. Peoria, Ill. Public Library (brick), 76+135, $70,000. Smiley Memorial Library, Redlands, Cal. (brick), 96+100, $50,000. Reuben Hoar Library, Littleton, Mass. (brick),

50+57, 25,000 vols., $25,000.   Rogers Memorial Library, Southworth, N. Y. 70+100, 20,000 vols., $20,000.   Belfast (Me.) Free Library (granite), 27+54, $10,000.   Gail-Borden Public Library, Elgin, Ill. (brick), 28+52, $9,000. Warwick, Mass. Public Library (wood), 45+60, 5,000 vols., $5,000.

The largely increased number of public library buildings erected in recent years is a most cheering sign of the times.   Since 1895, eleven extensive new library buildings have been opened: namely, the Library of Congress, the Boston Public Library, the Pratt Institute Library, Brooklyn, the Columbia University Library, New York, the Princeton, N. J. University Library, the Hart Memorial Library, of Troy, N. Y. the Carnegie Library, Pittsburgh, the Chicago Public Library, the Peoria, Ill. Public Library, the Kansas City, Mo. Public Library, and the Omaha, Neb. Public Library.

And there are provided for eight more public library buildings, costing more than $100,000 each; namely, the Providence, R. I. Public Library, the Lynn, Mass. Public Library, the Fall River, Mass. Public Library, the Newark, N. J. Free Public Library, the Milwaukee, Wis. Public Library and Museum, the Wisconsin State Historical Society Library, Madison, the New York Public Library, and the Jersey City Public Library.

To these will be added within the year 1900, as is confidently expected, the Washington City Public Library, the gift of Andrew Carnegie, to cost $300,000.

No philanthropist can ever find a nobler object for his fortune, or a more enduring monument to his memory, than the founding of a free public library.   The year 1899 has witnessed a new gift by Mr. Carnegie of a one hundred thousand dollar library to Atlanta, the Capital of Georgia, on condition that the city will provide a site, and $5,000 a year for the maintenance of the library. Cities in the east are emulating one another in providing public library buildings of greater or less cost. If the town library cannot have magnificence, it need not have meanness. A competition among architects selected to submit plans is becoming the favorite method of preparing to build. Five of the more extensive libraries have secured competitive plans of late from which to select—namely, the New York Public Library, the Jersey City Public Library, the Newark Free Public Library, the Lynn Public Library, and the Phoebe Hearst building for the University of California, which is to be planned for a library of 750,000 volumes. It is gratifying to add that in several recent provisions made for erecting large and important structures, the librarian was made a member of the building committee— *i. e.*, in the New York Public Library, the Newark Free Public Library, and the Lynn Public Library.

CHAPTER 17.

LIBRARY MANAGERS OR TRUSTEES.

We now come to consider the management of libraries as entrusted to boards of directors, trustees or library managers. These relations have a most intimate bearing upon the foundation, the progress and the consequent success of any library. Where a liberal intelligence and a hearty coöperation are found in those constituting the library board, the affairs of the institution will be managed with the best results. Where a narrow-minded and dictatorial spirit is manifested, even by a portion of those supervising a public library, it will require a large endowment both of patience and of tact in the librarian, to accomplish those aims which involve the highest usefulness.

Boards of library trustees vary in number, usually from three to nine or more. A board of three or five is found in practice more active and efficient than a larger number. The zeal and responsibility felt is apt to diminish in direct proportion to the increased numbers of the board. An odd number is preferable, to avoid an equal division of opinion upon any question to be determined.

In town or city libraries, the mode of selection of library trustees varies much. Sometimes the mayor appoints the library board, sometimes they are chosen by the city council, and sometimes elected by the people, at the annual selection of school or municipal officers. The term of service (most usually three years) should be so arranged that retirement of any members should always leave two at least who have had experience on the board. Library trustees serve without salary, the high honor of so serving the public counting for much.

The librarian is often made secretary of the trustees, and then he keeps the record of their transactions. He should never be made treasurer of the library funds, which would involve labor and responsibility incompatible with the manifold duties of the superintendent of a library. In case of a library supported by municipal taxation, the town treasurer may well serve as library treasurer also, or the trustees can choose one from their own board. The librarian, however, should be empowered to collect book fines or other dues, to be deposited with the treasurer at regular intervals, and he should have a small fund at disposal for such petty library expenses as constantly arise. All bills for books and other purchases, and all salaries of persons employed in the library should be paid by the treasurer.

The meetings of the trustees should be attended by the librarian, who must always be ready to supply all information as to the workings of the library, the needs for books, etc. Frequently the trustees divide up the business before them, appointing sub-committees on book selections, on library finances, on administration, furnishings, &c., with a view to prompt action.

If a library receives endowments, money gifts or legacies, they are held and administered by the trustees as a body corporate, the same as the funds annually appropriated for library maintenance and increase. Their annual report to the council, or municipal authorities, should exhibit the amount of money received from all sources in detail, and the amount expended for all purposes, in detail; also, the number of books purchased in the year, the aggregate of volumes in the library, the number of readers, and other facts of general interest.

All accounts against the library are first audited by the proper sub-committee, and payment ordered by the full board, by order on the treasurer. The accounts for all these expenditures should be kept by the treasurer, who should inform the librarian periodically as to balances.

The selection of books for a public library is a delicate and responsible duty, involving wider literary and scientific knowledge than falls to the lot of most trustees of libraries. There are sometimes specially qualified professional men or widely read scholars on such boards, whose services in recruiting the library are of great value. More frequently there are one or more men with hobbies, who would spend the library funds much too freely upon a class of books of no general interest. Thus, one trustee who plays golf may urge the purchase of all the various books upon that game, when one or at most two of the best should supply all needful demands. Another may want to add to the library about all the published books on the horse; another, who is a physician, may recommend adding a lot of medical books to the collection, utterly useless to the general reader. Beware of the man who has a hobby, either as librarian or as library trustee; he will aim to expend too much money on books which suit his own taste, but which have little general utility. Two mischiefs result from such a course: the library gets books which very few people read, and its funds are diverted from buying many books that may be of prime importance.

Trustees, although usually, (at least the majority of them) persons of culture and intelligence, cannot be expected to be bibliographers, nor to be familiar with the great range of new books that continually pour from the press. They have their own business or profession to engage them, and are commonly far too busy to study catalogues, or to follow the journals of the publishing world. So these busy men, charged with the oversight of the library interests, call to their aid an expert, and that expert is the librarian. It is his interest and his business to know far more than they do both of what the library already contains, and what it most needs. It is his to peruse the critical journals and reviews, as well as the literary notices of the select daily press, and to be prepared to recommend what works to purchase. He must always accompany his lists of wants with the prices, or at least the approximate cost of each, and the aggregate amount. If the trustees or book committee think the sum too large to be voted at any one time from the fund at their disposal, the librarian must know what can best be postponed, as well as what is most indispensable for the immediate wants of the library. If they object to any works on the list, he should be prepared to explain the quality and character of those called in question, and why the library, in his judgment, should possess them. If the list is largely cut down, and he considers himself hardly used, he should meet the disappointment with entire good humor, and try again when the members of the committee are in better mood, or funds in better supply.

It is very customary for boards of library officers to assume the charge of the administration so far as regards the library staff, and to make appointments, promotions or removals at their own pleasure. In most libraries, however, this power is exercised mainly on the advice or selection of the librarian, his action being confirmed when there is no serious objection. In still other cases, the librarian is left wholly free to choose the assistants. This is perhaps the course most likely to secure efficient service, since his judgment, if he is a person of tried capacity and mature experience, will lead to the selection of the fittest candidates, for the work which he alone thoroughly knows. No library trustee can put himself fully in the place of a librarian, and see for himself the multitude of occasions arising in the daily work of the library, where promptness, tact, and wide knowledge of books will make a success, and the want of any of these qualities a failure. Still less can he judge the competency or incompetency of one who is to be employed in the difficult and exact work of cataloguing books. Besides, there is always the hazard that trustees, or some of them, may have personal favorites or relatives to prefer, and will use their influence to secure the appointment or promotion of utterly uninstructed persons, in place of such candidates as are known to the librarian to be best qualified. In no case should any person be employed without full examination as to fitness for library work, conducted either by the librarian, or by a committee of which the librarian is a member or chief examiner. A probationary trial should also follow before final appointment.

The power of patronage, if unchecked by this safeguard, will result in filling any library with incompetents, to the serious detriment of the service on which its usefulness depends. The librarian cannot keep a training school for inexperts: he has no time for this, and he indispensably needs and should have assistants who are competent to their duties, from their first entrance upon them. As he is held responsible for all results, in the conduct of the library, both by the trustees and by the public, he should have the power, or at least the approximate power, to select the means by which those results are to be attained.

In the Boston Public Library, all appointments are made by the trustees upon nomination by the librarian, after an examination somewhat similar to that of the civil service, but by a board of library experts. In the British Museum Library, the selection and promotion of members of the staff are passed upon by the trustees, having the recommendation of the principal librarian before them. In the Library of Congress, appointments are made directly by the librarian after a probationary trial, with previous examination as to education, former experience or employments, attainments, and fitness for library service.

In smaller libraries, both in this country and abroad, a great diversity of usage prevails. Instances are rare in which the librarian has the uncontrolled power of appointment, promotion and removal. The requirement of examinations to test the fitness of candidates is extending, and since the establishment of five or six permanent schools of library science in the United States, with their graduates well equipped for library work, there is no longer any excuse for putting novices in charge of libraries —institutions where wide knowledge and thorough training are more indispensable than in any other profession whatever.

In State libraries, no uniformity prevails as to control. In some States, the governor has the appointment of the librarian, while in others, he is an elective officer, the State Legislature being the electors. As governors rarely continue in office longer than two or three years, the tenure of a librarian under them is precarious, and a most valuable officer may at any time be superseded by another who would have to learn all that the other knows. The result is rarely favorable to the efficient administration of the library. In a business absolutely demanding the very largest compass of literary and scientific knowledge, frequent rotation in office is clearly out of place. In a public or State library, every added year of experience adds incalculably to the value of a librarian's services, provided he is of active habits, and full of zeal to make his acquired knowledge constantly useful to those who use the library. Partizan politics, with their frequent changes, if suffered to displace a tried librarian and staff, will be sure to defeat the highest usefulness of any library. What can a political appointee, a man totally without either library training or library experience, do with the tools of which he has never learned the use? It will take him years to learn, and by the time he has learned, some other political party coming uppermost will probably displace him, to make room for another novice, on the principle that "to the victors belong the spoils" of office. Meanwhile, "the hungry sheep look up and are not fed," as Milton sings—that is, readers are deprived of expert and intelligent guidance.

This bane of political jobbery has not been confined to the libraries of States, but has invaded the management of many city and town libraries also. We have yet to learn of any benefit resulting to those who use the libraries.

In the case of a few of the State libraries, trustees or library commissioners or boards of control have been provided by law, but in others, a joint library committee, composed of members of both houses of the Legislature, has charge of the library interests. This is also the case in the Library of Congress at Washington, where three Senators and three Representatives constitute the Joint Committee of both Houses of Congress on the Library. The membership of this committee, as of all others in Congress, is subject to change biennially. It has been proposed to secure a more permanent and careful supervision of this National Library by adding to the Joint Committee of Congress three or more trustees of eminent qualifications, elected by Congress, as the Regents of the Smithsonian Institution now are, for a longer term of years. The trustees of the British Museum are appointed by the Crown, their tenure of office being for life.

In several States the librarian is appointed by the supreme court, as the State libraries are composed more largely of law books, than of miscellaneous literature, and special knowledge of case law, and the principles of jurisprudence, is demanded of the librarian.

Where the trustees of a public library are elected by the people, they have in their own hands the power of choosing men who are far above party considerations, and they should exercise it. In no department of life is the maxim —"the tools to the hands that can use them," more important than in the case of librarians and boards of managers of libraries. The value of skilled labor over the unskilled is everywhere recognized in the business of the world, by more certain employment and larger compensation: and why should it not be so in libraries?

CHAPTER 18.

LIBRARY REGULATIONS.

No feature in library administration is more important than the regulations under which the service of the library is conducted. Upon their propriety and regular enforcement depends very much of the utility of the collection.

Rules are of two kinds, those which concern the librarian and assistants, and those which concern the public resorting to the library. Of the first class are the regulations as to hours, division of labor, leaves or vacations of employees, &c. The larger the library, and consequently the force employed, the more important is a careful adjustment of relative duties, and of the times and seasons to be devoted to them. The assignment of work to the various assistants will naturally depend upon their respective qualifications. Those who know Latin, and two or more of the modern languages, would probably be employed upon the catalogue. Those who are familiar with the range of books published, in literature and science, will be best qualified for the service of the reading-room, which involves the supply of books and information. In direct proportion to the breadth of information possessed by any one, will be his usefulness in promptly supplying the wants of readers. Nothing is so satisfactory to students in libraries, or to the casual seekers of information of any kind, as to find their wants immediately supplied. The reader whom an intelligent librarian or assistant answers at once is grateful to the whole establishment; while the reader who is required to wait ten to twenty minutes for what he wants, becomes impatient and sometimes querulous, or leaves the library unsatisfied.

One rule of service at the library desk or counter should be that every assistant there employed should deem it his duty to aid immediately any one who is waiting, no matter what other concerns may engage his attention.   In other words, the one primary rule of a public library should be that the service of the public is always paramount.   All other considerations should be subordinate to that.

It is desirable that assistants in every library should learn all departments of library work, cataloguing, supplying books and information, preparing books for the shelves, etc.   This will enable each assistant to take the place of another in case of absence, a most important point. It will also help to qualify the more expert for promotion.

A second rule for internal adminstration in any library should be that all books are to be distributed, or replaced upon their shelves, daily.   If this is not systematically done, the library will tend to fall into chaos.   And even a small number of volumes not in their places will embarrass the attendants seeking them, and often deprive readers of their use—a thing to be always sedulously avoided.

In the Library of Congress, the replacement of books upon the shelves is carried out much more frequently than once daily.   As fast as books come in at the central desk by the returns of readers, they are sent back through the book-carriers, to the proper floors, where the outside label-numbers indicate that they belong, and replaced by the attendant there on their proper shelves.   These mechanical book-carriers run all day, by electric power, supplied by a dynamo in the basement, and, with their endless chain and attached boxes constantly revolving, they furnish a near approach to perpetual motion.   Thus I have seen a set of Macaulay's England, called for by ticket from the reading-room, arrive in three minutes from the outlying book-repository or iron stack, several hundreds of feet distant on an upper floor, placed on the reader's table, referred to, and returned at once, then placed in the book-carrier by the desk attendant, received back on its proper floor, and distributed to its own shelf by the attendant there, all within half an hour after the reader's application. Another rule to be observed by the reading-room attendants is to examine all call-slips, or readers' tickets, remaining uncalled for at the close of each day's business, and see if the books on them are present in the library. This precaution is demanded by the security of the collection, as well as by the good order and arrangement of the library. Neglect of it may lead to losses or misplacements, which might be prevented by careful and unremitting observance of this rule.

Another rule of eminent propriety is that librarians or assistants are not to read newspapers during library hours. When there happen to be no readers waiting to be helped, the time should be constantly occupied with other library work. There is no library large enough to be worthy of the name, that does not have arrears of work incessantly waiting to be done. And while this is the case, no library time should be wasted upon periodicals, which should be perused only outside of library hours. If one person employed in a library reads the newspaper or magazine, the bad example is likely to be followed by others. Thus serious inattention to the wants of readers, as well as neglect of library work postponed, will be sure to follow.

A fourth rule, resting upon the same reason, should prevent any long sustained gossip or conversation during library hours. That time belongs explicitly to the public or to the work of the library. The rule of silence which is enforced upon the public in the interest of readers should not be broken by the library managers themselves. Such brief question and answer as emergency or the need-

ful business of the library requires should be conducted in
a low tone, and soon ended. Library administration is a
business, and must be conducted in a business way. No
library can properly be turned into a place of conversation.

All differences or disputes between attendants as to the
work to be done by each, or methods, or any other question
leading to dissension, should be promptly and decisively
settled by the librarian, and of course cheerfully submitted
to by all. Good order and discipline require that there
should be only one final authority in any library. Controversies are not only unseemly in themselves, but they
are time-consuming, and are liable to be overheard by
readers, to the prejudice of those who engage in them.

Another rule to be observed is to examine all books returned, as carefully as a glance through the volume will
permit, to detect any missing or started leaves, or injury
to bindings. No volume bearing marks of dilapidation of
any kind should be permitted to go back to the shelves, or
be given to readers, but placed in a bindery reserve for
needful repairs.

It should hardly be necessary to say that all those connected with a public library should be carefully observant
of hours, and be always in their places, unless excused.
The discipline of every library should be firm in this respect, and dilatory or tardy assistants brought to regard
the rule of prompt and regular service. "No absence without leave" should be mentally posted in the consciousness
and the conscience of every one.

Another rule should limit the time for mid-day refreshment, and so arrange it that the various persons employed
go at different hours. As to time employed, half-an-hour
for lunch, as allowed in the Washington departments, is
long enough in any library.

Furloughs or vacations should be regulated to suit the

library service, and not allow several to be absent at the same time. As to length of vacation time, few libraries can afford the very liberal fashion of twelve months wages for eleven months work, as prevalent in the Washington Departments. The average vacation time of business houses—about two weeks—more nearly corresponds to that allowed in the smaller public libraries. Out of 173 libraries reporting in 1893, 61 allowed four weeks or more vacation, 27 three weeks, 54 two weeks, and 31 none. But in cases of actual illness, the rule of liberality should be followed, and no deduction of wages should follow temporary disability.

Where many library attendants are employed, all should be required to enter on a daily record sheet or book, the hour of beginning work. Then the rule of no absence without special leave should be enforced as to all during the day.

We now come to such rules of library administration as concern the readers, or the public. The rule of silence, or total abstinence from loud talking, should be laid down and enforced. This is essential for the protection of every reader from annoyance or interruption in his pursuits. The rule should be printed on all readers' tickets, and it is well also to post the word SILENCE, in large letters, in two or more conspicuous places in the reading-room. This will give a continual reminder to all of what is expected, and will usually prevent any loud conversation. While absolute silence is impossible in any public library, the inquiries and answers at the desk can always be made in a low and even tone, which need attract no attention from any readers, if removed only a few feet distant. As there are always persons among readers who will talk, notwithstanding rules, they should be checked by a courteous reminder from the librarian, rather than from any subordinate. This—for the obvious reason that admonition from the highest authority carries the greatest weight.

Another rule, which should always be printed on the call-slips, or readers' tickets, is the requirement to return books and receive back their tickets always before leaving the library. This duty is very commonly neglected, from the utter carelessness of many readers, who do not realize that signing their ticket for any book holds them responsible for it until it is returned. Many are unwilling to spend a moment's time in waiting for a ticket to be returned to them. Many will leave their books on tables or seats where they were reading, and go away without reclaiming their receipts. While complete observance of this rule is of course hopeless of attainment in a country where free and easy manners prevail, every librarian should endeavor to secure at least an approximate compliance with a rule adopted alike for the security and good order of the library, and the efficient service of the reader.

All readers should be privileged to reserve books from day to day which they have not completed the use of, and instructed always to give notice of such reservation before leaving the library. This saves much time, both to the reader and to the librarian in sending repeatedly for books put away needlessly.

In a circulating library, a fixed rule limiting the time for which a book may be kept, is essential. This may be from three days to two weeks, according to the demand for the book, but it should not exceed the latter period. Still, a renewal term may be conceded, provided the book is not otherwise called for. A small fine of so much a day for each volume kept out beyond the time prescribed by the rule, will often secure prompt return, and is the usage in most libraries where books are lent out. In the Boston Public Library no renewals are allowed. A rule requiring the replacement or repair of books damaged while in the hands of a reader should be printed and enforced. It may properly be waived where the damage is slight or unavoidable.

In public circulating libraries, a rule of registration is required, and in some libraries of reference also; but in the Library of Congress all readers over sixteen are admitted without any formality or registration whatever.

In popular libraries, the need of a registry list of those entitled to borrow books, is obvious, to prevent the issue to improper or unauthorized persons; as, for example, residents of another town, or persons under the prescribed age of admission to library privileges. A printed library card should be issued to each person privileged to draw books; corresponding in number to the page or index-card of the library record. Each card should bear the full name and address of the applicant, and be signed with an obligation to obey the rules of the library. On this card all books drawn may be entered, always with month and day date, and credited with date of return, the parallel entries being at the same time made in the library charging record.

Library cards of registration should be issued for a limited period, say twelve months, in order to bring all persons to a systematic review of their privilege, and should be renewed annually, so long as the holder is entitled to registration. No books should be issued except to those presenting registration cards, together with a call-slip or ticket for the book wanted.

Another rule should fix a limit to the number of volumes to be drawn by any reader. Two volumes out at any one time would be a fair limit. If made more to all readers, there is likely to be sometimes a scarcity of books to be drawn upon; and if a few readers are permitted to draw more than others, the charge of undue favoritism will be justified.

Another rule should be that any incivility or neglect on the part of any library attendant should be reported to the librarian. In such cases, the attendant should always be heard, before any admonition or censure is bestowed.

An almost necessary rule in most libraries is that no book should be taken from the shelves by any person not employed in the library. The exceptions are of course, the books provided expressly for the free and open reference of the readers.

Another essential rule is that no writing or marks may be made in any library book or periodical; nor is any turning down of leaves permitted. A printed warning is important to the effect that any cutting or defacing of library books or periodicals is a penal offense, and will be prosecuted according to law.

The regulations for admission to library privileges are important. In this country the age limitation is more liberal than in Europe. The Boston Public Library, for example, is free to all persons over twelve years of age. In the Library of Congress, the age limit is sixteen years or upward, to entitle one to the privileges of a reader. In the Astor Library, none are admitted under nineteen, and in the British Museum Library none below twenty-one years.

The hours during which the library is open should be printed as part of the regulations.

All the library rules should be printed and furnished to the public. The most essential of them, if carefully expressed in few words, can be grouped in a single small sheet, of 16mo. size or less, and pasted in the inside cover of every book belonging to the library. Better still, (and it will save expense in printing) let the few simple rules, in small but legible type, form a part of the book plate, or library label, which goes on the left-hand inner cover of each volume. Thus every reader will have before him, in daily prominence, the regulations which he is to observe, and no excuse can be pleaded of ignorance of the rules.

As no law is ever long respected unless it is enforced, so no regulations are likely to be observed unless adhered to in every library. Rules are a most essential part of library administration, and it should be a primary object of every librarian or assistant to see that they are observed by all.

CHAPTER 19.

LIBRARY REPORTS AND ADVERTISING.

We now come to consider the annual reports of librarians. These should be made to the trustees or board of library control, by whatever name it may be known, and should be addressed to the chairman, as the organ of the board. In the preparation of such reports, two conditions are equally essential—conciseness and comprehensiveness. Every item in the administration, frequentation, and increase of the library should be separately treated, but each should be condensed into the smallest compass consistent with clear statement. Very long reports are costly to publish, and moreover, have small chance of being read. In fact, the wide perusal of any report is in direct proportion to its brevity.

This being premised, let us see what topics the librarian's report should deal with.

1. The progress of the library during the year must be viewed as most important. A statistical statement of accessions, giving volumes of books, and number of pamphlets separately, added during the year, should be followed by a statement of the aggregate of volumes and pamphlets in the collection. This is ascertained by actual count of the books upon the shelves, adding the number of volumes charged out, or in the bindery, or in readers' hands at the time of the enumeration. This count is far from a difficult or time-consuming affair, as there is a short-hand method of counting by which one person can easily arrive at the aggregate of a library of 100,000 volumes, in a single day of eight to ten hours. This is done by counting by twos or threes the rows of books as they stand on the shelves, passing the finger rapidly along the backs, from left to right and from top to bottom of the shelves. As fast as one hundred volumes are counted, simply write down a figure one; then, at the end of the second hundred, a figure two, and so on, always jotting down one figure the more for each hundred books counted. The last figure in the counter's memorandum will represent the number of hundreds of volumes the library contains. Thus, if the last figure is 92, the library has just 9,200 volumes. This rapid, and at the same time accurate method, by which any one of average quickness can easily count two hundred volumes a minute, saves all counting up by tallies of five or ten, and also all slow additions of figures, since one figure at the end multiplied by one hundred, expresses the whole.

2. Any specially noteworthy additions to the library should be briefly specified.

3. A list of donors of books during the year, with num-

ber of volumes given by each, should form part of the report. This may properly come at the end as an appendix.

4. A brief of the money income of the year, with sources whence derived, and of all expenditures, for books, salaries, contingent expenses, etc., should form a part of the report, unless reported separately by a treasurer of the library funds.

5. The statistics of a librarian's report, if of a lending library, should give the aggregate number of volumes circulated during the year, also the number of borrowers recorded who have used and who have not used the privilege of borrowing. The number of volumes used by readers in the reference or reading-room department should be given, as well as the aggregate of readers. It is usual in some library reports to classify the books used by readers, as, so many in history, poetry, travels, natural science, etc., but this involves labor and time quite out of proportion to its utility. Still, a comparative statement of the aggregate volumes of fiction read or drawn out, as against all other books, may be highly useful as an object lesson, if embodied in the library report.

6. A statement of the actual condition of the library, as to books, shelving accommodations, furniture, etc., with any needful suggestions for improvement, should be included in the annual report.

7. A well-considered suggestion of the value of contributions to the library in books or funds to enrich the collection, should not be overlooked.

8: The librarian should not forget a word of praise for his assistants, in the great and useful work of carrying on the library. This will tend to excite added zeal to excel, when the subordinates feel that their services are appreciated by their head, as well as by the public.

The preparation of an annual report affords some test

of the librarian's skill and judgment. It should aim at plain and careful statement, and all rhetoric should be dispensed with. Divided into proper heads, a condensed statement of facts or suggestions under each should be made, and all repetition avoided.

Such a library report should never fail to set forth the great benefit to the community which a free use of its treasures implies, while urging the importance of building up the collection, through liberal gifts of books, periodicals, or money, thus enabling it to answer the wants of readers more fully, year by year. It will sometimes be a wise suggestion to be made in a librarian's report, that the library still lacks some specially important work, such as Larned's "History for Ready Reference," or the extensive "Dictionary of National Biography," or Brunet's *Manuel du Libraire*, or a set of Congressional Debates from the beginning; and such a suggestion may often bear fruit in leading some public-spirited citizen to supply the want by a timely contribution.

Of course, the annual report of every public library should be printed, and as pamphlets are seldom read, and tend rapidly to disappear, its publication in the newspapers is vastly more important than in any other form. While a pamphlet report may reach a few people, the newspaper reaches nearly all; and as a means of diffusing information in any community, it stands absolutely without rival. Whether the library reports shall be printed in pamphlet form or not is a matter of expediency, to be determined by the managing board. Funds are rarely ample enough, in the smaller town libraries, to justify the expense, in view of the small circulation which such reports receive, and it is much better to put the money into printing library catalogues, which every body needs and will use, than into library reports, which comparatively few will make any use of. A judicious compromise may be usefully made, by inducing some newspaper, which would print a liberal share of the report free of charge, as news, for public information, to put the whole in type and strike off a few hundred copies in sheet form or pages, at a moderate charge.

This would enable the library officers to distribute a goodly number, and to keep copies of each annual report for reference, without the expense of a pamphlet edition.

In some of the larger and more enterprising of city libraries, reports are made quarterly or monthly by the librarian. These of course are much more nearly up to date, and if they publish lists of books added to the library, they are correspondingly useful. Frequently they contain special bibliographies of books on certain subjects. Among these, the monthly bulletins of the Boston Public Library, Harvard University Library, New York Public Library, Salem, Mass., Public Library, and the Providence Public Library are specially numerous and important.

The relations of a public library to the local press of the city or town where it is situated will now be noticed. It is the interest of the librarian to extend the usefulness of the library by every means; and the most effective means is to make it widely known. In every place are found many who are quite ignorant of the stores of knowledge which lie at their doors in the free library. And among those who do know it and resort to it, are many who need to have their interest and attention aroused by frequent notices as to its progress, recent additions to its stores, etc. The more often the library is brought before the public by the press, the more interest will be taken in it by the community for whose information it exists.

It is of the utmost importance that the library conductors should have the active good will of all the newspaper

editors in its vicinity. This will be acquired both by aiding them in all researches which the daily or frequent
wants of their profession render necessary; and also, by
giving them freely and often items of intelligence about
the library for publication. Enterprising journals are
perpetually on the hunt for new and varied matter to fill
their columns. They send their reporters to the library
to make "a story," as it is called, out of something in it
or about it. These reporters are very seldom persons
versed in books, or able to write understandingly or attractively about them. Left to themselves to construct
"a story" out of a half hour's conversation with the librarian, the chances are that an article will be produced which
contains nearly as many errors as matters of fact, with the
names of authors or the titles of their books mis-spelled or
altered, and with matters manufactured out of the reporter's fancy which formed no part of the interview, while
what did form important features in it are perhaps omitted. The remedy, or rather the preventive of such inadequate reports of what the librarian would say to the
public is to become his own reporter. The papers will
willingly take for publication short "library notes," as
they may be called, containing information about the library or its books, carefully type-written. This course at
once secures accurate and authentic statements, and saves
the time of the press reporters for other work.

Bear in mind always that the main object of such library
notices is to attract attention, and encourage people to use
the library. Thus there should be sought frequent opportunities of advertising the library by this best of all possible
means, because it is the one which reaches the largest
number. To do it well requires some skill and practice,
and to do it often is quite as essential as to do it well.
Keep the library continually before the public. What are

the business houses which are most thronged with customers? They are those that advertise most persistently and attractively. So with the library; it will be more and more resorted to, in proportion as it keeps its name and its riches before the public eye.

A certain timeliness in these library notices should be cultivated. The papers are eager to get anything that illustrates what is uppermost in the public mind. If a local fair is in progress or preparing, give them a list of the best books the library has in that field; the history of the Philadelphia Exposition, the Chicago World's Fair, the Paris Expositions, &c. On another day, set forth the books on manufactures, horses, cattle, domestic animals, decorative art, &c. If there is a poultry exhibition, or a dog show, call public attention to the books on poultry or dogs. If an art exhibition, bring forward the titles of books on painting, sculpture, drawing, and the history of art, ancient and modern.

If some great man has died, as Bismarck or Gladstone, give the titles of any biographies or books about him, adding even references to notable magazine articles that have appeared. When the summer vacation is coming around, advertise your best books of travel, of summer resorts, of ocean voyages, of yachting, camping, fishing and shooting, golf and other out-door games, etc. If there is a Presidential campaign raging, make known the library's riches in political science, the history of administrations, and of nominating conventions, lives of the Presidents, books on elections, etc. If an international dispute or complication is on foot, publish the titles of your books on international law, and those on the history or resources of the country or countries involved; and when a war is in progress, books on military science, campaigns, battles, sieges, and the history of the contending nations will be timely and interesting.

Whatever you do in this direction, make it short and at-tractive.   Organize your material, describe a specially in-teresting work by a reference to its style, or its illustra-tions, or its reputation, etc.   Distribute your library notes impartially; that is, if several papers are published, be care-ful not to slight any of them.   Find out the proper days to suit their want of matter, and never send in your notes when the paper is overcrowded.   Always read a proof-slip of each article; time spent in going to a newspaper office to correct proof is well spent, for misprints always await the unwary who trusts to the accuracy of types.

If the library acquires any extensive or notable book, whether old or new, do not fail to make it known through the press.   If any citizen gives a number of volumes to the library, let his good deeds have an appreciative notice, that others may go and do likewise.

Another feature of library advertising is the publication in the press of the titles of new books added to the library. As this is merely catalogue printing, however abbreviated in form the titles may be, it will usually (and very prop-erly) be charged for by the newspapers.   But it will pay, in the direction of inducing a much larger use of the li-brary, and as the sole object of the institution is to con-tribute to public intelligence, it becomes library managers not to spare any expense so conducive to that result.

CHAPTER 20.

THE FORMATION OF LIBRARIES.

In the widely extended and growing public interest in libraries for the people, and in the ever increasing gatherings of books by private collectors, I may be pardoned for some suggestions pertaining specially to the formation of libraries. I do not refer to the selection of books, which is treated in the first chapter, nor to the housing and care of libraries, but to some important points involved in organizing the foundation, so to speak, of a library.

The problem, of course, is a widely different one for the private collector of an individual or family library, and for the organizers of a public one. But in either case, it is important, first of all, to have a clearly defined and well considered plan. Without this, costly mistakes are apt to be made, and time, energy and money wasted, all of which might be saved by seeing the end from the beginning, and planning accordingly.

Let us suppose that a resident in a community which has never enjoyed the benefit of a circulating library conceives the idea of using every means to secure one. The first question that arises is, what are those means? If the State in which his residence lies has a Library law, empowering any town or city to raise money by taxation for founding and maintaining a free library, the way is apparently easy, at first sight. But here comes in the problem —can the requisite authority to lay the tax be secured? This may involve difficulties unforeseen at first. If there is a city charter, does it empower the municipal authorities (city council or aldermen) to levy such a tax? If not, then appeal must be made to a popular vote, at some election of municipal officers, at which the ballots for or against a Library tax should determine the question. This will at once involve a campaign of education, in which should be enlisted (1) The editors of all the local papers. (2) The local clergymen, lawyers and physicians. (3) All literary men and citizens of wealth or influence in the community. (4) All teachers in the public schools and other institutions of learning. (5) The members of the city or town government. These last will be apt to feel any impulse of public sentiment more keenly than their own individual opinions on the subject. In any case, the public-spirited man who originates the movement should enlist as many able coadjutors as he can. If he is not himself gifted with a ready tongue, he should persuade some others who are ready and eloquent talkers to take up the cause, and should inspire them with his own zeal. A public meeting should be called, after a goodly number of well-known and influential people are enlisted (not before) and addresses should be made, setting forth the great advantage of a free library to every family. Its value to educate the people, to furnish entertainment that will go far to supplant idleness and intemperance, to help on the work of the public schools, and to elevate the taste, improve the morals, quicken the intellect and employ the leisure hours of all, should be set forth.

With all these means of persuasion constantly in exercise, and unremitting diligence in pushing the good cause through the press and by every private opportunity, up to the very day of the election, the chances are heavily in favor of passing the library measure by a good majority. It must be a truly Bœotian community, far gone in stupidity or something worse, which would so stand in its own light as to vote down a measure conducing in the high-

est degree to the public intelligence.   But even should it
be defeated, its advocates should never be discouraged.
Like all other reforms or improvements, its progress may
be slow at first, but it is none the less sure to win in the
end.   One defeat has often led to a more complete victory
when the conflict is renewed.   The beaten party gathers
wisdom by experience, finds out any weakness existing in
its ranks or its management, and becomes sensible where
its greatest strength should be put forth in a renewal of
the contest.   The promoters of the measure should at once
begin a fresh agitation.   They should pledge every friend
of the library scheme to stand by it himself, and to secure
at least one new convert to the cause.   And the chances
are that it will be carried triumphantly through at the
next trial, or, if not then, at least within no long time.

But we should consider also the case of those communities where no State Library law exists.   These are unhappily not a few; and it is a remarkable fact that even so old,
and rich, and well-developed a State as Pennsylvania had
no such provision for public enlightenment until within
three years.   In the absence of a law empowering local
governments or voters to lay a tax for such a purpose, the
most obvious way of founding a library is by local subscription.   This is of course a less desirable method than
one by which all citizens should contribute to the object
in proportion to their means.   But it is better to avail of
the means that exist in any place than to wait an indefinite period for a State Legislature to be educated up
to the point of passing measures which would render the
formation of libraries easy in all places.

Let the experiment be tried of founding a library by
individual effort and concert.   With only two or three
zealous and active promoters, even such a plan can be carried into successful operation in almost any community.

A canvass should be made from house to house, with a
short prospectus or agreement drawn up, pledging the
subscribers to give a certain sum toward the foundation
of a library. If a few residents with large property can
be induced to head the list with liberal subscriptions, it
will aid much in securing confidence in the success of the
movement, and inducing others to subscribe. No contributions, however small, should fail to be welcomed, since
they stand for a wider interest in the object. After a
thorough canvass of the residents of the place, a meeting of
those subscribing should be called, and a statement put before them of the amount subscribed. Then an executive
committee, say of three or five members, should be chosen
to take charge of the enterprise. This committee should
appoint a chairman, a secretary, and a treasurer, the latter
to receive and disburse the funds subscribed. The chairman should call and preside at meetings of the committee,
of which the secretary should record the proceedings in a
book kept for the purpose.

The first business of the Library committee should be
to confer and determine upon the ways and means of
organizing the library. This involves a selection of books
suitable for a beginning, a place of deposit for them, and
a custodian or librarian to catalogue them and keep the
record of the books drawn out and returned. Usually, a
room can be had for library purposes in some public building or private house, centrally located, without other expense than that of warming and lighting. The services of
a librarian, too, can often be secured by competent volunteer aid, there being usually highly intelligent persons with
sufficient leisure to give their time for the common benefit,
or to share that duty with others, thus saving all the funds
for books to enrich the library.

The chief trouble likely to be encountered by a Library

committee will lie in the selection of books to form the nucleus or starting point of the collection. Without repeating anything heretofore suggested, it may be said that great care should be taken to have books known to be excellent, both interesting in substance and attractive in style. To so apportion the moderate amount of money at disposal as to give variety and interest to the collection, and attract readers from the start, is a problem requiring good judgment for its solution. Much depends upon the extent of the fund, but even with so small a sum as two or three hundred dollars, a collection of the very best historians, poets, essayists, travellers and voyagers, scientists, and novelists can be brought together, which will furnish a range of entertaining and instructive reading for several hundred borrowers. The costlier encyclopaedias and works of reference might be waited for until funds are recruited by a library fair, or lectures, or amateur concerts, plays, or other evening entertainments.

Another way of recruiting the library which has often proved fruitful is to solicit contributions of books and magazines from families and individuals in the vicinity. This should be undertaken systematically some time after the subscriptions in money have been gathered in. It is not good policy to aim at such donations at the outset, since many might make them an excuse for not subscribing to the fund for founding the library, which it is to the interest of all to make as large as possible. But when once successfully established, appeals for books and periodicals will surely add largely to the collection, and although many of such accessions may be duplicates, they will none the less enlarge the facilities for supplying the demands of readers. Families who have read through all or nearly all the books they possess will gladly bestow them for so useful a purpose, especially when assured of reaping reciprocal benefit by the opportunity of freely perusing a great variety of choice books, new and old, which they have never read. Sometimes, too, a public-spirited citizen, when advised of the lack of a good cyclo-paedia, or of the latest extensive dictionary, or collective biography, in the library, will be happy to supply it, there-by winning the gratitude and good will of all who frequent the library. All donations should have inserted in them a neat book-plate, with the name of the donor inscribed, in connection with the name of the Library.

Many a useful library of circulation has been started with a beginning of fifty to a hundred volumes, and the little acorn of learning thus planted has grown up in the course of years to a great tree, full of fruitful and wide-spreading branches.

CHAPTER 21.

CLASSIFICATION.

If there is any subject which, more than all others, di-vides opinion and provokes endless controversy among li-brarians and scholars, it is the proper classification of books. From the beginning of literature this has been a well-nigh insoluble problem. Treatise after treatise has been written upon it, system has been piled upon system, learned men have theorised and wrangled about it all their lives, and successive generations have dropped into their graves, leaving the vexed question as unsettled as ever.

Every now and then a body of *savans* or a convention of librarians wrestles with it, and perhaps votes upon it,

"And by decision more embroils the fray"

since the dissatisfied minority, nearly as numerous and quite as obstinate as the majority, always refuses to be bound by it. No sooner does some sapient librarian, with the sublime confidence of conviction, get his classification house of cards constructed to his mind, and stands rapt in admiration before it, when there comes along some wise man of the east, and demolishes the fair edifice at a blow, while the architect stands by with a melancholy smile, and sees all his household gods lying shivered around him.

Meanwhile, systems of classification keep on growing, until, instead of the thirty-two systems so elaborately described in Edwards's Memoirs of Libraries, we have almost as many as there are libraries, if the endless modifications of them are taken into account. In fact, one begins to realise that the schemes for the classification of knowledge are becoming so numerous, that a classification of the systems themselves has fairly become a desideratum. The youthful neophyte, who is struggling after an education in library science, and thinks perhaps that it is or should be an exact science, is bewildered by the multitude of counsellors, gets a head-ache over their conflicting systems, and adds to it a heart-ache, perhaps, over the animosities and sarcasms which divide the warring schools of opinion.

Perhaps there would be less trouble about classification, if the system-mongers would consent to admit at the outset that no infallible system is possible, and would endeavor, amid all their other learning, to learn a little of the saving grace of modesty. A writer upon this subject has well observed that there is no man who can work out a scheme of classification that will satisfy permanently even himself.

Much less should he expect that others, all having their favorite ideas and systems, should be satisfied with his. As there is no royal road to learning, so there can be none to classification; and we democratic republicans, who stand upon the threshold of the twentieth century, may rest satisfied that in the Republic of Letters no autocrat can be allowed.

The chief difficulty with most systems for distributing the books in a library appears to lie in the attempt to apply scientific minuteness in a region where it is largely inapplicable. One can divide and sub-divide the literature of any science indefinitely, in a list of subjects, but such exhaustive sub-divisions can never be made among the books on the shelves. Here, for example, is a "Treatise on diseases of the heart and lungs." This falls naturally into its two places in the subject catalogue, the one under "Heart," and the second under "Lungs;" but the attempt to classify it on the shelves must fail, as regards half its contents. You cannot tear the book to pieces to satisfy logical classification. Thousands of similar cases will occur, where the same book treats of several subjects. Nearly all periodicals and transactions of societies of every kind refuse to be classified, though they can be catalogued perfectly on paper by analysing their contents. To bring all the resources of the library on any subject together on the shelves is clearly impossible. They must be assembled for readers from various sections of the library, where the rule of analogy or of superior convenience has placed them.

What is termed close classification, it will be found, fails by attempting too much. One of the chief obstacles to its general use is that it involves a too complicated notation. The many letters and figures that indicate position on the shelves are difficult to remember in the direct ratio of their number. The more minute the classification, the more signs of location are required. When they become very numerous, in any system of classification, the system breaks down by its own weight. Library attendants consume an undue amount of time in learning it, and library cataloguers and classifiers in affixing the requisite signs of designation to the labels, the shelves, and the catalogues. Memory, too, is unduly taxed to apply the system. While a superior memory may be found equal to any task imposed upon it, average memories are not so fortunate. The expert librarian, in whose accomplished head the whole world of science and literature lies coördinated, so that he can apply his classification unerringly to all the books in a vast library, must not presume that unskilled assistants can do the same.

One of the mistakes made by the positivists in classification is the claim that their favorite system can be applied to all libraries alike. That this is a fallacy may be seen in an example or two. Take the case of a large and comprehensive Botanical library, in which an exact scientific distribution of the books may and should be made. It is classified not only in the grand divisions, such as scientific and economic botany, etc., but a close analytical treatment is extended over the whole vegetable kingdom. Books treating of every plant are relegated to their appropriate classes, genera, and species, until the whole library is organised on a strictly scientific basis. But in the case, even of what are called large libraries, so minute a classification would be not only unnecessary, but even obstructive to prompt service of the books. And the average town library, containing only a shelf or two of botanical works, clearly has no use for such a classification. The attempt to impose a universal law upon library arrangement, while the conditions of the collections are endlessly varied, is foredoomed to failure.

The object of classification is to bring order out of confusion, and to arrange the great mass of books in science
and literature of which every library is composed, so that
those on related subjects should be as nearly as possible
brought together. Let us suppose a collection of some
hundred thousand volumes, in all branches of human
knowledge, thrown together without any classification or
catalogue, on the tables, the shelves, and the floor of an
extensive reading-room. Suppose also an assemblage of
scholars and other readers, ready and anxious to avail
themselves of these literary treasures, this immense library
without a key. Each wants some certain book, by some
author whose name he knows, or upon some subject upon
which he seeks to inform himself. But how vain and hopeless the effort to go through all this chaos of learning, to
find the one volume which he needs! This illustration
points the prime necessity of classification of some kind,
before a collection of books can be used in an available way.

Then comes in the skilled bibliographer, to convert this
chaos into a cosmos, to illumine this darkness with the light
of science. He distributes the whole mass, volume by
volume, into a few great distinct classes; he creates families
or sub-divisions in every class; he assembles together in
groups all that treat of the same subject, or any of its
branches; and thus the entire scattered multitude of volumes is at length coördinated into a clear and systematic
collection, ready for use in every department. A great library is like a great army: when unorganized, your army
is a mere undisciplined mob: but divide and sub-divide it
into army corps, divisions, brigades, regiments, and com-
panies, and you can put your finger upon every man.

To make this complete organization of a library successful, one must have an organising mind, a wide acquaintance with literature, history, and the outlines, at least, of

all the sciences; a knowledge of the ancient and of various modern languages; a quick intuition, a ripe judgment, a cultivated taste, a retentive memory, and a patience and perseverance that are inexhaustible.

Even were all these qualities possessed, there will be in the arrangement elements of discord and of a failure. A multitude of uncertain points in classification, and many exceptions will arise; and these must of necessity be settled arbitrarily. The more conversant one becomes with systems of classification, when reduced to practice, the more he becomes assured that a perfect bibliographical system is impossible.

Every system of classification must find its application fraught with doubts, complications, and difficulties; but the wise bibliographer will not pause in his work to resolve all these insoluble problems; he will classify the book in hand according to his best judgment at the moment it comes before him. He can no more afford to spend time over intricate questions of the preponderance of this, that, or the other subject in a book, than a man about to walk to a certain place can afford to debate whether he shall put his right foot forward or his left. The one thing needful is to go forward.

Referring to the chapter on bibliography for other details, I may here say that the French claim to have reached a highly practical system of classification in that set forth in J. C. Brunet's *Manuel du Libraire*. This is now generally used in the arrangement of collections of books in France, with some modifications, and the book trade find it so well adapted to their wants, that classified sale and auction catalogues are mostly arranged on that system. It has only five grand divisions: Theology, Law, Arts and Sciences, Belles-lettres, and History. Each of these classes has numerous sub-divisions. For example, geography and voyages and travels form a division of history, between the philosophy of history and chronology, etc.

The classification in use in the *Bibliothèque nationale* of France places Theology first, followed by Law, History, Philosophy and Belles-lettres. The grand division of Philosophy includes all which is classified under Arts and Sciences in the system of Brunet.

In the Library of the British Museum the classification starts with Theology, followed by 2. Jurisprudence; 3. Natural History (including Botany, Geology, Zoölogy, and Medicine); 4. Art (including Archaeology, Fine Arts, Architecture, Music, and Useful Arts); 5. Philosophy (including Politics, Economics, Sociology, Education, Ethics, Metaphysics, Mathematics, Military and Naval Science, and Chemistry; 6. History (including Heraldry and Genealogy); 7. Geography (including Ethnology); 8. Biography (including Epistles); 9. Belles-lettres (including Poetry, Drama, Rhetoric, Criticism, Bibliography, Collected Works, Encyclopaedias, Speeches, Proverbs, Anecdotes, Satirical and facetious works, Essays, Folklore and Fiction); 10. Philology.

Sub-divisions by countries are introduced in nearly all the classes.

In the Library of Congress the classification was originally based upon Lord Bacon's scheme for the division of knowledge into three great classes, according to the faculty of the mind employed in each. 1. History (based upon memory); 2. Philosophy (based upon reason); 3. Poetry (based upon imagination). This scheme was much better adapted to a classification of ideas than of books. Its failure to answer the ends of a practical classification of the library led to radical modifications of the plan, as applied to the books on the shelves, for reasons of logical arrangement, as well as of convenience. A more thorough and systematic re-arrangement is now in progress.

Mr. C. A. Cutter has devised a system of "Expansive classification," now widely used in American libraries. In this, the classes are each indicated by a single letter, followed by numbers representing divisions by countries, and these in turn by letters indicating sub-divisions by subjects, etc. It is claimed that this method is not a rigid unchangeable system, but adaptable in a high degree, and capable of modification to suit the special wants of any library. In it the whole range of literature and science is divided into several grand classes, which, with their sub-classes, are indicated by the twenty-six letters of the alphabet. Thus Class A embraces Generalia; B to D, Spiritual sciences (including philosophy and religion); E to G, Historical sciences (including, besides history and biography, geography and travels); H to K, Social sciences (including law and political science and economics); L to P, Natural sciences; Q, Medicine; and R to Z, Arts (including not only mechanical, recreative and fine arts, but music, languages, literature, and bibliography).

The sub-divisions of these principal classes are arranged with progressive fullness, to suit smaller or larger libraries. Thus, the first classification provides only eleven classes, suited to very small libraries: the second is expanded to fifteen classes, the third to thirty classes, and so on up to the seventh or final one, designed to provide for the arrangement of the very largest libraries.

This is the most elaborate and far-reaching library classification yet put forth, claiming superior clearness, flexibility, brevity of notation, logical coördination, etc., while objections have been freely made to it on the score of over-refinement and aiming at the unattainable.

What is known as the decimal or the Dewey system of

classification was originally suggested by Mr. N. B. Shurt-leff's "Decimal system for the arrangement and administration of libraries," published at Boston in 1856. But in its present form it has been developed by Mr. Melvil Dewey into a most ingenious scheme for distributing the whole vast range of human knowledge into ten classes, marked from 0 to 9, each of which sub-divides into exactly ten sub-classes, all divisible in their turn into ten minor divisions, and so on until the material in hand, or the ingenuity of the classifier is exhausted. The notation of the books on the shelves corresponds to these divisions and sub-divisions. The claims of this system, which has been quite extensively followed in the smaller American libraries, and in many European ones, are economy, simplicity, brevity of nota-tion, expansibility, unchanging call-numbers, etc. It has been criticised as too mechanical, as illogical in arrange-ment of classes, as presenting many incongruities in its divisions, as procrustean, as wholly inadequate in its clas-sification of jurisprudence, etc. It is partially used by librarians who have had to introduce radical changes in portions of the classification, and in fact it is understood that the classification has been very largely made over both in Amherst College library and in that of Columbia Uni-versity, N. Y., where it was fully established.

This only adds to the cumulative proofs that library classification cannot be made an exact science, but is in its nature indefinitely progressive and improvable. Its main object is not to classify knowledge, but books. There be-ing multitudes of books that do not belong absolutely to any one class, all classification of them is necessarily a com-promise. Nearly all the classification schemers have made over their schemes—some of them many times. I am not arguing against classification, which is essential to the practical utility of any library. An imperfect classification is much better than none: but the tendency to erect classification into a fetish, and to lay down cast-iron rules for it, should be guarded against. In any library, reasons of convenience must often prevail over logical arrangement; and he who spends time due to prompt library service in worrying over errors in a catalogue, or vexing his soul at a faulty classification, is as mistaken as those fussy individuals who fancy that they are personally responsible for the obliquity of the earth's axis.

It may be added that in the American Library Association's Catalogue of 5,000 books for a popular library, Washington, 1893, the classification is given both on the Dewey (Decimal) system, and on the Cutter expansive system, so that all may take their choice.

The fixed location system of arrangement, by which every book is assigned by its number to one definite shelf, is objectionable as preventing accessions from being placed with their cognate books. This is of such cardinal importance in every library, that a more elastic system of some kind should be adopted, to save continual re-numbering. No system which makes mere arithmetical progression a substitute for intrinsic qualities can long prove satisfactory.

The relative or movable location on shelves is now more generally adopted than the old plan of numbering every shelf and assigning a fixed location to every volume on that shelf. The book-marks, if designating simply the relative order of the volumes, permit the books to be moved along, as accessions come in, from shelf to shelf, as the latter become crowded. This does not derange the numbers, since the order of succession is observed.

For small town libraries no elaborate system of classification can properly be attempted. Here, the most convenient grouping is apt to prove the best, because books

are most readily found by it.   Mr. W. I. Fletcher has outlined a scheme for libraries of 10,000 volumes or less, as
follows:

A. Fiction (appended, J. Juvenile books); B. English and
American literature; C. History; D. Biography; E. Trav-
els; F. Science; G. Useful arts; H. Fine and recreative arts;
I. Political and social science; K. Philosophy and religion;
L. Works on language and in foreign languages; R. Ref-
erence books.

Numerous sub-divisions would be required to make such
a scheme (or indeed any other) fit any collection of books.

In arranging the main classes, care should be taken to
bring those most drawn upon near to the delivery desk, or
charging system of the library.

The alphabet is usefully applied in the arrangement of
several of the great classes of books, and in many sub-divisions of other classes.   Thus, all English and American
fiction may be arranged in a single alphabet of authors, including English translations of foreign works.   All collected works, or polygraphy, may form an alphabet, as
well as poetry, dramatic works, collections of letters, and
miscellanea, arranged by authors' names.   In any of these
classes, sub-divisions by languages may be made, if desired.

The class biography may best be arranged in an alphabet of the subjects of the biographies, rather than of writers, for obvious reasons of convenience in finding at once
the books about each person.

CHAPTER 22.

CATALOGUES.

Catalogues of libraries are useful to readers in direct proportion to their fulfilment of three conditions: (1) Quick and ready reference. (2) Arranging all authors' names in an alphabet, followed by titles of their works. (3) Subjects or titles in their alphabetical order in the same alphabet as the authors. This is what is known as a "Dictionary catalogue"; but why is it preferable to any other? Because it answers more questions in less time than any other.

The more prevalent styles of catalogues have been, 1. A list of authors, with titles of their works under each. 2. A catalogue of subjects, in a classified topical or alphabetical order, the authors and their works being grouped under each head. 3. A catalogue attempting to combine these two, by appending to the author-catalogue a classed list of subjects, with a brief of authors under each, referring to the page on which the titles of their works may be found; or else, 4. Appending to the subject-catalogue an alphabet of authors, with similar references to pages under subjects.

Each of these methods of catalogue-making, while very useful, contrives to miss the highest utility, which lies in enabling the reader to put his finger on the book he wants, at one glance of the eye. The catalogue of authors will not help him to subjects, nor will the catalogue of subjects, as a rule, give the authors and titles with the fullness that may be needed. In either case, a double reference becomes necessary, consuming just twice the time,

and in a two-column catalogue, three times the time required in a dictionary catalogue.

The reader who wants Darwin's "Origin of Species" finds
it readily enough by the author-catalogue; but he wants,
at the same time, to find other works on the same subject,
and all the author-catalogues in the world will not help
him to them. But give him a dictionary catalogue, and
he has, in the same alphabet with his Darwin, (if the
library is large) dozens of books discussing the theory of
that great naturalist, under species, evolution, Darwinism,
etc.

Thus he finds that there is no key which so quickly un-
locks the stores of knowledge which a library contains, as
a dictionary catalogue.

The objections to it are chiefly brought by minds school-
ed in systems, who look askance on all innovations, and instinctively prefer round-about methods to short-hand ones.
Ask such an objector if he would prefer his dictionary
of the English language arranged, not alphabetically, but
subjectively, so that all medical terms should be defined
only under medicine, all species of fish described only under fishes, etc., and he will probably say that there is no
analogy in the case. But the analogy becomes apparent
when we find, in what are called systematic catalogues, no
two systems alike, and the finding of books complicated by
endless varieties of classification, with no common alphabet to simplify the search. The authors of systems doubtless understand them themselves, but no one else does, until he devotes time to learn the key to them; and even
when learned, the knowledge is not worth the time lost in
acquiring it, since the field covered in any one catalogue
is so small. Alphabetical arrangement, on the other hand,
strictly adhered to, is a universal key to the authors and
subjects and titles of all the books contained in the library

it represents. The devotee of a bibliographical system may be as mistaken as the slave of a scientific terminology. He forgets that bibliography is not a school for teaching all departments of knowledge, but a brief and handy index to books that may contain that knowledge. A student who has once made a thorough comparative test of the merits, as aids to wide and rapid research, of the old-fashioned bibliographies and the best modern dictionary catalogues, will no more deny the superiority of the latter, than he will contest the maxim that a straight line is the nearest road between two points. Meantime, "while doctors disagree, disciples are free;" and the disciples who would follow the latest guides in the art "how to make and use a catalogue," must get rid of many formulas.

The reader will find in the chapter on bibliography, notes on some classes of catalogues, with the more notable examples of them. We are here concerned with the true method of preparing catalogues, and such plain rules as brevity will permit to be given, will be equally adapted to private or public libraries. For more ample treatment, with reasons for and against many rules laid down, reference is made to the able and acute work, "Rules for a Dictionary Catalogue," by C. A. Cutter, published by the U. S. Bureau of Education, 3d ed. 1891.

CONDENSED RULES FOR AN AUTHOR AND TITLE CATALOGUE.

Prepared by the Co-operation Committee of the American Library Association.

ENTRY.

Books are to be entered under the:

Surnames of authors when ascertained, the abbreviation "*Anon.*" being added to the titles of anonymous works.

Initials of authors' names when these only are known, the last initial being put first.

Pseudonyms of the writers when the real names are not ascertained.

Names of editors of collections, each separate item to be at the same time sufficiently catalogued under its own heading.

Names of countries, cities, societies, or other bodies which are responsible for their publication.

First word (not an article or serial number) of the titles of periodicals and of anonymous books, the names of whose authors are not known. And a motto or the designation of a series may be neglected when it begins a title, and the entry may be made under the first word of the real title following.

Commentaries accompanying a text, and translations, are to be entered under the heading of the original work; but commentaries without the text under the name of the commentator. A book entitled "Commentary on ...." and containing the text, should be put under both.

The Bible, or any part of it (including the Apocrypha), in any language, is to be entered under the word Bible.

The Talmud and Koran (and parts of them) are to be entered under those words; the sacred books of other religions are to be entered under the names by which they are generally known; references to be given from the names of editors, translators, etc.

The respondent or defender of an academical thesis is to be considered as the author, unless the work unequivocally appears to be the work of the *praeses*.

Books having more than one author to be entered under the one first named in the title, with a reference from each of the others.

Reports of civil actions are to be entered under the name of the party to the suit which stands first on the title page. Reports of crown and criminal proceedings are to be entered under the name of the defendant. Admiralty proceedings relating to vessels are to be put under the name of the vessel.

Noblemen are to be entered under their titles, unless the family name is decidedly better known.

Ecclesiastical dignitaries, unless popes or sovereigns, are to be entered under their surnames.

Sovereigns (other than Greek or Roman), ruling princes, Oriental writers, popes, friars, persons canonized, and all other persons known *only* by their first name, are to be entered under this first name.

Married women, and other persons who have changed their names, are to be put under the last well-known form.

A pseudonym may be used instead of the surname (and only a reference to the pseudonym made under the surname) when an author is much more known by his false than by his real name. In case of doubt, use the real name.

A society is to be entered under the first word, not an article, of its corporate name, with references from any other name by which it is known, especially from the name of the place where its headquarters are established, if it is often called by that name.

REFERENCES.

When an author has been known by more than one name, references should be inserted from the name or names not to be used as headings to the one used.

References are also to be made to the headings chosen:

from the titles of all novels and plays, and of poems likely to be asked for by their titles;

from other striking titles;

from noticeable words in anonymous titles, especially from the names of subjects of anonymous biographies;

from the names of editors of periodicals, when the periodicals are generally called by the editor's name;

from the names of important translators (especially poetic translators) and commentators;

from the title of an ecclesiastical dignitary, when that, and not the family name, is used in the book catalogued;

and in other cases where a reference is needed to insure the ready finding of the book.

HEADINGS.

In the heading of titles, the names of authors are to be given in full, and in their vernacular form, except that the Latin form may be used when it is more generally known, the vernacular form being added in parentheses; except, also, that sovereigns and popes may be given in the English form.

English and French surnames beginning with a prefix (except the French de and d') are to be recorded under the prefix; in other languages under the word following.

English compound surnames are to be entered under the last part of the name; foreign ones under the first part.

Designations are to be added to distinguish writers of the same name from each other.

Prefixes indicating the rank or profession of writers may be added in the heading, when they are part of the usual designation of the writers.

Names of places to be given in the English form. When both an English and a vernacular form are used in English works, prefer the vernacular.

TITLES.

The title is to be an exact transcript of the title-page, neither amended, translated, nor in any way altered, except that mottos, titles of authors, repetitions, and matter of any kind not essential, are to be omitted. Where great accuracy is desirable, omissions are to be indicated by three dots (...). The titles of books especially valuable for antiquity or rarity may be given in full, with all practicable precision. The phraseology and spelling, but not necessarily the punctuation, of the title are to be exactly copied.

Any additions needed to make the title clear are to be supplied, and inclosed by brackets.

Initial capitals are to be given in English:

to proper names of persons and personifications, places, bodies, noted events, and periods (each separate word not an article, conjunction, or preposition, may be capitalized in these cases);

to adjectives and other derivatives from proper names when they have a direct reference to the person, place, etc., from which they are derived;

to the first word of every sentence and of every quoted title;

to titles of honor when standing instead of a proper name (e. g., the Earl of Derby, but John Stanley, earl of Derby);

In foreign languages, according to the local usage;

In doubtful cases capitals are to be avoided.

Foreign languages.—Titles in foreign characters may be transliterated. The languages in which a book is written are to be stated when there are several, and the fact is not apparent from the title.

IMPRINTS.

After the title are to be given, in the following order, those in [ ] being optional:

the edition;

the place of publication;

[and the publisher's name] (these three in the language of the title);

the year as given on the title-page, but in Arabic figures;

[the year of copyright or actual publication, if known to be different in brackets, and preceded by c. or p. as the case may be];

the number of volumes, or of pages if there is only one volume;

[the number of maps, portraits, or illustrations not included in the text];

and either the approximate size designated by letter, or the exact size in centimeters;

the name of the series to which the book belongs is to be given in parentheses after the other imprint entries.

After the place of publication, the place of printing may be given if different. This is desirable only in rare and old books.

The number of pages is to be indicated by giving the last number of each paging, connecting the numbers by the sign +; the addition of unpaged matter may be shown by a +, or the number of pages ascertained by counting may be given in brackets. When there are more than three pagings, it is better to add them together and give the sum in brackets.

These imprint entries are to give the facts, whether ascertained from the book or from other sources; those which are usually taken from the title (edition, place, publisher's name, and series) should be in the language of the title, corrections and additions being inclosed in brackets. It is better to give the words, "maps," "portraits," etc., and the abbreviations for "volumes" and "pages," in English.

CONTENTS, NOTES.

Notes (in English) and contents of volumes are to be given when necessary to properly describe the works. Both notes and lists of contents to be in a smaller type.

MISCELLANEOUS.

A single dash or indent indicates the omission of the preceding heading; a subsequent dash or indent indicates the omission of a subordinate heading, or of a title.

A dash connecting numbers signifies to and including; following a number it signifies continuation.

A ? following a word or entry signifies probably.

Brackets inclose words added to titles or imprints, or changed in form.

Arabic figures are to be used rather than Roman; but small capitals may be used after the names of sovereigns, princes, and popes.

A list of abbreviations to be used was given in the Library journal, Vol. 3: 16-20.

ARRANGEMENT.

The surname when used alone precedes the same name used with forenames; where the initials only of the forenames are given, they are to precede fully written forenames beginning with the same initials (e. g., Brown, Brown, J.; Brown, J. L.; Brown, James).

The prefixes M and Mc, S., St., Ste., Messrs., Mr., and Mrs., are to be arranged as if written in full, Mac, Sanctus, Saint, Sainte, Messieurs, Mister, and Mistress.

The works of an author are to be arranged in the following order:

1. Collected works.

2. Partial collections.

3. Single works, alphabetically, by the first word of the title.

The order of alphabeting is to be that of the English alphabet.

The German ae, oe, ue, are always to be written as ä, ö, ü, and arranged as a, o, u.

Names of persons are to precede similar names of places, which in turn precede similar first words of titles.

A few desirable modifications or additions to these rules may be suggested.

1. In title-entries, let the year of publication stand last, instead of the indication of size.

2. Noblemen to be entered under their family names, with reference from their titles.

3. Instead of designations of title, profession, residence, or family, to distinguish authors, let every name be followed by the chronology, as—

> James (Henry) 1811-82.
>
> James (Henry) 1843-

It is highly desirable to give this information as to the author's period in every title-heading, without exception, when ascertainable. If unknown, the approximate period to be given, with a query.

4. All titles to be written in small letters, and printed in lower case, whether in English, German, or any other language, avoiding capitals except in cases named in the rule.

5. Works without date, when the exact date is not found, are to be described conjecturally, thus:

> [1690?] or [about 1840.]

6. In expressing collations, use commas rather than the sign $+$ between the pagings, as—xvi, 452, vii pp.—not xvi+452+vii pp.

7. Forenames should be separated from the surnames which precede them by parenthesis rather than commas, as a clearer discrimination: as—

> Alembert (Jean Baptiste le Rond d')—not
>
> Alembert, Jean Baptiste le Rond d'.

The printed catalogue of the British Museum Library follows this method, as well as that in the preceding paragraph.

8. All books of history, travels, or voyages to have the period covered by them inserted in brackets, when not expressed in the title-page.

9. All collected works of authors, and all libraries or collections of different works to be analysed by giving the

contents of each volume, either in order of volumes, or alphabetically by authors' names.

Of course there are multitudes of points in catalogue practice not provided for in the necessarily brief summary preceding: and, as books on the art abound, the writer gives only such space to it as justice to the wide range of library topics here treated permits.

Probably the most important question in preparing catalogue titles, is what space to give to the author's frequently long-drawn-out verbiage in his title-page. There are two extremes to be considered: (1) Copying the title literally and in full, however prolix; and (2) reducing all title-pages, by a Procrustean rule, to what we may call "one-line titles." Take an example:

"Jones (Richard T.) A theoretical and practical treatise on the benefits of agriculture to mankind. With an appendix containing many useful reflections derived from practical experience. iv, 389 pp. 8°. London, MDCCXLIV." As abridged to a short title, this would read: "Jones (Richard T.) Benefits of agriculture. iv, 389 pp. 8°. Lond. 1744." Who will say that the last form of title does not convey substantially all that is significant of the book, stripped of superfluous verbiage? But we need not insist upon titles crowded into a single line of the catalogue, whether written or printed. This would do violence to the actual scope of many books, by suppressing some significant or important part of their titles. The rule should be to give in the briefest words selected out of the title (never imported into it) the essential character of the book, so far as the author has expressed it. Take another example:

"Bowman (Thomas) A new, easy, and complete Hebrew course; containing a Hebrew grammar, with copious Hebrew and English exercises, strictly graduated: also, a Hebrew-English and English-Hebrew lexicon. In two parts. Part I. Regular verbs. Edinburgh, 1879."

This might be usefully condensed thus:

Bowman, (Thomas) Hebrew course: grammar, exercises, lexicon, [&c.] Part I. Regular verbs. Edinburgh, 1879.

One objection brought against the dictionary catalogue is that it widely separates subjects that belong together. In the Boston Athenæum catalogue, for example, the topic Banks is found in Vol. 1, while Money is in Vol. 3; and for Wages, one must go to Vol. 5, while Labor is in Vol. 3. But there are two valid reasons for this. First, the reader who wants to know about banks or wages may care nothing about the larger topics of money or of labor; and secondly, if he does want them, he is sent to them at once by cross-reference, where they belong in the alphabet; whereas, if they were grouped under Political Economy, as in classed catalogues, he must hunt for them through a maze of unrelated books, without any alphabet at all.

It is often forgotten by the advocates of systematic subject catalogues rather than alphabetical ones, that catalogues are for those who do not know, more than for those who do. The order of the alphabet is settled and familiar; but no classification by subjects is either familiar or settled. Catalogues should aim at the greatest convenience of the greatest number of readers.

It is noteworthy that the English Catalogue (the one national bibliography of the current literature of that country) has adopted, since 1891, the dictionary form of recording authors, titles and subjects in one alphabet, distinguishing authors' names by antique type. It is hoped that the American Catalogue, an indispensable work in all libraries, will adopt in its annual and quinquennial issues the time-saving method of a single alphabet.

It is not claimed that the dictionary catalogue possesses

fully all the advantages in educating readers that the best classed catalogues embody. But the chief end of catalogues being to find books promptly, rather than to educate readers, the fact that the dictionary catalogue, though far from perfect, comes nearer to the true object than any other system, weighs heavily in its favor. Edward Edwards said—"Many a reader has spent whole days in book-hunting [in catalogues] which ought to have been spent in book-reading." It is to save this wasted time that catalogues should aim.

Nothing can be easier than to make a poor catalogue, while nothing is more difficult than to make a good one. The most expert French bibliographers who have distinguished themselves by compiling catalogues have been most severely criticised by writers who no doubt would have been victimized in their turn if they had undertaken similar work. Byron says

"A man must serve his time to every trade,
    Save censure;—critics all are ready made."

When De Bure and Van Praet, most accomplished bibliographers, published the catalogue of the precious library of the duke de La Vallière, the abbé Rive boasted that he had discovered a blunder in every one of the five thousand titles of their catalogue. Barbier and Brunet have both been criticised for swarms of errors in the earlier editions of their famous catalogues. The task of the exact cataloguer is full of difficulty, constantly renewed, and demanding almost encyclopaedic knowledge, and incessant care of minute particulars.

The liability to error is so great in a kind of work which, more than almost any other, demands the most scrupulous accuracy, lest a catalogue should record a book with such mistakes as to completely mislead a reader, that rules are imperatively necessary. And whatever rules are adopted, a rigid adherence to them is no less essential, to avoid misapprehension and confusion. A singular instance of imperfect and misleading catalogue work was unwittingly furnished by Mr. J. Payne Collier, a noted English critic, author, and librarian, who criticised the slow progress of the British Museum catalogue, saying that he could himself do "twenty-five titles an hour without trouble." His twenty-five titles when examined, were found to contain almost every possible error that can be made in cataloguing books. These included using names of translators or editors as headings, when the author's name was on the title-page; omitting christian names of authors; omitting to specify the edition; using English instead of foreign words to give the titles of foreign books; adopting titled instead of family names for authors (which would separate Stanhope's "England under Queen Anne" from the same writer's "History of England," published when he was Lord Mahon); errors in grammar, etc. These ridiculous blunders of a twenty-five-title-an-hour man exemplify the maxim "the more haste, the worse speed," in catalogue-making.

That our British brethren are neither adapted nor inclined to pose as exemplars in the fine art of cataloguing, we need only cite their own self-criticisms to prove. Here are two confessions found in two authors of books on catalogue-making, both Englishmen. Says one: "We are deficient in good bibliographies. It is a standing disgrace to the country that we have no complete bibliography of English authors, much less of English literature generally." Says another: "The English are a supremely illogical people. The disposition to irregularity has made English bibliography, or work on catalogues, a by-word among those who give attention to these matters."

An American may well add, "They do these things better in France and Germany," while declining to claim the meed of superiority for the United States.

Too much prominence should not be given to place-numbers in library catalogues. The tendency to substitute mere numerical signs for authors and subjects has been carried so far in some libraries, that books are called for and charged by class-numbers only, instead of their distinctive names. An English librarian testifies that assistants trained in such libraries are generally the most ignorant of literature. When mechanical or mnemonical signs are wholly substituted for ideas and for authors, is it any wonder that persons incessantly using them become mechanical? Let catalogue and classification go hand in hand in bringing all related books together, and library assistants will not stunt their intellects by becoming bond-slaves to the nine digits, nor lose the power of thought and reflection by never growing out of their a b c's.

There are two forms of catalogue not here discussed, which are adjuncts to the library catalogue proper. The accession catalogue, kept in a large volume, records the particulars regarding every volume, on its receipt by the library. It gives author, title, date, size, binding, whence acquired, cost, etc., and assigns it an accession number, which it ever after retains. The shelf catalogue (or shelf-list) is a portable one divided into sections representing the cases of shelves in the library. It gives the shelf classification number, author, brief title and number of volumes of each book, as arranged on the shelves; thus constituting an inventory of each case, or stack, throughout the library.

To check a library over is to take an account of stock of all the books it should contain. This is done annually in some libraries, and the deficiencies reported. All libraries lose some books, however few, and these losses will be small or great according to the care exercised and the safe-guards provided. The method is to take one division of the library at a time, and check off all books on the shelves by their numbers on the shelf-list, supplemented by care-ful examination of all numbers drawn out, or at bindery, or in other parts of the library. Not a volume should be absent unaccounted for. Those found missing after a cer-tain time should be noted on the shelf-list and accession book, and replaced, if important, after the loss is definitely assured.

The reason for writing and printing all catalogue titles in small letters, without capitals (except for proper names) is two-fold. First, there can be no standard prescribing what words should or should not be capitalized, and the cataloguer will be constantly at a loss, or will use capitals in the most unprincipled way. He will write one day, perhaps, "The Dangers of great Cities," and the next, "The dangers of Great cities"—with no controlling reason for either form. Secondly, the symmetry of a title or a sentence, whether written or printed, is best attained by the uniform exclusion of capitals. That this should be applied to all languages, notwithstanding the habit of most German typographers of printing all nouns with capitals, is borne out by no less an authority than the new Grimm's *Deutsches Wörterbuch*, which prints all words in "lower case" type except proper names. Nothing can be more unsightly than the constant breaking up of the har-mony of a line by the capricious use of capitals.

To discriminate carefully the various editions of each work is part of the necessary duty of the cataloguer. Many books have passed through several editions, and as these are by no means always specified on the title-page, one should establish the sequence, if possible, by other means. The first edition is one which includes all copies printed from the plates or the type as first set; the second, one which is reprinted, with or without changes in the text or the title. First editions often acquire a greatly enhanced value, in the case of a noted author, by reason of changes made in the text in later issues of the work. For though the latest revision may and should be the author's best improved expression, his earliest furnishes food for the hunters of literary curiosities. Every catalogue should distinguish first editions thus [1st ed.] in brackets.

In the arrangement of titles in catalogues, either of the various works of the same writer, or of many books on the same subject, some compilers follow the alphabetical order, while others prefer the chronological—or the order of years of publication of the various works. The latter has the advantage of showing the reader the earlier as distinguished from the recent literature, but in a long sequence of authors (in a subject-catalogue) it is more difficult to find a given writer's work, or to detect its absence.

The task of accurately distributing the titles in a catalogue of subjects would be much simplified, if the books were all properly named. But it is an unhappy failing of many writers to give fanciful or far-fetched titles to their books, so that, instead of a descriptive name, they have names that describe nothing. This adds indefinitely to the labor of the cataloguer, who must spend time to analyse to some extent the contents of the book, before he can classify it. This must be done to avoid what may be gross errors in the catalogue. Familiar examples are Ruskin's Notes on Sheep-folds (an ecclesiastical criticism) classified under Agriculture; and Edgeworth's Irish Bulls under Domestic animals.

The work of alphabeting a large number of title-cards is much simplified and abbreviated by observing certain obvious rules in the distribution. (1) Gather in the same pile all the cards in the first letter of the alphabet, A, followed in successive parallel rows by all the B's, and so on, to the letter Z. (2) Next, pursue the same course with all the titles, arranging under the second letter of the alphabet, Aa, Ab, Ac, etc., and so with all the cards under B. C. &c. for all the letters. (3) If there still remain a great many titles to distribute into a closer alphabetic sequence, the third operation will consist in arranging under the third letter of the alphabet, *e. g.*, Abb, Abc, Abd, etc. The same method is pursued throughout the entire alphabet, until all the title-cards are arranged in strict order.

Too much care cannot be taken to distinguish between books written by different authors, but bearing the same name. Many catalogues are full of errors in this respect, attributing, for example, works written by Jonathan Edwards, the younger, (1745-1801) to Jonathan Edwards the elder, (1703-58); or cataloguing under Henry James, Jr., the works of his father, Henry James. The abundant means of identification which exist should cause such errors to be avoided; and when the true authorship is fixed, every author's chronology should appear next after his name on every card-title: *e. g.* James (Henry, 1811-82) Moralism and Christianity, New York, 1850. James (Henry, 1843-) Daisy Miller, N. Y. 1879.

The designation of book sizes is a vexed question in catalogues. The generally used descriptions of size, from folio down to 48mo. signify no accurate measurement whatever, the same book being described by different catalogues as 12mo. 8vo, crown 8vo. &c., according to fancy; while the same cataloguer who describes a volume as octavo to-day, is very likely to call it a duodecimo to-morrow. Library catalogues are full of these heterogeneous descriptions, and the size-notation is the *bête noir* of the veteran bibliographer, and the despair of the infant librarian. Yet it is probable that the question has excited a discussion out of all proportion to its importance. Of what consequence is the size of a book to any one, except to the searcher who has to find it on the shelves? While the matter has been much exaggerated, some concert or uniformity in describing the sizes of books is highly desirable.

A Committee of the American Library Association agreed to a size-notation, figured below, adopting the metric system as the standard, to which we add the approximate equivalents in inches.

Sizes.	Size abbreviations.	Centimetres outside height.	Inches.
Folio, F°.	F	40	16
Quarto, 4°.	Q	30	12
Octavo, 8°.	O	25	10
Duodecimo, 12°.	D	20	8
Sixteen mo., 16°.	S	17.5	7
Twenty-four mo., 24°.	T	15	6
Thirty-two mo., 32°.	Tt	12.3	5
Forty-eight mo., 48°.	Fe	10	4

It will be understood that the figure against each size indicated represents the maximum measure: e. g. a volume is octavo when above 20 and below 25 centimetres (8 to 10 inches high).

As this question of sizes concerns publishers and booksellers, as well as librarians, and the metric system, though established in continental Europe, is in little use in the United States and England, it remains doubtful if any general adherence to this system of notation can be reached—or, indeed, to any other. The Publishers' Weekly (N. Y.) the organ of the book trade, has adopted it for the titles of new books actually in hand, but follows the publishers' descriptions of sizes as to others. Librarian J. Winter Jones, of the British Museum, recommended classing all books above twelve inches in height as folios, those

between ten and twelve inches as quartos, those from seven
to ten inches as octavos, and all measuring seven inches
or under as 12mos. Mr. H. B. Wheatley, in his work,
"How to Catalogue a Library," 1889, proposed to call all
books small octavos which measure below the ordinary
octavo size. As all sizes "run into each other," and the
former classification by the fold of the sheets is quite obsolete, people appear to be left to their own devices in describing the sizes of books. While the metric notation
would be exact, if the size of every book were expressed in
centimetres, the size-notation in the table given is wholly
wanting in precision, and has no more claim to be adopted
than any other arbitrary plan. Still, it will serve ordinary
wants, and the fact that we cannot reach an exact standard is no reason for refusing to be as nearly exact as we can.

And while we are upon the subject of notation may be
added a brief explanation of the method adopted in earlier
ages, (and especially the years reckoned from the Christian
era) to express numbers by Roman numerals. The one
simple principle was, that each letter placed after a figure
of greater equal value adds to it just the value which itself
has; and, on the other hand, a letter of less value placed
before (or on the left of) a larger figure, diminishes the
value of that figure in the same proportion. For example:
These letters—VI represent six; which is the same as
saying V+I. On the contrary, these same letters reversed
represent four; thus—IV: that is V—I=4. Nine is represented by IX, i. e., X—I, ten minus one. On the same
principle, LX represents 60—or L+X: whereas XL means
40—being L—X. Proceeding on the same basis, we find
that LXX=L+XX=70; and LXXX or L+XXX is 80.
But when we come to ninety, instead of adding four X's
to the L, they took a shorter method, and expressed it in
two figures instead of five, thus, XC, i. e. 100 or C—X=90.

The remarkable thing about this Roman notation is that only six letters sufficed to express all numbers up to one thousand, and even beyond, by skilful and simple combinations: namely the I, the V, the X, the L, the C, and the M, and by adding or substracting some of these letters, when placed before or after another letter, they had a whole succession of numbers done to their hand—thus:

I,	 1	XX,	. . . 20	CC,	. . .	200
II,	 2	XXX,	. . . 80	CCC,	. . .	800
III,	 8	XL,	. . . 40	CCCC,	. . .	400
IV,	 4	L,	. . . 50	D,	. . .	500
V,	 5	LX,	. . . 60	DC,	. . .	600
VI,	 6	LXX,	. . . 70	DCC,	. . .	700
VII,	 7	LXXX,	. . . 80	DCCC,	. . .	800
VIII,	 8	XC,	. . . 90	CM,	. . .	900
IX,	 9	C (centum),	. . 100	M, (mille),		1,000
X,	 10					

Now, when the early printers came to apply dates of publication to the books they issued, (and here is where their methods of notation become most important to librarians) they used precisely these methods. For example, to express the year 1695, they printed it thus: MDCVC, that is—1000+500+100+100—5. But the printers of the 15th century and later, often used complications of letters, dictated by caprice rather than by any fixed principles, so that it is sometimes difficult to interpret certain dates in the colophons or title-pages of books, without collateral aid of some kind, usually supplied to the librarian by bibliographies. One of the simpler methods of departure from the regular notation as above explained, was to substitute for the letter D (500) two letters, thus—IƆ, an I and a C inverted, supposed to resemble the letter D in outline. Another fancy was to replace the M, standing for 1,000, by the symbols CIƆ—which present a faint approach to the outline of the letter M, for which they stand. Thus, to express the year 1610, we have this combination— CIƆ IƆ CX, which would be indecipherable to a modern reader, uninstructed in the numerical signs anciently used, and their values. In like manner, 1548 is expressed thus: MDXLIIX, meaning 1000+500+40+10—2. And for 1626, we have CIƆ IƆ C XXVI.

As every considerable library has early printed books, a librarian must know these peculiarities of notation, in order to catalogue them properly, without mistake as to their dates. In some books, where a capricious combination of Roman numerals leaves him without a precedent to guide him to the true date, reference must be had to the bibliographies of the older literature, (as Hain, Panzer, etc.), which will commonly solve the doubt.

As to the mechanics of catalogue-making, widely different usages and materials prevail. In America, the card or title-slip system is well nigh univeral, while in England it is but slowly gaining ground, as against the ledger or blank book catalogue. Its obvious advantage lies in affording the only possible means of maintaining a strict alphabetical sequence in titles, whether of authors or subjects. The title-cards should be always of uniform size, and the measure most in vogue is five inches in length by three inches in breadth. They should not be too stiff, though of sufficient thickness, whether of paper or of thin card board, to stand upright without doubling at the edges. They may be ruled or plain, at pleasure, and kept in drawers, trays, or (in case of a small catalogue) in such paste-board boxes as letter envelopes come in.

The many advantages of the card system, both for catalogues and indexes, should not lead us to overlook its palpable defects. These are (1) It obliges readers to manipulate many cards, to arrive at all the works of an author, or all the books on any subject, instead of having them under his eye at once, as in printed catalogues. (2) It can be used only in the library, and in only one place in the library, and by only one person at a time in the same spot, while a printed catalogue can be freely used anywhere, and by any numbers, copies being multiplied. (3) It entails frequent crowding of readers around the catalogue drawers, who need to consult the same subjects or authors at the same time. (4) It requires immeasurably more room than a printed catalogue, and in fact, exacts space which in some libraries can be ill afforded. (5) It obliges readers to search the title-cards at inconvenient angles of vision, and often with inadequate light. (6) It is cumbersome in itself, and doubly cumbersome to searchers, who must stand up instead of sitting to consult it, and travel from drawer to drawer, interfering with other searchers almost constantly, or losing time in waiting. (7) To this is added the inconvenience of constant insertion of new title-cards by members of the library staff, and the time-consuming process of working the rods which keep the cards in place, if they are used, and if not used, the risk of loss of titles, or misplacement equivalent to loss for a time.

Says Mr. H. B. Wheatley: "I can scarcely imagine anything more maddening than a frequent reference to cards in a drawer." But it is to be considered that all systems have defects, and the problem of choosing the least defective is ever before us. Most of the suggested defects of the card catalogue, as concerns the readers, can be obviated by making a two-fold catalogue, the type-written titles being manifolded, and one set arranged in card-drawers for the use of the library staff, while another is mounted on large sheets in bound volumes for use of the public. This would secure the advantages of a printed catalogue, with no more expense than the manuscript titles would cost. If desired, a number of copies could be bound up for reading-room use. Accessions of new books could be incorporated from month to month, by leaving the right-hand pages blank for that purpose. This would be near enough to alphabetical order for most readers, with the immense advantage of opening at one glance before the eye, any author or subject. It would go far to solve the problem how to unite the flexibility and perfect alphabeting of the card system, with the superior comfort, safety, and ease of reference of the book. It would also be a safe-guard against the loss or displacement of titles, a danger inherent in the card system, as they could be replaced by copying missing titles from the catalogue volumes.

While the undoubted merits of the card system have been much overrated, it would be as unwise to dispense with it as the complete official catalogue of the library, as it would be to tie down the public to its use, when there is a more excellent way, saving time and patience, and contributing to the comfort of all.

To print or not to print? is a vital question for libraries, and it is in most cases decided to forego or to postpone printing, because of its great expense. Yet so manifest are the advantages of a printed catalogue, that all public libraries should make every effort to endow their readers with its benefits. These advantages are (1) Greater facility of reading titles. (2) Much more rapid turning from letter to letter of the catalogue alphabet. (3) Ability to consult it outside of the library. (4) Unlimited command of the catalogue by many readers at once, from the number of copies at hand, whereas card catalogues or manuscript volumes involve loss of time in waiting, or interfering with the researches of others. A part of these advantages may be realized by printing type-written copies of all titles in duplicate, or by carbon paper in manifold, thus furnishing the library with several copies of its catalogue:

but why not extend this by multiplying copies through the ingenious processes now in use, by which the printing of titles can be effected far more cheaply than in any printing office? Might not every library become its own printer, thus saving it from the inconvenience and risk of sending its titles outside, or the great expense of copying them for the printer?

The titles thus manifolded could be combined into volumes, by cutting away all superfluous margins and mounting the thin title-slips alphabetically on paper of uniform size, which, when bound, would be readily handled. All the titles of an author's works would be under the eye at a glance, instead of only one at a time, as in the card catalogue. And the titles of books on every subject would lie open, without slowly manipulating an infinite series of cards, one after another, to reveal them to the eye. The classification marks could be readily placed against each title, or even printed as a part of the manifold card titles.

Not that the card catalogue system would be abolished: it would remain as the only complete catalogue of the library, always up to date, in a single alphabet. Daily accessions inserted in it would render it the standard of appeal as to all that the library contained, and it would thus supplement the printed catalogue.

Of course, large and increasing accessions would require to be combined in occasional supplementary volumes of the catalogue; and in no long number of years the whole might be re-combined in a single alphabet, furnishing a printed dictionary catalogue up to its date.

The experience of the great British Museum Library in this matter of catalogues is an instructive one. After printing various incomplete author-catalogues in the years from 1787 to 1841, the attempt to print came to a full stop. The extensive collection grew apace, and the management got along somehow with a manuscript catalogue, the titles of which (written in script with approximate fullness) were pasted in a series of unwieldy but alphabetically arranged volumes. To incorporate the accessions, these volumes had continually to be taken apart by the binder, and the new titles combined in alphabetical order, entailing a literally endless labor of transcribing, shifting, relaying and rebinding, to secure even an imperfect alphabetical sequence. In 1875, the catalogue had grown to over two thousand thick folio volumes, and it was foreseen, by a simple computation of the rate of growth of the library, that in a very few years its catalogue could no longer be contained in the reading-room. The bulky manuscript catalogue system broke down by its own weight, and the management was compelled to resort to printing in self defence. Before the printing had reached any where near the concluding letters of the alphabet, the MS. catalogue had grown to three thousand volumes, and was a daily and hourly incubus to librarians and readers.

This printed catalogue of the largest library in the world, save one, is strictly a catalogue of authors, giving in alphabetical order the names, followed by the titles of all works by each writer which that library possesses. In addition, it refers in the case of biographies or comments upon any writer found in the index, to the authors of such works; and also from translators or editors to the authors of the translated or edited work. The titles of accessions to the library (between thirty and forty thousand volumes a year) were incorporated year by year as the printing went on. All claim to minute accuracy had to be ignored, and the titles greatly abridged by omitting superfluous words, otherwise its cost would have been prohibitory. The work was prosecuted with great energy and diligence by the staff of able scholars in the service of the

Museum Library. As the catalogue embraces far more titles of books, pamphlets, and periodicals than any other ever printed, it is a great public boon, the aid it affords to all investigators being incalculable. And any library possessing it may find, with many titles of rare and unattainable works, multitudes of books now available by purchase in the market, to enrich its own collection. It is said to contain about 3,500,000 titles and cross-references. It is printed in large, clear type, double columns, well spaced, and its open page is a comfort to the eye. Issued in paper covers, the thin folios can be bound in volumes of any thickness desired by the possessor.

It has several capital defects: (1) It fails to discriminate authors of the same name by printing the years or period of each; instead of which it gives designations like "the elder", "the younger", or the residence, or occupation, or title of the author. The years during which any writer flourished would have been easily added to the name in most cases, and the value of such information would have been great, solving at once many doubts as to many writers. (2) The catalogue fails to print the collations of all works, except as to a portion of those published since 1882, or in the newer portions issued. This omission leaves a reader uncertain whether the book recorded is a pamphlet or an extensive work. (3) The letters I and J and U and V are run together in the alphabet, after the ancient fashion, thus placing Josephus before Irving, and Utah after Virginia; an arrangement highly perplexing, not to say exasperating, to every searcher. To follow an obsolete usage may be defended on the plea that it is a good one, but when it is bad as well as outworn, no excuse for it can satisfy a modern reader. (4) No analysis is given of the collected works of authors, nor of many libraries made up of monographs. One cannot find in it the contents of the volumes of any of Swift's Works, nor even of Milton's Prose Writings. (5) It fails to record the names of publishers, except in the case of some early or rare books.

The printing of this monumental catalogue began in 1881, the volumes of MS. catalogue being set up by the printer without transcription, which would have delayed the work indefinitely, and it is now substantially completed. Its total cost will be not far from £50,000. There are about 374 volumes or parts in all. Only 250 copies were printed, part of which were presented to large libraries, and others were offered for sale at £3.10 per annum, payable as issued, so that a complete set costs about £70. One learns with surprise that only about forty copies have been subscribed for. This furnishes another evidence of the low estate of bibliography in England, where, in a nation full of rich book-collectors and owners of fine libraries, almost no buyers are found for the most extensive bibliography ever published, a national work, furnishing so copious and useful a key to the literature of the world in every department of human knowledge.

CHAPTER 23.

COPYRIGHT AND LIBRARIES.

The preservation of literature through public libraries has been and will ever be one of the most signal benefits which civilization has brought to mankind. When we consider the multitude of books which have perished from the earth, from the want of a preserving hand, a lively sense of regret comes over us that so few libraries have been charged with the duty of acquiring and keeping every publication that comes from the press. Yet we owe an immeasurable debt to the wisdom and far-sightedness of those who, centuries ago, provided by this means for the perpetuity of literature.

The earliest step taken in this direction appears to have been in France. By an ordinance proclaimed in 1537, regulating the printing of books, it was required that a copy of each work issued from the press should be deposited in the royal library. And it was distinctly affirmed that the ground of this exaction was to preserve to posterity the literature of the time, which might otherwise disappear.* This edict of three centuries and a half ago was the seed-grain from which has grown the largest library yet gathered in the world—the *Bibliothèque Nationale* of France. It antedated by more than two hundred years, any similar provision in England for the preservation of the national literature.

It is a notable fact that the United States of America

---

*G. H. Putnam, "Books and their makers in the Middle Ages," N. Y. 1897, vol. 2, p. 447.

was the first nation that ever embodied the principle of protection to the rights of authors in its fundamental law. "The Congress shall have power to promote the progress of science and useful arts, by securing for limited times to authors and inventors the exclusive right to their respective writings and discoveries." Thus anchored in the Constitution itself, this principle has been further recognized by repeated acts of Congress, aimed in all cases at giving it full practical effect.

If it is asked why the authors of the Constitution gave to Congress no plenary power, which might have authorized a grant of copyright in perpetuity, the answer is, that in this, British precedent had a great, if not a controlling influence. Copyright in England, by virtue of the statute of Anne, passed in 1710 (the first British copyright act), was limited to fourteen years, with right of renewal, by a living author, of only fourteen years more; and this was in full force in 1787, when our Constitution was framed. Prior to the British statute of 1710, authors had only what is called a common law right to their writings; and however good such a right might be, so long as they held them in manuscript, the protection to printed books was extremely uncertain and precarious.

It has been held, indeed, that all copyright laws, so far from maintaining an exclusive property right to authors, do in effect deny it (at least in the sense of a natural right), by explicitly limiting the term of exclusive ownership, which might otherwise be held (as in other property) to be perpetual. But there is a radical distinction between the products of the brain, when put in the concrete form of books and multiplied by the art of printing, and the land or other property which is held by common law tenure. Society views the absolute or exclusive property in books or inventions as a monopoly. While a monopoly may be justified for a reasonable number of years, on the obvious ground of securing to their originators the pecuniary benefit of their own ideas, a perpetual monopoly is generally regarded as odious and unjust. Hence society says to the author or inventor: "Put your ideas into material form, and we will guarantee you the exclusive right to multiply and sell your books or your inventions for a term long enough to secure a fair reward to you and to your family; after that period we want your monopoly, with its individual benefits, to cease in favor of the greatest good of all." If this appears unfair to authors, who contribute so greatly to the instruction and the advancement of mankind, it is to be considered that a perpetual copyright would (1) largely increase the cost of books, which should be most widely diffused for the public benefit, prolonging the enhanced cost indefinitely beyond the author's lifetime; (2) it would benefit by a special privilege, prolonged without limit, a class of book manufacturers or publishers who act as middle-men between the author and the public, and who own, in most cases, the entire property in the works of authors deceased, and which they did not originate; (3) it would amount in a few centuries to so vast a sum, taxed upon the community who buy books, that the publishers of Shakespeare's works, for example, who under perpetual copyright could alone print the poet's writings, might have reaped colossal fortunes, perhaps unequalled by any private wealth yet amassed in the world.

If it is said that copyright, thus limited, is a purely arbitrary right, it may be answered that all legal provisions are arbitrary. That which is an absolute or natural right, so long as held in idea or in manuscript, becomes, when given to the world in multiplied copies, the creature of law. The most that authors can fairly claim is a sufficiently prolonged exclusive right to guarantee them for a lifetime the just reward of their labors, with a reversion for their immediate heirs. That such exclusive rights should run to their remotest posterity, or, *a fortiori*, to mere merchants or artificers who had no hand whatever in the creation of the intellectual work thus protected, would be manifestly unjust. The judicial tribunals, both in England and America, have held that copyright laws do not affirm an existing right, but create a right, with special privileges not before existing, and also with special limitations.

The earliest copyright enactment of 1790 granted the exclusive privilege of printing his work to the author or his assigns for 14 + 14, or twenty-eight years in all.

The act further required entry of the title, before publication, in the office of the Clerk of the United States District Court in the State where the author or proprietor resided.

This remained the law, with slight amendment, until 1831, when a new copyright act extended the duration of copyright from fourteen to twenty-eight years for the original, or first term, with right of renewal to the author (now first extended to his widow or children, in case of his decease) for fourteen additional years, making forty-two years in all.

By the same act the privilege of copyright was extended to cover musical compositions, as it had been earlier extended (in 1802) to include designs, engravings, and etchings. Copyright was further extended in 1856 to dramatic compositions, and in 1865 to photographs and negatives thereof. In 1870 a new copyright code, to take the place of all existing and scattered statutes, was enacted, and there were added to the lawful subjects of copyright, paintings, drawings, chromos, statues, statuary, and models or designs intended to be perfected as works of the fine arts. And finally, by act of March 3, 1891, the benefits of copyright were extended so as to embrace foreign authors. In 1897, Congress created the office of Register of Copyrights, but continued the Copyright office, with its records, in the Library of Congress.

In 1846, the first enactment entitling the Library of the United States Government to a copy of every work protected by copyright was passed. This act, to establish the Smithsonian Institution, required that one copy of each copyright publication be deposited therein, and one copy in the Library of Congress. No penalties were provided, and in 1859, on complaint of the authorities of the Smithsonian Institution that the law brought in much trash in the shape of articles which were not books, the law was repealed, with the apparent concurrence of those in charge of the Congressional Library.

This left that Library without any accessions of copyright books until 1865, when, at the instance of the present writer, the Library Committee recommended, and Congress passed an act restoring the privilege to the Library of Congress. But it was found to require, in order to its enforcement, frequent visits to the records of the clerks of United States District Courts in many cities, with costly transcripts of records in more than thirty other offices, in order to ascertain what books had actually been copyrighted. To this was added the necessity of issuing demands upon delinquent authors or publishers for books not sent to the Library; no residence of the delinquents, however, being found in any of the records, which simply recorded those claiming copyright as "of the said District."

It resulted that no complete, nor even approximate compliance with the law was secured, and after five years' trial, the Librarian was obliged to bring before the committees of Congress the plan of a copyright registry at the seat of government, as had been the requirement in the case of Patents from the beginning.

The law of copyright, as codified by act of July 8, 1870, made an epoch in the copyright system of the United States. It transferred the entire registry of books and other publications, under copyright law, to the city of Washington, and made the Librarian of Congress sole register of copyrights, instead of the clerks of the District Courts of the United States. Manifold reasons existed for this radical change, and those which were most influential with Congress in making it were the following:

1. The transfer of the copyright records to Washington it was foreseen would concentrate and simplify the business, and this was a cardinal point. Prior to 1870 there were between forty and fifty separate and distinct authorities for issuing copyrights. The American people were put to much trouble to find out where to apply, in the complicated system of District Courts, several of them frequently in a single State, to enter titles for publication. They were required to make entry in the district where the applicant resided, and this was frequently a matter of doubt. Moreover, they were required to go to the expense and trouble of transmitting a copy of the work, after publication, to the District clerk, and another copy to the Library of Congress. Were both copies mailed to Washington (post-free by law) this duty would be diminished by one-half.

2. A copyright work is not an invention nor a patent; it is a contribution to literature. It is not material, but intellectual, and has no natural relation to a department which is charged with the care of the mechanic arts; and it belongs rather to a national library system than to any other

department of the civil service. The responsibility of caring for it would be an incident to the similar labors already devolved upon the Librarian of Congress; and the receipts from copyright certificates would much more than pay its expense, thus leaving the treasury the gainer by the change.

3. The advantage of securing to our national library a complete collection of all American copyright publications can scarcely be over-estimated. If such a law as that enacted in 1870 had been enforced since the beginning of the government, we should now have in the Library of Congress a complete representation of the product of the American mind in every department of science and literature. Many publications which are printed in small editions, or which become "out of print" from the many accidents which continually destroy books, would owe to such a library their sole chance of preservation. We ought to have one comprehensive library in the country, and that belonging to the nation, whose aim it should be to preserve the books which other libraries have not the room nor the means to procure.

4. This consideration assumes additional weight when it is remembered that the Library of Congress is freely open to the public day and evening throughout the year, and is rapidly becoming the great reference library of the country, resorted to not only by Congress and the residents of Washington, but by students and writers from all parts of the Union, in search of references and authorities not elsewhere to be found. The advantage of having all American publications accessible upon inquiry would be to build up at Washington a truly national library, approximately complete and available to all the people.

These considerations prevailed with Congress to effect the amendment in copyright registration referred to.

By enactment of the statute of 1870 all the defects in the methods of registration and deposit of copies were obviated. The original records of copyright in all the States were thenceforward kept in the office of the Librarian of Congress. All questions as to literary property, involving a search of records to determine points of validity, such as priority of entry, names and residence of actual owners, transfers or assignments, timely deposit of the required copies, etc., could be determined upon inquiry at a single office of record. These inquiries are extremely numerous, and obviously very important, involving frequently large interests in valuable publications in which litigation to establish the rights of authors, publishers or infringers has been commenced or threatened. By the full records of copyright entries thus preserved, moreover, the Library of Congress (which is the property of the nation) has been enabled to secure what was before unattainable, namely, an approximately complete collection of all American books, etc., protected by copyright, since the legislation referred to went into effect. The system has been found in practice to give general satisfaction; the manner of securing copyright has been made plain and easy to all, the office of record being now a matter of public notoriety; and the test of experience during thirty years has established the system so thoroughly that none would be found to favor a return to the former methods.

The Act of 1870 provided for the removal of the collection of copyright books and other publications from the over-crowded Patent Office to the Library of Congress. These publications were the accumulations of about eighty years, received from the United States District Clerks' offices under the old law. By request of the Commissioner of Patents all the law books and a large number of technical works were reserved at the Department of the

Interior. The residue, when removed to the Capitol, were found to number 23,070 volumes, a much smaller number than had been anticipated, in view of the length of time during which the copy tax had been in operation. But the observance of the acts requiring deposits of copyright publications with the Clerks of the United States District Courts had been very defective (no penalty being provided for non-compliance), and, moreover, the Patent Office had failed to receive from the offices of original deposit large numbers of publications which should have been sent to Washington. From one of the oldest States in the Union not a single book had been sent in evidence of copyright. The books, however, which were added to the Congressional Library, although consisting largely of school books and the minor literature of the last half century, comprised many valuable additions to the collection of American books, which it should be the aim of a National Library to render complete. Among them were the earliest editions of the works of many well-known writers, now out of print and scarce.

The first book ever entered for copyright privileges under the laws of the United States was "The Philadelphia Spelling Book," which was registered in the Clerk's Office of the District of Pennsylvania, June 9, 1790, by John Barry as author. The spelling book was a fit introduction to the long series of books since produced to further the diffusion of knowledge among men. The second book entered was "The American Geography," by Jedediah Morse, entered in the District of Massachusetts on July 10, 1790, a copy of which is preserved in the Library of Congress. The earliest book entered in the State of New York was on the 30th of April, 1791, and it was entitled "The Young Gentleman's and Lady's Assistant, by Donald Fraser, Schoolmaster."

Objection has occasionally, though rarely, been made to what is known as the copy-tax, by which two copies of each publication must be deposited in the National Library. This requirement rests upon two valid grounds: (1) The preservation of copies of everything protected by copyright is necessary in the interest of authors and publishers, in evidence of copyright, and in aid of identification in connection with the record of title; (2) the library of the government (which is that of the whole people) should possess and permanently preserve a complete collection of the products of the American press, so far as secured by copyright. The government makes no unreasonable exaction in saying to authors and publishers: "The nation gives you exclusive right to make and sell your publication, without limit as to quantity, for forty-two years; give the nation in return two copies, one for the use and reference of Congress and the public in the National Library, the other for preservation in the copyright archives, in perpetual evidence of your right."

In view of the valuable monopoly conceded by the public, does not the government in effect give far more than a *quid pro quo* for the copy-tax? Of course it would not be equitable to exact even one copy of publications not secured by copyright, in which case the government gives nothing and gets nothing; but the exaction of actually protected publications, while it is almost unfelt by publishers, is so clearly in the interest of the public intelligence, as well as of authors and publishers themselves, that no valid objection to it appears to exist. In Great Britain five copies of every book protected by copyright are required for five different libraries, which appears somewhat unreasonable.

Regarding the right of renewal of the term of copyright, it is a significant fact that it is availed of in comparatively

few instances, compared with the whole body of publications. Multitudes of books are published which not only
never reach a second edition, but the sale of which does
not exhaust more than a small part of the copies printed
of the first. In these cases the right of renewal is waived
and suffered to lapse, from defect of commercial value in
the work protected. In many other cases the right of renewal expires before the author or his assigns bethink
them of the privilege secured to them under the law. It
results that more than nine-tenths, probably, of all books
published are free to any one to print, without reward or
royalty to their authors, after a very few years have elapsed.
On the other hand, the exclusive right in some publications of considerable commercial value is kept alive far beyond the forty-two years included in the original and the
renewal term, by entry of new editions of the work, and
securing copyright on the same. While this method may
not protect any of the original work from republication by
others, it enables the publishers of the copyright edition
to advertise such unauthorized reprints as imperfect, and
without the author's or editor's latest revision or additions.

The whole number of entries of copyright in the United
States since we became a nation considerably exceeds a
million and a half. · It may be of interest to give the aggregate number of titles of publications entered for copyright in each year since the transfer of the entire records
to Washington in 1870.

COPYRIGHTS REGISTERED IN THE UNITED STATES,
1870-1899.

1870.... 5,600	1874....16,283	1878....15,798
1871....12,688	1875....14,364	1879....18,125
1872....14,164	1876....14,882	1880....20,686
1873....15,352	1877....15,758	1881....21,075

1882....22,918	1888....38,225	1894....62,762
1883....25,273	1889....40,777	1895....67,572
1884....26,893	1890....42,758	1896....72,470
1885....28,410	1891....48,908	1897....74,321
1886....31,241	1892....54,735	1898....76,874
1887....35,083	1893....58,936	1899....86,492

Total, 30 years, ...1,079,445

It will readily be seen that this great number of copyrights does not represent books alone. Many thousands of entries are daily and weekly periodicals claiming copyright protection, in which case they are required by law to make entry of every separate issue. These include a multitude of journals, literary, political, scientific, religious, pictorial, technical, commercial, agricultural, sporting, dramatic, etc., among which are a number in foreign languages. These entries also embrace all the leading monthly and quarterly magazines and reviews, with many devoted to specialties—as metaphysics, sociology, law, theology, art, finance, education, and the arts and sciences generally. Another large class of copyright entries (and the largest next to books and periodicals) is musical compositions, numbering recently some 20,000 publications yearly. Much of this property is valuable, and it is nearly all protected by entry of copyright, coming from all parts of the Union. There is also a large and constantly increasing number of works of graphic art, comprising engravings, photographs, photogravures, chromos, lithographs, etchings, prints, and drawings, for which copyright is entered. The steady accumulation of hundreds of thousands of these various pictorial illustrations will enable the government at no distant day, without a dollar of expense, to make an exhibit of the progress of the arts of design in America, which will be highly interesting and instructive. An art gallery of ample dimensions for this purpose is provided in the new National Library building.

It remains to consider briefly the principles and practice of what is known as international copyright.

Perhaps there is no argument for copyright at all in the productions of the intellect which is not good for its extension to all countries. The basis of copyright is that all useful labor is worthy of a recompense; but since all human thought when put into material or merchantable form becomes, in a certain sense, public property, the laws of all countries recognize and protect the original owners, or their assigns to whom they may convey the right, in an exclusive privilege for limited terms only. Literary property therefore is not a natural right, but a conventional one. The author's right to his manuscript is, indeed, absolute, and the law will protect him in it as fully as it will guard any other property. But when once put in type and multiplied through the printing-press, his claim to an exclusive right has to be guarded by a special statute, otherwise it is held to be abandoned (like the articles in a newspaper) to the public. This special protection is furnished in nearly all civilized countries by copyright law.

What we call "copyright" is an exclusive right to multiply copies of any publication for sale. Domestic copyright, which is all we formerly had in this country, is limited to the United States. International copyright, which has now been enacted, extends the right of American authors to foreign countries, and recognizes a parallel right of foreign authors in our own. There is nothing in the constitutional provision which restrains Congress from granting copyright to other than American citizens. Patent right, coming under the same clause of the Constitution, has been extended to foreigners. Out of over 20,-000 patents annually issued, about 2,500 (or 12 per cent.)

are issued to foreigners, while American patents are similarly protected abroad. If we have international patent right, why not international copyright? The grant of power is the same; both patent right and copyright are for a limited time; both rights during this time are exclusive; and both rest upon the broad ground of the promotion of science and the useful arts. If copyright is justifiable at all, if authors are to be secured a reward for their labors, they claim that all who use them should contribute equally to this result. The principle of copyright once admitted, it cannot logically be confined to State lines or national boundaries. There appears to be no middle ground between the doctrine of common property in all productions of the intellect—which leads us to communism by the shortest road—and the admission that copyright is due, while its limited term lasts, from all who use the works of an author, wherever found.

Accordingly, international copyright has become the policy of nearly all civilized nations. The term of copyright is longer in most countries than in the United States, ranging from the life of the author and seven years beyond, in England, to a life term and fifty years additional in France and Russia. Copyright is thus made a life tenure and something more in all countries except our own, where its utmost limit is forty-two years. This may perhaps be held to represent a fair average lifetime, reckoned from the age of intellectual maturity. There have not been wanting advocates for a perpetual copyright, to run to the author and his heirs and assigns forever. This was urged before the British Copyright Commission in 1878 by leading British publishers, but the term of copyright is hitherto, in all nations, limited by law.

Only brief allusion can be made to the most recent (and in some respects most important) advance step which has been taken in copyright legislation in the United States. This act of Congress is aimed at securing reciprocal protection to American and foreign authors in the respective countries which may comply with its provisions. There is here no room to sketch the hitherto vain attempt to secure to authors, here and abroad, an international protection to their writings. Suffice it to say that a union of interests was at last effected, whereby authors, publishers and manufacturers are supposed to have secured some measure of protection to their varied interests. The measure is largely experimental, and the satisfaction felt over its passage into law is tempered by doubt in various quarters as to the justice, or liberality, or actual benefit to authors of its provisions. What is to be said of a statute which was denounced by some Senators as a long step backward toward barbarism, and hailed by others as a great landmark in the progress of civilization?

The main features added to the existing law of copyright by this act, which took effect July 1, 1891, are these:

1. All limitation of the privilege of copyright to citizens and residents of the United States is repealed.

2. Foreigners applying for copyright are to pay fees of $1 for record, or $1.50 for certificate of copyright.

3. Importation of books, photographs, chromos or lithographs entered here for copyright is prohibited, except two copies of any book for use and not for sale.

4. The two copies of books, photographs, chromos or lithographs deposited with the Librarian of Congress must be printed from type set, or plates, etc., made in the United States. It follows that all foreign works protected by American copyright must be wholly manufactured in this country.

5. The copyright privilege is restricted to citizens or subjects of nations permitting the benefit of copyright to

Americans on substantially the same terms as their own citizens, or of nations who have international agreements providing for reciprocity in the grant of copyright, to which the United States may at its pleasure become a party.

6. The benefit of copyright in the United States is not to take effect as to any foreigner until the actual existence of either of the conditions just recited, in the case of the nation to which he belongs, shall have been made known by a proclamation of the President of the United States.

One very material benefit has been secured through international copyright. Under it, authors are assured the control of their own text, both as to correctness and completeness. Formerly, republication was conducted on a "scramble" system, by which books were hastened through the press, to secure the earliest market, with little or no regard to a correct re-production. Moreover, it was in the power of the American publisher of an English book, or of a British publisher of an American one, to alter or omit passages in any work reprinted, at his pleasure. This license was formerly exercised, and imperfect, garbled, or truncated editions of an author's writings were issued without his consent, an outrage against which international copyright furnishes the only preventive.

Another benefit of copyright between nations has been to check the relentless flood of cheap, unpaid-for fiction, which formerly poured from the press, submerging the better literature. The Seaside and other libraries, with their miserable type, flimsy paper, and ugly form, were an injury alike to the eyesight, to the taste, and in many cases, to the morals of the community. More than ninety per cent. of these wretched "Libraries" were foreign novels. An avalanche of English and translated French novels of the "bigamy school" of fiction swept over the land, until the cut-throat competition of publishers, after exhausting the stock of unwholesome foreign literature, led to the failure of many houses, and piled high the counters of book and other stores with bankrupt stock. Having at last got rid of this unclean brood, (it is hoped forever) we now have better books, produced on good paper and type, and worth preserving, at prices not much above those of the trash formerly offered us.

At the same time, standard works of science and literature are being published in England at prices which tend steadily toward increased popular circulation. Even conservative publishers are reversing the rule of small editions at high prices, for larger editions at low prices. The old three-volume novel is nearly supplanted by the one volume, well-printed and bound book at five or six shillings. Many more reductions would follow in the higher class of books, were not the measure of reciprocal copyright thus far secured handicapped by the necessity of re-printing on this side at double cost, if a large American circulation is in view.

The writers of America, with the steady and rapid progress of the art of making books, have come more and more to appreciate the value of their preservation, in complete and unbroken series, in the library of the government, the appropriate conservator of the nation's literature. Inclusive and not exclusive, as this library is wisely made by law, so far as copyright works are concerned, it preserves with impartial care the illustrious and the obscure. In its archives all sciences and all schools of opinion stand on equal ground. In the beautiful and ample repository, now erected and dedicated to literature and art through the liberal action of Congress, the intellectual wealth of the past and the present age will be handed down to the ages that are to follow.

CHAPTER 24.

POETRY OF THE LIBRARY.

THE LIBRARIAN'S DREAM.

1.

He sat at night by his lonely bed,
  With an open book before him;
And slowly nodded his weary head,
  As slumber came stealing o'er him.

2.

And he saw in his dream a mighty host
  Of the writers gone before,
And the shadowy form of many a ghost
  Glided in at the open door.

3.

Great Homer came first in a snow-white shroud,
  And Virgil sang sweet by his side;
While Cicero thundered in accents loud,
  And Caesar most gravely replied.

4.

Anacreon, too, from his rhythmical lips
  The honey of Hybla distilled,
And Herodotus suffered a partial eclipse,
  While Horace with music was filled.

5.

The procession of ancients was brilliant and long,
  Aristotle and Plato were there,
Thucydides, too, and Tacitus strong,
  And Plutarch, and Sappho the fair.

6.

Aristophanes elbowed gay Ovid's white ghost,
  And Euripides Xenophon led,
While Propertius laughed loud at Juvenal's jokes,
  And Sophocles rose from the dead.

(417)

7.

Then followed a throng to memory dear,
  Of writers more modern in age,
Cervantes and Shakespeare, who died the same year,
  And Chaucer, and Bacon the sage.

8.

Immortal the laurels that decked the fair throng,
  And Dante moved by with his lyre,
While Montaigne and Pascal stood rapt by his song,
  And Boccaccio paused to admire.

9.

Sweet Spenser and Calderon moved arm in arm,
  While Milton and Sidney were there,
Pope, Dryden, and Molière added their charm,
  And Bunyan, and Marlowe so rare.

10.

Then Gibbon stalked by in classical guise,
  And Hume, and Macaulay, and Froude,
While Darwin, and Huxley, and Tyndall looked wise,
  And Humboldt and Comte near them stood.

11.

Dean Swift looked sardonic on Addison's face,
  And Johnson tipped Boswell a wink,
Walter Scott and Jane Austen hobnobbed o'er a glass,
  And Goethe himself deigned to drink.

12.

Robert Burns followed next with Thomas Carlyle,
  Jean Paul paired with Coleridge, too,
While De Foe elbowed Goldsmith, the master of style,
  And Fielding and Schiller made two.

13.

Rousseau with his eloquent, marvellous style,
  And Voltaire, with his keen, witty pen,
Victor Hugo so grand, though repellent the while,
  And Dumas and Balzac again.

14.

Dear Thackeray came in his happiest mood,
　And stayed until midnight was done,
Bulwer-Lytton, and Reade, and Kingsley and Hood,
　And Dickens, the master of fun.

15.

George Eliot, too, with her matter-full page,
　And Byron, and Browning, and Keats,
While Shelley and Tennyson joined youth and age,
　And Wordsworth the circle completes.

16.

Then followed a group of America's best,
　With Irving, and Bryant, and Holmes,
While Bancroft and Motley unite with the rest,
　And Thoreau with Whittier comes.

17.

With his Raven in hand dreamed on Edgar Poe,
　And Longfellow sweet and serene,
While Prescott, and Ticknor, and Emerson too,
　And Hawthorne and Lowell were seen.

18.

While thus the assembly of witty and wise
　Rejoiced the librarian's sight,
Ere the wonderful vision had fled from his eyes,
　From above shone a heavenly light:

19.

And solemn and sweet came a voice from the skies,
　"All battles and conflicts are done,
The temple of Knowledge shall open all eyes,
　And law, faith, and reason are one!"

When the radiant dawn of the morning broke,
From his glorious dream the librarian woke.

THE LIBRARY.

That place that does contain my books,
My books, the best companions, is to me,
A glorious court, where hourly I converse
With the old sages and philosophers;
And sometimes, for variety I confer
With kings and emperors, and weigh their counsels.

BEAUMONT AND FLETCHER.

The bard of every age and clime,
Of genius fruitful and of soul sublime,
Who from the glowing mint of fancy pours
No spurious metal, fused from common ores,
But gold to matchless purity refined,
And stamped with all the Godhead in his mind.

JUVENAL.

Books, we know,
Are a substantial world, both pure and good;
Round these, with tendrils strong as flesh and blood,
Our pastime and our happiness will grow.

WORDSWORTH.

QUAINT LINES ON A BOOK-WORM.

The Bokeworme sitteth in his celle,
He studyethe all alone,
And burnethe oute the oile,
'Till ye midnight hour is gone
Then gethe he downe upon his bedde,
Ne mo watch will he a-keepe,
He layethe his heade on ye pillowe,
And eke he tryes to sleepe.
Then swyfte there cometh a vision grimme,
And greetythe him sleepynge fair,
And straighte he dreameth of grislie dreames,
And dreades fellowne and rayre.
Wherefore, if cravest life to eld
Ne rede longe uppe at night,
But go to bed at Curfew bell
And ryse wythe mornynge's lyte.

BALLADE OF THE BOOK-HUNTER.

In torrid heats of late July,
In March, beneath the bitter *bise*,
He book-hunts while the loungers fly,—
He book-hunts, though December freeze;
In breeches baggy at the knees,
And heedless of the public jeers,
For these, for these, he hoards his fees,—
Aldines, Bodonis, Elzevirs.

No dismal stall escapes his eye,
He turns o'er tomes of low degree,
There soiled romanticists may lie,
Or Restoration comedies;
Each tract that flutters in the breeze
For him is charged with hopes and fears,
In mouldy novels fancy sees
Aldines, Bodonis, Elzevirs.

With restless eyes that peer and spy,
Sad eyes that heed not skies nor trees,
In dismal nooks he loves to pry,
Whose motto evermore is *Spes!*
But ah! the fabled treasure flees;
Grown rarer with the fleeting years,
In rich men's shelves they take their ease,—
Aldines, Bodonis, Elzevirs!

Prince, all the things that tease and please,—
Fame, hope, wealth, kisses, jeers and tears,
What are they but such toys as these—
Aldines, Bodonis, Elzevirs? ANDREW LANG.

'Tis in books the chief
Of all perfections to be plain and brief.
SAMUEL BUTLER.

Of all those arts in which the wise excel,
Nature's chief master-piece is writing well.
BUCKINGHAM.

Books should to one of these four ends conduce:
For wisdom, piety, delight, or use.
SIR JOHN DENHAM.

My Books.

Oh, happy he who, weary of the sound
Of throbbing life, can shut his study door,
Like Heinsius, on it all, to find a store
Of peace that otherwise is never found!
Such happiness is mine, when all around
My dear dumb friends in groups of three or four
Command my soul to linger on the shore
Of those fair realms where they reign monarchs crowned.
To-day the strivings of the world are naught,
For I am in a land that glows with God,
And I am in a path by angels trod.
Dost ask what book creates such heavenly thought?
Then know that I with Dante soar afar,
Till earth shrinks slowly to a tiny star.

                                        J. WILLIAMS

Thoughts in a Library.

Speak low! tread softly through these halls;
  Here genius lives enshrined;
Here reign in silent majesty
  The monarchs of the mind.

A mighty spirit host they come
  From every age and clime;
Above the buried wrecks of years
  They breast the tide of time.

Here shall the poets chant for thee
  Their sweetest, loftiest lays,
And prophets wait to guide thy steps
  In Wisdom's pleasant ways.

Come, with these God-anointed kings
  Be thou companion here;
And in the mighty realm of mind
  Thou shalt go forth a peer!

                        ANNE C. LYNCH BOTTA.

Verses in a Library.

Give me that book whose power is such
That I forget the north wind's touch.

Give me that book that brings to me
Forgetfulness of what I be.

Give me that book that takes my life
In seeming far from all its strife.

Give me that book wherein each page
Destroys my sense of creeping age.

John Kendrick Bangs.

A Book by the Brook.

Give me a nook and a book,
And let the proud world spin round;
Let it scramble by hook or by crook
For wealth or a name with a sound.
You are welcome to amble your ways,
Aspirers to place or to glory;
May big bells jangle your praise,
And golden pens blazon your story;
For me, let me dwell in my nook,
Here by the curve of this brook,
That croons to the tune of my book:
Whose melody wafts me forever
On the waves of an unseen river.

William Freeland.

The love of learning, the sequestered nooks,
And all the sweet serenity of books.

H. W. Longfellow.

Oh for a booke and a shady nooke
    Eyther in door or out,
With the greene leaves whispering overhead,
    Or the streete cryes all about:
Where I maie reade all at my ease
    Both of the newe and olde,
For a jollie goode booke whereon to looke
    Is better to me than golde!

To Daniel Elzevir.

(*From the Latin of Ménage.*)

What do I see! Oh! gods divine
And Goddesses—this Book of mine—
This child of many hopes and fears,
Is published by the Elzevirs!
Oh Perfect publishers complete!
Oh dainty volume, new and neat!
The Paper doth outshine the snow,
The Print is blacker than the crow,
The Title-page, with crimson bright,
The vellum cover smooth and white,
All sorts of readers to invite;
Ay, and will keep them reading still,
Against their will, or with their will!
Thus what of grace the Rhymes may lack
The Publisher has given them back,
As Milliners adorn the fair
Whose charms are something skimp and spare.

Oh dulce decus, Elzevirs!
The pride of dead and dawning years,
How can a poet best repay
The debt he owes your House to-day?
May this round world, while aught endures,
Applaud, and buy, these books of yours.
May purchasers incessant pop,
My Elzevirs, within your shop,
And learned bards salute, with cheers,
The volumes of the Elzevirs,
Till your renown fills earth and sky,
Till men forget the Stephani,
And all that Aldus wrought, and all
Turnebus sold in shop or stall,
While still may Fate's (and Binders') shears
Respect, and spare, the Elzevirs!

Blessings be with them, and eternal praise,
Who gave us nobler loves and nobler cares!
The Poets, who on earth have made us heirs
Of truth and pure delight by heavenly lays.

WORDSWORTH.

COMPANIONS.

But books, old friends that are always new,
Of all good things that we know are best;
They never forsake us, as others do,
And never disturb our inward rest.
Here is truth in a world of lies,
And all that in man is great and wise!
Better than men and women, friend,
That are dust, though dear in our joy and pain,
Are the books their cunning hands have penned,
For they depart, but the books remain.

RICHARD HENRY STODDARD.

THE PARADOX OF BOOKS.

I'm strange contradictions; I'm new and I'm old,
I'm often in tatters, and oft decked with gold.
Though I never could read, yet lettered I'm found;
Though blind, I enlighten; though loose, I am bound.
I'm always in black, and I'm always in white;
I am grave and I'm gay, I am heavy and light.
In form too I differ,—I'm thick and I'm thin;
I've no flesh and no bone, yet I'm covered with skin;
I've more points than the compass, more stops than the flute;
I sing without voice, without speaking confute;
I'm English, I'm German, I'm French, and I'm Dutch;
Some love me too fondly, some slight me too much;
I often die soon, though I sometimes live ages,
And no monarch alive has so many pages.

HANNAH MORE.

I love my books as drinkers love their wine;
The more I drink, the more they seem divine;
With joy elate my soul in love runs o'er,
And each fresh draught is sweeter than before:
Books bring me friends where'er on earth I be,—
Solace of solitude, bonds of society.

I love my books! they are companions dear,
Sterling in worth, in friendship most sincere;
Here talk I with the wise in ages gone,

And with the nobly gifted in our own:
If love, joy, laughter, sorrow please my mind,
Love, joy, grief, laughter in my books I find.

FRANCIS BENNOCH.

MY LIBRARY.

All round the room my silent servants wait,—
My friends in every season, bright and dim
Angels and seraphim
Come down and murmur to me, sweet and low,
And spirits of the skies all come and go
Early and late;
From the old world's divine and distant date,
From the sublimer few,
Down to the poet who but yester-eve
Sang sweet and made us grieve,
All come, assembling here in order due.
And here I dwell with Poesy, my mate,
With Erato and all her vernal sighs,
Great Clio with her victories elate,
Or pale Urania's deep and starry eyes.
Oh friends, whom chance or change can never harm,
Whom Death the tyrant cannot doom to die,
Within whose folding soft eternal charm
I love to lie,
And meditate upon your verse that flows,
And fertilizes wheresoe'er it goes.

BRYAN WALLER PROCTER.

RATIONAL MADNESS.

A Song, for the Lover of Curious and Rare Books.

Come, boys, fill your glasses, and fill to the brim,
Here's the essence of humor, the soul, too, of whim!
Attend and receive (and sure 'tis no vapour)
A "hap' worth of wit on a pennyworth of paper."

Those joys which the Bibliomania affords
Are felt and acknowledged by Dukes and by Lords!
And the finest estate would be offer'd in vain
For an exemplar bound by the famed Roger Payne!

To a proverb goes madness with love hand in hand,
But our senses we yield to a double command;
The dear frenzy in both is first rous'd by fair looks,—
Here's our sweethearts, my boys! not forgetting our books!

Thus our time may we pass with rare books and rare friends,
Growing wiser and better, till life itself ends:
And may those who delight not in black-letter lore,
By some obsolete act be sent from our shore!

BALLADE OF TRUE WISDOM.

While others are asking for beauty or fame,
Or praying to know that for which they should pray,
Or courting Queen Venus, that affable dame,
Or chasing the Muses the weary and grey,
The sage has found out a more excellent way—
To Pan and to Pallas his incense he showers,
And his humble petition puts up day by day,
For a house full of books, and a garden of flowers.

Inventors may bow to the God that is lame,
And crave from the fire on his stithy a ray;
Philosophers kneel to the God without name,
Like the people of Athens, agnostics are they;
The hunter a fawn to Diana will slay,
The maiden wild roses will wreathe for the Hours;
But the wise man will ask, ere libation he pay,
For a house full of books, and a garden of flowers.

Oh grant me a life without pleasure or blame
(As mortals count pleasure who rush through their day
With a speed to which that of the tempest is tame)
O grant me a house by the beach of a bay,
Where the waves can be surly in winter, and play
With the sea-weed in summer, ye bountiful powers!
And I'd leave all the hurry, the noise, and the fray,
For a house full of books, and a garden of flowers.

ENVOY.

Gods, grant or withhold it; your "yea" and your "nay"
Are immutable, heedless of outcry of ours:

But life is worth living, and here we would stay
For a house full of books, and a garden of flowers.

ANDREW LANG.

THE LIBRARY.

They soothe the grieved, the stubborn they chastise,
Fools they admonish, and confirm the wise:
Their aid they yield to all: they never shun
The man of sorrow, nor the wretch undone:
Unlike the hard, the selfish, and the proud,
They fly not sullen from the suppliant crowd;
Nor tell to various people various things,
But show to subjects, what they show to kings.

Blest be the gracious Power, who taught mankind
To stamp a lasting image of the mind!

With awe, around these silent walks I tread;
These are the lasting mansions of the dead:—
"The dead!" methinks a thousand tongues reply;
"These are the tombs of such as cannot die!
"Crown'd with eternal fame, they sit sublime,
"And laugh at all the little strife of time."

Lo, all in silence, all in order stand,
And mighty folios first, a lordly band;
Then quartos their well-order'd ranks maintain,
And light octavos fill a spacious plain:
See yonder, rangèd in more frequent rows,
A humbler band of duodecimos;
While undistinguished trifles swell the scene,
The last new play and fritter'd magazine.

Here all the rage of controversy ends,
And rival zealots rest like bosom friends:
An Athanasian here, in deep repose,
Sleeps with the fiercest of his Arian foes;
Socinians here with Calvinists abide,
And thin partitions angry chiefs divide;
Here wily Jesuits simple Quakers meet,
And Bellarmine has rest at Luther's feet.

GEORGE CRABBE.

ETERNITY OF POETRY.

For deeds doe die, however noblie donne,
And thoughts do as themselves decay;
But wise words, taught in numbers for to runne
Recorded by the Muses, live for ay;
Ne may with storming showers be washt away,
Ne bitter breathing windes with harmful blast,
Nor age, nor envie, shall them ever wast.

SPENSER.

THE OLD BOOKS.

The old books, the old books, the books of long ago!
Who ever felt Miss Austen tame, or called Sir Walter slow?
We did not care the worst to hear of human sty or den;
We liked to love a little bit, and trust our fellow-men.
The old books, the old books, as pure as summer breeze!
We read them under garden boughs, by fire-light on our knees,
They did not teach, they did not preach, or scold us into good;
A noble spirit from them breathed, the rest was understood.

The old books, the old books, the mother loves them best;
They leave no bitter taste behind to haunt the youthful
     breast:
They bid us hope, they bid us fill our hearts with visions fair;
They do not paralyze the will with problems of despair.
And as they lift from sloth and sense to follow loftier planes,
And stir the blood of indolence to bubble in the veins:
Inheritors of mighty things, who own a lineage high,
We feel within us budding wings that long to reach the sky:
To rise above the commonplace, and through the cloud to soar,
And join the loftier company of grander souls of yore.

THE SPECTATOR.

CHAPTER 25.

HUMORS OF THE LIBRARY.*

SOME THOUGHTS ON CLASSIFICATION.

By Librarian F. M. Crunden.

Classification is vexation,
    Shelf-numbering is as bad;
      The rule of D
      Doth puzzle me;
    Mnemonics drives me mad.

Air—The Lord Chancellor's Song.

When first I became a librarian,
    Says I to myself, says I,
I'll learn all their systems as fast as I can,
    Says I to myself, says I;
The Cutter, the Dewey, the Schwartz, and the Poole,
The alphabet, numeral, mnemonic rule,
The old, and the new, and the eclectic school,
    Says I to myself, says I.

Class-numbers, shelf-numbers, book-numbers, too,
    Says I to myself, says I,
I'll study them all, and I'll learn them clear thro',
    Says I to myself, says I;
I'll find what is good, and what's better and best,
And I'll put two or three to a practical test;
And then—if I've time—I'll take a short rest,
    Says I to myself, says I.

But art it is long and time it doth fly,
    Says I to myself, says I,
And three or four years have already passed by,
    Says I to myself, says I;
And yet on those systems I'm not at all clear,
While new combinations forever appear,
To master them all is a life-work, I fear,
    Says I to myself, says I.

---

*Mostly from the Library Journal, New York.

Classification in a Library in Western New York: Gail Hamilton's "Woolgathering," under Agriculture.

Book asked for. "An attack philosopher in Paris."

A changed title. A young woman went into a library the other day and asked for the novel entitled "She combeth not her head," but she finally concluded to take "He cometh not, she said."

Labor-saving devices. The economical catalogue-maker who thus set down two titles—

"Mill on the Floss,"
  do. Political economy."

has a sister who keeps a universal scrap-book into which everything goes, but which is carefully indexed. She, too, has a mind for saving, as witness:

"Patti, Adelina.
  do. Oyster."

From a New York auction catalogue:

"267. Junius Stat Nominis Umbrii, with numerous splendid portraits."

At the New York Free Circulating Library, a youth of twenty said Shakespeare made him tired. "Why couldn't he write English instead of indulging in that *thee* and *thou* business?" Miss Braddon he pronounced "a daisy". A pretty little blue-eyed fellow "liked American history best of all," but found the first volume of Justin Winsor's history too much for him. "The French and German and Hebrew in it are all right, but there's Spanish and Italian and Latin, and I don't know those."

A gentleman in Paris sent to the bookbinder two volumes of the French edition of "Uncle Tom's Cabin." The title in French is "L'Oncle Tom," and the two volumes were returned to him marked on their backs:

L'Oncle,	L'Oncle,
Tome I.	Tome II.

How a Bibliomaniac Binds His Books.

I'd like my favorite books to bind
So that their outward dress
To every bibliomaniac's mind
Their contents should express.

Napoleon's life should glare in red,
John Calvin's life in blue;
Thus they would typify bloodshed
And sour religion's hue.

The Popes in scarlet well may go;
In jealous green, Othello;
In gray, Old Age of Cicero,
And London Cries in yellow.

My Walton should his gentle art
In salmon best express,
And Penn and Fox the friendly heart
In quiet drab confess.

Crimea's warlike facts and dates
Of fragrant Russia smell;
The subjugated Barbary States
In crushed Morocco dwell.

But oh! that one I hold so dear
Should be arrayed so cheap
Gives me a qualm; I sadly fear
My Lamb must be half-sheep!

IRVING BROWNE.

In a Wisconsin library, a young lady asked for the "Life of National Harthorne" and the "Autograph on the breakfast table."

"Have you a poem on the Victor of Manengo, by Anon?"

Library inquiry—"I want the catalogue of temporary literature."

Query—What did she want?

A friend proposes to put Owen's "Footfalls on the Boundaries of Another World" in Travels. Shall we let him?

A poet, in Boston, filled out an application for a volume of Pope's works, an edition reserved from circulation, in the following tuneful manner:

"You ask me, dear sir, to a reason define
Why you should for a fortnight this volume resign
To my care.—*I am also a son of the nine*."

A worthy Deutscher, confident in his mastery of the English tongue, sent the following quaint document across the sea:

"I send you with the Post six numbers, of our Allgemeine Militär-Zeitung, which is published in the next year to the fifty times. Excuse my bath english I learned in the school and I forgot so much. If you have interest to german Antiquariatskataloge I will send to you some. I remain however yours truly servant."

A gentlemanly stranger once asked the delivery clerk for "a genealogy." "What one?" she asked. "Oh! any," he said. "Well—Savage's?" "No; white men."

Said Melvil Dewey: "To my thinking, a great librarian must have a clear head, a strong hand, and, above all, a great heart. Such shall be greatest among librarians; and, when I look into the future, I am inclined to think that most of the men who will achieve this greatness will be women."

A LIBRARY HYMN.

By an Assistant Librarian.

I have endeavored to clothe the dull prose of the usual Library Rules with the mantle of poetry, that they may be more attractive, and more easily remembered by the great public whom we serve.

Gently, reader, gently moving,
Wipe your feet beside the door;
Hush your voice to whispers soothing,
Take your hat off, I implore!
Mark your number, plainly, rightly,
From the catalogue you see;

With the card projecting slightly,
Then your book bring unto me.
    Quickly working,
    With no shirking,
Soon another there will be.

If above two weeks you've left me,
Just two cents a day I'll take,
And, unless my mind's bereft me,
Payment you must straightway make.
Treat your books as if to-morrow,
Gabriel's trump would surely sound,
And all scribbling, to your sorrow,
'Gainst your credit would be found.
    Therefore tear not,
    Spot and wear not
All these books so neatly bound.

These few simple rules abiding,
We shall always on you smile:
There will be no room for chiding,
No one's temper will you rile.
And when Heaven's golden portals
For you on their hinges turn,
With the books for all immortals,
There will be no rules to learn.
    Therefore heed them,
    Often read them,
Lest your future weal you spurn.

TITLES OF BOOKS ASKED FOR BY WRITTEN SLIPS IN A POPULAR LIBRARY.

Aristopholus translated by Buckley.
Alfreri Tragedus.
Bertall Lavie Hors De Ches Soi.
Cooke M. C. M. A. L. L. D. their nature and uses. Edited by Rev. J. M. Berkeley M. A. F. R. S. (Fungi.)
Caralus Note Book (A Cavalier's).
Gobden Club-Essays.
Specie the origin of Darwin.
An Epistropal Prayer Book.

Blunders in Cataloguing.

Gasparin. The uprising of a great many people.
Hughes, Tom. The scouring of the White House.
Mayhew. The pheasant boy.
Wind in the lower animals (Mind.)

Recent Calls for Books at a Western Library.

Account of Monte Cristo.
Acrost the Kontinent by Boles.
Bula.
Count of Corpus Cristy.
Dant's Infernal comedy.
Darwin's Descent on man.
Feminine Cooper's works.
Infeleese.
Less Miserable.
Some of Macbeth's writings.
Something in the way of friction.
Squeal to a book.

In Vol. 3 of Laporte's "Bibliographie contemporaine," Dibdin's famous book is entered thus: "Bibliomania, or boock, madness: a bibliographical romance...illustrated with cats."

A well-known librarian writes:

"The Catalogue of the Indiana State Library for the year 1859 has long been my wonder and admiration. "Bank's History of the Popes" appears under the letter B. Strong in the historical department, it offers a choice between the "Life of John Tyler, by Harper & Brothers," "Memoirs of Moses Henderson, by Jewish Philosophers," "Memoirs and Correspondence of Viscount Castlereach, by the Marquis of Londonderry," and "Memoirs of Benvenuto, by Gellini." In fiction, you may find "Tales of My Landlord by Cleishbotham," and "The Pilot, by the Author of the Pioneers;" while, if your passion for plural authorship is otherwise unappeasable—if Beaumont and Fletcher or Erckman-Chatrian seem to you too feeble a combination of talents—you may well be captivated by the title "Small Arms, by the United States Army."

Prince of Peace, Boston, 1809." How Godoy should become McKinley, or McKinley should become the Prince of Peace, is a problem for psychologists.

CONFUSION OF KNOWLEDGE.

The following are some specimens of answers to Examinations of candidates for Library employment, given within the past five years:

"A sonnet is a poem which is adapted to music, as Petrarch's sonnets"; "a sonnet is a short poem sometimes and sometimes a long one and generally a reflection, or thoughts upon some inanimate thing, as Young's 'Night thoughts.'" "An epic is a critical writing, as 'Criticism on man'"; "an epic is a literary form written in verse, and which teaches us some lesson not necessarily of a moral nature"; "an epic is a dramatic poem."

Epigrammatic writing is very clearly defined as "critical in a grammatical way." "Allegory is writing highly colored, as Pope's works"; "allegory is writing of something that never happened, but it is purely imaginary, often a wandering from the main point." A common mistake regarding the meaning of the word bibliography results in such answers as "bibliography—a study of the Bible;" or "gives the lives of the people in the Bible." An encyclopædia was aptly defined as "a storehouse of knowledge for the enlightenment of the public," while another answer reads "Book of Books, giving the life of famous persons, life and habits of animals and plants, and some medical knowledge." A collection of works of any author is termed "an anthropology." "Anthology is the study of insects." Folklore is defined as "giving to animals and things human sense"; an elegy means "a eulogy," oratory, "the deliverance of words." Belles-lettres is to one applicant "beautiful ideas," to another "the title of a book," to another "short stories"; again "are the letters of French writers," and still another writes "French for prominent literature and light literature." A concordance "is the explication or definition of something told in a simpler form," is the extremely lucid answer to one question, which was answered by another candidate as "a table of reference at back of book."

The titles of books are too seldom associated with their

authors' names, resulting in such answers as "Homer is the author of the Aeneid"; "Lalla Rookh" was written by James Blackmore; "Children of the Abbey," by Walter Besant (while another attributed it to Jane Porter): "Bow of orange Ribbon," by George Meredith; "Hon. Peter Stirling," by Fielding; "Quo Vadis," by Browning; "Pamela," by Frank Stockton (according to another by Marie Edgworth); "Love's Labour's Lost," by Bryant (another gives Thomas Reade as the author, while still another guesses Schiller); "Descent of Man," by Alexander Pope (another gives Dryden); "The Essay on Man," by Francis Bacon.

One candidate believes "Hudibras" to be an early Saxon poem; another that "Victor Hugo's best known work is William Tell"; another that "Aesop's Fables is a famous allegory." Charlotte Brontë is described as an "American— nineteenth century—children's book." Cicero was "known for Latin poetry." "Dante is an exceedingly bitter writer; he takes you into hell and describes Satan and his angels. He wrote his play for the stage." Another's idea of the Divine Comedy is "a play which could be acted by the priests on the steps of a church for the benefit of the poorer class."

Civil service in the mind of one young woman was "the service done by the government in a country, domesticly."

A Christian socialist is "an advocate of Christian science." "A limited monarchy is a kingdom whose ruler is under the ruler of another country." Legal tender is "the legal rate of interest"; another considers it "Paper money." In economics, some of the answers were "profit-sharing, a term used in socialism, the rich to divide among the poor." "Monopolies is the money gained by selling church properties"; while "a trust is usually a place where a person puts some money where it will be safe to keep it."

About noted personages and historic events and places the answers are equally startling. "Molière was a French essayist and critic" (also "a French writer of the nineteenth century,") Cecil Rhodes, "the founder of Bryn Mawr College"; "Seth Low—England, eighteenth century;" Attila "a woman mentioned in the Bible for her great cruelty to her child;" Warren Hastings "was a German soldier" (also "was a discoverer; died about 1870"); "Nero was a Roman emperor B. C.

450." Perhaps the most unique guess in this line was "Richard Wagner invented the Wagner cars;" Abbotsford is "the title of a book by Sir Walter Scott;" "Vassar College is a dream, high-up and unattainable;" "Tammany Hall is a political meeting place in London;" "the Parthenon, an art gallery in Athens."

Pedagogy seemed one of the most perplexing of words. It was defined by one as "the science of religion," by another as "learned pomposity;" but the most remarkable of all was "pedagogy is the study of feet."

SONG OF SOME LIBRARY SCHOOL SCHOLARS.

Three little maids from school are we,
Filled to the brim with economy—
Not of the house but library,
Learnt in the Library School

1st Maid—I range my books from number one.
2nd Maid—Alphabetically I've begun.
3rd Maid—In regular classes mine do run.
All—Three maids from the Library School.

All—Three little maidens all unwary,
Each in charge of a library,
Each with a system quite contrary
To every other school.

Our catalogues, we quite agree,
From faults and errors must be free,
If only we our way can see
To find the proper rule.

Boy's remark on returning a certain juvenile book to the library: "I don't want any more of them books. The girls is all too holy."

"Half the books in this library are not worth reading," said a sour-visaged, hypercritical, novel-satiated woman.—"Read the other half, then," advised a bystander.

THE WOES OF A LIBRARIAN.

Let us give a brief rehearsal
Of the learning universal,
Which men expect to find
In Librarians to their mind.

He must undergo probation,
Before he gets a situation;
Must begin at the creation,
When the world was in formation,
And come down to its cremation,
In the final consummation
Of the old world's final spasm:
He must study protoplasm,
And bridge over every chasm
In the origin of species,
Ere the monkey wore the breeches,
Or the Simian tribe began
To ascend from ape to man.

He must master the cosmology,
And know all about psychology,
And the wonders of biology,
And be deep in ornithology,
And develop ideology,
With the aid of craniology.
He must learn to teach zoölogy,
And be skilled in etymology,
And the science of philology,
And calculate chronology,
While he digs into geology,
And treats of entomology,
And hunts up old mythology,
And dips into theology,
And grows wise in sociology,
And expert in anthropology.

He must also know geography,
And the best works on photography,
And the science of stenography,
And be well up on cosmography,
And the secrets of cryptography.
Must interpret blind chirography,

Know by heart all mens' biography,
And the black art of typography,
And every book in bibliography.

These things are all essential
And highly consequential.

If he's haunted by ambition
For a library position,
And esteems it a high mission,
To aspire to erudition;
He will find some politician
Of an envious disposition,
Getting up a coalition
To secure his non-admission,
And send him to perdition.
Before he's reached fruition.

If he gets the situation,
And is full of proud elation
And of fond anticipation,
And has in contemplation
To enlighten half the nation,
He may write a dissertation
For the public information
On the laws of observation,
And the art of conversation.

He must know each famed oration,
And poetical quotation,
And master derivation,
And the science of translation,
And complex pagination,
And perfect punctuation,
And binomial equation,
And accurate computation,
And boundless permutation,
And infinite gradation,
And the craft of divination,
And Scripture revelation,
And the secret of salvation.

He must know the population
Of every separate nation,

The amount of immigration,
And be wise in arbitration,
And the art of navigation,
And colonial annexation,
And problems Australasian.

He must take his daily ration
Of catalogue vexation,
And endless botheration
With ceaseless complication
Of decimal notation,
Or Cutter combination.

To complete his education,
He must know the valuation
Of all the publications
Of many generations,
With their endless variations,
And true interpretations.

When he's spent a life in learning,
If his lamp continues burning,
When he's mastered all philosophy,
And the science of theosophy,
Grown as learned as Mezzofanti,
As poetical as Dante,
As wise as Magliabecchi
As profound as Mr. Lecky—
Has absorbed more kinds of knowledge
Than are found in any college;
He may take his full degree
Of Ph. or LL. D.
And prepare to pass the portal
That leads to life immortal.

CHAPTER 26.

Rare Books.

There is perhaps no field of inquiry concerning literature in which so large an amount of actual mis-information or of ignorance exists as that of the rarity of many books. The makers of second-hand catalogues are responsible for much of this, in describing the books which they wish to sell as "rare," "very scarce," etc., but more of it proceeds from absolute ignorance of the book-markets of the world. I have had multitudes of volumes offered for sale whose commercial value was hardly as many cents as was demanded in dollars by their ill-informed owners, who fancied the commonest book valuable because they "had never seen another copy." No one's ideas of the money value of any book are worth anything, unless he has had long experimental knowledge of the market for books both in America and in Europe.

What constitutes rarity in books is a question that involves many particulars. Thus, a given book may be rare in the United States which is abundant in London; or rare in London, when common enough in Germany. So books may be rare in one age which were easily found in another: and again, books on certain subjects may be so absorbed by public demand when events excite interest in that subject, as to take up most of the copies in market, and enhance the price of the remainder. Thus, Napoleon's conquering career in Egypt created a great demand for all books on Egypt and Africa. The scheme for founding a great French colony in Louisiana raised the price of all books and pamphlets on that region, which soon after fell into the possession of the United States. President Lincoln's assassination caused a demand for all accounts of the murder of the heads of nations. Latterly, all books on Cuba, the West Indies, and the Philippines have been in unprecedented demand, and dealers have raised the prices, which will again decline after the recent public interest in them has been supplanted by future events.

There is a broad distinction to be drawn between books which are absolutely rare, and those which are only relatively scarce, or which become temporarily rare, as just explained. Thus, a large share of the books published in the infancy of printing are *rare;* nearly all which appeared in the quarter century after printing began are *very* rare; and several among these last are *superlatively* rare. I may instance the Mazarin Bible of Gutenberg and Schoeffer (1455?) of which only twenty-four copies are known, nearly all in public libraries, where they ought to be; the Mentz Psalter of the same printers, 1457, the first book ever printed with a date; and the first edition of Livy, Rome [1469] the only copy of which printed on vellum is in the British Museum Library.

One reason of the scarcity of books emanating from the presses of the fifteenth century is that of many of them the editions consisted of only two hundred to three hundred copies, of which the large number absorbed in public libraries, or destroyed by use, fire or decay, left very few in the hands of booksellers or private persons. Still, it is a great mistake to infer that all books printed before A. D. 1500 are rare. The editions of many were large, especially after about 1480, many were reprinted in several editions, and of such incunabula copies can even now be picked up on the continent at very low prices.

Contrary to a wide-spread belief, mere age adds very little to the value of any book, and oft-times nothing at

J. L. Humfreville, were destroyed by fire in a Hartford printing office in 1899, except two, which had been deposited in the Library of Congress, to secure the copyright. The whole edition of the *Machina coelestis* of Hevelius was burned, except the few copies which the author had presented to friends before the fire occurred. The earlier issues in Spanish of the Mexican and Peruvian presses prior to 1600 are exceedingly rare. And editions of books printed at places in the United States where no books are now published are sought for their imprint alone and seldom found.

(3) Many books have become rare because proscribed and in part destroyed by governmental or ecclesiastical authority. This applies more especially to the ages that succeeded the application of printing to the art of multiplying books. The freedom of many writers upon politics and popular rights led to the suppression of their books by kings, emperors or parliaments. At the same time, books of church history or doctrinal theology which departed, in however slight a degree, from the standard of faith proclaimed by the church, were put in the Index Expurgatorius, or list of works condemned in whole or in part as heretical and unlawful to be read. A long and melancholy record of such proscriptions, civil and ecclesiastical, is found in Gabriel Peignot's two volumes—*Dictionnaire des livres condamnés au feu, supprimés, ou censurés,* etc. Works of writers of genius and versatile ability were thus proscribed, until it gave rise to the sarcasm among the scholars of Europe, that if one wanted to find what were the books best worth reading, he should look in the Index Expurgatorius. It appears to have been quite forgotten by those in authority that persecution commonly helps the cause persecuted, and that the best way to promote the circulation of a book is to undertake to suppress it. This

age finds itself endowed with so many heretics that it is no longer possible to find purchasers at high prices for books once deemed unholy. Suppressed passages in later editions lead to a demand for the uncastrated copies which adds an element of enhanced cost in the market.

(4) Another source of rarity is the great extent and cost of many works, outrunning the ability of most collectors to buy or to accommodate them on their shelves. These costly possessions have been commonly printed in limited numbers for subscribers, or for distribution by governments under whose patronage they were produced. Such are some of the notable collections of early voyages, the great folios of many illustrated scientific works on natural history, local geography, etc. That great scholar, Baron von Humboldt, used jocosely to say that he could not afford to own a set of his own works, most of which are folios sumptuously printed, with finely engraved illustrations. The collection known as the "*Grands et petits Voyages*" of De Bry, the former in 13 volumes, relating to America, and finely illustrated with copper-plates produced in the highest style of that art, are among the rarest sets of books to find complete. The collection of voyages by Hulsius is equally difficult to procure. A really perfect set of Piranesi's great illustrated work on the art and architecture of ancient Rome is very difficult to acquire. The *Acta Sanctorum*, in the original edition, is very seldom found. But there is no room to multiply examples.

(5) What adds to the rarity and cost o. certain books is the peculiarly expensive style or condition in which they are produced or preserved. Some few copies of an edition, for example, are printed on vellum, or on China or India or other choice paper, in colored ink or bronze, on colored paper, (rose-tinted, or green, blue or yellow,) on large paper, with broad margins, etc. Uncut copies always fetch

a higher price than those whose edges are trimmed down in binding. To some book-collecting amateurs cut edges are an abomination. They will pay more for a book "in sheets," which they can bind after their own taste, than for the finest copy in calf or morocco with gilt edges. Some books, also, are exceptionally costly because bound in a style of superior elegance and beauty, or as having belonged to a crowned head or a noble person, ("books with a pedigree") or an eminent author, or having autographs of notable characters on the fly-leaves or title-pages, or original letters inserted in the volume. Others still are "extra-illustrated" works, in which one volume is swelled to several by the insertion of a multitude of portraits, autographs, and engravings, more or less illustrative of the contents of the book. This is called "Grangerising," from its origin in the practice of thus illustrating Granger's Biographical History of England. Book amateurs of expensive tastes are by no means rare, especially in England, France, and America, and the great commercial value placed upon uncut and rarely beautiful books, on which the highest arts of the printer and book-binder have been lavished, evinces the fact.

(6) The books emanating from the presses of famous printers are more sought for by collectors and libraries than other publications, because of their superior excellence. Sometimes this is found in the beauty of the type, or the clear and elegant press-work; sometimes in the printers' marks, monograms, engraved initial letters, head and tail-pieces, or other illustrations; and sometimes in the fine quality of the choice paper on which the books are printed. Thus, the productions of the presses of Aldus, Giunta, Bodoni, Etienne, Elzevir, Froben, Gutenberg, Fust and Schoeffer, Plantin, Caxton, Wynkyn de Worde, Bulmer, Didot, Baskerville, Pickering, Whittingham, and

others, are always in demand, and some of the choicer specimens of their art, if in fine condition, bring great prices in the second-hand book-shops, or the auction room. An example of Caxton's press is now almost unattainable, except in fragmentary copies. There are known to be only about 560 examples of Caxtons in the world, four-fifths of which are in England, and thirty-one of these are unique. His "King Arthur" (1485) brought £1950 at auction in 1885, and the Polychronicon (1482) was sold at the Ives sale (N. Y.) in 1891, for $1,500.

(7) In the case of all finely illustrated works, the earlier impressions taken, both of text and plates, are more rare, and hence more valuable, than the bulk of the edition. Thus, copies with "proofs before letters" of the steel engravings or etchings, sometimes command more than double the price of copies having only the ordinary plates. Each added impression deteriorates a little the sharp, clear outlines and brilliant impressions which are peculiar to the first copies printed.

(8) Of some books, certain volumes only are rare, and very costly in consequence. Thus, Burk's History of Virginia is common enough in three volumes, but volume 4 of the set, by Jones and Girardin, (1816,) is exceedingly rare, and seldom found with the others. The fifth and last volume of Bunsen's Egypt's Place in Universal History is very scarce, while the others are readily procured. Of De Bry's Voyages, the 13th or final part of the American voyages is so rare as to be quite unattainable, unless after long years of search, and at an unconscionable price.

(9) The condition of any book is an unfailing factor in its price. Many, if not most books offered by second-hand dealers are shop-worn, soiled, or with broken bindings, or some other defect. A pure, clean copy, in handsome condition without and within, commands invariably an extra

price. Thus the noted Nuremberg Chronicle of 1493, a
huge portly folio, with 2,250 wood-cuts in the text, many
of them by Albert Dürer or other early artists, is priced
in London catalogues all the way from £7.15 up to £35, for
identically the same edition. The difference is dependent
wholly on the condition of the copies offered. Here is part
of a description of the best copy: "Nuremberg Chronicle,
by Schedel, printed by Koberger, first edition, 1493, royal
folio, with fine original impressions of the 2,250 large wood-
cuts of towns, historical events, portraits, etc., very tall
copy, measuring $18\frac{1}{2}$ inches by $12\frac{1}{4}$, beautifully bound in
morocco super extra, full gilt edges, by Riviere, £35. All
the cuts are brilliant impressions, large and spirited. The
book is genuine and perfect throughout; *no washed leaves*,
and all the large capitals filled in by the rubricator by
different colored inks: it has the six additional leaves at
end, which Brunet says are nearly always wanting."

(10) The first editions printed of many books always
command high prices. Not only is this true of the *editio
princeps* of Homer, Virgil, Tacitus and other Greek and
Roman writers, published in the infancy of printing, but
of every noted author, of ancient or modern date. The
edition printed during the life of the writer has had his
own oversight and correction. And when more than one
issue of his book has thus appeared, one sees how his ma-
turer judgment has altered the substance or the style of
his work. First editions of any very successful work always tend to become scarce, since the number printed is
smaller, as a rule, and a large part of the issue is absorbed
by public libraries. The earliest published writings of
Tennyson, now found with difficulty, show how much of
emendation and omission this great poet thought proper
to make in his poems in after years. A first edition of
Ivanhoe, 3 vols., 1820, brings £7 or more, in the original

boards, but if rebound in any style, the first Waverley novels can be had at much less, though collectors are many.

(11) Another class of rare books is found in many local histories, both among the county histories of Great Britain, and those of towns and counties in the United States. Jay Gould's History of Delaware County, N. Y., published in 1856, and sought after in later times because of his note as a financier, is seldom found. Of family genealogies, too, printed in small editions, there are many which cannot be had at all, and many more which have risen to double or even quadruple price. The market value of these books, always dependent on demand, is enhanced by the wants of public libraries which are making or completing collections of these much sought sources of information.

(12) There is a class of books rarely found in any reputable book shop, and which ought to be much rarer than they are—namely, those that belong to the domain of indecent literature. Booksellers who deal in such wares often put them in catalogues under the head of *facetiae*, thus making a vile use of what should be characteristic only of books of wit or humor. Men of prurient tastes become collectors of such books, many of which are not without some literary merit, while many more are neither fit to be written, nor printed, nor read.

(13) There is a large variety of books that are sought mainly on account, not of their authors, nor for their value as literature, but for their illustrators. Many eminent artists (in fact most of those of any period) have made designs for certain books of their day. The reputation of an artist sometimes rests more upon his work given to the public in engravings, etchings, wood-cuts, etc., that illustrate books, than upon his works on canvas or in marble. Many finely illustrated works bear prices enhanced by the

eagerness of collectors, who are bent upon possessing the designs of some favorite artist, while some amateurs covet a collection of far wider scope. This demand, although fitful, and sometimes evanescent, (though more frequently recurrent,) lessens the supply of illustrated books, and with the constant drafts of new libraries, raises prices. Turner's exquisite pictures in Rogers's Italy and Poems (1830-34) have floated into fame books of verse which find very few readers. Hablot K. Browne ("Phiz") designed those immortal Wellers in Pickwick, which have delighted two whole generations of readers. The "Cruikshankiana" are sought with avidity, in whatever numerous volumes they adorn. Books illustrated with the designs of Bartolozzi, Marillier, Eisen, Gravelot, Moreau, Johannot, Grandville, Rowlandson, Bewick, William Blake, Stothard, Stanfield, Harvey, Martin, Cattermole, Birket Foster, Mulready, Tenniel, Maclise, Gilbert, Dalziel, Leighton, Holman Hunt, Doyle, Leech, Millais, Rossetti, Linton, Du Maurier, Sambourne, Caldecott, Walter Crane, Kate Greenaway, Haden, Hamerton, Whistler, Doré, Anderson, Darley, Matt Morgan, Thos. Nast, Vedder, and others, are in constant demand, especially for the early impressions of books in which their designs appear.

(14) Finally, that extensive class of books known as early *Americana* have been steadily growing rarer, and rising in commercial value, since about the middle of the nineteenth century. Books and pamphlets relating to any part of the American continent or islands, the first voyages, discoveries, narratives or histories of those regions, which were hardly noted or cared for a century ago, are now eagerly sought by collectors for libraries both public and private. In this field, the keen competition of American Historical Societies, and of several great libraries, besides the ever increasing number of private col-

lectors with large means, has notably enhanced the prices of all desirable and rare books. Nor do the many reprints which have appeared much affect the market value of the originals, or first editions.

This rise in prices, while far from uniform, and furnishing many examples of isolated extravagance, has been marked. Witness some examples. The "Bay Psalm Book," Cambridge, Mass., A. D. 1640, is the Caxton of New England, so rare that no perfect copy has been found for many years. In 1855, Henry Stevens had the singular good fortune to find this typographical gem sandwiched in an odd bundle of old hymn books, unknown to the auctioneers or catalogue, at a London book sale. Keeping his own counsel, he bid off the lot at nine shillings, completed ar imperfection in the book, from another imperfect copy, had it bound in Bedford's best, and sold it to Mr. Lenox's library at £80. In 1868, Stevens sold another copy to George Brinley for 150 guineas, which was bought for $1,200 in 1878, by C. Vanderbilt, at the Brinley sale.

John Smith's folio "Historie of Virginia," 1st ed., 1624, large paper, was sold to Brinley in 1874 at $1,275, and resold in 1878 for $1,800 to Mr. Lenox. In 1884 a copy on large paper brought £605 at the Hamilton Library sale in London. In 1899, a perfect copy of the large paper edition was presented to the Library of Congress by Gen. W. B. Franklin. Perfect copies of Smith's Virginia of 1624 on small paper have sold for $1,000, and those wanting some maps at $70 to $150.

The earlier English tracts relating to Virginia and New England, printed between 1608 and 1700, command large prices: e. g., Lescarbot's New France, [Canada,] 1609, $50 to $150; Wood's New England's Prospect, 1635, $50 to $320; Hubbard's Present State of New England, Boston, 1677, $180 to $316.

It is curious to note, in contrast, the following record of prices at the sale of Dr. Bernard's Library in London, in 1686:

T. Morton's New England, 1615, eight pence; Lescarbot's New France, 1609, ten pence; Wood's New England's Prospect, 1635, and three others, 5 s. 8 d.; nine Eliot Tracts, &c., 5 s. 2 d.; Hubbard's Present State of New England, 1677, 1 s.; Smith's Historie of Virginia, 1624, 4 s. 2 d.

The numerous and now rare works of Increase and Cotton Mather, printed from 1667 to 1728, though mostly sermons, are collected by a sufficient number of libraries to maintain prices at from $4 to $25 each, according to condition. They number over 470 volumes.

Several collections have been attempted of Frankliniana, or works printed at Benjamin Franklin's press, and of the many editions of his writings, with all books concerning the illustrious printer-statesman of America. His "Poor Richard's Almanacs," printed by him from 1733 to 1758, and by successors to 1798, are so rare that Mr. P. L. Ford found a visit to three cities requisite to see all of them. The Library of Congress possesses thirty-five years of these issues.

A word may be added as to early newspapers, of some special numbers of which prices that are literally "fabulous" are recorded. There are many reprints afloat of the first American newspaper, and most librarians have frequent offers of the Ulster County, (N. Y.) Gazette of Jan. 10, 1800, in mourning for the death of Washington, a genuine copy of which is worth money, but the many spurious reprints (which include all those offered) are worth nothing.

Of many rare early books reprints or facsimiles are rife in the market, especially of those having but few leaves;

these, however, are easily detected by an expert eye, and need deceive no one.

Of some scarce books, it may be said that they are as rare as the individuals who want them: and of a very few, that they are as rare as the extinct dodo. In fact, volumes have been written concerning extinct books, not without interest to the bibliomaniac who is fired with the passion for possessing something which no one else has got. Some books are quite at worthless as they are rare. But books deemed worthless by the common or even by the enlightened mind are cherished as treasures by many collectors. The cook-book, entitled *Le Pastissier françois*, an Elzevir of 1655, is so rare as to have brought several times its weight in gold. Nearly all the copies of some books have been worn to rags by anglers, devout women, cooks, or children.

When a book is sold at a great price as "very rare," it often happens that several copies come into the market soon after, and, there being no demand, the commercial value is correspondingly depressed. The books most sure of maintaining full prices are first editions of master-pieces in literature. Fitzgerald's version of Omar Khayyam was bought by nobody when Quaritch first published it in 1859. After eight years, he put the remainder of the edition,—a paper-covered volume—down to a penny each. When the book had grown into fame, and the many variations in later issues were discovered, this first edition, no longer procurable, rose to £21, the price actually paid by Mr. Quaritch himself at a book auction in 1898!

Auction sales of libraries having many rare books have been frequent in London and Paris. The largest price yet obtained for any library was reached in 1882-3, when that of Mr. Wm. Beckford brought £73,551, being an average of nearly $40 a volume. But W. C. Hazlitt says of this sale, "the Beckford books realized perfectly insane prices, and were afterwards re-sold for a sixth or even tenth of the amount, to the serious loss of somebody, when the barometer had fallen."

The second-hand bookseller, having the whole range of printed literature for his field, has a great advantage in dealing with book collectors over the average dealer, who has to offer only new books, or such as are "in print."

It may be owned that the love of rare books is chiefly sentimental. He who delights to spend his days or his nights in the contemplation of black-letter volumes, quaint title-pages, fine old bindings, and curious early illustrations, may not add to the knowledge or the happiness of mankind, but he makes sure of his own.

The passion for rare books, merely because of their rarity, is a low order of the taste for books. But the desire to possess and read wise old books which have been touched by the hoar frost of time is of a higher mood. The first impression of Paradise Lost (1667) with its quarto page and antique orthography, is it not more redolent of the author's age than the elegant Pickering edition, or the one illustrated by John Martin or Gustave Doré? When you hold in your hand Shakespeare's "Midsommer Night's Dream" (A. D. 1600) and read with fresh admiration and delight the exquisite speeches of Oberon and Titania, may not the thought that perhaps that very copy may once have been held in the immortal bard's own hand send a thrill through your own?

When you turn over the classic pages of Homer illustrated by Flaxman, that "dear sculptor of eternity," as William Blake called him, or drink in the beauty of those delicious landscapes of Turner, that astonishing man, who shall wonder at your desire to possess them?

The genuine book lover is he who reads books; who values them for what they contain, not for their rarity, nor for the preposterous prices which have been paid for them. To him, book-hunting is an ever-enduring delight. Of all the pleasures tasted here below, that of the book lover in finding a precious and long sought volume is one of the purest and most innocent. In books, he becomes master of all the kingdoms of the world.

CHAPTER 27.

BIBLIOGRAPHY.

To the book collector and the Librarian, books of bibliography are the tools of the profession. Without them he would be lost in a maze of literature without a clue. With them, his path is plain, and, in exact proportion to his acquaintance with them, will his knowledge and usefulness extend. Bibliography may be defined as the science which treats of books, of their authors, subjects, history, classification, cataloguing, typography, materials (including paper, printing and binding) dates, editions, etc. This compound word, derived from two Greek roots, *Biblion*, book, and *graphein*, to write, has many analogous words, some of which, ignorantly used to express a bibliographer, may be set down for distinction: as, for example—Bibliopole—a seller of books, often erroneously applied to a librarian, who buys but never sells: Bibliophile, a lover of books, a title which he should always exemplify: Bibliopegist, a book-binder: Bibliolater, a worshipper of books: Bibliophobe, a hater of books: Bibliotaph, a burier of books—one who hides or conceals them: Bibliomaniac, or bibliomane, one who has a mania or passion for collecting books. (Bibliomania, some one has said, is a disease: Bibliophily is a science: The first is a parody of the second.) Bibliophage, or bibliophagist, a book-eater, or devourer of books. Bibliognost, one versed in the science of books. Biblioklept, a book thief. (This, you perceive, is from the same Greek root as kleptomaniac.) Bibliogist, one learned about books, (the same nearly as bibliographer); and finally, Bibliothecary, a librarian.

This brings me to say, in supplementing this elementary list (needless for some readers) that *Bibliotheca* is Latin for a library; *Bibliothèque* is French for the same; *Bibliothécaire* is French for Librarian, while the French word *Libraire* means book seller or publisher, though often mistaken by otherwise intelligent persons, for librarian, or library.

The word "bibliotechny" is not found in any English dictionary known to me, although long in use in its equivalent forms in France and Germany. It means all that belongs to the knowledge of the book, to its handling, cataloguing, and its arrangement upon the shelves of a library. It is also applied to the science of the formation of libraries, and their complete organization. It is employed in the widest and most extended sense of what may be termed material or physical bibliography. Bibliotechny applies, that is to say, to the technics of the librarian's work—to the outside of the books rather than the inside—to the mechanics, not the metaphysics of the profession. The French word "*Bibliothéconomie*," much in use of late years, signifies much the same thing as *Bibliotechnie*, and we translate it, not into one word, but two, calling it "library economy." This word "economy" is not used in the most current sense—as significant of saving—but in the broad, modern sense of systematic order, or arrangement.

There are two other words which have found their way into Murray's Oxford Dictionary, the most copious repository of English words, with illustrations of their origin and history, ever published, namely, Biblioclast— a destroyer of books (from the same final root as iconoclast) and Bibliogony, the production of books. I will add that out of the fifteen or more words cited as analogous to Bibliography, only three are found used earlier than the last quarter century, the first use of most having been this side of 1880. This is a striking instance of the phenomenal growth of new words in our already rich and flexible English tongue. Carlyle even has the word "Bibliopoesy," the making of books,—from *Biblion,* and *poiein*—to make.

Public libraries are useful to readers in proportion to the extent and ready supply of the helps they furnish to facilitate researches of every kind. Among these helps a wisely selected collection of books of reference stands foremost. Considering the vast extent and opulence of the world of letters, and the want of experience of the majority of readers in exploring this almost boundless field, the importance of every key which can unlock its hidden stores becomes apparent. The printed catalogue of no single library is at all adequate to supply full references, even to its own stores of knowledge; while these catalogues are, of course, comparatively useless as to other stores of information, elsewhere existing. Even the completest and most extensive catalogue in the world, that of the British Museum Library, although now extended to more than 370 folio volumes in print, representing

3,000 volumes in manuscript, is not completed so as to embrace the entire contents of that rich repository of knowledge.

From lack of information of the aid furnished by adequate books of reference in a special field, many a reader goes groping in pursuit of references or information which might be found in some one of the many volumes which may be designated as works of bibliography. The diffidence and reserve of many students in libraries, and the mistaken fear of giving trouble to librarians, frequently deprives them of even those aids which a few words of inquiry might bring forth from the ready knowledge of the custodians in charge.

That is the best library, and he is the most useful librarian, by whose aid every reader is enabled to put his finger on the fact he wants, just when it is wanted. In attaining this end it is essential that the more recent, important, and valuable aids to research in general science, as well as in special departments of each, should form a part of the library. In order to make a fit selection of books (and all libraries are practically reduced to a selection, from want of means to possess the whole) it is indispensable to know the relative value of the books concerned. Many works of reference of great fame, and once of great value, have become almost obsolete, through the issue of more extensive and carefully edited works in the same field. While a great and comprehensive library should possess every work of reference, old or new, which has aided or may aid the researches of scholars, (not forgetting even the earlier editions of works often reprinted), the smaller libraries, on the other hand, are compelled to exercise a close economy of selection. The most valuable works of reference, among which the more copious and extensive bibliographies stand first, are frequently expensive treasures, and it is important to the librarian furnishing a limited and select library to know what books he can best afford to do without. If he cannot buy both the *Manuel du libraire* by Brunet, in five volumes, and the *Trésor des livres rares et précieux* of Graesse, seven volumes, both of which are dictionaries of the choicer portions of literature, it is important to know that Brunet is the more indispensable of the two. From the 20,000 reference books lying open to the consultation of all readers in the great rotunda of the British Museum reading room, to the small and select case of dictionaries, catalogues, cyclopaedias, and other works of reference in a town or subscription library, the interval is wide indeed. But where we cannot have all, it becomes the more important to have the best; and the reader who has at hand for ready reference the latest and most copious dictionary of each of the leading languages of the world, two or three of the best general bibliographies, the most copious catalogue raisonné of the literature in each great department of science, the best biographical dictionaries, and the latest and most copious encyclopaedias issued from the press, is tolerably well equipped for the prosecution of his researches.

Next in importance to the possession in any library of a good selection of the most useful books of reference, is the convenient accessibility of these works to the reading public. Just in proportion to the indispensability and frequency of use of any work should be the facility to the reader of availing himself of its aid. The leading encyclopaedias, bibliographies, dictionaries, annuals, and other books of reference should never be locked up in cases, nor placed on high or remote shelves. There should be in every library what may be termed a central bureau of reference. Here should be assembled, whether on circular cases made to revolve on a pivot, or on a rectangular case, with volumes covering both sides, or in a central alcove forming a portion of the shelves of the main library, all those books of reference, and volumes incessantly needed by students in pursuit of their various inquiries. It is important that the custodians of all libraries should remember that this ready and convenient supply of the reference books most constantly wanted, serves the double object of economizing the time of the librarian and assistants for other labor, and of accommodating in the highest degree the readers, whose time is also economized. The misplacement of volumes which will thus occur is easily rectified, while the possibility of loss through abstraction is so extremely small that it should not be permitted to weigh for a moment in comparison with the great advantages resulting from the rule of liberality in aiding the wants of readers.

Bibliography, in its most intimate sense, is the proper science of the librarian. To many it is a study—to some, it is a passion. While the best works in bibliography have not always been written by librarians, but by scholars enamored of the science of books, and devotees of learning, it is safe to say that the great catalogues which afford such inestimable aid to research, have nearly all been prepared in libraries, and not one of the books worthy of the name of bibliography, could have been written without their aid.

In viewing the extensive field of bibliographies, regard for systematic treatment requires that they be divided into classes. Beginning first with general bibliographies, or those claiming to be universal, we should afterwards consider the numerous bibliographies of countries, or those devoted to national literature; following that by the still more numerous special bibliographies, or those embracing works on specially designated subjects. The two classes last named are by far the most numerous.

Although what may be termed a "universal catalogue" has been the dream of scholars for many ages, it is as far as ever from being realized—and in fact much farther than ever before, since each year that is added to the long roll of the past increases enormously the number of books to be dealt with, and consequently the difficulties of the problem. We may set down the publication of a work which should contain the titles of all books ever printed, as a practical impossibility. The world's literature is too vast and complex to be completely catalogued, whether on the coöperative plan, or any other. Meanwhile the many thousands of volumes, each of which has been devoted to some portion of the vast and ever-increasing stores of literature and science which human brains have put in print, will serve to aid the researches of the student, when rightly guided by an intelligent librarian.

Notwithstanding the hopeless nature of the quest, it is true that some men of learning have essayed what have been termed universal bibliographies. The earliest attempt in this direction was published at Zürich in 1545, under the title of "Bibliotheca Universalis," by Conrad Gesner, a Swiss scholar whose acquisition of knowledge was so extensive that he was styled "a miracle of learning." This great work gave the titles of all books of which its author could find trace, and was illustrated by a mass of bibliographical notes and criticism. It long held a high place in the world of letters, though it is now seldom referred to in the plethora of more modern works of bibliography. In 1625, the bookseller B. Ostern put forth at Frankfort, his *Bibliothèque Universelle*, a catalogue of all books from 1500 to 1624. In 1742, Th. Georgi issued in eleven folio volumes, his *Allgemeines Europäisches*

Bücher-lexikon, claiming to represent the works of nearly
all writers from 1500 down to 1739. This formidable catalogue may perhaps be said to embrace more forgotten
books than any other in the literary history of the world.

Almost equally formidable, however, is the bibliography
of that erudite scholar, Christian G. Jöcher, who put forth
in 1750, at Leipzig, his *Allgemeines Gelehrten-lexicon,* in
which, says the title page, "the learned men of all classes
who have lived from the beginning of the world up to
the present time, are described." This book, with its
supplement, by Adelung and Rotermund, (completed only
to letter R), makes ten ponderous quarto volumes, and
may fairly be styled a thesaurus of the birth and death
of ancient scholars and their works. It is still largely
used in great libraries, to identify the period and the full
names of many obscure writers of books, who are not commemorated in the catalogues of universal bibliography,
compiled on a more restrictive plan.

We come now to the notable catalogues of early-printed
books, which aim to cover all the issues of the press from
the first invention of printing, up to a certain period.
One of the most carefully edited and most readily useful
of these is Hain, (L.) *Repertorium Bibliographicum,* in
four small and portable octavo volumes, published at
Stuttgart in 1826-38. This gives, in an alphabet of authors, all the publications found printed (with their variations and new editions), from A. D. 1450 to A. D. 1500.

More extensive is the great catalogue of G. W. Panzer,
entitled *Annales Typographici,* in eleven quarto volumes,
published at Nuremberg from 1793 to 1803. This work,
which covers the period from 1457 (the period of the first
book ever printed with a date) up to A. D. 1536, is not
arranged alphabetically (as in Hain's Repertorium) by
the names of authors, but in the order of the cities or

places where the books catalogued were printed. The bibliography thus brings together in one view, the typographical product of each city or town for about eighty years after the earliest dated issues of the press, arranged in chronological order of the years when printed. This system has undeniable advantages, but equally obvious defects, which are sought to be remedied by many copious indexes of authors and printers.

Next in importance comes M. Maittaire's *Annales Typographici, ab artis inventae origine ad annum 1664*, printed at The Hague (Hagae Comitum) and completed at London, from 1722-89, in eleven volumes, quarto, often bound in five volumes. There is besides, devoted to the early printed literature of the world, the useful three volume bibliography by La Serna de Santander, published at Brussels in 1805, entitled *Dictionnaire bibliographique choisie du quinzième siècle*, Bruxelles, 1803, embracing a selection of what its compiler deemed the more important books published from the beginning of printing up to A. D. 1500. All the four works last named contain the titles and descriptions of what are known as *incunabula*, or cradle-books (from Latin *cunabula*, a cradle) a term applied to all works produced in the infancy of printing, and most commonly to those appearing before 1500. These books are also sometimes called fifteeners, or 15th century books.

Of general bibliographies of later date, only a few of the most useful and important can here be named. At the head of these stands, deservedly, the great work of J. C. Brunet, entitled *Manuel du Libraire et de l'amateur des livres*, the last or 5th edition of which appeared at Paris in 1860-64, in five thick octavo volumes. The first edition of Brunet appeared in 1810, and every issue since has exhibited not only an extensive enlargement, but great improvement in careful, critical editorship. It embraces most of the choicest books that have appeared in the principal languages of Europe, and a supplement in two volumes, by P. Deschamps and G. Brunet, appeared in 1878.

Next to Brunet in importance to the librarian, is J. G. T. Graesse's *Trésor des Livres rares et précieux*, which is more full than Brunet in works in the Teutonic languages, and was published at Dresden in six quarto volumes, with a supplement, in 1861-69. Both of these bibliographies aim at a universal range, though they make a selection of the best authors and editions, ancient and modern, omitting however, the most recent writers. The arrangement of both is strictly alphabetical, or a dictionary of authors' names, while Brunet gives in a final volume a classification by subjects. Both catalogues are rendered additionally valuable by the citation of prices at which many of the works catalogued have been sold at book auctions in the present century.

In 1857 was published at Paris a kind of universal bibliography, on the plan of a *catalogue raisonné*, or dictionary of subjects, by Messrs. F. Denis, Pinçon, and De Martonne, two of whom were librarians by profession. This work of over 700 pages, though printed in almost microscopic type, and now about forty years in arrears, has much value as a ready key to the best books then known on nearly every subject in science and literature. It is arranged in a complete index of topics, the books under each being described in chronological order, instead of the alphabetical. The preponderance is given to the French in the works cited on most subjects, but the literature of other nations is by no means neglected. It is entitled *Nouveau Manuel de Bibliographie universelle*, and being a subjective index, while Brunet and Graesse are arranged by authors' names, it may be used to advantage in connection with these standard bibliographies.

While on this subject, let me name the books specially devoted to lists of bibliographical works—general and special. These may be termed the catalogues of catalogues,—and are highly useful aids, indeed indispensable to the librarian, who seeks to know what lists of books have appeared that are devoted to the titles of publications covering any period, or country, or special subject in the whole circle of sciences or literatures. The first notably important book of reference in this field, was the work of that most industrious bibliographer, Gabriel Peignot, who published at Paris, in 1812, his *Repertoire bibliographique universelle*, in one volume. This work contains the titles of most special bibliographies, of whatever subject or country, published up to 1812, and of many works bibliographical in character, devoted to literary history.

Dr. Julius Petzholdt, one of the most learned and laborious of librarians, issued at Leipzig in 1866, a *Bibliotheca bibliographica*, the fuller title of which was "a critical catalogue, exhibiting in systematic order, the entire field of bibliography covering the literature of Germany and other countries." The rather ambitious promise of this title is well redeemed in the contents: for very few catalogues of importance issued before 1866, are omitted in this elaborate book of 931 closely printed pages. Most titles of the bibliographies given are followed by critical and explanatory notes, of much value to the unskilled reader. These notes are in German, while all the titles cited are in the language of the books themselves. After giving full titles of all the books in general bibliography, he takes up the national bibliographies by countries, citing both systematic catalogues and periodicals devoted to the literature of each in any period. This is followed by a distributive list of scientific bibliographies, so full as to leave little to be desired, except for later issues of the press.   One of the curiosities of this work is its catalogue of all the issues of the "Index Librorum Prohibitorum", or books forbidden to be read, including 185 separate catalogues, from A. D. 1510 to A. D. 1862.

The next bibliographical work claiming to cover this field was in the French language, being the *Bibliographie des bibliographies* of Léon Vallée, published in 1883 at Paris.   This book, though beautifully printed, is so full of errors, and still fuller of omissions, that it is regarded by competent scholars as a failure, though still having its uses to the librarian.   It is amazing that any writer should put forth a book seventeen years after the great and successful work of Petzholdt, purporting to be a catalogue of bibliographies, and yet fail to record such a multitude of printed contributions to the science of sciences as Vallée has overlooked.

Some ten years later, or in 1897, there came from the French press, a far better bibliographical work, covering the modern issues of books of bibliography more especially, with greater fullness and superior plan.   This is the *Manuel de Bibliographie générale*, by Henri Stein.   Thus work contains, in 915 well-printed pages, 1st. a list of universal bibliographies: 2d. a catalogue of national bibliographies, in alphabetical order of countries: 3d. a list of classified bibliographies of subjects, divided into seventeen classes, namely, religious sciences, philosophical sciences, juridical, economic, social, and educational sciences, pure and applied sciences, medical sciences, philology and belles lettres, geographical and historical sciences, sciences auxiliary to history, archaeology and fine arts, music, and biography. Besides these extremely useful categories of bibliographical aids, in which the freshest publications of catalogues and lists of books in each field are set forth, M. Stein gives us a complete geographical bibliography of printing, on a new plan. This he entitles "*Géographie bibliographique,*" or systematic lists of localities in every part of the world which possessed a printing press prior to the 19th century. It gives, after the modern or current name of each place, the Latin, or ancient name, the country in which located, the year in which the first printed publication appeared in each place, and finally, the authority for the statement. This handy-list of information alone, is worth the cost of the work, since it will save much time of the inquirer, in hunting over many volumes of Panzer, Maittaire, Hain, Dibdin, Thomas, or other authors on printing, to find the origin of the art, or early name of the place where it was introduced. The work contains, in addition, a general table of the periodicals of all countries, (of course not exhaustive) divided into classes, and filling seventy-five pages. It closes with a "repertory of the principal libraries of the entire world," and with an index to the whole work, in which the early names in Latin, of all places where books were printed, are interspersed in the alphabet, distinguished by italic type, and with the modern name of each town or city affixed. This admirable feature will render unnecessary any reference to the *Orbis Latinus* of Graesse, or to any other vocabulary of geography, to identify the place in which early-printed books appeared. Stein is by no means free from errors, and some surprising omissions. One cardinal defect is the absence of any full index of authors whose books are cited.

There are also quite brief catalogues of works on bibliography in J. Power's Handy Book about Books, London, 1870, and in J. Sabin's Bibliography: a handy book about

books which relate to books, N. Y., 1877. The latter
work is an expansion of the first-named.

We come now to the second class of our bibliographies,
viz: those of various countries. Here the reader must be
on his guard not to be misled into too general an inter-
pretation of geographical terms. Thus, he will find many
books and pamphlets ambitiously styled "*Catalogue Américaine*", which are so far from being general bibliographies of books relating to America, that they are merely
lists of a few books for sale by some book-dealer, which
have something American in their subject. To know
what catalogues are comprehensive, and what period they
cover, as well as the limitations of nearly all of them, is
a necessary part of the training of a bibliographer, and is
essential to the librarian who would economize his time
and enlarge his usefulness.

Let us begin with our own country. Here we are met
at the outset by the great paucity of general catalogues
of American literature, and the utter impossibility of finding any really comprehensive lists of the books published
in the United States, during certain periods. We can get
along tolerably well for the publications within the last
thirty years, which nearly represent the time since systematic weekly bibliographical journals have been published, containing lists of the current issues of books. But
for the period just before the Civil War, back to the year
1775, or for very nearly a century, we are without any
systematic bibliography of the product of the American
press. The fragmentary attempts which have been made
toward supplying an account of what books have been
published in the United States from the beginning, will
hereafter be briefly noted. At the outset, you are to observe the wide distinction that exists between books treating of America, or any part of it, and books printed in

America. The former may have been printed anywhere, at any time since 1492, and in any language: and to such books, the broad significant term "*Americana*" may properly be applied, as implying books relating to America. But this class of works is wholly different from that of books written or produced by Americans, or printed in America. It is these latter that we mean when we lament the want of a comprehensive American catalogue. There have been published in the United States alone (to go no farther into America at present) thousands of books, whose titles are not found anywhere, except widely scattered in the catalogues of libraries, public and private, in which they exist. Nay, there are multitudes of publications which have been issued in this country during the last two hundred years, whose titles cannot be found anywhere in print. This is not, generally, because the books have perished utterly,—though this is unquestionably true of some, but because multitudes of books that have appeared, and do appear, wholly escape the eye of the literary, or critical, or bibliographical chronicler. It is, beyond doubt true even now, that what are commonly accepted as complete catalogues of the issues of the press of any year, are wofully incomplete, and that too, through no fault of their compilers. Many works are printed in obscure towns, or in newspaper offices, which never reach the great eastern cities, where our principal bibliographies, both periodical and permanent, are prepared. Many books, too, are "privately printed," to gratify the pride or the taste of their authors, and a few copies distributed to friends, or sometimes to selected libraries, or public men. In these cases, not only are the public chroniclers of new issues of the press in ignorance of the printing of many books, but they are purposely kept in ignorance. Charles Lamb, of humorous and perhaps immortal memory, used to com-

plain of the multitudes of books which are no books; and
we of to-day may complain, if we choose, of the vast number of publications that are not published.

Take a single example of the failure of even large and
imposing volumes to be included in the "American Catalogue," for whose aid, librarians are so immeasurably indebted to the enterprise of its publishers. A single publishing house west of New York, printed and circulated in
about four years time, no less than thirty-two elaborate
and costly histories, of western counties and towns, not
one of which was ever recorded by title in our only comprehensive American bibliography. Why was this? Simply because the works referred to were published only as
subscription books, circulated by agents, carefully kept out
of booksellers' hands, and never sent to the Eastern press
for notice or review. When circumstances like these exist
as to even very recent American publications (and they are
continually happening) is it any wonder that our bibliographies are incomplete?

Perhaps some will suggest that there must be one record
of American publications which is complete, namely, the
office of Copyright at Washington. It is true that the
titles of all copyright publications are required by law to
be there registered, and copies deposited as soon as printed.
It is also true that a weekly catalogue of all books and
other copyright publications is printed, and distributed by
the Treasury, to all our custom-houses, to intercept piratical re-prints which might be imported. But the books
just referred to were not entered for copyright at all, the
publishers apparently preferring the risk of any rival's reprinting them, rather than to incur the cost of the small
copyright fee, and the deposit of copies. In such cases,
there is no law requiring publishers to furnish copies of
their books. The government guarantees no monopoly of

publication, and so cannot exact a *quid pro quo.*, however much it might inure to the interest of publisher and author to have the work seen and noticed, and preserved beyond risk of perishing (unless printed on wood-pulp paper) in the Library of the United States.

If such extensive omissions of the titles of books sometimes important, can now continually occur in our accepted standards of national bibliography, what shall we say of times when we had no critical journals, no publishers' trade organs, and no weekly, nor annual, nor quinquennial catalogues of American books issued? Must we not allow, in the absence of any catalogues worthy of the name, to represent such periods, that all our reference books are from the very necessity of the case deplorably incomplete? Only by the most devoted, indefatigable and unrewarded industry have we got such aids to research as to the existence of American publications, as Haven's Catalogue of American publications prior to 1776, Sabin's Bibliotheca Americana, and the American Catalogues of Leypoldt, Bowker, and their coadjutors.

These illustrations are cited to guard against the too common error of supposing that we have in the numerous American catalogues that exist, even putting them all together, any full bibliography of the titles of American books. While it cannot be said that the *lacunae* or omissions approach the actual entries in number, it must be allowed that books are turning up every day, both new and old, whose titles are not found in any catalogue. The most important books—those which deserve a name as literature, are found recorded somewhere—although even as to many of these, one has to search many alphabets, in a large number of volumes, before tracing them, or some editions of them.

One principal source of the great number of titles of

books found wanting in American catalogues, is that many
books were printed at places remote from the great cities,
and were never announced in the columns of the press at
all.   This is especially true as to books printed toward the
close of the 18th century, and during the first quarter of
the 19th.   Not only have we no bibliography whatever of
American issues of the press, specially devoted to covering
the long period between 1775 and 1820, but multitudes of
books printed during that neglected half-century, have
failed to get into the printed catalogues of our libraries.
As illustrations we might give a long catalogue of places
where book-publication was long carried on, and many
books of more or less importance printed or reprinted, but
in which towns not a book has been produced for more
than three-quarters of a century past.   One of these towns
was Winchester, and another Williamsburg, in Virginia;
another was Exeter, New Hampshire, and a fourth was
Carlisle, Pa.   In the last-named place, one Archibald Loudon printed many books, between A. D. 1798, and 1813,
which have nearly all escaped the chroniclers of American
book-titles.   Notable among the productions of his press,
was his own book, A History of Indian Wars, or as he
styled it in the title page, "A selection of some of the most
interesting narratives of outrages committed by the Indians in their wars with the white people."   This history
appeared in two volumes from the press of A. Loudon, Carlisle, Pa., in 1808 and 1811.   It is so rare that I have failed to find its title anywhere except in Sabin's Bibliotheca
Americana, Field's Indian Bibliography, and the Catalogue
of the Library of Congress.   Not even the British Museum
Library, so rich in Americana, has a copy.   Sabin states
that only six copies are known, and Field styles it, "this
rarest of books on America," adding that he could learn of

only three perfect copies in the world. A Harrisburg reprint of 1888 (100 copies to subscribers) is also quite rare.

Continuing the subject of American bibliography, and still lamenting the want of any comprehensive or finished work in that field which is worthy of the name, let us see what catalogues do exist, even approximating completeness for any period. The earlier years of the production of American books have been partially covered by the "Catalogue of publications in what is now the United States, prior to 1776." This list was compiled by an indefatigable librarian, the late Samuel F. Haven, who was at the head of the Library of the American Antiquarian Society, at Worcester, Mass. It gives all titles by sequence of years of publication, instead of alphabetical order, from 1639 (the epoch of the earliest printing in the United States) to the end of 1775. The titles of books and pamphlets are described with provoking brevity, being generally limited to a single line for each, and usually without publishers' names, (though the places of publication and sometimes the number of pages are given) so that it leaves much to be desired. Notwithstanding this, Mr. Haven's catalogue is an invaluable aid to the searcher after titles of the early printed literature of our country. It appeared at Albany, N. Y., in 1874, as an appendix [in Vol 2] to a new (or second) edition of Isaiah Thomas's History of Printing in America, which was first published in 1810. In using it, the librarian will find no difficulty, if he knows the year when the publication he looks for appeared, as all books of each year are arranged in alphabetical order. But if he knows only the author's name, he may have a long search to trace the title, there being no general alphabet or index of authors. This chronological arrangement has certain advantages to the literary inquirer or historian, while for ready reference, its disadvantages are obvious.

While there were several earlier undertakings of an American bibliography than Haven's catalogue of publications before the American revolution, yet the long period which that list covers, and its importance, entitled it to first mention here. There had, however, appeared, as early as the year 1804, in Boston, "A Catalogue of all books, printed in the United States, with the prices, and places where published, annexed." This large promise is hardly redeemed by the contents of this thin pamphlet of 91 pages, all told. Yet the editor goes on to assure us—

"This Catalogue is intended to include all books of general sale printed in the United States, whether original, or reprinted; that the public may see the rapid progress of book-printing in a country, where, twenty years since, scarcely a book was published. Local and occasional tracts are generally omitted. Some of the books in the Catalogue are now out of print, and others are scarce. It is contemplated to publish a new edition of this Catalogue, every two years, and to make the necessary additions and corrections; and it is hoped the time is not far distant, when useful Libraries may be formed of American editions of Books, well printed, and handsomely bound.

Printed at Boston, for the Book sellers, Jan., 1804."

The really remarkable thing about this catalogue is that it was the very first bibliographical attempt at a general catalogue, in separate form, in America. It is quite interesting as an early booksellers' list of American publications, as well as for its classification, which is as follows: "Law, Physic, Divinity, Bibles, Miscellanies, School Books, Singing Books, Omissions."

The fact that no subsequent issues of the catalogue appeared, evinces the very small interest taken in bibliographic knowledge in those early days.

This curiosity of early American bibliography gives the titles of 1338 books, all of American publication, with prices in 1804. Here are samples: Bingham's Columbian Orator, 75 cts.: Burney's Cecilia, 3 vols. $3: Memoirs of

Pious Women, $1.12: Belknap's New Hampshire, 3 vols. $5: Mrs. Coghlan's Memoirs, 62½ cts.: Brockden Brown's Wieland, $1: Federalist, 2 vols. $4.50: Dilworth's Spelling Book, 12½ cts.: Pike's Arithmetic, $2.25.

The number of out-of-the-way places in which books were published in those days is remarkable. Thus, in Connecticut, we have as issuing books, Litchfield, New London and Fairhaven: in Massachusetts, Leominster, Dedham, Greenfield, Brookfield, and Wrentham; in New Hampshire, Dover, Walpole, Portsmouth, and Exeter: in Pennsylvania, Washington, Carlisle, and Chambersburg: in New Jersey, Morristown, Elizabethtown, and Burlington. At Alexandria, Va., eight books are recorded as published.

This historical nugget of the Boston bookmongers of a century ago is so rare, that only two copies are known in public libraries, namely, in the Library of Congress, and in that of the Massachusetts Historical Society. It was reprinted in 1898, for the Dibdin Club of New York, by Mr. A. Growoll, of the Publishers' Weekly, to whose curious and valuable notes on "Booktrade Bibliography in the United States in the 19th century," it forms a supplement.

The next catalogue of note claiming to be an American catalogue, or of books published in America, was put forth in 1847, at Claremont, N. H., by Alexander V. Blake. This was entitled, "The American Bookseller's complete reference trade-list, and alphabetical catalogue of books, published in this country, with the publishers' and authors' names, and prices." This quarto volume, making 351 pages (with its supplement issued in 1848) was the precursor of the now current "Trade List Annual," containing the lists of books published by all publishers whose lists could be secured. The titles are very brief, and are arranged in the catalogue under the names of the respective publishers, with an alphabetical index of authors and of anonymous titles at the end. It served well its purpose of a book-trade catalogue fifty years ago, being the pioneer in that important field. It is now, like the catalogue of 1804, just noticed, chiefly interesting as a bibliographical curiosity, although both lists do contain the titles of some books not elsewhere found.

Mr. Orville A. Roorbach, a New York bookseller, was the next compiler of an American bibliography. His first issue of 1849 was enlarged and published in 1852, under this title: "Bibliotheca Americana: a catalogue of American publications, including reprints and original works, from 1820 to 1852, inclusive." This octavo volume of 663 pages, in large, clear type, closely abbreviates nearly all titles, though giving in one comprehensive alphabet, the authors' names, and the titles of the books under the first word, with year and place of publication, publisher's name, and price at which issued. No collation of the books is given, but the catalogue supplies sufficient portions of each title to identify the book. It is followed in an appendix by a catalogue of law books, in a separate alphabet, and a list of periodicals published in the United States in 1852.

Roorbach continued his catalogue to the year 1861, by the issue of three successive supplements: (1) covering the American publications of 1853 to 1855: (2) from 1855 to 1858: (3) from 1858 to 1861. These four catalogues, aiming to cover, in four different alphabets, the issues of the American press for forty years, or from 1820 to 1861, are extremely useful lists to the librarian, as finding lists, although the rigorously abbreviated titles leave very much to be desired by the bibliographer, and the omissions are exceedingly numerous of books published within the years named, but whose titles escaped the compiler.

Following close upon Roorbach's Bibliotheca Americana in chronological order, we have next two bibliographies covering American book issues from 1861 to 1871. These were compiled by a New York book dealer named James Kelly, and were entitled The American Catalogue of Books, (original and reprint) published in the United States from Jan., 1861, to Jan., 1866, [and from Jan., 1866, to Jan., 1871] with date of publication, size, price, and publisher's name. The first volume contained a supplement, with list of pamphlets on the civil war, and also a list of the publications of learned societies. These very useful and important catalogues cover ten years of American publishing activity, adding also to their own period many titles omitted by Roorbach in earlier years. Kelly's catalogues number 307 and 444 pages respectively, and, like Roorbach's, they give both author and title in a single alphabet. Names of publishers are given, with place and year of publication, and retail price, but without number of pages, and with no alphabet of subjects.

Next after Kelly's catalogue came the first issue of the "American Catalogue," which, with its successive volumes (all published in quarto form) ably represents the bibliography of our country during the past twenty-five years. The title of the first volume, issued in 1880, reads "American Catalogue of books in print and for sale (including reprints and importations) July 1, 1876. Compiled under direction of F. Leypoldt, by L. E. Jones." This copious repository of book-titles was in two parts: (1) Authors, and (2) Subject-index. Both are of course in alphabetical order, and the titles of books are given with considerable abbreviation. The fact that its plan includes many titles of books imported from Great Britain, (as supplying information to book-dealers and book-buyers) prevents it from being considered as a bibliography of strictly American publications. Still, it is the only approxmiately full American bibliography of the publications current twenty-

five years ago.   As such, its volumes are indispensable
in every library, and should be in its earliest purchase of
works of reference.   The limitation of the catalogue to
books still in print—i. e., to be had of the publishers at
the time of its issue, of course precludes it from being
ranked as a universal American bibliography.

The first issue in 1880 was followed, in 1885, by the
"American Catalogue, 1876-1884: books recorded (including reprints and importations, under editorial direction of
R. R. Bowker, by Miss A. I. Appleton."   This appeared in
one volume, but with two alphabets; one being authors
and titles, and the other an alphabet of subjects.   As this
volume included eight years issues of the American press,
the next bibliography published covered the next ensuing
six years, and included the books recorded from July, 1884
to July, 1890.   This appeared in 1891, edited with care
by Miss Appleton and others.

In 1896 appeared its successor, the "American Catalogue, 1890-95.   Compiled under the editorial direction
of R. R. Bowker."   This catalogue records in its first
volume, or alphabet of authors: (1) author; (2) size of
book; (3) year of issue; (4) price; (5) publisher's name.
The names of places where published are not given with
the title, being rendered unnecessary by the full alphabetical list of publishers which precedes, and fixes the city or
town where each published his books.   This same usage is
followed in succeeding issues of the American Catalogue.

This indispensable bibliography of recent American
books, in addition to its regular alphabets of authors and
titles (the latter under first words and in the same alphabet
with the authors) and the succeeding alphabet of subjects,
prints a full list of the publications of the United States
government, arranged by departments and bureaus; also

a list of the publications of State governments, of Societies, and of books published in series.

This last issue has 939 pages. Its only defects (aside from its inevitable omissions of many unrecorded books) are the double alphabet, and the 'want of collation, or an indication of the number of pages in each work, which should follow every title. Its cost in bound form is $15, at which the two preceding American catalogues 1876-84, and 1884 to 1890 can also be had, while the catalogue of books in print in 1876, published in 1880, is quite out of print, though a copy turns up occasionally from some book-dealer's stock.

The American Catalogue has now become a quinquennial issue, gathering the publications of five years into one alphabet; and it is supplemented at the end of every year by the "Annual American Catalogue," started in 1886, which gives, in about 400 pages, in its first alphabet, collations of the books of the year (a most important feature, unfortunately absent from the quinquennial American Catalogue.) Its second alphabet gives authors, titles, and sometimes subject-matters, but without the distribution into subject-divisions found in the quinquennial catalogue; and the titles are greatly abridged from the full record of its first alphabet. Its price is $3.50 each year.

And this annual, in turn, is made up from the catalogues of titles of all publications, which appear in the *Publishers' Weekly*, the carefully edited organ of the book publishing interests in the United States. This periodical, which will be found a prime necessity in every library, originated in New York, in 1855, as the "American Publishers' Circular," and has developed into the recognized authority in American publications, under the able management of R. R. Bowker and A. Growoll. For three dollars a year, it supplies weekly and monthly alphabetical lists of whatever comes from the press, in book form, as completely as the titles can be gathered from every source. It gives valuable notes after most titles, defining the scope and idea of the work, with collations, features which are copied into the Annual American Catalogue.

I must not omit to mention among American bibliographies, although published in London, and edited by a foreigner, Mr. N. Trübner's "Bibliographical Guide to American literature: a classed list of books published in the United States during the last forty years." This book appeared in 1859, and is a carefully edited bibliography, arranged systematically in thirty-two divisions of subjects, filling 714 pages octavo. It gives under each topic, an alphabet of authors, followed by titles of the works, given with approximate fullness, followed by place and year of publication, but without publishers' names. The number of pages is also given where ascertained, and the price of the work quoted in sterling English money. This work, by a competent German-English book-publisher of London, is preceded by a brief history of American literature, and closes with a full index of authors whose works are catalogued in it.

We come now to by far the most comprehensive and ambitious attempt to cover not only the wide field of American publications, but the still more extensive field of books relating to America, which has ever yet been made. I refer to the "Bibliotheca Americana; a dictionary of books relating to America," by Joseph Sabin, begun more than thirty years ago, in 1868, and still unfinished, its indefatigable compiler having died in 1881, at the age of sixty. This vast bibliographical undertaking was originated by a variously-gifted and most energetic man, not a scholar, but a bookseller and auctioneer, born in England. Mr. Sabin is said to have compiled

more catalogues of private libraries that have been
brought to the auctioneer's hammer, than any man who
ever lived in America. He bought and sold, during nearly
twenty years, old and rare books, in a shop in Nassau street,
New York, which was the resort of book collectors and
bibliophiles without number. He made a specialty of
Americana, and of early printed books in English literature, crossing the Atlantic twenty-five times to gather
fresh stores with which to feed his hungry American
customers. During all these years, he worked steadily at
his *magnum opus*, the bibliography of America, carrying
with him in his many journeys and voyages, in cars or
on ocean steamships, copy and proofs of some part of the
work. There have been completed about ninety parts,
or eighteen thick volumes of nearly 600 pages each; and
since his death the catalogue has been brought down to
the letter S, mainly by Mr. Wilberforce Eames, librarian
of the Lenox Library, New York. Though its ultimate
completion must be regarded as uncertain, the great value
to all librarians, and students of American bibliography
or history, of the work so far as issued, can hardly be over-
estimated. Mr. Sabin had the benefit in revising the
proofs of most of the work, of the critical knowledge and
large experience of Mr. Charles A. Cutter, the librarian
of the Boston Athenaeum Library, whose catalogue of the
books in that institution, in five goodly volumes, is a
monument of bibliographical learning and industry.
Sabin's Dictionary is well printed, in large, clear type,
the titles being frequently annotated, and prices at auction sales of the rarer and earlier books noted. Every
known edition of each work is given, and the initials of
public libraries in the United States, to the number of
thirteen, in which the more important works are found,
are appended. In not a few cases, where no copy was

known to the compiler in a public collection, but was found in a private library, the initials of its owner were given instead.

This extensive bibliography was published solely by subscription, only 635 copies being printed at $2.50 a part, so that its cost to those subscribing was about $225 unbound, up to the time of its suspension. The first part appeared January 1, 1867, although Vol. I. bears date New York, 1868. It records most important titles in full, with (usually) marks denoting omissions where such are made. In the case of many rare books relating to America (and especially those published prior to the 18th century) the collations are printed so as to show what each line of the original title embraces, i. e. with vertical marks or dashes between the matter of the respective lines. This careful description is invaluable to the bibliographical student, frequently enabling him to identify editions, or to solve doubts as to the genuineness of a book-title in hand. The collation by number of pages is given in all cases where the book has been seen, or reported fully to the editor. The order of description as to each title is as follows: (1) Place of publication (2) publisher (3) year (4) collation and size of book. Notes in a smaller type frequently convey information of other editions, of prices in various sales, of minor works by the same writer, etc.

The fullness which has been aimed at in Sabin's American bibliography is seen in the great number of sermons and other specimens of pamphlet literature which it chronicles. It gives also the titles of most early American magazines, reviews, and other periodicals, except newspapers, which are generally omitted, as are maps also. As an example of the often minute cataloguing of the work, I may mention that no less than eight pages are occupied with a list of th: various publications and editions of books by Dr. Jedediah Morse, an author of whom few of the present generation of Americans have ever heard. He was the earliest American geographer who published any comprehensive books upon the subject, and his numerous Gazetteers and Geographies, published from 1784 to 1826, were constantly reprinted, until supplanted by more full, if not more accurate works.

Upon the whole, Sabin's great work, although so far from being finished, is invaluable as containing immeasurably more and fuller titles than any other American bibliography. It is also the only extensive work on the subject which covers all periods, although the books of the last thirty years must chiefly be excepted as not represented. As a work of reference, while its cost and scarcity may prevent the smaller public libraries from possessing it, it is always accessible in the libraries of the larger cities, where it is among the foremost works to be consulted in any research involving American publications, or books of any period or country relating to America, or its numerous sub-divisions.

I may now mention, much more cursorily, some other bibliographies pertaining to our country. The late Henry Stevens, who died in 1886, compiled a "Catalogue of the American Books in the Library of the British Museum." This was printed by the Museum authorities in 1856, and fills 754 octavo pages. Its editor was a highly accomplished bibliographer and book-merchant, born in Vermont, but during the last forty years of his life resided in London, where he devoted himself to his profession with great learning and assiduity. He published many catalogues of various stocks of books collected by him, under such titles as "Bibliotheca historica," "Bibliotheca Americana," etc., in which the books were carefully described, often with notes illustrating their history or their value. He became an authority upon rare books and early editions, and made a valuable catalogue of the Bibles in the Caxton exhibition at London, in 1877, with bibliographical commentary. He was for years chief purveyor of the British Museum Library for its American book purchases, and aided the late James Lenox in building up that rich collection of Americana and editions of the Scriptures which is now a part of the New York Public Library. His catalogue of the American books in the British Museum, though now over forty years old, and supplanted by the full alphabetical catalogue of that entire library since published, is a valuable contribution to American bibliography.

Mr. Stevens was one of the most acute and learned bibliographers I have known. He was a man of marked individuality and independent views; with a spice of eccentricity and humor, which crept into all his catalogues, and made his notes highly entertaining reading. Besides his services to the British Museum Library, in building up its noble collection of Americana, and in whose rooms he labored for many years, with the aid of Panizzi and his successors, whom he aided in return, Stevens collected multitudes of the books which now form the choice treasures of the Lenox library, the Carter Brown library, at Providence, the Library of Congress, and many more American collections. To go with him through any lot of Americana, in one of his enterprising visits to New York, where he sometimes came to market his overflowing stores picked up in London and on the continent, was a rare treat. Every book, almost, brought out some verbal criticism, anecdote or reminiscence of his book-hunting experiences, which began in America, and extended all over Europe.

He was not only an indefatigable collector, but a most industrious and accurate bibliographer, doing more work in that field, probably, than any other American. He wrote a singularly careful, though rapid hand, as plain and condensed as print, and in days before modern devices for manifolding writing were known, he copied out his invoices in duplicate or triplicate in his own hand, with titles in full, and frequent descriptive notes attached. His many catalogues are notable for the varied learning embodied. He was a most intelligent and vigilant book collector for more than forty years, his early labors embracing towns in New York and New England, as purveyor for material for Peter Force, of Washington, whose American Archives were then in course of preparation. Among the library collectors who absorbed large portions of his gathered treasures, were James Lenox, Jared Sparks, George Livermore, John Carter Brown, Henry C. Murphy, George Brinley, the American Geographical Society, and many historical societies. He was an authority on all the early voyages, and wrote much upon them. No one knew more about early Bibles than Henry Stevens.

His enterprise and ambition for success led him to bold and sometimes extensive purchases. He bought about 1865, the library of Baron von Humboldt, and this and other large ventures embarrassed him much in later years. He became the owner of the Franklin manuscripts, left in London by the great man's grandson, and collected during many years a library of Frankliniana, which came to the Library of Congress when the Franklin manuscripts were purchased for the State Department in 1881.

He was proud of his country and his State, always signing himself "Henry Stevens, of Vermont." His bookplate had engraved beneath his name, the titles, "G. M. B.: F. S. A." The last, of course, designated him as Fellow of the Society of Antiquaries of London, but the first puzzled even his friends, until it was interpreted as signifying "Green Mountain Boy." His brother used jocosely to assure me that it really meant "Grubber of Musty Books."

As to his prices for books, while some collectors complained of them as "very stiff," they appear, when compared with recent sales of Americana, at auction and in sale catalogues, to be quite moderate. The late historian Motley told me that Mr. Stevens charged more than any one for Dutch books relating to America; but Mr. Motley's measure of values was guaged by the low prices of Dutch booksellers which prevailed during his residence in the Netherlands, for years before the keen demand from America had rendered the numerous Dutch tracts of the West India Company, etc., more scarce and of greater commercial value than they bore at the middle of this century.

As treating of books by American authors, though not so much a complete bibliography of their works, as a critical history, with specimens selected from each writer, Duyckincks "Cyclopaedia of American Literature" deserves special mention. The last edition appeared at Philadelphia, in 1875, in two large quarto volumes. Equally worthy of note is the compilation by E. C. Stedman and Ellen M. Hutchinson, in eleven volumes, entitled "Library of American Literature," New York, 1887-90. A most convenient hand-book of bibliographical reference is Oscar F. Adams's "Dictionary of American Authors," Boston, 1897, which gives in a compact duodecimo volume, the name and period of nearly every American writer, with a brief list of his principal works, and their date of publication, in one alphabet.

Of notable catalogues of books relating to America.

rather than of American publications, should be named White Kennet's "Bibliotheca Americana primordia," the earliest known catalogue devoted to American bibliography, London, 1713; O. Rich, Catalogue of Books relating to America, 1500-1700, London, 1832; Rich, "Bibliotheca Americana nova," books printed between 1700 and 1844, two volumes, London, 1835-46; H. Harrisse, "Bibliotheca Americana vetustissima," New York, 1866, and its supplement, Paris, 1872, both embracing rare early Americana, published from 1492 to 1551. This is a critically edited bibliography of the rarest books concerning America that appeared in the first half century after its discovery.

The important field of American local history has given birth to many bibliographies. The earliest to be noted is H. E. Ludewig's "Literature of American Local History," New York, 1846. Thirty years later came F. B. Perkins's "Check List for American Local History," Boston, 1876; followed by A. P. C. Griffin's "Index of articles upon American Local History in historical collections," Boston, 1889, and by his "Index of the literature of American local history in collections published in 1890-95," Boston, 1896. Closely allied to the catalogues of city, town, and county histories, come the bibliographies of genealogies and family histories, of which the last or 4th edition of D. S. Durrie's "Bibliographia genealogica Americana; an alphabetical index to American genealogies in county and town histories, printed genealogies, and kindred works," Albany, 1895, is the most comprehensive and indispensable. This work gives us an alphabet of family names, under each of which are grouped the titles of books in which that special name is treated, with citation of the page. It also gives the name and date of publication of the special family genealogies which are separately printed, whether book or pamphlet, with number of pages in each. The work is by a librarian, to whose laborious diligence Americans are deeply indebted.

Among other bibliographies of genealogy are Munsell's "American Genealogist: a catalogue of family histories," Albany, 1897. This work aims to give the titles of all separately printed American genealogies, in an alphabet of family names, giving titles in full, with place and year of publication, name of publisher, and collation, or number of pages.

For the multitudinous public documents of the United States, consult B. P. Poore's "Descriptive catalogue of the government publications of the United States, 1775-1881," Washington, 1885, and F. A. Crandall, Check list of public documents, debates and proceedings from 1st to 53d Congress (1789-1895), Washington, 1895; also,

Comprehensive index to the publications of the United States government, 1889-1893. The same—United States Catalogue of Public Documents, 1893 to 1895, Washington, 1896. Several biennial or annual lists of United States Documents have followed.

As supplementing these extensive catalogues, we have in the Appendix to the "American Catalogue" of 1885 a List of United States Government publications from 1880 to 1884; in that of 1891 a List from 1884 to 1890; and in that of 1896 a List covering the years 1891 to 1895.

A most important recent bibliography is found in H. C. Bolton's "Catalogue of Scientific and Technical Periodicals, 1665-1895," Washington, 1897.

There are also many sale catalogues of American books, with prices, some of which may be noted, e. g. J. R. Smith, Bibliotheca Americana, London, 1865; F. Müller, Catalogue of books and pamphlets relating to America, Amsterdam, 1877, and later years. Ternaux-Compans, "Bibliothèque Américaine;" books printed before 1700, Paris,

1837: P. Trömel, "Bibliothèque Américaine," Leipzig, 1861: D. B. Warden, "Bibliothèque Américaine," Paris, 1840: R. Clarke & Co., "Bibliotheca Americana," Cincinnati, 1874, 1878, 1887, 1891, and 1893.

There are, besides, important catalogues of some private libraries, devoted wholly or chiefly to books relating to America. Among these, the most extensive and costly is John R. Bartlett's catalogue of the library of J. Carter Brown, of Providence, in four sumptuous volumes, with fac-similes of early title-pages, of which bibliography only fifty copies were printed. It is entitled, "Bibliotheca Americana: a catalogue of books relating to North and South America," 1482-1800, 4 vols. large 8vo., Providence, 1870-82. The Carter Brown Library is now the richest collection of Americana in any private library in the world.

Among catalogues of libraries sold by auction, and composed largely of American books, are those of John A. Rice, New York, 1870: W. Meuzies, New York, 1875: George Brinley, in five volumes, sold 1878 to 1886: Henry C. Murphy, New York, 1884: S. L. M. Barlow, New York, 1889: and Brayton Ives, New York, 1891.

The wide field of bibliography of English literature has given birth to many books. Only the more comprehensive can here be noted.

R. Watt's Bibliotheca Britannica, in four quarto volumes, Edinburgh, 1824, although now old, is still an indispensable work of reference, giving multitudes of titles of English books and pamphlets not found in any other bibliography. It of course abounds in errors, most of which have been copied in Allibone's Dictionary of English literature. This extensive work is a monument of labor, to which the industrious compiler devoted many years, dying of too intense study, at Glasgow, at the early age of forty-five, in the year 1819. The issue of the work in 1824, being thus posthumous, its errors and omissions are largely accounted for by the author's inability to correct the press. The plan of the work is unique. Vols. I and 2 contain the alphabet of authors and titles, with dates and publishers' prices when known. Vols. 3 and 4 contain an alphabet of subjects, in which the titles reappear, with a key alphabet in italic letters attached to each title, by which reference is made to the author-catalogue, at a fixed place, where all the works of the author are recorded.

The work is printed in small type, with two crowded columns on a page, thus containing an enormous amount of matter. The key is quickly learned, and by its aid, and the alphabet of subjects, the librarian can find out the authors of many anonymous books. Watt is the only general bibliography of English literature which gives most of the obscure writers and their works.

Lowndes' Bibliographer's Manual of English Literature, in its second edition, enlarged by H. G. Bohn, is a most indispensable bibliography. This work is arranged alphabetically by authors' names, and aims to record all important books published in Great Britain, from the earliest times to about A. D. 1834. It is in eleven parts, or 6 vols. 16 mo. of very portable size, Lond., 1857-65. While it gives collations of the more important works, with publishers and dates, it fails to record many editions of the same work. Its quoted prices represent the original publisher's price, with very frequent additions of the sale prices obtained at book auctions. The chief defect of Lowndes' Manual is its total lack of any index of subjects.

S. Austin Allibone's "Critical Dictionary of English literature," Philadelphia, 1858-71, 3 volumes, with sup-

plement by John F. Kirk, in 2 vols., Philadelphia, 1891,
is a copious reference book, which, in spite of its many
errors and crudities, should be in all libraries.   It contains in abbreviated form most of the titles in Watt and
Lowndes, with the addition of American authors, and of
British books published since the period covered by
Lowndes.   The three volumes of Allibone accompany
the titles of works by noted authors with many critical
remarks, copied mostly from reviews and literary journals.
This feature of the book, which makes it rather a work of
literary history and criticism than a bibliography pure
and simple, has been dropped in Mr. Kirk's supplement,
which thus becomes properly a bibliography.   The publications of England and America, from about 1850 to 1890,
are more fully chronicled in this work of Kirk than in any
other bibliography.

The important "English Catalogue of Books," from A.
D. 1835 to 1897, in 5 vols., with its valuable Index of Subjects, in 4 vols., from 1857 up to 1889, is so constantly
useful as to be almost indispensable in a public library,
It records, in provokingly brief one-line titles, with publisher's name, year of issue, and price, all books published
in Great Britain whose titles could be secured.   It thus
subserves the same purpose for English publications,
which the American Catalogue fulfills for those of the
United States.   Both are in effect greatly condensed bibliographies, enabling the librarian to locate most of the
published literature in the English language for many
years back.   The English catalogue, from 1897 to date, is
supplemented by its annual issues, entitled "the English
Catalogue of Books for 1898," etc.

I have said that accuracy should be one of the cardinal
aims of the librarian: and this because in that profession
it is peculiarly important.   Bibliography is a study which

approaches very nearly to the rank of an exact science;
and the practice of it, in application to the daily work of
the librarian, is at once a school of accuracy, and a test
of ability. A habit of analytical methods should be assiduously cultivated, without which much time will be lost
in fruitless searches in the wrong books to find what one
wants. As a single illustration of this need of method,
suppose that you want to find the title of a certain book
with its full description, a want likely to occur every hour
in the day, and sometimes many times an hour. The book
is perhaps Sir Walter Scott's Life of Napoleon,—9 vols.,
London, 1827, and your object is to trace its title, published price, etc., among the numerous bibliographies of
literature. You begin by a simple act of analysis—thus.
This is a London, not an American book—hence it is useless to look in any American catalogue. It is written in
English, so you are dispensed from looking for it in any
French or other foreign bibliography. Its date is 1827,
London. Therefore among the three leading English reference books in bibliography, which are Watt's Bibliotheca
Britannica, Lowndes' Bibliographer's Manual, and the
English Catalogue, you at once eliminate the former as
not containing the book. Why do you do this? Because
Watt's great work, in four huge quartos, though invaluable for the early English literature, stops with books published before the date of its issue, 1824. Your book is
published in 1827, and of course could not appear in a
catalogue of 1824. Shall you refer then to the English
Catalogue for its title? No, because the five volumes of
that useful work (though some imperfect book lists were
published earlier), begin with the year 1835, and the book
you seek bears date of 1827. You are then reduced, by
this simple process of analyzing in your mind the various

sources of information, and rejecting all except one, namely Lowndes' Bibliographer's Manual, to a search in a single catalogue for your title. This simplifies matters
greatly, and saves all the time which might otherwise have
been lost in hunting fruitlessly through several works of
reference. Lowndes' invaluable Manual was published in
1834, and though a second edition, edited by Bohn, appeared thirty years later, it does not contain books pub-
ished after that date, unless they are later editions of
works issued earlier. You find in it your Scott's Napoleon,
date 1827, with its published price, £4. 14. 6, and an
account of other later editions of the book. Of
course you will observe that it is necessary to know
what period of years is covered by the various bibliographies, and to carry those dates perpetually in your
memory, in order thus to simplify searches, and save time.
Once learned, you will have the comfort of knowing where
to turn for light upon any book, and the faculty of accurate memory will reward the pains taken to acquire it.

I must not omit to include, in noting the more useful
and important English bibliographies, the very copious
list of works appended to each biography of British
writers, in the new "Dictionary of National Biography,"
Lond., 1885-1900. This extensive work is nearly finished in about 65 volumes, and constitutes a rich thesaurus
of information about all British authors, except living
ones.

Living characters, considered notable, and brief note of
their books, are recorded in "Men and Women of the
Time," 15th ed. London, 1899—but this book, although
highly useful, is far from being a bibliography.

I should not omit to mention among useful librarians'
aids, the "Book Prices Current; record of prices at which
books have been sold at auction." This London publica-

tion began with the year 1887. No sales are reported
of books bringing less than one pound sterling. The
book-sales of 1898 were reported in 1899 of this issue,
and the book is published in each case the next year. The
similar catalogue entitled "American Book Prices Current" was begun with 1895, being compiled from the sale
catalogues of American auctioneers, for that year, and
the prices brought at auction in New York, Boston, Philadelphia, and Chicago, are recorded for all notable books,
but limited to works bringing as much as $3 or upward.
Five years' reports, in as many volumes, have now been
issued, and the publication is to be continued. Its utility
of course consists in informing librarians or collectors of
the most recent auction values of books. At the same
time, a word of caution is required, since it is not safe to
judge of average commercial values, from any isolated bid
at an auction sale.

A very useful classed catalogue, published by the British
Museum library, and edited by G. K. Fortescue, an assistant librarian, is the so-called "Subject-index to modern
works," of which three volumes have appeared, beginning
with the accessions of 1880-85, each covering five years
additions of new works, in all European languages, to that
library. The third volume embraces the years 1890 to
1895, and appeared in 1896. As this is not confined to
works in English, it should be classed with universal
bibliography. As containing most of the latest books of
any note, all three volumes are important aids to research.
They are printed in large type, in which it is a refreshment
to the eye to read titles, after the small and obscure print
of Watt's Bibliotheca Britannica, and the but little better
type of Lowndes' Manual, and of the English Catalogue.
A collation of pages is also added in most cases, and the
importance of this can hardly be overrated. These cata-

logues of the British Museum Library abound in pamphlets, English, French, German, Italian, etc., evincing how large a share of attention is given to the minor literature coming from the press in the more recent years.

W. H. D. Adams's "Dictionary of English Literature," London, 1880, and later, in a compact volume, gives authors and titles of the more important English and American books. Also, in the same alphabet, an index to the titles, as well as authors, by the first word, and to many sayings or quotations, with their original sources. It is a highly useful book, although its small bulk leaves it far from being a comprehensive one.

Chambers' Cyclopaedia of English Literature, in 2 vols., London, 1876, has an account of the most notable British writers, with specimens of their works, and forms what may be termed an essential part of the equipment of every public library.

The Library Association of the United Kingdom, since 1888, the date of its organization, has published Transactions and Proceedings; also, since 1889, "The Library," a periodical with bibliographical information.

It may be noted, without undue expression of pride, that America first set the example of an organized national association of Librarians (founded in 1876) followed the same year by a journal devoted to Library interests. That extremely useful periodical, the *Library Journal*, is now in its twenty-fourth volume. Its successive issues have contained lists of nearly all new bibliographical works and catalogues published, in whatever language.

The London Publisher's Circular, first established in 1838, is a weekly organ of the book-publishing trade, aiming to record the titles of all British publications as they appear from the press. It gives, in an alphabet by authors' names, the titles in much abbreviated form, with publisher, size in inches, collation, price, and date, with a fairly good index of titles or subjects, in the same alphabet. Covering much the same ground, as a publishers' periodical, is "The Bookseller," issued monthly since 1858, with lists of the new issues of the British press, and critical notices. In addition to the English catalogue, there is the extensive Whitaker's "Reference catalogue of current literature," published every year, which now makes two large volumes, and embraces the trade catalogues of English publishers, bound up in alphabetical order, with a copious index, by authors and titles, in one alphabet, prefixed.

While on English bibliographies, I must note the important work on local history, by J. P. Anderson, "Book of British Topography," London, 1881. This gives, in an alphabet of counties, titles of all county histories or descriptive works of England, Scotland, Ireland, and Wales, followed in each county by a list of town histories or topographical works. The arrangement under each town is chronological. Its only want is a collation of the books. British genealogy, or the history of families, is treated bibliographically in G. W. Marshall's "The Genealogist's Guide," London, 1893, which gives an alphabet of family names, with references in great detail to county and town histories, pedigrees, heralds' visitations, genealogies, etc., all over Great Britain, in which any family is treated.

The wide field of foreign bibliography, by countries, cannot here be entered upon, nor can I now treat of the still more extensive range of works devoted to the bibliography of various subjects.

INDEX.

(501)

AUTHORS AND PUBLISHERS

A MANUAL OF SUGGESTIONS FOR BEGINNERS IN LITERATURE

Comprising a description of publishing methods and arrangements, directions for the preparation of MSS. for the press, explanations of the details of book-manufacturing, instructions for proof-reading, specimens of typography, the text of the United States Copyright Law, and information concerning International Copyrights, together with general hints for authors. By G. H. P. and J. B. P.

Seventh Edition, re-written with additional material.
8°, gilt top . . . . . . *net, $1.75*

CHIEF CONTENTS

PART I.—Publishing arrangements—Books published at the risk and expense of the publisher—Books published for the account of the author, *i. e.*, at the author's risk and expense, or in which he assumes a portion of the investment—Publishing arrangements for productions first printed in periodicals or cyclopædias—The literary agent—Authors' associations—Advertising—On securing copyright.

PART II.—The Making of Books—Composition—Electrotyping—Presswork—Bookbinding—Illustrations.

" Full of valuable information for authors and writers. . . . A most instructive and excellent manual."—GEORGE WM. CURTIS in *Harper's Magazine.*
" This handy and useful book is written with perfect fairness and abounds in hints which writers will do well to ' make a note of.' . . . There is a host of other matters treated succinctly and lucidly which it behoves beginners in literature to know, and we can recommend it most heartily to them."—*London Spectator.*

G. P. PUTNAM'S SONS, NEW YORK AND LONDON

BY GEO. HAVEN PUTNAM

AUTHORS AND THEIR PUBLIC IN ANCIENT TIMES

A Sketch of Literary Conditions and of the Relations with the
Public of Literary Producers, from the Earliest Times
to the Fall of the Roman Empire.
Second edition, revised, 12°, gilt top, $1.50.

The book abounds in information, is written in a delightfully succinct and
agreeable manner, with apt comparisons that are often humorous, and with
scrupulous exactness to statement, and without a sign of partiality either from
an author's or a publisher's point of view.—*New York Times.*

BOOKS AND THEIR MAKERS DURING THE MIDDLE AGES

A Study of the Conditions of the Production and Distribution of
Literature from the Fall of the Roman Empire to the
Close of the Seventeenth Century.
In two volumes, 8°, cloth extra (sold separately), each $2.50
Vol. I., 476–1600—Vol. II., 1500–1709.

It is seldom that such wide learning, such historical grasp and insight, have
been employed in their service.—*Atlantic Monthly.*
It is a book to be studied rather than merely praised. . . . That its
literary style is perfect is acceptable as a matter of course, and equally of
course is it that the information it contains bears the stamp of historical verification.—*N. Y. Sun.*

THE QUESTION OF COPYRIGHT

Comprising the text of the Copyright Law of the United States,
and a summary of the Copyright laws at present in force in
the chief countries of the world ; together with a report of the
legislation now pending in Great Britain, a sketch of the contest in the United States, 1837–1891, in behalf of International Copyright, and certain papers on the development of
the conception of literary property and on the results of the
American law of 1891.
Second edition, revised, with additions, and with the record of
legislation brought down to March, 1896.   8°, gilt top, $1.75.

A perfect arsenal of facts and arguments, carefully elaborated and very effectively presented. . . . Altogether it constitutes an extremely valuable
history of the development of a very intricate right of property, and it is as
interesting as it is valuable.—*N. Y. Nation.*

G. P. PUTNAM'S SONS
New York : 27 West 23d Street.   London : 24 Bedford St., Strand.

LANGUAGE.

SOME COMMON ERRORS OF SPEECH.

Suggestions for the Avoiding of Certain Classes of Errors, together with Examples of Bad and of Good Usage. By ALFRED G. COMPTON, Professor in College of the City of New York. 12° . $ .75

"The book calls up many interesting, not to say fascinating, lapses from strict grammar, and is very valuable. In its index expurgatorius will be found many surprises by the self-supposed learned."—*Chicago Times-Herald*.

A SIMPLE GRAMMAR OF ENGLISH NOW IN USE.

By JOHN EARLE, A.M., LL.D., Professor of Anglo-Saxon, University of Oxford, author of "English Prose: Its Elements, History, and Usage." 12° $1.50

"The book is a clear, careful, and scholarly treatise on the English Language and its use, rather than a work of science. It is a book that will be valuable to teachers and to students of language everywhere."—*Washington Times*.

THE ENGLISH LANGUAGE AND ENGLISH GRAMMAR.

An Historical Study of the Sources, Development, and Analogies of the Language, and of the Principles Covering its Usages. Illustrated by Copious Examples by Writers of all Periods. By SAMUEL RAMSEY. 8° $2 00

"Mr. Ramsey's work will appeal especially to those that desire to know something more about the history and philology, the growth and mistakes of their native tongue than is given in the ordinary text-books."—*Baltimore Sun*.

ORTHOMETRY.

A Treatise on the Art of Versification and the Technicalities of Poetry, with a New and Complete Rhyming Dictionary. By R. F. BREWER, B.A. 12°, pp. xv. + 376 . . . . $2.00

"It is a good book for its purpose, lucid, compact, and well arranged. It lays bare, we believe, the complete anatomy of poetry. It affords interesting quotations, in the way of example, and interesting comments by distinguished critics upon certain passages from the distinguished poets."—*N. Y. Sun*.

MANUAL OF LINGUISTICS.

An Account of General and English Phonology. By JOHN CLARK, A.M. 8°, pp. lxiii. + 314 . . . . $2.00

"Mr. Clark has traced the English language back to its foundations in his work 'Manual of Linguistics.' It is an interesting theme, and his book will prove very useful for reference, for he has culled from many sources and gone over a wide territory." —*Detroit Free Press*.

COMPOSITION IN THE SCHOOL-ROOM.

A Practical Treatise. By E. GALBRAITH. 16°, cloth . . $1.00

"The author has drawn fully from the best writers on the subject, and her book is an epitome of the best thought of all."—*Boston Transcript*.

G. P. PUTNAM'S SONS, NEW YORK AND LONDON.

Lightning Source UK Ltd.
Milton Keynes UK
UKOW022003030412

190117UK00008B/64/P